Odyssey *of a* Wandering Mind

Odyssey *of a* Wandering Mind

The Strange Tale of Sara Mayfield, Author

JENNIFER HORNE

THE UNIVERSITY OF ALABAMA PRESS
Tuscaloosa

The University of Alabama Press
Tuscaloosa, Alabama 35487-0380
uapress.ua.edu

Typeface: Adobe Caslon

Cover images: (*top*) James Mayfield Jr. and Sara Mayfield on
bicycles in London; (*bottom*) materials from the Sara Mayfield
Papers in the University of Alabama Libraries Special Collections,
used with the permission of James Mayfield and the Sara Mayfield
Estate; (*background*) photo by Ireland Rogers on unsplash.com
Cover design: Lori Lynch

Cataloging-in-Publication data is available
from the Library of Congress.
ISBN: 978-0-8173-2136-9 (cloth)
ISBN: 978-0-8173-6136-5 (paper)
E-ISBN: 978-0-8173-9418-9

Dedicated to the memory of Sara, Sara, Zelda, and Tallulah

By some odd chance, I was born in the hurricane
season and have lived in one ever since.

—SARA MAYFIELD

Contents

Figures

Author's Note

REGARDING MY SOURCE CITATION, USAGE, AND APPROACH TO THE material, it may be helpful for readers to know a few things before beginning:

Over the course of a decade I read through and took extensive notes on the Sara Mayfield Papers in the W. S. Hoole Special Collections Library at the University of Alabama. Comprising 19.4 linear feet, the collection includes Sara Mayfield's journals, from childhood on; thousands of letters (those she wrote, which she kept copies of throughout her life, and those written to her); manuscripts of the books, plays, and articles she wrote, some published, some not; and a wide range of other materials, including family history, research notes, memorabilia from various trips, newspaper clippings, class notes, and photographs. When not otherwise noted in text or cited as an endnote, quoted material is from the Mayfield Papers. My other primary source was Sara Mayfield's patient files from her time in Bryce Hospital, 1948 to 1965, obtained by permission from the Health Information Management office at Bryce Hospital in Tuscaloosa, Alabama. Sara's two published literary biography-memoirs, of the Menckens (*The Constant Circle*) and the Fitzgeralds (*Exiles from Paradise*), provided additional biographical material. All thoughts, conversations, and actions attributed to Sara Mayfield in this book can be found in a specific statement in her writings or were learned through interviews with those who knew her. A full list of other works consulted can be found in a chapter-by-chapter summary, for readers who want to skim sources in a particular chapter, and in the bibliography.

Sara's legal name was spelled "Sara," not "Sarah," and as an adult, she always spelled her name without the "h." But some legal documents and notes in her patient files refer to her as "Sarah," and I have not corrected that spelling. Speaking of Saras, Sara Mayfield's good friend Sara Haardt appears frequently in this book. When necessary to avoid confusion, I have referred to them as "Sara M." and "Sara H." Sara's friend Elisabeth Thigpen Hill spelled her name with an "s," but Sara always spelled it "Elizabeth," and I have not changed that when quoting her. Finally, when there are omissions or errors of spelling in Sara's letters, journals, or other papers, I have made bracketed corrections or noted the error with [*sic*], except in some of her childhood letters and journal entries that are clearly the work of a beginning speller.

Although Sara lived through several major historical eras—the Roaring Twenties, the Great Depression, World War II, and the Civil Rights Era—and her life touches on issues of feminism, race, upper-class white southern culture, mental illness, and sexuality, this is, more than anything else, Sara's singular story, based on the words she left behind. Many of those words were written while she was a patient at Bryce Hospital (formerly Alabama Insane Hospital). Thus her mental state throughout her adult life becomes one of the main subjects of this book.

My bedrock principle in telling her story has been to go no further in my assertions than either direct evidence from a primary source or reasonable conclusion based on a variety of sources could take me. In narrating and analyzing Sara Mayfield's commitments for the treatment of mental illness, and her family's role in those, I have read all of the family's letters in her papers and in her patient files from Bryce Hospital and have talked to the few remaining people who might have some insight into her being committed. Although I began my investigation into Sara Mayfield's life suspicious of her family's motives, I ended with the conclusion that her family did what they thought they needed to do for Sara. At the time of her commitment in 1948 there were no antipsychotic drugs available, certainly none of the many psychopharmaceuticals now used to treat mental illness. There is no question in my mind that she had delusional episodes, sometimes hallucinated, believed in conspiracies in which people were out to get her, and as a result of what I think of as her mind's misinterpretations of reality could become very angry at what she thought was being done to her. Unfortunately, beyond the phrase in her patient files about her "violent and ungovernable behavior" and her notes to herself about a possible "homicidal attack" on her mother, further evidence and information regarding the reasons for her 1940 and 1948 commitments are not available.

It might have been better, more admirable and unselfish, for her mother and brother to have had her released to live at home, despite the possibility of occasional episodes of ill health. At the time, however, having a mentally ill relative committed (or people committing themselves voluntarily) was often seen as the best option for care until the person improved. Sara's mother, Victorian and conventional, would have followed "doctor's orders" about Sara's care. Sara was not abandoned by her family; they made sure she had whatever food, clothes, books, and art supplies she wanted, and regularly took her to visit other family members or to shop and eat out.

In retrospect, and certainly by contemporary standards of care, it seems possible that, while Sara's paranoia persisted throughout her years at Bryce, she was sufficiently functional that she might have been able to live on her own, perhaps with the need for occasional treatment and some family support. As I've studied her life and writings, I've wished she had had the chance to find out, but it's impossible to know how things would have gone for Sara. Indeed, with greater autonomy during that period, her life could have been worse, rather than better, had she become unable to look out for her own well-being. On her own, she might simply have become one of the town's eccentrics or, without consistent treatment and a set schedule, she might have receded further and further from reality, to the point of being self-destructive or endangering others. It's frustrating not to know more, but that is where I find myself as her biographer—having investigated all there is to investigate, I am left with some ambiguities that cannot be resolved.

I have used Sara's phrase "odyssey of a wandering mind" as a guide for showing the peripatetic, often picaresque nature of her life, as she oscillates geographically between her home in Alabama and Baltimore or between home and New York City, travels to many other places in the US and abroad, and symbolically oscillates between the aesthetic and the ethically driven life, between traditional and unconventional attitudes and actions, between functionality and poor mental health, between insisting on her own way and adapting to what others need or require.

Balancing and acknowledging the complexities of her life and personality may be less satisfying than framing her story in a more straightforward way. But I believe this approach is the best way to tell her story and the way that is truest to the facts as I have found them. I offer this biography of an extraordinary woman, hoping that in accommodating the complexity of Sara's life, I will encourage readers to make room for ambiguity and complexity in the telling of their own lives and those of others.

Chapter 1

"Montgomery's a Peach"

*Sara is introduced. A Deep South Childhood in a Notable Family. Travels with
Girls from Miss Booth's School around Europe, and a Misunderstanding.*

AFTER SEVENTEEN YEARS AS A PATIENT AT BRYCE HOSPITAL FOR
the Insane in Tuscaloosa, Alabama, Sara Mayfield walked out of its
doors a free woman. Not quite sixty in early 1965, she was ready to live the
rest of her life, however long that might be, as she chose.

First, she'd get the declaration of sanity, eliminating her cousin's guardianship and restoring her financial affairs to her control. She had her book on
Sara and H. L. Mencken to finish, and after that the one on Scott and Zelda
Fitzgerald. Some friends were long gone, Sara Haardt Mencken and Zelda
Sayre Fitzgerald among them, and she'd heard Tallulah was hooked on pills
and booze. But some were still around and would be there for her: her oldest
and best friend, Liz Thigpen Hill; her new friend, Sidney Landman, who'd
helped her get out; and a host of friends near and far who'd cheered her on in
her long struggle to leave the hospital, with its bad food, crowded buildings,
and frequent persecution.

Now she could eat what she wanted when she wanted to, go to bed when
she decided the light should be turned out. She could come and go with no
one's permission but her own. Perhaps she'd even go back to Europe. She
sometimes thought of her first trip abroad with other girls from Miss Margaret Booth's school in Montgomery, Alabama. After the journey across the
Atlantic by ship, they'd taken a tugboat to the port; gone through customs
(she'd been frightened, for no good reason, that she would get caught doing
something forbidden); and then, after a train ride on "the queerest little train"

in which the French countryside flashed by, looking vaguely foreign, arrived in Paris. Really, truly, Paris. It was a long way from Alabama, and she was only sixteen. The year was 1922 and the city was alive with writers and artists and musicians, and she meant to experience all she could. Her best friend, Liz, a few years older but, Sara was convinced, her soul mate, was on the trip as well. Sara had hoped to show Liz how mature and intelligent and sophisticated she was, now that Liz, the daughter of a prominent Montgomery physician, had spent a year away in college.

So much had happened since those early, innocent days. There were stories she could tell, and stories she couldn't; things she wanted to remember, and things she didn't. Upon Sara's release from the hospital and for decades afterward, stories circulated around Tuscaloosa about why and how she'd been institutionalized: her family—mother and brother—had had her committed against her will because they wanted the family money for themselves, or because she was a lesbian, or because she was an alcoholic, or because she flouted the norms of the day for appropriate upper-class white female behavior. There were bits of truth in all those stories, but the story that gained widest circulation was the one Sara floated herself: that shortly after her commitment in 1948, the doctors had realized she was perfectly well, and thereafter had let her keep a room at the hospital while being free to come and go as she pleased during the day. They couldn't release her due to a state, or national, or international political conspiracy against Sara and her family, a conspiracy with roots in Sara's World War II propaganda work, or perhaps because of her lawyer brother's battle with the Dixiecrats and other political forces, or perhaps because of the local powerbrokers' resolve to stop her from starting a rival newspaper—her fertile brain looked for explanations everywhere.

Sara was a lifelong writer: of letters, diaries, poems, plays, short stories, novels, newspaper articles, biographies. Her greatest work, however, was the story of her life, endlessly revised, often retold, always crafted as a plucky heroine's struggle against adversity, with Sara starring as a victim of sinister machinations and absurd occurrences who would never give her persecutors the satisfaction of knowing they'd hurt her.

Throughout her life, Sara Mayfield created a record of her existence, a treasure trove of information about a singular and adventurous life: her childhood in Montgomery, at the turn of the century; the expatriate world of Paris and London in the twenties; town and farm life in Tuscaloosa, alternating with theater work in New York City in the thirties; a stateside war correspondent's stories in the forties; life in a mental hospital in the fifties; and literary life in the South in the sixties and seventies. Throughout, she had friendships and acquaintanceships with the famous and talented: Virginia Woolf, Leslie Howard, Tallulah Bankhead, Ernest Hemingway, Zelda and Scott Fitzgerald, H. L. Mencken, Sara Haardt, and dozens of other writers, actors, publishers, and politicians.

In 1970, Sara wrote in a letter about a "young friend" who showed up at her house with a tape recorder, wanting to write a biography of her. "I said, 'Absolutely, no, Bob! I'm not important, and I'm not dead! No biographies should ever be written about people who aren't both.' 'But someday you will be,' he replied hopefully."

She might have imagined that someday, when she was dead, there would be a book about her. She donated the bulk of her papers, the ones she didn't destroy to protect her famous friends' privacy, to the University of Alabama library. In the margins of her journals and notes, she left what amount to notes for a future biographer, sometimes in red ink: "Imp." She left commentaries: "If I had had any barbiturates, they were given me without my knowledge or consent." She wrote dates on old letters and filled in the names of correspondents. Schooled in a culture of literacy and history, she believed in the power of words to record, order, and make sense of a life.

Her own life began in 1905, as the first child of an Alabama lawyer and judge, James J. Mayfield, and a young woman from Arkansas, Susie Fitts Martin, described as "a beautiful blonde of Little Rock." Sara learned to read and write early, encouraged by her mother and father. The newspaper article on her parents' wedding in 1897 described the match as "a union of brains and a union of hearts." Susie enrolled in graduate school as one of the first females to attend the University of Alabama. Sara was born in Tuscaloosa. Revealing the elitism she was born into, Sara described it as "a sleepy old river town, the northern gateway of the Black Belt, one of the last strongholds of the cotton kingdom, the citadel of a homogeneous group of Anglo-Saxons, a race apart, still known as the Confederates. Tuskaloosa and Idlewyld were not separated from the garish subdivisions along the Birmingham Highway and the Alabama State Hospital by actual distance as by the chasm of time and the unbridgeable gulf that divides the planters of Alabama's Black Belt from the rednecks of its hills."[1] Sara's father, a graduate of the University of Alabama law school who had also tutored at the university in physics and astronomy, was a specialist in state constitutional law. In 1908, when Sara was turning three, he became an associate justice on the state supreme court. The family moved to Montgomery but kept their home, called Idlewyld, in

Tuscaloosa. Judge Mayfield served alongside Zelda Sayre's father and the two occupied adjoining offices, where they often played chess at the end of the day. Sara's mother was active in the Alabama Democratic Party as well as in women's groups, including the Daughters of the American Revolution, the United Daughters of the Confederacy, and the Alabama Chapter of the National Society of the Colonial Dames of America, of which she was a charter member.

FIGURE 1. Sara Mayfield as a child

Born in 1905, Sara Martin Mayfield grew up in Montgomery, Alabama, the first-born child of Susie Mayfield, an Arkansas debutante who attended graduate school at the University of Alabama after her marriage, and James J. Mayfield, an Alabama Supreme Court justice. Judge Mayfield and another justice, Anthony Sayre, father of Zelda, had adjoining offices, and the two often played chess at the end of the day. (University of Alabama Libraries Special Collections)

FIGURE 2. Sara Mayfield as a child with the women of her family

Sara Mayfield (*center*) with her mother, (*left*) grandmother (*in rear*), and great-grandmother (*right*). An article in the *Montgomery Advertiser* noted that Sara "enjoys the unusual distinction of having for her 'guide, philosopher and friend' her great-grandmother, Mrs. Martin, who makes her home with the Mayfields. Between these two people there is the most beautiful comradeship imaginable." (University of Alabama Libraries Special Collections)

Pictures of Sara as a young child, dressed in white finery, with bows on her shoes or in her hair, show a winsome, gently smiling, but somehow serious little face, framed by soft curls. In one four-generation photograph, she is the shining center of a triad of women, her mother on the left, her grandmother standing behind her, her great-grandmother on the right. All four look straight toward the camera with confidence and belonging. She is their precious, ringleted, lace- and frill-bedecked child. Living in Montgomery, educated, owning large tracts of land outside of Tuscaloosa and Montgomery, white, well-to-do, the Mayfields were at the top of Alabama's social ladder. In 1910, when Sara was five, about two-thirds of the state's population was employed in agriculture; Montgomery was one of only three cities with a population greater than twenty-five thousand; and only one in ten of the state's citizens was an urban dweller.

Readers of the *Montgomery Advertiser* would have opened the newspaper on March 26, 1911, to a front-page article, taking up the whole page, "Children of the Alabama Judiciary." Written by Tallulah Bankhead's aunt Marie Bankhead Owen—sister to a senator, husband to the state archivist, and a formidable force in her own right—the piece described one of Sara's earliest attempts at publication: "When there was a request sent out for catchy slogans for the city, this little golden-haired child listened at the many suggestions that her grandmother read from the *Advertiser* and added her own slogan: 'Montgomery's a peach.'" Even earlier, at three or four, Sara had written a story about a horse named Prince Charlie and submitted it to the newspaper. As another daughter of a state supreme court justice, Zelda Sayre was featured in the front-page story as well. Zelda, nearing age eleven, proclaimed that she "dearly loved" storybooks, saying, "Reading is my favorite study at school because there are such beautiful tales in the books."

The former capital of the Confederacy, Montgomery in the early 1900s saw itself as a dynamic, flourishing city with a busy railway station and a citywide electric streetcar system. One of the reasons Zelda Sayre's father lived in the same neighborhood for so many years, according to Sara, was that he could ride the streetcar to and from work. In 1910 the Wright Brothers set up their flying school in a field outside of Montgomery. The school only lasted a few months, but crowds gathered to watch the flights, and Sara grew up with the sense of her town as a noteworthy place that these enterprising brothers would find attractive in promoting their new invention. Even as an adult, Sara remained smitten with the town she grew up in (although she somehow never managed to live there as an adult), writing glowingly, and, most would say, inaccurately: "As the first capital of the Confederate States of America, Montgomery was an international city, coequal with London, Rome, or Athens—and in the eyes of its proud citizens, *primus inter pares* . . . it combined the attractions of North and South, city and country, white and Negro, a former world capital and a quaint southern town." That Confederate heritage mattered to the Mayfields. One of the family treasures was the portrait of an ancestor who was sent to Alabama by President James Madison "to settle the land claims with the Indians before Alabama became a state." The portrait had a rip in it, purported to be from a Yankee bayonet; the family proudly left it unmended. Sara did not share the southern obsession with ancestry, writing of herself, "By some strange biological mutation, I was born among them with a feeling the pursuit of truth and beauty was the one important thing in the world and, that one's ancestors had little or nothing to do with the attainment of ideals. I realized that in one sense I was comically like them, in another, wholly different, and resolved the conquest in humor for the most part."[2] When Sara was five, she visited family in Memphis, Tennessee, and was given a brown leather journal with gilt edging to record the events of her trip: "Memphis. Tuesday. Oct. 1910: Freddie has given me a diary to keep my records and expenses in. Little girls living with their grandparents do not have very much fun or expenses either. Lallie and Freddie buy everything for me and give me a qua[r]ter. I bought some jaw-breakers for five cents."

Having started the habit early, Sara kept diaries throughout her childhood and indeed all her life. In one diary, an entry for September 1911 reads, "I am six years old now. Mother wants me to go to Miss Gussie's to school. All the other children I know go there." Sara, bright as she was, didn't like school at first. The next month she wrote, "Nobody not even Daddy can make me go to school any more. If you move without holding up your hand or talk you have to go up and sit by Miss Gussie. . . . You even have to hold up you[r] hand to be excused and that is not nice when there are lots of boys in the room." In her resistance to formal education, she was like her older friend Zelda, who had also refused to go back to first grade. On November 1, Sara wrote, "My report was 100% in everything but I am not going to school any more. . . . I read all the reader the first day." She did go back to school, but also received extra learning at home, tutored by her father and other family members.

Sara's brother, James, was born in November 1911. Before that, a cousin, Mark, had come to live with them, after his father died. Sara wrote in her journal about the boys as well. With her new little brother on the way, Sara wrote, "I hope my new brother won't be as mean as Mark is. He chunks china berries at me and makes fun of my dolls." When James was born, she wrote, "My baby brother was born this morning before I woke up. He is the cutest thing my life [has] ever seen. His name is James Jefferson Mayfield Junior like Fathers."

She kept diaries on trips up north to visit family members, describing travels around Boston, including Bunker Hill and Plymouth Rock, and to West Point, and beginning her penchant for writing about her journeys with a mixture of the observational and the personal. Of West Point, she wrote: "There are no children to play with and no body to read to me, but Uncle Forrest took me up to see old Fort Putnam where a battle was fought during the revolution." Sara also began her life as a letter-writer early. At ten, on the Boston trip, she wrote her father: "My Darling Dady, Many happy returns of your birthday. Well Dady you may be growing be growing [sic] Old in years but not at heart. Dady, do you miss me much. Today Aunt Hun and I went to Boston and I got a very pretty grey purse (which Mother told me to get). I think it is very pretty. I have not spent any money on trash. Dady you would have enjoyed [the] Museum of Fine Arts immincily. Well I will soon be turning my head homeward. Though Uncle Forrest and Aunt Hun have been awfully sweet to me, I [will] be mighty glad to be home-ward bound. This may sound ungreatfull, but I can't help but wanting to get home for 'There is no place like home be it ever so isolated.' Give my love to all especially Mother and Jim and wishing a happy birthday to the Dearest Dady in the world. Your most very lovingist Girle. Nobody told me to write or told me it was your birthday."

In 1917, now twelve, Sara kept notes on their country place outside of Montgomery, tales of bird dogs and rifles and fights with her brother and cousin. In an entry that prefigured her later conflicts with her mother over how well Sara conformed to conventional standards of femininity, she wrote: "Last night I heard Mother tell Father that I was growing up to be a wild comanche. This morning I looked in the mirror to see whether it was true or not. My skin is still white and my nose turns up but I am an Indian at heart." Because her father mandated that she both read and help around the house, Sara figured out how to get her work done while reading the novels of Sir Walter Scott, Charles Dickens, and William Makepeace Thackeray. Tasked with churning butter, she attached a sewing machine wheel to the churn and pedaled it with her foot, reading and churning at the same time. Requiring his daughter to do physical work was somewhat unusual for those of their time and place; in turn-of-the-century Alabama, for whites who could afford it, the mentality would have been that Black servants should do all the physical labor.

Far from being a "wild comanche" or even helping with chores, an upper-class white girl growing up in early twentieth-century Alabama was expected to be demure, polite, and pleasant at all times. Sara Mayfield's friend Sara Haardt, a teacher, a writer, and "Little Sara's" intellectual mentor, presents a model of southern womanhood in her short story "Little Lady," when the twelve-year-old Jean is given a grand "coming-out" party by her Aunt Eugenia. After the party, Jean "slipped down off the golden chair, and curtseyed before Aunt Eugenia but in her mind under all the glory of being a little lady was the tiredness, the weariness of soul that comes from making an effort to be nice and amusing in order to be a belle. Instead of thanking Aunt Eugenia now for giving her such a lovely party she wanted to ask if such tiredness of body and soul was the price she must pay for being a little lady. Yet, somehow, she could not do it. She merely murmured her thanks prettily, and said she must be going." Sara M. described the set of expected behaviors, reinforced since childhood, as the "no ladies" rules: "No lady ever sits with her limbs crossed (and limbs, it was; legs was still a four-letter word); no lady ever lets her back touch the back of the chair; no lady ever goes out without a clean linen handkerchief in her purse; no lady ever leaves the house until the last button on her gloves is fastened; no lady ever lets her bare foot touch the bare floor, and so forth."[3] In a reversal of Oscar Wilde's bon mot, "I don't say we ought to misbehave, but we should look as though we could," it wasn't enough to behave: you also needed to look like you would.

Sara's circle of friends in their neighborhood on the tree-shaded streets of Montgomery included Sara Haardt, born 1898; Zelda Sayre, born 1900; and Tallulah Bankhead, born 1902 and, along with her sister, Eugenia, raised in part by her aunt Marie Bankhead in Montgomery after the girls' mother died. All grew up within walking distance of one another at the turn of the century in the state's capital. Raised to be belles but resistant to conform, all four girls struggled with the roles they were expected to play. In her autobiography, *Outside the Magic Circle*, another contemporary, Virginia Foster Durr, described the three options for "a well-brought-up young Southern white woman": "She could be the actress, playing out the stereotype of the Southern Belle . . . and offering a sweet, winning smile to the world. . . . If she had a spark of independence or worse, creativity, she could go crazy—on the dark, shadowy street traveled by more than one stunning Southern Belle. Or she could be the rebel. She could step outside the magic circle, abandon privilege, and challenge this

FIGURE 3. Zelda Sayre

Zelda Sayre, five years older than Sara Mayfield, was like a big sister to the admiring Sara. Growing up in the same Montgomery neighborhood, they often played outdoors with other children. Zelda made up games for them and once saved Sara from a bad roller-skating accident by swooping up and pulling her away from a cobblestoned street at the last minute. (*The Oracle* [yearbook of Sidney Lanier High School, Montgomery, AL], Alabama Department of Archives and History)

way of life. Ostracism, bruises of all sorts, and defamation would be her lot."[4] In that description are echoes of Zelda, Tallulah, Sara H., and Sara M., playing the roles of actress, creative gone crazy, and rebel.

Zelda was physically brave, and Sara, wanting to impress, tried to keep up with her. One day, trying out new roller skates on a hill in their neighborhood, Sara began to lose control as she gained speed, and Zelda, seeing she was in trouble, swooped in, pulled her away from the cobblestones she was about to fly onto, and let Sara hold onto her the next time so that she could get the hang of skating. Zelda also taught Sara how to dive, invented games for the neighborhood children, and slipped their daddies' mint julep cups away when they were finished so that she could drain off the mint-and-bourbon flavored sugar. One letter Sara received much later, when she was researching Zelda's life, describes Zelda as a young woman and suggests how easy it was to be shocking in those days. Sara's correspondent, Harold T. Council, of Cedar Lane Farms in Greenville, Mississippi, writes that he only knew Zelda slightly, but: "I do know of one instance in 1920 when Farnell Blair, whom I ran with, invited her up to Sewanee for some dances. When she arrived at Tuckaway Inn where she was to stay, her pocketbook flew open and several packages of cigarettes fell out. Of course, everybody was all eyes as back in 1920 very few girls smoked. As I remember her, she was most intelligent and was a very popular girl."[5]

Sara was coming of age as young people were ever more autonomous, spending time with one another alone, driving cars, reading magazine articles and seeing films with romantic, even erotic, content.[6] When Sara M. was a teenager, she and Sara Haardt liked to go on drives in the early evening in the Ford Racer that Judge Mayfield had given his daughter, talking about everything under the sun, and not just the life of the mind but the life of the body, as they discussed men and what they both thought they knew of them. They also played guitars together: jazz, blues, and ragtime, "Salty Dog" and "Mama Don't 'Low" and "Lovesick Blues." Sara M. wrote, "Jazz had a double meaning among the negroes and was incontestably not a word that ladies used in those days."[7]

Perhaps hoping to tame their daughter as she became an adolescent— Sara once wrote that her mother had sent her to a finishing school when peach tree switches couldn't make her behave—the Mayfields sent Sara to the very proper Margaret Booth School in Montgomery, a college preparatory school for girls. It was under Miss Booth's chaperonage that Sara first went to Europe. At sixteen and a half, when less-privileged girls her age in Alabama would have been working in fields or factories, perhaps already married, Sara was applying for a passport. Her application listed plans to visit "France, Spain, Italy, Germany, Austria, Czecho-slovakia, Holland, Belgium and British Isles." Along with other girls from the Margaret Booth School, Sara sailed from New York on June 3, 1922, and returned to the States on September 30, arriving in New York from Plymouth, England. On September 10 she turned seventeen abroad.

On the trip, Sara kept a travel diary, a notebook bound in red leather in which she writes, "I hope in my declining years it will be a great source of amusement to me and mine." She recorded the various places they visited and what she enjoyed and also described her feelings and concerns regarding the other girls. Despite the excitement of seeing so many new places, she found group travel stressful at times: in one entry she vents her frustrations over a fight with Liz Thigpen and remarks several times that the day "was hell." In Nice, two weeks after their arrival, she complains that "Elizabeth and I are [in the] same room & I can tell she hates it. Somehow I feel she doesn't like me so much as she used to. She has just realized how ignoble I am & how just plain sad." A few days later, she writes that the girls had tried to plan a party—presumably involving alcohol—but that Miss Margaret had gotten wind of their plans and forbidden it. Sara and Liz were friends partly because their mothers, Susie and Daisy—Suze and Daze—were great friends, so their friendship mattered to Sara not only for itself but also as part of the near-familial network that bound them together, just as their mothers' nicknames for them, Seraphim and Cherubim, signaled an almost divinely inspired connection.

Something else happened on that trip to Europe that haunted Sara the rest of her life, some accusation, real or imagined, that Miss Booth made regarding Sara and Liz's friendship. The group was staying in Cornwall, England, at the King Arthur Hotel, where waves broke against the rocks on the shore and a storm blew up, literally and figuratively. Many years later in a letter to Liz, Sara described what Miss Booth had said as "unthinkable," a "projection" they were "too young to understand," but something that made them pull the covers over their heads and cry. Their friendship was "noble" and "one for which the Greeks had a word. And the word was *agape* rather than *philia*." Given the context, the mention of projection, and the assertion that theirs was a higher love, it seems likely that Margaret Booth had implied—or Sara had inferred from something she said—that there was a sexual affection between the two girls. Although it's not possible to know, at this remove, whether any physical relationship between the two ever occurred, it is clear from Sara's letters over a lifetime that Sara always *loved* Liz, idealized her, and was devoted to the idea of her. Sara often opened her letters with "Darling B," or "Dearest B"—the *B* standing for "Beloved"—or sometimes to "Seraphim," signed "Cherubim." Sara had no sister and was only briefly married, and for all her life, Liz would be sister and celibate spouse and seraphic spirit, all rolled into one.

Such endearments, and even passionate attachments, were common between women in the nineteenth century, without any assumed implication of sexual intimacy, according to the authors of *Intimate Matters: A History of Sexuality in America*. By the 1880s, however, same-sex attraction was beginning to be seen as a defining identity rather than a discrete sexual act, and the "medical labeling of same-sex intimacy as perverse conflated an entire range of relationships and stigmatized all of them as a single, sexually deviant personal identity." Theories about the source of deviance ranged from it being an acquired degenerative illness, inborn, or psychologically derived. "By the 1920s, Freudian theories of sexual development as well as the writings of other sexologists had completed the redefinition of same-sex pairings as homosexual and labeled them morbid and pathological."[8] At sixteen, Sara was no expert on writers such as Krafft-Ebing, Havelock Ellis, or Freud, but she had absorbed, like many other young women in the twenties, the idea that attraction to another woman was seen by others as abnormal, and perhaps had internalized that perception as well.

Apart from those interpersonal ups and downs, however, Sara still took great pleasure from seeing so many new places and faces. It was in Paris that she first saw Ernest Hemingway, just beginning to make a name for himself as a writer. She had slipped away from Miss Booth and the rest of the girls, who were having tea at the stylish Rumplemayer's, and asked a journalist she knew to take her to the Rotonde café. There, the newspaperman pointed out a young man slouched in a corner, reading a racing sheet. She was not impressed, writing of him that "even among the broad black hats and the flowing ties, the paint-smeared smocks and mandarin coats jammed together at the sidewalk tables, his clothes were conspicuously sloppy. He wore a dirty singlet, a pair of old corduroy trousers, grimy sneakers, and no hat." As Sara and her friend watched him "scowl over the francs and centimes marked on the saucers before him as he totted up the bill," they gossiped about his spartan living conditions, his wife's money, how he drove an ambulance in the war and was wounded.[9]

In Italy, she met a more congenial spirit, Hudson Strode, an English professor at the University of Alabama who became well-known both as a teacher of Shakespeare and a writer of travel books. Strode, on leave from teaching, was spending the summer of 1922 in Sorrento, Italy, with an apartment on the Bay of Naples. He and Miss Booth were friends, and when she became ill, she asked for help from Professor Strode to take the girls to the Blue Grotto. As Strode described his chaperonage, "Because of the low-hanging rock at the entrance of the eerie Grotto, I had to lie down with one of the girls in a small boat. This girl, then in her late teens, was Sara Mayfield, the daughter of an Alabama Supreme Court judge."[10]

When the girls returned to the States and their ship docked in New York City, Sara's mother met her for further travels to Baltimore and Washington, DC, before going back to Alabama. In New York, her friend Zelda Sayre, now married to the writer F. Scott Fitzgerald, after a courtship in Montgomery where he was stationed during World War I, met Sara at the chic Palm Court of the Plaza Hotel. Sara expected cocktails but Zelda said she was too young for that, so, surrounded by palms and potted plants under a stained-glass dome, the two Montgomery girls settled in for a chat, with tea for Zelda and hot chocolate for Sara.

One topic of discussion might have been an incident that had happened at the Margaret Booth School in the past school year. Sara Haardt, having graduated from Goucher College in 1921 (she was described in her yearbook as a "soulful highbrow"), had come back home from Baltimore to teach at the Booth School. There, she became involved in a disagreement with Margaret Booth over what Sara M. described as a "clear cut case of cheating." As Sara M. understood it, Miss Booth had wished to overlook the academic misbehavior of a "prominent pupil" so as not to cause a scandal. When the mother of the cheating student demanded an apology from Miss Haardt and the student body president, Miss Booth told them to do so, and, said Sara, "the same moral and intellectual courage that Sara Haardt had shown in defending her fellow-suffragettes from the Montgomery police force asserted itself." Haardt and the student government officers arranged a hearing, in which Sara Mayfield and other girls were called to testify. As Sara described it, the student was found guilty of cheating, Miss Booth refused to expel her, the mother threatened legal action against Sara Haardt, Sara Haardt consulted Judge Mayfield, who supported her legal rights in the matter, and, said Sara M., "there the matter rested."[11]

Sara Haardt left Montgomery to return to Goucher College to teach, and her departure for Baltimore provided both an example and an excuse for Sara M. to leave Montgomery and get away from small-town pettiness. Having been abroad and gotten a taste of the wider world, Sara was likely chafing for more excitement and variety than she would ever find on the quiet, decorous streets of Montgomery, described by one historian as a "city consumed by politics, dominated by traditional values, and run by elite families who could trace their genealogy at least as far back as Jefferson Davis's brief residency in the 'capital of the Confederacy.'"[12]

Chapter 2

From "Something in the Literary Line"
to "The Line of Least Resistance"

*In which Sara wins a Writing Prize and meets a Famous Writer, leaves College
to marry a Hometown Suitor, and departs on another Trip to Europe when the
Marriage collapses.*

N O ONE WAS SURPRISED WHEN SARA MAYFIELD FOLLOWED SARA
Haardt to Goucher, a women's college founded in 1888 by the Meth-
odist Episcopal Church. She even took up residence in Sara Haardt's old
dorm room. The second Sara from Montgomery at Goucher quickly came to
be known as "Mayfield." Although she fit in just fine and pledged a sorority,
as with her initial effort at going to school, she didn't like it at first, writing
her mother in November of how miserable she was. She studied all the time,
but she couldn't seem to make much headway: "my brain is just too undevel-
oped for this stuff." Perhaps her mother spoke with Margaret Booth, Sara's
former school principal, to enlist her in encouraging Sara's studies. Despite
whatever dismay Sara had felt about the cheating scandal, she still kept in
touch with Miss Booth. In a letter to Sara that first semester at Goucher,
Miss Booth wrote, "You are a precious dear to have written me that clever,
attractive letter," recounted activities with girls at the Booth School, and then
closed her letter with that combination of affection, guilt, and lacy rhetoric in
which practiced southern ladies so excel: "I am so eager to see you. Be sure to
come right around when you arrive. I hope you are working because you can
do so very well if you will work. I miss you greatly and will be rejoiced to see
you in about four weeks. In the mean time do your very best and show your

father and your mother what the piece of humanity that they love best in the world can do."

The adjustment to college was difficult at first, but Sara began to find encouragement for her writing. She wrote her father of one teacher's advice: "There is no news here except that yesterday I had a conference with my English teacher and she said she thought that I ought to do something in the literary line and that I had been doing very well in class."[1] In December she was inducted into the Press Club, which carried with it the privilege of wearing a small gold pin in the shape of a quill, another sign that her writing abilities were being acknowledged.[2]

Also by December, she began to feel she was getting the hang of school: "I eat, sleep, and work, all mechanically, but I am beginning to like Goucher much more." Setting a pattern for future letters to her mother, she sat at her dormitory desk writing letter after letter home, of how much she misses her, of how she feels bad at being criticized for not writing more frequently, and of how she needs food or clothes or money, as in a letter in her first year when

FIGURE 4. Sara Mayfield and the staff of the *Goucher Weekly*

At Goucher College, Sara (*front row, far right*) joined the staff of the *Goucher Weekly* her freshman year, 1922; her hometown friend Sara Haardt (*back row, third from left*) was alumnae editor. In December, Sara was inducted into the Press Club, which carried with it the privilege of wearing a small gold pin in the shape of a quill. (Courtesy of Goucher College Special Collections and Archives)

she writes, "If you don't send me some food I am not going to write anymore even though I do love you the most in the world."

When Sara took the train back to Goucher from Montgomery after Christmas break, she wrote her parents that her friend Dottie Tilton had been surprised to see her when she arrived, her friends having decided she was done with college life. By the end of the month, during exams, she was living on coffee and "dope" (Coca-Colas), not getting any sleep, and on top of everything had to have two teeth pulled and abscesses in two wisdom teeth lanced to drain and clear the infection. She closed one letter, "I have been up all night long, so if this letter is crazy don't blame me." In the spring, Sara was still worried that her parents were disappointed in her, but her mother wrote with typical endearment, "My darling child, I am so distressed that you thought I had written you a 'hard letter' for such was certainly not my intention & you simply misinterpreted it. I have nothing but praise for you & your work this year you have exceeded my fondest expectations." Sara saved at least one hundred letters from her mother, and that likely represents only a fraction of those written. All her life, from Sara's childhood and on into her years in Bryce Hospital, Susie faithfully wrote Sara with encouragement, news of family and friends, discussions of finances and clothes and food. Sara seemed to need her mother's steadfastness, and even when Sara was angry with her, Susie Mayfield served as a fixed point from which Sara measured where she was in the world, and where she'd come from.

Sara's father encouraged her as well, but few letters from him survive. In one, in the spring of her freshman year at Goucher, he wrote, "My Darling Sara, We were so glad to know you arrived well and safe. That was, I am proud to say, a well-deserved compliment paid you by your Critical teacher. It shows she is a good Judge, and a sagacious critic.

"If you knew how much pleasure your work at college afforded your mother & father it would make your tasks easier." After discussing football (he was delighted to report that the University of Alabama had just defeated the professional team of Rochester, New York), and court news, he closes, "The woods here are beautiful. The dogwood, . . . yellow Jasmine and all wild flowers are now at their peak. Lovingly, Dad." Surely that letter made her miss home more than ever.

The brightest spot in her freshman year was winning a short story contest judged by the editorial board of the Goucher literary magazine. Earning her a twenty-dollar gold piece, Sara's story, "When the Prodigal Returns," is well-crafted but fairly maudlin: a young man returns home from five years in "the city" to find that his father has taken up making moonshine; happy to find alcohol on the premises, he secretly drinks some, and, tragically, goes blind when it turns out to be a bad batch. Recruited to hand out the literary prizes at the awards ceremony was the Sage of Baltimore, literary critic and gadfly H. L. Mencken. Sara Haardt herself had won that same freshman contest in 1917 with a story titled "The Rattle-Snake: Being the Romance of a Clown," in which Mary Elizabeth Smith, a girl with "a baby mouth and blue eyes," is hired by a circus to be "Sari, The Snake Charmer" and to handle a huge rattlesnake from Alabama known as the "King Rattler." The character of Sari,

Figure 5. Sara Haardt

Sara Haardt, eight years older than Sara Mayfield, was Sara's teacher at the Margaret Booth School in Montgomery and again at Goucher. A suffragist, writer, and clear-eyed social observer of the South, Haardt was a dear friend as well as an intellectual mentor to the younger Sara. (Photograph by Stanley Paulger, 1919; courtesy of Goucher College Special Collections and Archives)

which was one of Sara H.'s names for Sara M., is likely a playful homage to the younger girl.

Because it would have been considered improper for the young Sara to go out to dinner with the older Mencken after the prize-giving, Sara Haardt agreed to serve as chaperone, along with Sara M.'s English professor, Harry T. Baker. Sara M. later remembered the dinner as being at Otto Schellhase's restaurant, where "the city's glitterati met"; it became Mencken's favorite hangout, the place he met literary and artistic friends for beer and conversation on a Saturday night.[3] They must have eaten somewhere else that first night, though, as Schellhase didn't open his restaurant until 1924. Mencken, who had coined the phrase "Sahara of the Bozart" to describe the cultural sterility and provinciality of the South, was famously antimarriage, but he was strongly attracted to Sara Haardt. After the initial dinner, Mencken asked Haardt out by asking Sara M. to bring her along when novelist Joseph Hergesheimer, at the time incredibly successful though now little remembered, came to Baltimore. Sara H. was supposedly along to keep Joe company, but at dinner Sara M. and Joe talked about writing while, wrote Sara M., "Sara and Mencken had been engaged in exploratory talks. They shared a distaste for evangelists, gospel singers, Holy Rollers, actors, literary fakirs, politicians, athletics, Prohibition, terrestrial redemption, the Oxford movement, the New Humanism, and other such non-Euclidean theologies." As the intellectual and romantic sparks continued to fly between Haardt and Mencken, Mencken encouraged both young women in their writing. At one point he encouraged them to live together to keep each other company, writing to Sara H. that "it is impossible to bang away at the typewriter for more than five or six hours a day. Even under the best conditions. The great curse of authors is loneliness." He also included them in gatherings of visiting writers and publishers (mostly male), including James Branch Cabell, author of the bestseller *Jurgen*, Sherwood Anderson, James M. Cain, and Edgar Lee Masters. Mencken appreciated the fact that these two Montgomery girls were smart in both senses of the word—intelligent *and* well-dressed— and he let them know which men to watch out for with phrases like "'he's a charming fellow but a chicken-chaser.'"[4] Sara M. and Henry Mencken learned that they had birthdays just two days apart—the tenth and twelfth of September—and, throughout her life, whenever Sara was in Baltimore they split the difference and celebrated with friends on the eleventh.

As Sara M. grew up, she and the older Sara became even closer friends. Sara M. wrote that "among friends there is usually such a thing as mine and thine." But, in their friendship, "If one had money, we both had it. If we didn't have it, we just didn't have it."⁵ Sara H. also enlisted the energetic younger woman as "chef, girl Friday and chauffeur."⁶ Even though she was studying hard, Sara had mastered the discipline of college and found time to play, sometimes sitting on the floor at Sara Haardt's place, having an illicit drink and smoke with her and another teacher, Marjorie Nicolson, sometimes going down to the naval academy at Annapolis for dances and even weekends.

In high school she'd had at least one big romance, with a boy named Tommy, away at boarding school. In September, when she had just turned sixteen, she wrote, "Tommy even when the initials on my arm are gone the rememberence [*sic*] of you won't be gone from my heart"; in October she wrote, "Tommy you [are] my joy I couldn't live without you"; in November she addressed him as "Tommy Darling"; and in December she said she'd have committed suicide if she hadn't gotten a letter from him. On January 25, after receiving a photograph of him, she gushed, "It is the best looking picture in the world & the living breathing image of you. Likeness is no word for it. I love the size, color, paper, shades & the man himself."

Meanwhile, she was breaking someone's heart in Tuscaloosa: One anguished letter from a beau reads, "Sara, for the love of Pete, don't treat me this way. The reason for my saying the few simple things that I did was not that I did not care for you, because I do, Little Girl, more than you'll ever know or believe, but because it is terribly humiliating to fall in love with a girl and then get brutally jilted." Another fellow, from Montgomery, wrote more jauntily to her when she went off to college, "I expect when you come back, there'll be a trail of Yankee letters that'll reach around the world, but young lady let it be *letters only*. I couldn't stand having a bunch of Yankee jellies on your trail."

At Goucher, she dated men in Baltimore and Annapolis, and, when she was home, she continued to play the dating game with men in Montgomery. Among them was a physician she called "Doc" who was ten years older than she and gave her candies, magazines, roses, and, for a while, his heart, before realizing she was not yet serious about getting married. While home for the Christmas holidays, Sara M. and Sara H. double-dated with John Sellers and Peyton Mathis, known around Montgomery as the Gold Dust Twins. Sara M. wrote that "Peyton, who had all the charm of an older man with a romantic past, was the proprietor of the Montgomery Marble Works and creator of such distinguished monuments in Oakwood Cemetery as 'The Broken Column' and 'The Wings of Death.'"⁷ Perhaps what Sara refers to as Peyton's "romantic past" is the loss of his wife, Laura, who died in November 1916 after giving birth to a son in May, leaving behind the baby boy and a little girl. When Peyton was a man-about-town in Sara's adolescence and young adulthood, and periodically dating Sara H., he was already a father and a widower. Born in 1890, he was truly an "older man," fifteen years Sara M.'s senior, but only eight years older than Sara H., who, while being pursued by Mencken, also recognized his reluctance to commit to marriage and was careful to let him know she could see other men.

John Sellers, born in 1900, was five years older than Sara Mayfield. She once described him as "tall, blond, immaculate, and distinguished by what Peyton called 'maxillary regions similar to a Pontiac chief's.'" She went on, "His mother was dead, but the wife of his father's partner was one of the Twenty-Twos, the Montgomery equivalent of New York's Four Hundred, which by local standards made John highly eligible." John had been infatuated with Zelda, but Zelda had married Scott, so John turned his attentions to Sara Mayfield. Sara wrote of the two that, "Like all Southern gentlemen, Peyton and John were past masters at putting their girls on pedestals, glorifying them, and abasing themselves."[8]

A darker story of the two men than the one Sara tells has been proposed in later biography and literary criticism. Zelda biographer Sally Cline, based on a scene in Zelda's unpublished novel "Caesar's Things" and on her interpretation of Scott's letters, hypothesizes that Sellers and Mathis sexually assaulted Zelda in some way when she was fifteen. In the novel, characters named Dan and Anton convince the main character, Janno, to go with them to a deserted schoolyard by threatening her with being socially ostracized if she doesn't. Cline quotes "Caesar's Things": "They went up to the haunted schoolyard so deep in shadows and creaking with felicities of murder to the splintery old swing and she was so miserable and trusting that her heart broke and for many years after she didn't want to live: but it was better to keep going." Building on Cline's interpretation, Kendall Taylor in *The Gatsby Affair* conjectures that Zelda's strong interest in personal hygiene was consistent with the behavior of someone who had experienced sexual assault. If some kind of sexual coercion or assault did happen to Zelda, something similar to what she alluded to for her character Janno, the "boys" may well not have considered it significant, though what Cline describes as "one of the most savage scenes in Zelda's adolescence" would have haunted her. Added to sexual trauma would be the misguided sense of culpability: girls of her station were expected to be the ones to say no to sexual intercourse, as virginity was seen as preserving their greater "value" to a future husband. They were to keep their heads clear despite whatever arousal they might feel; losing control, letting go, was for boys only. Sara later explained this expectation as the result of the near-medieval societal structure of the southern white elite and land-based wealth: "Men of property insisted on the chastity of their womenfolk to insure the legitimacy of their heirs and assigns. Consequently, the technique of Southern ladies was to proceed so far and no farther; their brinksmanship did not 'go the limit.' . . . As long as she retained the equivocal virtue of 'a technical virgin,' . . . [she] could proceed quite a distance, if she kept quiet about it. The sin was in the saying."[9]

In one of her letters home from college, Sara gave evidence of this double standard. Writing to her mother of a return trip to Goucher on the train, she reported on the behavior of some girls she knew who had "picked up these boys on the train that they had never seen before." One girl, Mary, seemed to have "lost her mind, bearings, and perspective," hanging all over one of the boys. But, knowing how dangerous it was for a girl to get a bad reputation, Sara cautioned her mother, "*Don't mention this* [to anyone we know]." The book *Intimate Matters: A History of Sexuality in America* affirms the widespread double standard upheld by whites in the South, with "an emphasis on female purity" that "served as a means of both racial and gender control that allowed white men to attack their black counterparts for the flimsiest reasons and kept white women confined in their activities, with all of it resting on the access that white males had to black women." White women were to be "virtually untouchable, exemplifying a purity that was beyond corruption." Surveys at the time showed that, if young women of the 1920s did have sex before marriage, it was generally with one partner, and with the expectation that marriage would follow.[10]

Although Sara M. and her friends played the field at dating, the game was expected to end in choosing an appropriate man to marry. At home were Doc and John. At Annapolis was one special boyfriend, an ensign, E. E. "Monty" Berthold. He and Sara met at Annapolis in the fall of 1922, and he fell hard for her, writing that even though they'd only spent a short amount of time together, he was eager to see her, and "if I keep this up much longer I'll be falling in love with you thru correspondence." They dated for two years and became engaged, but, unbeknownst to Sara, Monty was sent to Guantanamo naval base in Cuba, where he was nearly killed in an airplane accident and was hospitalized for months. Why Sara didn't try to find out from mutual acquaintances at Annapolis the reason Monty might have fallen silent that summer is a mystery—but perhaps it was pride. Having fallen in love herself, she assumed he was not, after all, in love with her and had regretted his engagement.

John Sellers had continued to pursue Sara. He sent her a telegram at Goucher in April 1924: "Have just gotten back to Montgomery and this first opportunity to write unusually busy for this season of year have missed you like everything and do not see how I can survive the next six weeks." After learning of Sara's broken engagement with Monty, John redoubled his courtship, pushing his advantage, and, although she could have simply returned to Goucher in the fall, Sara relented and became engaged to him instead. It was an appropriate match for the life she convinced herself, only nineteen at the time, she was meant to have. She may also have begun to acknowledge to herself that she could be attracted to women, in which case the marriage served as a proclamation of her heterosexuality and, perhaps, an escape from unacceptable desires. If, as some have concluded, Zelda was sexually assaulted by John and Peyton Mathis, Zelda must never have spoken of it to Sara before the wedding. She may have learned more at some point, however: in an early draft of her book on the Fitzgeralds many years later, Sara would write, cryptically, of "stories about John by which Scott broke up Zelda's romance with him and which eventually did as much as John's drinking to break up my marriage to him."

When Mencken heard of Sara's engagement to John, he wrote to congratulate her and tell her he approved of her marrying a businessman instead of a writer. As Sara described his sentiments, Mencken believed that "women should avoid artists as they would the plague. . . . A wise girl's fancy should be confined to rich Babbitts and prosperous Rotarians; in a word, to men engaged in a sound and lucrative business."[11] Perhaps Mencken's approval made her feel she was making the right choice. But there is, finally, no clear answer why someone as independent as Sara would leave Goucher to get married, to John or Monty or Doc or anyone else.

Sara came of age at a time of women's activism on behalf of social reforms and suffrage, so she had models of Alabama women who did not marry but found meaning in work on behalf of a cause with kindred female spirits. The suffrage movement had, in the words of historian Anne Firor Scott, "provided an opportunity for strong women to become stronger, and for personalities to develop. This was particularly true in the South." Sara, though, was not temperamentally suited to group efforts and was unlikely to find her path in those pursuits. Scott notes that many southern activists "found it effective to operate within the ladylike tradition," a tradition Sara found stifling. Also, as Alabama historian Wayne Flynt has written, "For women born at the end of the 19th or early in the 20th century, many of the old social norms and institutional involvements seemed irrelevant and antiquated. Their rebellion was more rooted in personal liberation than in social change." Although one scholar, writing about views of women in the 1920s, notes that some contemporary observers saw flapper-dom as just a passing, rebellious stage, and expected most young women would revert to traditional roles of wife and mother, Sara might still have achieved escape velocity from Alabama. She might have moved to New York City or to Paris, where she could be freer, in whatever ways she chose, a model of the New Woman, educated, working, independent.[12]

And yet she married. By Sara's own account, she may simply have been both on the rebound and tired of school. At nineteen, life with the older, seemingly more sophisticated John might have sounded like a great deal more fun than taking classes. Marriage was a societally endorsed path to adulthood, and she was of marriageable age. (According to a report prepared

FIGURE 6. Sara Mayfield in her wedding dress

On November 12, 1924, Sara married John Sellers, but despite what seemed like initial happiness, the two were separated by 1926 and divorced in 1927. Sara vowed that she would never marry again, and didn't. (University of Alabama Libraries Special Collections)

by the US Census Bureau, in 1920 the median age for a woman to marry for the first time was twenty-one; that number held fairly steady through the 1970s before starting to rise.[13]) The year before, she had watched as even the strong-minded Sara Haardt had grown discouraged about her own literary career and considered giving it up and marrying a Montgomery boy. In a small blue notebook, Sara M. wrote of herself in the third person: "To Sara getting married was, society being what it is, simply following the line of least resistance." In a visual echo of the way she gave in to societal expectations, Sara in her wedding portrait seemed almost swallowed by the rococo staging—a young, round, unexpressive face in a sea of lace, silk, and a huge bridal bouquet with light-colored roses and abundant floral frou-frou, with a standing candelabrum behind her.

Novelist Anne Rivers Siddons, born in Georgia in 1936, raised by women from the same generation as Sara and Sara's mother, has spoken of this surrender to what was expected: "You see, we were raised to be belles. . . . We all knew—nobody ever told us, but we knew with a deeper wisdom than words—that the highest we could aspire to was capturing a husband who would then provide for us. And we believed that. At fourteen I was constantly in love. Our mothers and grandmothers believed it was the best they could give us, the protection of a man." Anne Firor Scott argues that the "southern lady" image had lost much of its power to shape a life by the 1920s and concludes that "a young woman of 1925 had before her eyes plenty of old fashioned homemakers, busy with their beaten biscuits, fanning themselves on front porches on hot summer evenings. But the front porch was no longer the limit of woman's sphere. She could also see businesswomen, political activists, teachers and social workers, librarians and newspaperwomen, lawyers and doctors."[14] Sara, marrying in 1924, was certainly one of those young women of whom Scott writes. But faced with a new set of choices and thus pressures, from work to marriage to some combination, Sara apparently decided to choose by barely choosing. She accepted John and became more societally acceptable by so doing.

The invitations to John and Sara's wedding were thick, cream-colored cardstock from Tiffany and Co., announcing that the ceremony would be held at nine o'clock in the morning at St. John's Episcopal Church on Wednesday, November 12, 1924; a reception followed at the Mayfields' home on South Perry Street, just a block from the Governor's Mansion. It was a mild, sunny fall day, with no rain to spoil the festivities. Not surprisingly, Sara's wedding had a traditional southern setting. The venerable St. John's was founded in 1834; as the Civil War opened, the Secession Convention of Southern Churches met there in 1861; and it was the church of Jefferson Davis, president of the Confederate States of America, and his wife while they lived in Montgomery. In 1865 the Union Army ordered it, along with the rest of the Episcopal churches in the state, closed. It reopened in 1866. None of this would have been in the least forgotten by 1924.

John Sellers chose Peyton Mathis, the Pride of the Confederacy, as his best man, which created some awkwardness for Sara Haardt, who had at one point dated Peyton semiseriously. Peyton had once wired Sara H. that he was headed to Baltimore with a ring but instead had gotten drunk on the train, and, wrote Sara Mayfield, "when he came to a week later in Charleston, South Carolina, he was legally married—but not to Sara Haardt."[15] For Sara M.'s wedding, Sara H., who suffered from lung troubles, used her health as an excuse for not coming to the wedding, offering instead to oversee guests' signing of the bride's book at the reception afterward.

Sara's erstwhile fiancé Monty was heartbroken when he recovered from the airplane accident and found out about the engagement to John. He wrote agonized letters, describing how he felt when he got Sara's letter breaking their engagement: "I locked my door and sat down to think just what had happened. Now three hours later and I'm trying to say something that never will be able to put into words." He wonders if he can try to be a "good sport," but concludes "I fear not." Vowing never to fall in love again, he writes, "My God, Sara! If you have ever cared for me as more than a passing fancy, please don't go back on me now." But it was too late. The plans were made, the church was booked, the dress was sewn, and all Montgomery knew Sara was going to marry John.

Mr. and Mrs. Sellers honeymooned in New York City, staying at the Commodore Hotel, a grand new hotel near Grand Central Station with a waterfall inside the lobby. They drove up to a Princeton football game, went to the theater in the city, saw friends, dined out, and took a drive into the country in an elegant Packard; it was chilly, so Sara wore her fur coat. Sara wrote her parents, professing her love for John: "I love John more and more every day, he is the most thoughtful, considerate darling in the world. Every day he goes out and buys me violets and candy. Yesterday I bought him a lovely dressing case with which he was delighted. I never realized before how companionable we are and how dear he is to me." A dinner was given at the Montgomery Country Club for the couple upon their return from their honeymoon, and, perhaps in that attempt to be a "good sport," or maybe just because he needed to see the competition, Monty showed up, a woebegone figure if ever there was one.

With the couple back in Montgomery, John left Sara for periods of time as he traveled the South on cotton business, but they corresponded regularly and affectionately. Still, the marriage suffered from his absences, and, according to Sara, it suffered when he was home due to John's heavy drinking and Sara's youth and, likely, boredom. Why had she given up college to sit at home and be Mrs. Sellers while John drank mint juleps on the porch? They fought over John's drinking and his wandering eye, but, years later, Sara accepted her part in the failure of their marriage, writing to him that she had been "young and dumb and stupid enough to have done my full share towards instigating the domestic warfare between us."[16]

They married in late 1924, and less than a year and half later, in 1926, Sara went abroad without him. She planned to stay in Paris as long as she could, then move to New York City and look for work—an indication she thought the marriage might be over. As Sara explained it, the occasion of her going away was her father's run for the US Senate. Given John's drinking, the family thought that his flouting of Prohibition laws could be used against her father, and Sara's separation from her husband might ameliorate the threat.

Learning and travel were Sara's two great sources of solace whenever her life was in turmoil, and Sara wrote her parents from Paris (where Miss Booth's sister was serving as pro forma chaperone for the still-married young woman) that "a lifetime isn't long enough to live in Paris. I have enjoyed this past week more than any other of my life." She went to lectures at the Sorbonne in the morning and the famous expat bars in the afternoons and evenings. At those, she observed Hemingway again, still unkempt: "His baggy tweed suit was patched at the elbows, and the pocket of his coat was torn from the notebooks jammed in it." She often saw him at Sylvia Beach's bookstore, Shakespeare and Company, but they never conversed beyond "bonjour."[17]

She also reconnected with the Fitzgeralds that spring and summer of 1926. In Paris she got caught up in a crazy night with Scott and a number of Princeton boys and Westport, Connecticut, girls, which, in the way of nights involving too much alcohol and an unstable mixture of personalities, devolved into drunken chaos. She was having drinks with friends at the Ritz Bar when Scott showed up with his gang. Scott insisted that Sara go with him to see Zelda in the hospital, where she was "'having her appendix removed,' according to Scott's euphemistic description of the operation"—which Sara suggests was an abortion. She decided to go along rather than incur his loud displeasure. There were more drinks and a stop at Harry's Bar to look for Hemingway, Scott commandeering a hearse when there were no cabs available; yet more drinks, and a stop by the Fitzgeralds' apartment to get some books for Zelda. When Sara convinced him that they would only upset Zelda by visiting her at what had become a very late hour, he refused to drop Sara off at her apartment and directed the hearse driver to drive at top speed to the market of Les Halles, all the while singing along with the Princetonians, who were still along for the ride. They ended up at an all-night bistro, but Scott passed out, and his friends left him in the hearse and hailed taxis for the rest of them. Said Sara, "And that was *that* night in Paris."[18]

But, all in all, Sara loved being in the City of Light. Traveling abroad, about to turn twenty-one, Sara wrote home to her mother, "Hug and kiss Father and Jim for me and tell the latter that I have wished for him a million times in the last two days and that I hope he will hurry and grow up so *we* can travel around to-gether." Sara once described herself as "gypsy-footed" and never worried about finding her way in a strange place—confident of her abilities and native wit, she was always at home in the world.

Sara met up with Zelda and Scott again on the Riviera; she was in Antibes, they in Juan-les-Pins. Sara visited them for parties and for sunbathing, but she found them arguing about Hemingway, about Scott's writing time, about money, and saw in each of them the loss of the relaxed ease and glow of youth. The day before Sara left, she watched as Scott, who had been drinking, struck Zelda and then defended himself to a group of friends, asking whether all men didn't get angry enough at their wives to strike them. Sara, escaping from her own failing marriage, her own drunken husband, felt the scene exposed the sadness beneath the glamorous facade: "For all the outward opulence of their life in Juan-les-Pins, it was apparent that they were both fast drifting into the emotional slum in which all too many expatriates ended up abroad—working too little, drinking too much, having transient love affairs, quarreling with their friends, roaming aimlessly about Europe in search of some romantic paradise, lost with the first flush of youth."[19]

Sara herself roamed farther before returning to the States, but, far from aimless, she made use of her travels in writing. Accompanied by the redoubtable Miss Booth as chaperone (rather than Miss Booth's sister, apparently with Sara's approval), she took a driving tour of Italy and then went to Corsica, Tunis, Algiers, Gibraltar, Seville, and Madrid. Sara wrote her mother, "This is the adventure of a lifetime for me and I am enjoying it immensely." She freelanced for the *Paris Herald Tribune*, writing pieces on Corsica and on the Rif War, a conflict that took place in the mountains of Morocco between the Rif, or Berber, people, and Spain, and later France, in the first half of the 1920s. After her travels, she returned home rather than to New York, feeling better than she had when she left and ready to make a decision about her marriage, one way or the other.

In a book about biographies of women, one literary critic writes of "the marriage plot" which "demands not only that a woman marry but that the marriage and its progeny be her life's absolute and only center" and theorizes that "for women who wish to live a quest plot, as men's stories allow, indeed encourage, them to do, some event must be invented to transform their lives, all unconsciously, apparently 'accidentally,' from a conventional to an eccentric story."[20] Sara was so much more suited to the quest than the marriage plot, and the breaking up of her marriage to John was a way to wrest the narrative away from the conventional, starting a new plot line that emphasized adventure over domesticity, individuality over family.

The self-inflicted wound of her marriage had thrown Sara off course for a time, but life seemed to be opening back up. She was traveling, she was writing, and, though her father had lost the Senate race, perhaps she thought family life with her parents and brother would resume pleasantly whenever she chose to be at home with them, and the awkwardness and discomfort of ending her marriage would pass. In a letter to her mother, she described the marriage as "a bad tooth that has to come out, one that ached so long that the pulling will be a relief."

Chapter 3

"The Young Lady Who Doesn't Present
Her Letters of Introduction"

*A Terrible Loss. Finishing an Interrupted Education. Romances abroad, Study in
London, and a Subsequent Return Home.*

THE UNIVERSITY OF ALABAMA FOOTBALL TEAM WAS FACING STAN-
ford in the Rose Bowl on New Year's Day, 1927, and Sara was listening
to the game on the radio with friends she was visiting in New York City.
Judge Mayfield was listening with friends in Montgomery. Said to have
bought the team their first uniforms, he was an ardent fan of the Crimson
Tide. As Alabama struggled, Judge Mayfield fumed, "Why don't they resort
to the pass?" This was just before halftime, and those were his last words.
News of his fatal heart attack spread so quickly that his death was reported
on the radio, later on in the game, and that was how Sara heard that her beloved father, her "dear Dady," had died. She rushed home from New York. A
banner headline on the front page of the *Montgomery Advertiser* the next day
proclaimed "Judge Mayfield Drops Dead at Radio Party."[1]

It is almost always painful to get the news of a parent's death, but for
Sara it was traumatic. She was devastated by the loss. No more conversations about books, no more discussions of the finer points of the law, never
again the greeting that made her feel all was well, no matter what. The shame
of her interrupted education and her failed marriage would go forever un-
resolved; her father would never know what she could become. Even worse
than her grief was her belief that her mother blamed John and her for Judge
Mayfield's death. As she later described that period in a letter, "My husband

was away on a bender at the time, I was in the process of getting a divorce, my mother in a state of hysterical collapse. Within a few hours, I lost all that made life worth living—father, husband, friends, money, position—coming on top of it, the shock of my mother's accusation was more than I could bear." Although Sara may have misinterpreted whatever it was her mother said to her, or taken a momentary expression for a settled opinion, she took what she understood to heart.

The family's grieving was public as well as private. Judge Mayfield's death was reported in the US as well as in the European edition of the *New York Herald Tribune* ("Alabama Judge Dies While 'Listening In'"), and he was mourned across Alabama: The state flag was flown at half staff; Capitol offices were closed during the hours of his funeral, 10:00 a.m. to noon on January third; and the governor's office was closed all day. Members of the Alabama House of Representatives passed a resolution extending their "heartfelt sympathy . . . to his grief-stricken family" and recounting the judge's many accomplishments. In the months to follow, friends sought a way to properly memorialize him, and on May 28, 1928, during commencement exercises, UA President George H. Denny spoke at the installation of a granite boulder by Farrah Hall, then home to the law school, in Judge Mayfield's honor. Denny said, "He loved the whole University, but he loved the Law School and the Athletic Field most. So, spontaneously, it came to our minds and hearts that the spot in proximity to the Law Building and the Athletic Field would be the most appropriate site on which to set this boulder."[2]

After her father's death Sara grieved mostly in solitude and experienced "a complete emotional paralysis and protracted lethargy," as she described it years later in a letter to a friend. In Sara's estimation, she had "retreated from reality to sleep as people often do when confronted with an intolerable shock." Her doctors, however, diagnosed her with sleeping sickness, or "encephalitis lethargica." Little known now except to those who have read Oliver Sacks's book on postencephalitis patients who exhibited near-paralysis or seen the film *Awakenings*, based on the book, the disease affected as many as 1 million people, first in Europe and then worldwide, from about 1917 to 1928. A case was reported in Montgomery, Alabama, as early as 1919. The National Institute of Neurological Disorders and Stroke of the US National Institutes of Health defines the illness as "a disease characterized by high fever, headache, double vision, delayed physical and mental response, and lethargy. In acute cases, patients may enter coma." The cause, whether viral, toxicological, or autoimmune, was never determined with certainty, and the disease largely disappeared after the 1920s. Postencephalitic patients who did not recover fully might suffer a variety of continuing symptoms. The journal *Brain* reports that, after the acute phase of the disease, the chronic phase could vary, occurring immediately, up to five years later, or even after a decade or more. In the chronic phase, sufferers might experience symptoms of parkinsonism, "but sleep disturbances, oculomotor abnormalities, involuntary movements, speech and respiratory abnormalities, and psychiatric disorders were also common features."[3]

Sara resisted the diagnosis because of her fear of the potential psychiatric effects of the disease, later writing to a friend that she "had not had encephalitis but an atypical case of typhus." But could the eventual psychiatric disorders, particularly the paranoia, that landed her in Bryce Hospital many years later, have been a feature of what was understood to be a physical illness? She had traveled in Europe, and the disease was widespread across the US as well. If her symptoms had been seen as such, might she, later, have encountered greater sympathy and different treatments? It is an alternate history both fascinating and frustrating to ponder. The diagnosis changed her, and in her own estimation she went from being "very independent in deed and thought" to being inclined to "doubt my every thought and inclined to be dependent upon the approval and encouragement of others."[4] Although for the next two years Sara "lived in hell with the fear of post-encephalitis insanity hanging over me," as she later wrote in a letter, she decided to go back to Goucher to finish her degree, putting herself back on a track of intellectual pursuits. She also decided it was time, finally, to divorce John. The divorce was granted March 18, 1927, and as part of the decree she was "hereby permitted to resume her maiden name." Dorothy Tilton, a friend from Goucher, acknowledged the change with more fanfare: "Mayfield, Miss Sara Martin. How excellently pleasant to be able to think and write that again. *Dear* Mayfield."

The judge who granted the divorce, Walter B. Jones, took the time to write a letter on official letterhead addressed "To Whom It May Concern." (It probably helped that he was also senior warden of the vestry at the Mayfields' church.) The letter, which Judge Jones clearly took some care with, states that he considers Sara to be "absolutely blameless" in the matter of the divorce, that she is "a young lady of culture and refinement and she enjoys the confidence and esteem of all who know her." Moreover, "Her family is one of the old families of this State and are honored and esteemed in all parts of the State. There are no better people in the State than the Mayfields." Her husband, wrote the judge, "could have been divorced on the ground of the violation of . . . the Mann Act, but as the wife desired to spare the family of her husband as much as possible, this ground was not urged against the husband." (The Mann Act, passed in 1910, is a federal law that criminalizes transportation of women or girls across state lines "for the purpose of prostitution or debauchery, or for any other immoral purpose.") Sellers, it would seem, had been unfaithful. But, wrote Judge Jones: "There was no publicity attendant upon the hearing of the case, the matter being submitted upon depositions and no mention of same being carried in the newspapers." Especially under such conditions, Sara would not necessarily have been stigmatized by getting a divorce, which had become more common in the 1920s than in previous decades, even though rates were lower in Alabama than the national average. (Divorce rates for married women in the US were 3 per 1,000 in 1890; 4.1 per 1,000 in 1900; 4.7 per 1,000 in 1910; 8.0 per 1,000 in 1920; and 7.8 per 1,000 in 1927, the year of Sara's divorce. In Alabama, however, the rates were lower: fewer than 1 per 1,000 in 1890 and 1900, rising to 1 per 1,000 in 1916 and 1.2 per 1,000 in 1930.[5]) Although the increase in divorces may have been a reflection of women's increased ability to support themselves and unwillingness to simply endure an unhappy marriage, statistics can shed only some light on any individual story.[6] In the small world of Montgomery society, the failure of Sara and John's marriage, and the reasons for it, likely would have been known by all.

Having gone back to Baltimore and Goucher in the winter of '27 to finish her degree, in addition to taking classes Sara assisted a psychology professor on several experiments and began to develop an interest in the subject. She also translated some papers from German on "the psychology of suggestion" for Sara Haardt, who was researching the subject at the time. Sara M. was finding a pattern for her life in times of stress, to escape into relentless work on a problem external to her own troubles, losing herself, in both the good and bad senses of the phrase. When she was asked by her old sorority, the Deltas, to come to a dance, she wrote her mother that "somehow I feel terribly old and out of the swim, it is a pardon to spend all of your life preparing to live it, especially when I know that my race is run, and life's sweetest days are long past. Just a drudgery, sixteen hours a day, seven days a week, and nothing to show for it, but it is a narcotic and after all that's the best I ask for." She was all of twenty-one.

During all Sara's travails, her friend Liz Thigpen had remained close, and Sara saved her letters for comfort. It might have been some reassurance to

Sara that Liz struggled with the question of marriage as well. In the spring of 1923, about to graduate from college, she had written to "My darling Sara" that she had broken up with Wiley C. Hill Jr. and that she planned to move to New York and would try to stop and see Sara in Baltimore on the way. She changed her mind about Hill, however, returning to Montgomery, marrying him, and, on October 19, 1924 (just before Sara's wedding to John Sellers), giving birth to a son, whom they named Wiley Croom Hill III. She would

FIGURE 7. Elisabeth Thigpen Hill

Elisabeth Thigpen, who married Wiley C. Hill Jr. and stayed in Montgomery, was a lifelong friend and reliable North Star to the peripatetic Sara. Sara often opened her letters to Liz with "Darling B," or "Dearest B"—the "B" standing for "Beloved"—or sometimes to "Seraphim," signed "Cherubim," childhood nicknames from their mothers. (Isabel Thigpen Hill)

remain in Montgomery the rest of her life, a cultured woman who kept a beautiful home and entertained regularly—the life Sara might have had, but chose not to.

Married or not, Liz relied on Sara for unqualified love and as an antidote to feeling dreary. After Judge Sellers died in 1927, Sara's mother had moved from Montgomery back to Idlewyld, their antebellum mansion in Tuscaloosa, and Sara lived there when she wasn't elsewhere. In an undated but early letter Liz wrote, "Believe it or not some fine day I am going to arrive bag & baggage at Tuskaloosa for an indefinite stay—I am simply swamped with depression & the hopelessness of life." When Sara had failed to write, she pleaded, "And now to you, Cherubim, my *dearest dearest* love—Please get normal & write me a long letter—tell me about your dreams—tell me about your date with P.R." In early 1926 she wrote a brief note on her mother's stationery, using Sara's nickname: "Dearest Sal—You know I thought about you all night & what a real friend you are & how I love you—My life could be utterly colourless without you—Please hold fast & don't forsake me—I need the stimulation of you—My love, my chère, Liz." On August 1, 1927, she sent Sara a telegram that she was planning to visit her in Chicago, where Sara, pushing hard to finish her degree at Goucher, was going to summer school at the University of Chicago, living within walking distance of campus and taking classes in economics, French, and English composition so that she could catch up and graduate "on time" in 1928. Whereas Sara's life continued on its often irregular trajectory, Liz's took on the familiar pattern of marriage, children, home, and church—what Sara liked to refer to with the German phrase "kinder, küche, kirche."

In Chicago, still suffering from the lethargy she experienced after her father's death, Sara had yet another romance, this time with Charles Miller, a University of Chicago instructor who wrote witty, erudite, and lengthy love letters to Sara after her Chicago sojourn. One letter, addressed "Divine Sara," is deliberately undated because "time no longer matters." He addresses her as "divine" because, "as you can see by the salutation, your adorer, following the usual practices of mankind, has very shortly after your departure raised you to minor sainthood." He told stories, filled his letters with sketches, used alternately red and black ink on his typewriter ribbon for highlights, and did everything in his power to woo her with words. Through the final year of Sara's studies at Goucher, Charles wrote, and wrote, and wrote. He tried to convince her to finish her undergraduate degree at Chicago and fretted over her well-being: "Your health still remains a matter of tremendous concern—between the Scylla of sleeping sickness and the Charybdis of nervous collapse you seem to have jolly rough going."

But Sara, though flattered and even perhaps "in love," had just escaped one marriage and was not eager to embark upon another. However buoying Charles's admiration was, she was not prepared to exchange her freedom for it, and she had learned the need to take care of herself, rather than relying on a man, either husband or father. Back at Goucher, living at the Calvert Court Apartments, a handsome new red-brick building, she studied hard but finally began to enjoy again the undergraduate feel of late nights with friends, returning to Calvert Court along its brick walkway, in winter between the snow-laden box hedges on a cold evening to a cozy apartment and hot chocolate, or, as the weather warmed, sitting next to a rotating fan hoping for a cool breeze on a hot night as she smoked and listened to classical music. Friends knew that she aspired to write, and one Goucher friend wrote to her "Hope your [sic] doing really big things—the great American novel must come from the pen of Sara Mayfield." She also enjoyed telling stories of Montgomery, what her friend Dorothy Tilton later evoked in a letter as "your marvellous stories of Zelda Fitzgerald, and the foreign exotic world of Montgomery, from the smell of Cape Jasmine to Negro shanty town to picnics by the river . . . the magical mythical era of Montgomery which you recreated with the full genius of Scott Fitzgerald himself for a wide eyed Yankee!"

Sara's Goucher transcript shows that she entered school on September 27, 1922, that she was away from Goucher for two and a half years, from August 1924 to February 1927, and that she graduated on June 4, 1928. A transcript is a dry document, but it tells the story of her departure from and return to college, during which time she went from college girl to married lady to divorcée and back to college student, though no longer a girl. In 1928, at the age of twenty-two, she was launched into the world, a college graduate, but already with a great deal more life experience than the fresh-faced young women around her.

Her bachelor's degree completed, graduate school beckoned, and, she thought, combined with travel, it would be the perfect antidote to any remaining grief and lethargy. After graduation in 1928, Sara headed overseas, planning first to travel in England and Europe and then to attend graduate school at the University of London. Her younger brother, James, enrolled at the University of London as well, and before starting classes, Sara and Jim took a trip across Europe, a trip they began by purchasing bicycles and cycling from London to the English Channel. Sara complained about the

FIGURE 8. Sara Mayfield in her senior year at Goucher College

Sara graduated from Goucher in June 1928. Reentering college in 1927 after divorcing John Sellers, she wrote her mother, "somehow I feel terribly old and out of the swim, it is a pardon to spend all of your life preparing to live it, especially when I know that my race is run, and life's sweetest days are long past." She was all of twenty-one. (Yearbook photos courtesy of Goucher College Special Collections and Archives)

discomfort of her bicycle seat but otherwise loved the freedom of their trip. They didn't try to make any kind of time at all, having picnics, sitting on the banks of the Thames and reading books they'd bought at old bookshops, even going for swims. They slept at inns, farmhouses, and pubs. One night, wrote Sara, they even slept in a haystack.

Their bicycle trip coincided with the age of the adventurous aviator, and Sara described, in a letter to Dorothy Tilton, a comical mix-up that resulted when they arrived by bicycle in Southampton: "As I walked into the hotel there, looking like a tramp, dressed in riding britches, high-laced boots and a leather jacket, the people began shouting and someone thrust a bouquet into my arms. After all of that pedaling, I knew that I deserved some flowers, but I thought they were going to be lilies." She continued: "It appears that the crowd had gathered to greet Miss Erwright, the trans-atlantic flyer, and had mistaken my costume for that of the higher arts." It was Amelia Earhart that Sara meant, not yet apparently a household name, or not to her. Earhart completed the first transatlantic flight by a woman, landing with her copilot in Wales, then arriving in Southampton on June 19, 1928.

FIGURE 9. James Mayfield Jr. and Sara Mayfield on bicycles in London

In the summer of 1928 Sara and her younger brother, James, went to England together. Before enrolling at the University of London, they traveled in Europe, beginning with a cycling trip from London to the English Channel. Sara wrote that they stayed "at old inns, farmhouses, pubs, even one night in a haystack. During the day we rode very little, as it was quite warm, that is unless we could find a beer truck to hang on behind. We lolled around on the banks of the Thames, reading Chaucer and Shelley, haunted the old book shops . . . had tea at every place we could find, swam whenever we felt like it and sometimes did a little riding." (University of Alabama Libraries Special Collections)

As summer eased into fall, Sara continued her travels before returning to London for school. In "The Odyssey of a Wandering Mind," notes she took about the trip, she writes of how she and her brother went through France together but parted as James headed to the Riviera, hoping to meet the writer

Somerset Maugham. She ran into the Fitzgeralds again in Paris, finding them jointly morose, and watched them argue as the three had drinks at the Café de la Paix.

When Sara and Zelda slipped away for a tête-à-tête, Zelda complained about Scott's Princeton friends and then asked Sara what had happened with John Sellers. Sara replied, "I married him—in the time of my innocence . . . and divorced him when I came of age." With Zelda's further prompting, she went on to explain what happened to Sellers: "Too many parties, too many hangovers, too much money."[7] A friend from Montgomery wrote Sara a long, chatty letter that summer, envying Sara's trip abroad, "doing what you please, as you please." In a postscript, the friend wrote, "Heard the other day that John has just returned to Montgomery from a sanitarium in Chicago. They say he is as crazy as ever. Although I have been over several times lately, I have not seen him."

On her own this trip, she went from Paris to the island of Corsica, re-searching and writing an article for the *Baltimore Sun* about "the Robin Hood of Corsica," Nonce Romanetti, killed in 1926 by gendarmes, and of the ven-detta that continued after his death. To her friend Henry Mencken, back in Baltimore, she sent a stiletto that supposedly had belonged to Romanetti. Mencken used it for a letter opener. Further brief notes from her trip, which retraced some of the places she had visited with Miss Booth in 1926, include: "Tunis—The Casbah—The Souks," fakirs, rope tricks, Sufis and prophecies, Algiers, Morocco, "the plague breaks out—Oran—cattle boat to Albania—storm." What adventures are suggested by this brief outline, what pluck.

Over the summer, Sara adventured romantically as well, with a newspa-perman and with a woman, a former classmate from Goucher. Among the bohemians of Paris and London, such behavior was unexceptional, but Sara's attraction to both men and women would have been outré (at best) in Ala-bama, and in her letters and journal entries she was careful to speak mostly in generalities. Copies of the letters to the woman, Anne Hackman, kept by Sara (she kept copies of all her letters throughout her life), are fond, warm, and heavily edited by Sara—with scissors, pen, and typewriter xxxx's to cover up declarations of affection and the kisses and hugs represented by "xxxs and ooos." Among the tales of her travels are frequent statements of affection for Anne. In one letter she speaks of her mother and brother and then says, "You understand me better than they and everyone else in the world. But that is only one of the reasons that"—and then she literally cut off the rest of her copy of the letter with scissors. In a letter from Nice, she begins, "Anne:—the morning mail arrived without a letter from you" then later marked out six lines with the typewriter. She writes, "The thought of being with anyone xxx xxx is loathsome." The marked-out words are "but you." And "for the love of charity write me. Xxxxxxxxxx." Beneath the x's are the words "I adore you." In a less-edited letter she writes, "Idealism is a mockery and memory a bitter sweet. . . . Oh Hell! Darling, you know only too well—you know my every thought. You know how unbearable life is without someone to talk to, someone to be with you when the nights are too beautiful for sleep, too intense for anything but a silent vigil, too vast to be alone."

But among these ardent letters to Anne are stories of another love, occurring simultaneously, with Joseph Becker Phillips—called, variably, Joseph, or Beck, or Phil, a journalist she had likely met in New York. Adopting what might now be called a polyamorous attitude, she wrote Anne that "I am halfway deeply in love with him, but I will see him in Paris and I suppose that like all of his ilk he is more attractive a thousand miles away. Wouldn't it be joyful to be carnal in mind as well as in body. For the last few months or so, I have wrestled with this damn business until I have succeeded in putting myself beyond good and evil, and now I am not so sure that it wasn't all a mistake. To say the least, the calm after the storm is monotonous." It seems almost certain that the "damn business" she was wrestling with was her attraction to Anne, as she had, years ago, wrestled with her attraction to Liz. Although Sara must have been aware that attraction to women would be seen by many, and especially by those at home, as unnatural, she also would likely have been aware of examples of college-educated women who had chosen to become couples, sometimes lifelong partners, for reasons of sexual attraction, supportive friendship, and intellectual companionship. A survey of twenty-two hundred women conducted by Katharine B. Davis in the 1920s found that "twenty-eight percent of the women's college graduates . . . had experienced intense ties with other women that included a physical component recognized as sexual" and "almost equal numbers" described relationships of "intense emotional attachments that involved kissing and hugging."[8] Sara, then, could have felt simultaneously "normal" and "abnormal," at ease with her attraction but pulled by her upbringing and her fear of censure to conceal her feelings from any but the object of her affection. That very summer, Radclyffe Hall's novel *The Well of Loneliness*, a groundbreaking novel about a lesbian relationship, was published in the US and England and greeted with charges of obscenity.

At the end of the summer, Sara stopped off in Paris and stayed for a bit while she did freelance work and completed travel pieces for the *Paris Herald Tribune*. She browsed through bookstalls, looking at prints and old books, thinking back, thinking forward: a twenty-two-year-old woman, divorced, fatherless, a woman free to fall in love, or not, with a man, or a woman, or just her own freedom. Sara, lost and found. She did reunite with Joseph Phillips, and she did allow herself to fall in love, in the Paris "of swift, floating kisses, sweeter for their swiftness, of days that were a song and nights that were a dream—a Paris that shelters Beck and nurtures an old-fashioned romance!" as she wrote Anne. Romance was thrilling to her, and Sara later wrote, "As far as I know, philosophers have never decided what the *summum bonum* of life is; but Zelda and I once agreed that we would settle for being young and in love in Paris in the springtime."[9] Sara's friend Dorothy Tilton once asked her if she was "*ever* out of love," and for a long time the answer was decidedly no.

Sara returned to England at the end of the summer, arriving with letters of introduction, including one from an acquaintance with a note saying, "I hope your trip will be most delightful, but don't decide to stay too long with the 'Furriners.'" Apparently, however, she wasn't in a rush to use those letters. One foggy day, she was sitting in the British Museum Library, studying drawings by Leonardo da Vinci, "when a bowlered, umbrella-carrying, properly attired Englishman approached her and said: 'I believe that you are the young lady who doesn't present her letters of introduction.'"[10] It was Leslie Howard, already famous as a stage actor; he would go on to be a film star, perhaps best known in the United States for playing Ashley Wilkes in 1939's *Gone with the Wind*. (His acquaintance with Sara might well have helped prepare him for the role.) Sara invited him home to tea with her mother, who was staying with her in London while she got settled. If Susie Mayfield was surprised to see this "tall and elegant young man, with fair skin, sharply chiseled features, and tight blonde curls, carefully slicked down" that her daughter had picked up at the library, she wouldn't have shown it. She would have risen to the standards of southern ladyhood and immediately become the gracious hostess.[11] She would have been helped in her hosting by newly hired servants. As Sara and her mother set up house in a rented flat on Tavistock Square, they attended to practical matters, contacting the water and gas companies and then going to auction houses and antique shops for their furniture and household goods, buying mahogany furniture along with linen sheets and towels and English chintzes. For help in running the household, they paid a shilling to put a card in the window of the local post office and were soon employing a cook and a maid, who worked full days, six days a week, with one afternoon off. They were, Sara wrote with aristocratic aplomb, "the most efficient servants we have ever had."[12]

On September 5, 1928, five days before her twenty-third birthday, Sara went to the Bow Street police station, about a twenty-minute walk from her flat at 43 Tavistock Square, passing the British Museum as she headed in the direction of Covent Garden. She went to register her residence in the UK and her intention to study in England for the time it took to earn a degree, first considering a thesis on the minor Romantic poet Thomas Lovell Beddoes but then settling on the better known John Donne.

Aspiring not only to study literature but to write it, Sara wrote and sold a play, "The Tables Turn," to comic actor Leslie Henson. She and new friend Leslie Howard spoke of her writing a play in verse on Leonardo da Vinci, which, many years later, would become the basis for her only published novel. With another writer, Jo H. Chamberlin, she signed a contract with actor Roy Langford for the option to produce a play titled "Man about Town," but it was never produced. From an early age, Sara always had multiple irons in the fire.

She also wrote funny, detailed letters home to Sara Haardt. She worried about Sara H.'s recent illness and, especially, that she hadn't heard anything from her. Wanting to send amusing news to her old friend, she described the people she was meeting and the parties she went to. Her Tavistock Square apartment was in the Bloomsbury neighborhood of London, and in one undated letter, Sara wrote of an encounter with a leading light of the literary and artistic circle known as the Bloomsbury Group: "Yesterday Virginia Woolfe [sic], whom I met in the garden we share, came to call, en grande tenue, white gloves, silver card case, and no tweeds! She asked us to tea to meet some of the Bloomsbury Group next Friday, a kind of hands-across-the-sea-question-and-answer period, she said."

Tea with the Woolfs and the Sitwells was "quite the thing." Both Edith Sitwell and Virginia Woolf had "an odd despondent air, deep-socketed eyes, and long, narrow equine faces, arresting in a hungry, patrician way." In the course of conversation, Sara and Woolf spoke about being a woman and a writer, and Woolf described how she was "working on a book in which she contends that women would be as creative as men, perhaps, if they had fixed incomes and a room of their own in which to work. To which, I say, Amen!" This work, of course, became feminist holy writ, one of Woolf's best-known extended essays, "A Room of One's Own."

She also wrote to Sara H. of seeing their childhood friend Tallulah Bankhead, then starring in the play titled *Her Cardboard Lover*, about which *Play*

Pictorial's reviewer noted that "the chief point about 'Her Cardboard Lover' [is that] Miss Bankhead frequently undresses. And she does it all very well."[13] Using their childhood nickname, she wrote, "Tallu has wowed London. Even the Pragger-Wagger, as the English call the Prince of Wales, is carried away with her." (The Montgomery girls were of the same generation as Edward, Prince of Wales—he who would abdicate to marry Wallis Simpson.) In the same letter, she tells the amusing anecdote (back then, it was practically a duty to tell amusing anecdotes in letters) of having "tea with Leslie Howard in his dressing room after the matinee last Wednesday. While I was waiting for him to change, Tallulah, who's appearing opposite him in *Her Cardboard*

FIGURE 10. Tallulah Bankhead

Tallulah Bankhead was another of Sara's childhood friends. Sara completed a manuscript about Tallulah's early years, "All My Love, Tallulah," but it was never published. (Photograph by Arnold Genthe, Genthe Photograph Collection, Library of Congress, Prints and Photographs Division, LC-DIG-agc-7a16411)

Lover, came in, raising a great fuss because she was not going to have enough time off for her Christmas holidays. As I was talking to Leslie, my back was turned to her as she came in the door. She came over and asked in that husky, mellifluous tone for which she's famous, 'Oh, darling, *where* did you get that *marvelous* voice?' 'The same place you did, Tallulah,' I replied, turning around. Thereupon, being a polititian's [*sic*] daughter she embraced me and asked me to come to her flat for cocktails next Sunday; and I, being another's, accepted."

While Sara M. was writing to Sara H., Henry Mencken wrote letters to Sara M. on the health and well-being of Sara H., as their extended courtship continued. Both Henry and Sara M. worried about Sara H. and conspired to keep her well. In one letter, Henry wrote: "I had lunch with Sara the other day. She looks to be in superb health and is very comfortable in her new apartment. I am sending her some fire wood to supplement yours. I have a pile of sawed up railroad ties. Each section weighs at least thirty pounds. Once it begins to burn it is good for a week. Thus, with one thing and another, I hope that she will not freeze to death during the winter!" Henry also tried to make sure she ate enough, writing later that fall, "I had the immense pleasure yesterday of seeing Sara get down the better part of a fried chicken, not to speak of half a bottle of Moselle."

Settled, more or less, into school and her Bloomsbury flat, Sara was nevertheless very unsettled in her love life. On her twenty-third birthday, September 10, 1928, she wrote Anne Hackman of her romance with Joseph Becker Phillips that she and her mother had just hosted Beck's mother and sister for tea, and that she was "so damned much in love" with Beck that it must be "too marvelous, too perfect, too calm, too tempestuous, too transcendental to last." A couple of weeks later she wrote Anne that her mother and Mrs. Phillips had "conspired to marry us off" and that "Beck" had arrived in London the day before with an armful of roses from Paris. She continued, "Of all maidens, I am most thrilled. 'Picture of Mayfield as thrilled over that.' I can hear your sarcasms." No letter from Anne in that period survives, so we can't know whether she truly minded or not.

But what of those passionate letters she had sent to Anne? Was Sara trying to make Anne jealous with her letters about Beck or just trying to fit into what society (in the person of her mother) expected? She yearned to unite the intellectual and the bodily, to find someone with whom she could be in complete communion—mental, physical, and spiritual—and that seemed to happen more easily with women than with men. Finally, she could not bring herself to commit to Beck, and Beck alone. On October first she wrote Anne, "As it was in the beginning, now and ever shall be; world without end—I love you." And on the third she wrote Sara Haardt that Beck, "has come and gone. Marriage is not for me. Once was enough for me."

She revealed her thoughts to Anne: "I thought that I had learned to be without you under the necessity of having to do so. But yesterday and to-day bear evidence to the contrary." She sees a coat that reminds her of Anne's and bemoans that there are two such coats in the world; she hears Kreisler's "Meditation from Thaïs" played and suddenly she's back in Baltimore, "sitting on the chaise longue beside you, seeing nothing but the blue smoke of cigarettes and the bluer mist of your troubled eyes." The internal struggle continued throughout the fall, and Sara wrote in her journal on Monday, November 4, 1928, "After Joseph left, I came home and burst with tears. I think that the excuse that I gave Mother was that I couldn't make a living even as a charwoman. Perhaps it was a reaction from Joseph's proposals—but I am not a household ornament. I may starve but I will never marry again—once was too much." The week passed, no doubt with many discussions of the matter with her mother, and Sara continued to relay her indecision to Anne, writing, "I don't love him at all, and yet I love him too much to make either a friend, or a fool out of him. . . . There are so many things I could say, and can't; but I think that you know what they are." And then six lines in Sara's copy of the letter are x-ed out, completely illegible.

Shortly afterward, on November 16, *The Well of Loneliness* would be determined obscene by a London court and ordered destroyed because the book "would tend to corrupt those into whose hands it should fall" and its publication was "an offense against public decency."[14] With her lifelong attentiveness to the news, Sara would certainly have been aware of the judgment and likely talked it over with friends, perhaps debating why anyone should feel that society was threatened by the fictional portrayal of two women in love. One answer comes from the authors of *Intimate Matters*: in the early twentieth century, the idea of female sexuality was still strongly yoked to the goal of procreation, and female couples, who "demonstrated the possibilities of love and passion entirely beyond a procreative framework . . . offered an implicit challenge to the delicate structure of middle-class civilized morality."[15]

Taking a brief escape from her studies and from London, Sara went up to Oxford one weekend to visit friends from home, among them Robert Jemison "Tee" Van de Graaff, at Queen's College on a Rhodes scholarship. A physicist from Tuscaloosa, he would invent the Van de Graaff generator.

Soon she was distracting herself with Tee. She wrote Sara Haardt: "Tee Van de Graff [*sic*] and Oxford rival Phil [Beck] and Paris for my affections. But as usual, my intentions are honorable but not serious." While not wanting to be trapped, Sara loved to be loved, and she had yet another beau, John, at Corpus Christi College in Cambridge, who wrote charming letters. "When are you coming to Cambridge, snow-bound, immeasurably remote from London?" He loves "how you suddenly say something serious; how you set your mouth with the most delicious care and I really don't know how self-consciously; and any number of things like that; that make you incredibly adorable." Sara, divorced, no longer a virgin, enjoyed her role of rebel but maintained the manner of a belle, keeping various men on various lines, ready to reel one in or catch and release as the spirit moved her. Escaping into the dramatic narrative of falling in and out of love, she satisfied convention while avoiding commitment. She did feel sexually attracted to Tee, writing him fairly early in their romance that "until now I have always thought that the physical part of love was an invention of Havelock Ellis. . . . I love you, love you, love you with my mind, body and soul, if I have one." Being attracted to him was so much more acceptable than her attraction to Anne, and as long as she was heterosexually involved, she did not have to fully break with convention by publicly declaring her love for a woman. Even more acceptable, she felt—at least in Montgomery—was not acknowledging sexual desire of any kind. For a time after her divorce, at the age of only twenty-one, she had simply chosen sexual sublimation, because, she later said, "due to the conventional environment" of her hometown, she "had no right to hurt my family by 'living my own life.'"[16] (Sara may also have recognized that, in living as an independent sexual being, she would also implicitly be rejecting important assumptions of upper-class white southern culture and thus run the risk of being ostracized in Montgomery. As one scholar has written, "When white girls expressed their own sexual interests, they rejected an ideal of the alluring but chaste southern belle, a class-specific image that elites nevertheless employed as representative of an idyllic South." Undermining that image "threatened the South's foundational association between chastity and whiteness" and a power structure that enforced ideas of racial as well as sexual purity.[17])

From England, Sara wrote to Sara Haardt in March 1929 that the damp, chill weather didn't agree with her and proclaimed, slightly tongue in cheek, that she was returning home to "sit in the sun, live like a lady, and lead a *dolce far niente* life in the Black Belt." She also, although she didn't emphasize it to

Sara H., was concerned for her friend's health, having received letters from Mencken that Sara H. was suffering a relapse of her tuberculosis, and after one particularly worrisome letter she booked passage home on the ship *Leviathan*. Perhaps the newness had worn off, as she was not unhappy to leave her London life behind, returning to the US on April 26, 1929. She hadn't finished her degree at the University of London but instead planned to enter the University of Alabama to complete an MA in English. Living in London was different from simply visiting there, and, she wrote, "after living there a few months one begins to find that our homes, clothing, food, servants and customs differ far more from those of the English than English novels would lead one to believe."[18]

Chapter 4

"The Adventure of Living"

Relates Sara's Struggle to settle into Adult Life. Various Jobs in New York City. An Experiment in Farming and a Cyclone.

HAVING RETURNED TO THE STATES, SARA OSCILLATED BETWEEN Tuscaloosa and Baltimore. She had suggested to Anne Hackman that they set up house together in Baltimore, where Anne could study music and Sara could write, and (referring to a Goucher professor), "We can put ourselves under Miss Winslow's eye and satisfy our families that our intentions are honorable." The two did live together briefly in the summer of 1929. Meanwhile, she wrote Tee of how she and Anne Hackman amused themselves flirting with stylish, shallow young men, and she used the slang of the day: "Hack and I goodtime the jelly beans once in ever so often. That is our art. It is about as tiresome as any other." Anne also visited Tuscaloosa with Sara, later writing of "basking in the romantic moons of Alabama, and having the most glorious time of my life." As she had done with Joseph Phillips, Sara was trying to balance a conventional relationship with a man while hoping for, or flirting with, a relationship with Anne.

With Sara now in her mid-twenties, her life was taking on its fixed patterns, not those of most women of her time, but fixed nevertheless. A conventional trajectory for women was marriage, child-bearing and child-rearing, and eventual grandmotherhood. A woman of her times might volunteer at church or establish some other community involvement. She might become a spinster teacher or a nurse. But Sara Mayfield, rejecting the traditional domestic path and not easily finding an independent literary professional one, had no such trajectory. Her life pattern consisted of loops: between intense romantic affairs and intense periods of work; between a comfortable life at home in Alabama and a more exciting but more difficult one in Baltimore or New York City or London or Paris; between wanting to be taken care of—and being prone to fray during periods of stress—and wanting to be strong and independent; and between almost defying the conventions she was raised with and being pulled back into the familiar, if constricting, behavior she enacted fairly well, until she didn't. The author of a book on women and madness describes how nonconforming women live on what she calls "the razor's edge of normality . . . held firm by cultural, social and personal beliefs and practices that collectively reinforce the idea that mental and emotional normality for women demands that they constantly, self-consciously and anxiously appraise their feelings and behavior to ensure that they remain within that small acceptable zone between deficiency and excess."[1]

An incident in Baltimore in the spring of 1929, when Sara had returned from London to stay with Sara Haardt and help take care of her, illustrates how close both women could come to teetering on that "razor's edge." Sara H. had encouraged her to stay abroad and advised her strongly against a move to Baltimore she was considering, to work for the newspaper there, because of poor pay and few opportunities for women. She wrote, "Of course I know you'll do what you damned please" but reminded Sara M. that she would soon be sick of Baltimore if she moved back there.

Sara didn't know where to land, but she did feel a sense of responsibility to help her friend and decided to spend some time in Baltimore with Sara H. For one period of several weeks, however, she was almost overcome with difficulties. As she wrote to Tee Van de Graaff, "Somehow I haven't been able to bring myself to write you, for of late life has been so disgusting that I like to think you aren't even connected with it. But, I might as well confess all and get it off my shoulders." First, a visiting friend, depressed over marital woes, tried to jump out of her window. "The next event on the program was for Sara [Haardt] to get the doldrums and want to bump herself off." Sara M. and Henry put Sara H. in the hospital "for a rest cure." Next there was trouble with her brother Jim's friends: "Bob Phillips came down from Yale to see Anne and brought another boy named Leigh Marlow with him. They behaved so badly that I went to bed and refused to see them. They kept ringing the phone and banging on the door so Jim took himself over to the Belvedere to make them keep quiet. While he was there Leigh Marlow jumped out of the eighth story window. Whiskey was found in the room. Jim and Bob were held under the Jones law. Anne almost got shipped for knowing them. I had to bury the dead, interview the coroner, console them [*sic*] family and get the criminals out of jail. It couldn't have been worse in any way. I don't even want to think about it long enough to narrate the details."

The episode took its toll. She wrote to Tee of Anne's mother: "When it was all over, Mrs. Hackman took us up to the hills to rest, and there I have been ever since, half out of my mind." She ends with what seems a veiled worry about suicide, herself: "I love you better than life, and until you come back life is just a matter of days." She signed the typed letter SM, and not having a pen handy used an orange crayon to scrawl her initials. It was like Sara to have taken care of everything, but her letter to Tee shows that her responsible nature, the feeling that because she was suited to do a thing she therefore *must* do it, drained her psychologically, especially after her own depression following her father's death.

Soon afterward, Henry Mencken wrote Sara M., visiting home in Tuscaloosa, of what Sara H. believed to be "a small local infection" but which the doctors were telling Henry might be an infected kidney, the result of a "tuberculous infection." Even with surgery imminent, Sara H. was not being told, and once again Henry implored Sara M. to come to Baltimore and be there to support her friend. Sara, of course, went. Afterward, Sara M. wrote Tee that the immediate crisis had passed, but that Sara H. was still in the hospital, that life was dull, and that she herself had taken to her bed, except for visits to the hospital with Henry.

Sara returned to Tuscaloosa prior to entering graduate school at the university in the fall of 1929. Anne went on to graduate school at Columbia, and both women ultimately became engaged to men, with Anne eventually marrying and Sara conducting an extended, but finally failed engagement with Tee. Whether the women Sara loved, loved her, in the way she wanted, is not entirely clear. After that summer of 1929, Sara and Anne continued to write back and forth, often at cross purposes and with hurt feelings, as when Anne wrote, "Mayfield you can't imagine how strange it is to be writing to you where I can't even know whether you will read the letter. I wish, if it has been my imagination that you really are giving me the hearty bounce, you would write soon. I'm such an ardent optimist that I refuse to believe you won't write. . . . I'm most too melancholy & blue to write without bursting into tears. Please, darling, write. Always, I love you, Anne." Reassuring Sara, who had heard she was engaged, Anne wrote that she had no intention of getting married and if she did, it would "be held in the very great future, of some seven or eight years, at which time I hope to have you for chief mourner, and counsellor de nuit." Thinking she might have offended Sara in regard to Tee Van de Graaff, Anne wrote: "He certainly is a sweet one—I take back all the foolish things I said about your marrying him." What "foolish things" might have been said by Anne, or what hopes either might have had for a life together, have gone unrecorded. Their paths diverged, their letters trailed off, and they would not meet again for another thirty-five years.

The first semester of Sara's studies at the University of Alabama coincided with the beginning of the Great Depression. After the stock market crash in late October, although campus life at the university continued much as usual, anyone venturing off campus in Tuscaloosa would see worried and angry men seeking employment, and frightened, hungry women driven to begging for food for their families. There were farmers who had seen the price of cotton plummet and had lost their land, factory workers who were laid off, Black domestic workers let go by the white families who could no longer afford to pay them. Sara, living with her mother and brother in their elegant old home near the newly established country club, were among those who still could afford "help," even though letters between them in the years to come would show concerns about money.

In those tumultuous times, Sara used the routine of school life to ground her, becoming reacquainted with English professor Hudson Strode, whom she had met as a teenager on the bottom of that boat in Italy, visiting the Blue Grotto, and deciding to write her thesis on "the influence of Dorothy Wordsworth on the poetry of Samuel Taylor Coleridge during the years 1797–1810," an approach that prefigured her later assessment of Zelda's influence on Scott's writing.

Sara Mayfield, no longer Sellers, was done with marriage, but in April 1930, the other Montgomery Sara, Sara Haardt, came home to Montgomery planning to tell her family that she and Henry Mencken, the determined bachelor almost eighteen years her senior, were to be married that August. With no explanation, Sara H. called Sara M. in Tuscaloosa and asked her to come down to Montgomery "at once"; when Sara couldn't get away, she feared her older friend was irked. But they soon smoothed things out, and when Sara did get to Montgomery, she learned that her friend had wanted to show her the engagement ring and discuss the wedding. In search of "furniture and ornaments" for the apartment Haardt and Mencken were to share, the two Saras shopped for "gold-leaf mirrors, lady chairs, tufted sofas, shell-work, wax flowers, china pin-boxes, and other such Victorian bric-a-brac in the antique shops of Montgomery." As they shopped, Sara Haardt dithered, "rehearsing the doubts about marriage that had beset her for the last seven years," while Sara M. served as sounding board.[2]

Sara H. went back to Baltimore and Henry, and away from Montgomery's disapproval of her marriage plans as well as its horror at her recently published article "in which she questioned General Pickett's conduct at Gettysburg."[3] In Baltimore, preparations for the wedding proceeded, and Mencken wrote Sara M. that "the lovely Sal is hard at work in the new Palazzo Mencken, nailing down carpets, washing windows, gilding the chandeliers, and getting my brewery in order. What a gal! I begin to believe that I am doing well to give up that rich widow in Hoboken, N.J." Sara Haardt and H. L. Mencken were married on August 27, 1930, but Sara was unable to be there, having stayed home with her mother, who was ill.[4]

In the next academic year, Sara completed an MA in English at the University of Alabama, graduating in 1931. Upon graduation, she was offered an instructorship at the university but declined it, citing poor pay and lack of academic freedom. When she complained of the situation to Sara Haardt Mencken, presumably expecting a sympathetic ear, Sara H. responded with clear-eyed cynicism: "Why you should be moved to indignation at the behavior of the professors, I can't understand. They are the same everywhere, Alabama, Goucher, or the University of London. Why should you teach at the University of Alabama anyway? You can find far more engaging things to do.

"Write me your dirt, and let me hear how you get on with the novel."

Sara probably would have been better off living at home or in Baltimore and working on becoming a successful writer. She might never have been one of the greats, but she had talent, an abundance of discipline, and the ability to work hard to make her writing better. Although successful female writers in America were not legion, Sara could have found role models in Edna Ferber, Willa Cather, or Dorothy Parker, to name some of the best known of their time. Three factors combined to interfere with her establishing a steady writing life, however: a social conscience based on a sense of noblesse oblige; her belief that her mother blamed her for her father's death—and, further, that the loss of income incurred should be made up, somehow, by Sara; and the beginnings of the mental illness that would ultimately lead to her commitment. With no more school in view, no job, and no firm travel plans, Sara began the most peripatetic and unfocused period of her life. Like a satellite with an irregular orbit around a planet, Sara described erratic loops around an ill-defined core of wanting to do something important but being pulled in various directions by her many interests and self-imposed responsibilities.

As a bright, ambitious, socially conscious young woman, Sara was trying to find her way at a time when the country seemed to have lost its way, and she was well aware that the economic difficulties of the thirties had caused many artists and intellectuals to question the structure of capitalist society. She remained attached to the South, a lifelong "Confederate" in her words, but felt cramped by its social limitations. Of what she referred to as the "Confederate aristocracy" of Alabama, she wrote, "Among them, 'new-fangled ideas,' particularly communism, immediately aroused suspicion. Intellectuals were known as 'highbrows,' and all artists and writers without a local pedigree were regarded as 'bohemians.' In polite society it was considered ill-bred to talk about money or the lack of it; discussions of religion and sex were taboo."[5] Sara, a writer who had lived and studied abroad and hobnobbed with intellectuals, Communists, and bohemians in the US and Europe, and was quite willing to talk about sex with the right company, was *of* her place but no longer exactly belonged there, even with her "local pedigree."

Sara knew lots of people, wrote lots of letters, went to lots of parties. She seesawed between the poles of the aesthetic and the ethical life: enjoying cocktails and literary gossip with the educated and privileged but also, during the Great Depression, fretting about the impoverished descendants of people who had been enslaved by her family prior to the Civil War, a number of whom worked for her family in town or out on their property north of the river. These conflicts led her to put greater stress upon herself to save the world, or at least her corner of it, to do *something* for her people, for the South: something that she could invent or create that would give the poor people of the South greater economic power.

In the fall of 1931, unable to figure out how she could stay in Tuscaloosa and earn any money for herself, her family, or those who worked for her, Sara moved to New York City to find a paying job, hoping for something in the theater but willing to do anything: she worked as a salesperson in a Virginia Craftsmen furniture showroom, briefly went into a decorating business with a friend, and did freelance research for an editor at *Fortune* magazine. While working at the Virginia Craftsman showroom, she lived above the shop and wrote home that she was "sleeping on a couch with a mattress stuffed with newspapers, and nothing but my ermine wrap and my suede coat for cover. I have to bathe in the tub with the paint buckets." There was no heat, and, ironically, for someone living above a furniture showroom, no furniture. She was ermine-rich but cash poor.

Finally getting a foothold in theater work, Sara became a playreader and casting director for directors Bela Blau and Marc Connelly but was paid irregularly. She hoped to get a steadier job in publishing and asked friends to write recommendations for her. On the letterhead of Mencken's magazine *American Mercury* are typed brief endorsements whose authors include Mencken, Bela Blau, Sara Haardt Mencken, novelist Robert Hillyer, and Carl Carmer, who had lived in Tuscaloosa for six years in the 1920s and was writing *Stars Fell on Alabama*, a travelogue/cultural commentary based on his years there. It was a terrible time to be looking for a job in publishing, however, a terrible time, period, to be an English major looking for work, and no jobs were forthcoming.

In early 1932, after one of her trips home, Sara stopped in Baltimore to visit the Menckens on the way back to New York. Scott Fitzgerald arrived in town the next day and lost no time, as Sara saw it, in making sure that she and Sara Haardt Mencken "had the story of his most recent difficulties with Zelda from him rather than from her." Scott had a few drinks and proceeded to hold forth about several of his favorite subjects: dramatizations of his "matrimonial disasters," military strategy, and Princeton football. In her book about the Fitzgeralds, Sara wrote that "no three subjects could have interested Mencken less. . . . As the door finally closed behind Fitzgerald, Henry stubbed out the cigar he had been chewing on and turned to us. 'Jesus!' was all he could say."[6] Zelda's father, Judge Sayre, had died the past fall, and Sara, with her experience of losing her own father, would have sympathized all the more with any troubles Zelda was having.

She also sympathized with her as a wife who had creative aspirations. The record of a conversation between Zelda, Scott, and her psychiatrist at their home in Baltimore in 1933 shows Zelda's silence in response to her psychiatrist asking whether "a successful professional life as an artist would be enough if she were on her own without her husband, implying that their impasse could lead to a divorce." Zelda will say only that it's a "silly question." A literary critic who read the entire 114-page transcript observes that "this resistance may have stemmed from the fact that the choice was not one that Fitzgerald was asked to make. As such, her silence was more than just a refusal to cooperate with her doctor; it is a repudiation of the idea that women must be either muse or artist . . . and that a creative woman can either be a talented amateur surrounded by friends and family or a successful professional who works in isolation from the rest of society, but should never expect to merge both worlds."[7] Sara's own choice was to "never marry again"—valuing personal freedom more highly than what she saw as the financially more secure but inevitably restrictive roles of wife and mother. She could not imagine how to navigate a course in which she was both married and a successful writer with all the time she needed to focus on her work.

Back in New York, Sara went to Scribner's to see editor Maxwell Perkins (who had worked with Scott Fitzgerald, Ernest Hemingway, and Thomas Wolfe) and show him some possibly valuable documents regarding the Civil War she had found among her family's papers. They talked about Zelda, and Sara was shocked to learn that, at the sanitarium Prangins, in Switzerland, Zelda had been diagnosed as schizophrenic. When Sara later passed through Baltimore on another trip back home, Zelda was being treated for mental illness there, first at the Phipps Clinic at Johns Hopkins and then at the Sheppard Pratt Institute, and Scott had rented a large Victorian known as La Paix. Sara found the house dark and depressing, but even more depressing was the state of the Fitzgeralds, physically drained and aged and looking it, maritally at odds in the same way they'd been in Paris, except that now it was over what Scott saw as Zelda's obsession with painting, while in Paris it had been his dislike of the time she devoted to practicing ballet. Sketches stacked against a wall included two of crucifixions. Sara wrote that "the face on the cross in one of them was unmistakably Zelda's. As Scott saw that Sara and I recognized the likeness, he turned abruptly and walked out of the room. If he could not face it, I could not forget it." When Zelda began telling them about an exhibition she hoped to have in New York, Scott rather obviously pulled Sara Haardt Mencken away to show her a stack of manuscript pages for his new novel. The tension between the two, Scott's whispered remark that Zelda was "mad," and his subsequent attempt to justify himself as he drove the two Saras back to town, only made things worse. Sara wrote, "We tried half a dozen times to change the subject, but it was impossible to stop his scathing criticisms of Zelda and her family." Back with Henry, they described the afternoon, to which he remarked, "Too bad Scott thought of having Zelda locked up first."[8]

Although Sara blamed Scott for not seeing Zelda's creative genius, her primary explanation for Zelda's difficulties, when she later came to write about her, was that, "removed from the warmth and security of a familiar environment, plunged into a maelstrom of conflicting emotions, and faced with more professional, financial, and marital problems than she—or anyone else of her background and temperament—could cope with, she broke down," proved by Sara's observation that "during the times when the pressures relaxed and when there was even relative harmony between her and Scott, she rebounded quickly and appeared to be her old self again."[9] Sara could have been referring to herself when she spoke of Zelda and how "anyone else of her background and temperament" would have been unable to cope with too many pressures at once. In the times when she felt pressed on all sides, misunderstood or not taken seriously, yet with the burden of sacrificing herself to save others, Sara, too, could lose her footing.

Whenever Sara tired of New York City and had a break from whatever work she had found, she took the train or bus to Tuscaloosa, where, as she described it in the manuscript of her unpublished autobiographical novel, "home was just as it had always been. Outside, the yellow jasmine was in bloom against the columns; inside, it was dim and filled with the musky odor of old mahogany, old books, and fresh fruit—smells as familiar as the stiff rustle of magnolia leaves or the sound of our cook's sweet black voice, singing as she beat the biscuits on an antique marble slab—once part of my great-great-great-grandfather's tombstone and as characteristic of home as the negroes in the yard, the portraits in the dining room, and the guests at the dinner table." In these images, Sara's nostalgia for a South in which wealthy white landowners lived gracious lives while Blacks did all the physical labor reveals her desire, however ambivalent, to belong to the place and tradition in which she had been raised—even if it was one that left many of its citizens in dire poverty and with no voice in government and that tended to regard Sara as, at best, an eccentric.

On one visit home, Sara—along with everyone else in Tuscaloosa County—experienced a terrifying event. In an autobiographical statement she wrote, "In the midst of the Depression, our plantations were devastated by a cyclone." That "cyclone" was the tornado outbreak of March 21, 1932, described by the National Weather Service as "one of the top ten weather events in the 20th century for Alabama." Across the state, 268 people died, and more than 1,800 were injured. In number of deaths, the storm was on a par with the April 27, 2011, tornado outbreak across Alabama.

Sara was home with her family at Idlewyld when the storm hit. In her autobiographical novel, the Sara character, "Mayfield," sees from the window of her house "a long black cloud, scudding rapidly across the horizon . . . writhing across the sky like a gigantic octopus" and tells how "it twisted itself into two dark funnels that must have swirled up from the depths of the inferno." Mayfield, her mother, brother, and his friends seek refuge in the basement as the funnels bear down, and powerful winds strike the trees around the house and make the wood of the old house groan. They all imagine they are about

FIGURE 11. Idlewyld

After Judge Mayfield's death in 1927, Sara's mother, Susie Mayfield, moved back to the family home in Tuscaloosa. An antebellum house known as Carson Place and called Idlewyld by the Mayfield family, it would be the home Sara left from and returned to. In 1939 it was photographed for the Carnegie Survey of the Architecture of the South. (Photograph by Frances Benjamin Johnston, Carnegie Survey of the Architecture of the South, Library of Congress, Prints and Photographs Division, LC-DIG-csas-00146)

to die—then it is quiet. The storm has damaged one of the large columns on the front porch and taken out a large tree in the back, but otherwise left the house intact.

Nearby, however, there is horrible wreckage and injury. "The negro quarter had been razed. Many of the cabins had been blown away; the others were torn and shattered." Having survived the storm's immediate blast, Mayfield and her family began helping their Black neighbors get free from the wreckage of their small wooden houses, bandaging wounds as possible and taking others to the hospital, now a scene of chaos and pain. Having done what they could near home, they turned to the plantation they owned on the north side of the Black Warrior River, crossing the bridge to find another scene of destruction: "The tornado had wrapped the heavy machinery of the cotton gin around the blasted sycamore trees and buried the workmen under the windrows of cotton, timber, and brick. Nothing but the black skeleton of the coal tipple was left. The horses and mules pinned under the wreckage of the stable whinnied and bellowed in agony. Negroes groaned and writhed under the beams of their ruined huts. As we turned off towards the Snow Place we almost ran over two men lying in the middle of the road. Their heads had been cut off by a flying timber and their shoes torn from their feet by the suction of the twister."

Having no chance of finding an ambulance, they "commandeered an ice truck, piled the dead in with the living, and turned back toward town. After stopping at the morgue to sort our gristly [sic] load, we followed the sirens of an ambulance through the procession of cars and trucks that milled towards the hospital, fighting our way against the crowds, the tailwinds of the gale, and the rain that lashed our faces. We were wet to the skin, caked with red mud, and shivering from the cold and the horror. Every muscle in our bodies twitched; every nerve screamed." At the hospital, everyone who was not injured was attempting to give aid. "The sight of the torn and bleeding bodies on the stretchers in the corridors would have made an experienced nurse turn white. Their clothes were so plastered with red clay they looked more like mummies than human beings. The white-tiled floors were shambles, tracked with mud and blood, and the air was stifling with ether and iodoform." The next day, Mayfield went to work in a relief station, dressing wounds, serving hot food, and issuing orders "for clothes and coffins." As a self-described "Bourbon" (a term used primarily for conservative Southern Democrats in the late nineteenth century), she is an elitist, but one who sees it as her responsibility to help the "negro fieldhands and poor white trash alike" who show up needing all kinds of assistance.

Sara worked and reworked drafts of the novel from which these scenes come, and in the foreword to one version described her approach: "With the exception of certain elisions of time and circumstance, which are necessary to transcribe a series of human events into a readable narrative, none of the happenings in this book are imaginary."[10] Taking the Mayfield character as a close stand-in for Sara, in her actions during the storm, Mayfield/Sara embodies the noblesse oblige of the white landed class who had condescendingly little faith in the intellectual ability of the Blacks who worked for them but who also felt a responsibility to provide work and a place to live, and to "rescue" them in tough times. In the novel, Sara's character has a moment of illumination in the immediate aftermath of the storm: "I called to the maid to draw my bath and bring me some cold cream. She came in crying because her boy had lost all his clothes in the cyclone. As I was trying to tell her what the storm had done to my bank balance, her eye caught the price tag on the jar of cold cream.

'How come you can pay five dollars for stuff like dis, L'il Miss, and can't buy my child no shoes?'

'Yes, how come?' I wondered, turning to the window. . . . Ever since we were children, we had been taught that we were responsible for the welfare of the negroes. Now, for the first time in our lives, we were unable to answer the question of responsibility and salve our conscience by giving them money. Reality had invaded our house."

Like the character in her novel, Sara realized that she must find a way "to strike some sort of balance between those born with a gold spoon in their mouths and those born with a hoe handle in their hands." She wrote: "I had to come to grips with economic necessity and provide not only for myself and family, but [also] for the negroes on the plantation. I could either have them cut timber, mine coal, and raise cotton; or I could go back to work in the theatre and trust to luck to wrest a living from Broadway producers and Black Belt overseers. In some mysterious way, I'd gotten what I'd wanted: 'The Adventure of Living.'"[11] She did go back to New York but sometime in late 1932 or early 1933 returned home to help run the family farm north of Tuscaloosa. She decided to call the Mayfield plantation Riverhead after a novel by Robert Hillyer, whom her old Goucher friend Dorothy Tilton had married.

Rather than sharecropping, a system she considered unfair, Sara's plan was to create an "unemployment colony," which would pay a third of the net income to the men who cut timber logged from the property, a third to the men who hauled it away, and keep a third for herself as owner and manager. Despite her mother's reservations about a young woman in her late twenties living alone in the woods, she moved out to Riverhead and lived simply in a cabin with ladder-back chairs made of dried hickory and a stretcher table of pine boards. Sara loved being out in the woods, hunting and fishing, sometimes alone, sometimes with friends of her brother. Wearing a green riding coat over her shirt and whipcord pants, with sturdy boots, she was as comfortable as could be. Nor was she afraid: she could shoot a gun, and was not afraid to use it. Though she put her main efforts into trying to run the plantation profitably, Sara continued to think of herself as a writer and researcher.

She worked on drafts of poems in a leather-bound notebook with "Sara May-field, Riverhead-on-the-Warrior, March 1, 1933" written just inside. She also collected songs from the Blacks who worked for her, which she had first be-gun doing in 1926. She worked in the style of musicologists such as John Lomax and his son Alan, or Ruby Pickens Tartt, a folklorist in west Ala-bama's Sumter County who gathered material for the WPA and from 1937 to 1940 hosted John Lomax on his trips to Alabama to gather music. Sara made many of her recordings in 1933, about the same time the Lomaxes set out to do field recordings for the Archive of American Folk Song (now the Archive of Folk Culture) at the Library of Congress, and prior to John Lo-max's work with Tartt. The records are ringed with grooves and solid as slices from a tree trunk, frozen sound, now almost a century old, voices produced by bodies long gone back to earth.

Finally, it was a life that felt like enough. As Sara later wrote in her auto-biographical novel, "Every time I rode into Tuskaloosa, I regretted it. All the news from the outside world was bad: the Michigan banks had closed; the Japs and Chinese were fighting in Manchuria; the Communists and Nazis in Germany." Meanwhile, "Out in the hills, there was unrest in the buds that brushed a faint green-gold over the stark line of Backbone Ridge; and a stir that quickened the earth, but that was all. The unemployment colony at Riv-erhead was flourishing." Sara felt a sense of optimism with the coming of spring. Even with the never fully forgotten sense of what she referred to as "that chimerical incubus of the Black Belt, the past that preys upon the pres-ent," days on the plantation had a clarity that those in the city lacked.

She would learn, though, that as much as she loved the simple if tiring challenge of making a living from the land, it was impossible to be completely removed from the conflicts of the outside world. Communist Party organizers met secretly with her workers; sexual jealousy among them caused conflict; one woman spread rumors that Sara was using supernatural powers to harm them; and racial violence in Tuscaloosa County touched her would-be Eden when Dan Pippen Jr., the nephew of a man who worked for her, was lynched.

In the summer of 1933, two years after the Scottsboro Boys had been accused and wrongly convicted of raping two white women on a train, the body of Vaudine Maddox, a young white woman, was found dead in a ravine not far from her family's house in the Big Sandy community near Tuscalo-osa. In *Thirteen Loops: Race, Violence, and the Last Lynching in America*, B. J. Hollars tells the story in full. The brutal outline is that two Black teenag-ers, Pippen, eighteen, and A. T. Harden, fifteen, were arrested for the murder.

A third man, also Black, Elmore "Honey" Clark, was subsequently arrested. There was scant to no evidence tying any of the men to the crime, but all three were held in the Tuscaloosa jail, accused of Maddox's rape and murder. Rumors of a lynch mob reached the circuit judge, who ordered that the men be transported from Tuscaloosa to Birmingham, some sixty miles away, for safety. On the way, however, the three were taken from the deputy sheriff's car by masked men waiting for them on a dark country road, lined up, and shot; Clark survived only because he was covered with Pippen's and Harden's bodies. No one was arrested for the lynching.

These events, along with a swirling mix of local defensiveness, denial, and fear, brought on in part by the involvement of International Labor Defense lawyers in the Maddox case, created a highly charged situation. As Sara described it in her autobiographical novel, Mayfield discovers that the Black men on the plantation have armed themselves, taking turns sitting up at night on guard, despite her telling them not to. They have decided that "with dees woods full of strikers and Ku Kluxers and Mr. Saul Jackson saying if you started up de mill again he's gonna put you six feet underground," they must be ready. It's for Sara's protection, but also for their own: "'cause you knows, just like us does, if one hair on your head was hurt, every [one of us] on this place would hang." The Ku Klux Klan rides the roads, leaving behind a trail of handbills reading "Blacks and Reds! Beware of the Invisible Empire. K.K.K." They burn crosses on the hills around town, and Mayfield and a friend, Carl (based on Carl Carmer, whose *Stars Fell on Alabama* has its own Klan scene), pull off away from the road in an attempt to avoid them: "A troop of thirty Klansmen galloped down the hill and safely past our hiding place. Their ghoulish hoods and their white robes fluttered in the wind. The Grand Cyclops of the den, who lead [*sic*] the procession, brandished a flaming cross. Behind him, rode the bugler and a guard of Nighthawks with lightwood torches in their hands and white trappings on their horses." Sara felt it was impossible to stay at Riverhead under the current circumstances, so she left the farm and moved back to Idlewyld.

Even though, like Mayfield, she had been heavily influenced by her upbringing to think of the South as a place apart, "consecrated by the blood of those who fought not to preserve slavery but to defend liberty of conscience," a place grounded in "loyalty between masters and servants . . . [and] the right of both to pursue their ways in peace," Sara, a born gadfly, couldn't help but ask questions. In her novel, when the Mayfield character's father, brother, and a former governor agree that the ILD lawyers should keep their mouths shut, she asks her law student brother, why, if there is free speech, "shouldn't the agitators enjoy it as well as everyone else?" His response is that she, too, should keep her mouth shut or "people will think you've lost your mind. . . . Honestly, Sis, you talk like you're crazy." When she drops the eggs she's about to cook and breaks out in a cold sweat, he apologizes, but in the novel Sara makes her point: that questioning the status quo, even from, or perhaps especially from, within, could get you branded as crazy.

Sara Mayfield was brought up to fit in, but she knew that in some ways she didn't. Part of her felt she should fit in, even though she didn't really want to. Sara was a belle who didn't want to be belled, a lady who mistrusted leisure, a "Confederate" who sought out New York City, London, and Paris but missed home when she was away. She was supposed to live up to her family's history of accomplishment without betraying southern conventions for women, and she, being who she was, was stuck between a rock and a hard place. Wedged. What was she to do?

Still hoping to find a regular job in New York, in the fall of 1933 she decided again to look for work in "either manuscript, theatre, or publicity," as she wrote in a boilerplate application letter, but again had little luck. With her "unemployment colony" closed, Sara was inspired to begin work on a project that surprised those around her. Although she had not previously trained as a scientist and had taken few science classes at Goucher, she began work on her own in what she described as "synthetic chemistry." She justified her new endeavor as helping the people who lived and worked on her plantation, and for whom she felt responsible. She was, she wrote, "convinced that the best solution [to] the South's agrarian problem lay in the development of chemurgy." By chance, she said, it was art that led her to science. In typed statements of her accomplishments, she wrote of how, while on the plantation, she had begun sculpting "the most interesting negro types" among her workers. Looking for a substitute for clay because the plantation was too remote to have the heads cast easily, she "began experimenting with utilizing southern waste products" to create "a medium for sculpturing that would not disintegrate." Back at Idlewyld, she began working to derive products from cotton and cotton stalks and later wrote that she eventually "derived almost as many new products . . . as George Carver did from peanuts, among them a synthetic rubber, a synthetic fuel, and a fine grade of newsprint from cottonstalks."

Sara wanted to be a writer and an intellectual. She also wanted to save southern agriculture and farm workers from the desperation of Depression-era poverty through innovative farm management and scientific invention.

Not fitting into the roles prescribed by her family and her culture created internal conflict as well as conflict with her immediate family; her mother and brother pressured her to conform, and she fought their efforts and, at the same time, tried to convince herself they meant well, wearing herself out in the process. When she did, her exhaustion was blamed on being a woman, not on the exhaustion of being a woman in that particular culture. As Jill Astbury, a researcher into women's mental health, writes, "It seems more feasible and more consistent with emerging evidence to regard much of women's depression and 'madness' as a manifestation of the emotional frustration and sense of futility and failure arising out of unsuccessful attempts to fit forcibly into an unaccommodating structure of culturally constructed meaning that claims to define and understand them."[12] The novelist Anne Rivers Siddons puts it more directly: "I have a theory that Southern madhouses are full of gifted women who were stifled."[13]

In the spring of 1934 Sara was still stuck in Tuscaloosa, and despite her new work with cotton byproducts, she was feeling discouraged. A beau at the time wrote to lift her spirits: "Your letter the other day made me want very much to drop everything and head for Tuscaloosa to get you and take you away with me for awhile to show you what a grand place the world is." He'd been listening to Beethoven's Fifth Symphony and wrote, "it seems to me peculiarly to tell your story. Right now you are living in the third movement with its haunting fears and uncertainties but soon, perhaps only relatively soon, without a pause, you burst into the glorious triumph of the fourth movement, the personal triumph of the individual over life and environment past and present. And it will be a living triumph not a dead one." His words seemed to Sara to have some deeper meaning, although she couldn't yet tell what, and Beethoven's Fifth would become a touchstone for her throughout the rest of her life.

Chapter 5

"Must I Live and Try to Write?"

Wherein Sara discovers a Possible Conspiracy while working in New York City. The Tragedy of losing Sal. A Play is performed at the University, and Sara travels to Hollywood.

PROHIBITION, INSTITUTED JANUARY 16, 1919, WAS REPEALED DEcember 5, 1933, and sometime in 1934 Sara found a job in New York City working for a company called National Distillers, producers of Old Grand Dad and Old Crow whiskies, among others. It wasn't publishing, but she was hired to write a sales manual and to work as an assistant to R. C. Treseder, a family acquaintance who had become a vice president at National Distillers after two decades with Coca-Cola in Atlanta.

National Distillers had survived Prohibition by staying in the legal alcohol business, making sacramental wine and industrial alcohol. Just before Prohibition ended and not long before Sara arrived to work for Treseder, *Time* magazine published an article titled "Rum Rush," which Sara might well have read. The article announced that "not since President Harrison flung open the Oklahoma Indian Territory has the U.S. seen anything like what it will see next week when Prohibition is stricken from the Constitution. . . . After months of jockeying and no little cursing, legitimate liquormen last week sought to hold the positions they had achieved. Square in the front rank were the whiskeymen—Seton Porter of National Distillers with more than 50% of all U.S. whiskey in his saddle bags."[1] The article details the competition between the whiskeymen for supplies, markets, bottles, and delivery trucks, along with political maneuverings to tax or even take over wholesale liquor sales. The atmosphere was charged with intrigue, and there were millions to be made.

Having lived abroad and spent considerable time in New York City, Sara, now twenty-eight, was no wide-eyed ingénue, no "country-come-to-town" provincial. But she was idealistic all her life and she would have scorned any behavior she saw as tawdry or low-class. Working at National Distillers, she believed she had uncovered a byzantine story of chicanery. She later wrote in a deposition that Treseder was under pressure at the office and "the more hold that alcohol and sedatives got on him, the more he tried to persuade me to drink." With Treseder out of town, and rumored to be in a sanitarium, Sara was asked to step in to lead the completion of the sales manual. Some of the corporate records were sent to her to finish the manual, but in looking at the records she believed she had found the reason that Treseder had become addicted to drugs and alcohol and tried to addict her as well: "I had had enough economics in college to discern very quickly why there had been such an effort to hang whiskey and dope addiction off on him and on the other employees: the corporation was crooked through and through." When her boss returned, she told him what she thought, but he "tried to convince me that I was crazy." Earlier, on a visit to Tuscaloosa, Treseder had expressed curiosity about the state mental hospital there, because, in Sara's words, her boss "had a morbid interest in insanity." Learning that her family knew the superintendent, W. D. Partlow, "he asked me if I would get Dr. Partlow to take us through the hospital. I told him that due to the fact of mistaken diagnosis of encephalitis once, that I had a horror of insanity and insane hospitals and never went inside the gates if I could help it, fond as I was of the Partlows and of Dr. Leach and Dr. Mayfield, two cousins of mine who were on the staff."[2] Surely, she thought, Treseder remembered what she'd said and was drawing on it to frighten her.

She quit National Distillers, but not before sending the records to one of the shareholders. She then gave a deposition to her brother, who was now a lawyer, recounting her perspective on the affair. She also wrote to a lawyer of her acquaintance, Frank Wisner, a native of Laurel, Mississippi, now with a law firm on Wall Street, detailing what she believed she was owed for overtime work on the sales manual, bottle designs, and ad designs and copy for the company. She believed she had grounds for a slander suit against Treseder, especially "his repeated statements to the effect that I was having hallucinations and that I had had a nervous breakdown. . . . Since I left National Stores, I have been in bed part of the time and under a doctor's care. Fortunately, the doctor himself has been present on several occasions when I have been tormented by phoney messages and, in fact, once had to help me make an escape." Whether there was indeed any corruption at her company or whether Sara had connected the dots to make an incorrect picture of what was happening there, her mention of "phoney messages" and the need for escape suggests early indications of a mental health problem, the first clear instance of it in her letters, journals, and other writings. Keeping up a good front, she had scoffed at Treseder's accusation of craziness, later writing in a letter that "the only breakdown I'd ever have was to breakdown laughing," but the experience shook her. Friends of hers, perhaps recognizing the strain she was under, took her to their country place to rest. Easing her fears, her friends reassured her, saying "that I had had a shock, not encephalitis, and that the continued drowsiness was due to the force of the doctors' suggestion made at a time when I was in a semi-hysterical state."

As she had with her experiment in running her family's farm, she transmuted her experience into fiction, this time into a play, "The Affair of the Fly in the Bottle," which she described as a "detective story with economic implications." The main character, Dana Pearce, of Alabama, sister to Lance Pearce, has been investigating "conjuration" or voodoo among Blacks on her family plantation but gets involved with a distilling company in New York City while visiting there. Barry Latham, who researches telepathy at Columbia, falls in love with her when she visits New York and follows her home. Dana disappears and Lance must figure out what has happened to her. Among the "emotional effects" Sara listed in her notes for the story are "Sympathy for Dana's struggle against ruthlessness cruelty and greed of the distillers."

At this low point in her life, as Sara tried to find her way yet again, she lost one of her main sources of stability and friendship. On May 31, 1935, just days after Sara M. wrote to Wisner about the National Distillers dispute, Sara Haardt Mencken died. As late as April 11, Mencken had written Sara M. that his wife was "making excellent progress" and that "I see no reason why she should be alarmed for the future." Sara's death came as yet another terrible shock.

The Mencken-Haardt marriage was happy, but cruelly brief. Haardt, who had suffered from tuberculosis and had had periods of ill health for much of her life, nursed at times in Baltimore by Sara M. and their beloved professor Marjorie Hope Nicolson, died of tubercular meningitis less than five years after marrying Mencken. Sara M. was twenty-nine and Sara H. only thirty-seven. Sara Haardt Mencken's last letter to her friend—perhaps the last letter she ever wrote to anyone—was short and handwritten, and it opened, "I think your play is simply elegant. What are you doing about it? Henry is going up to N.Y. tomorrow and will read it on the train."

It ends: "I wish we could see you in Alabam.

"I'm quite weary with my miseries and all.

"Let me hear your news. S."

During her friend's latest illness, Sara had been staying at the Waldorf Astoria in New York City, but, trying to work on a new play, "Earth Takes Its Toll," had decided to move to the Parkside Hotel so that she wouldn't be interrupted by friends coming and going. She learned of Sara's death when a cousin tracked her down at the Parkside, knocked on her hotel room door, and told her the news. Back at the Waldorf Astoria, there was a message, now useless, to call Henry. She had even missed the funeral as a result of getting the news too late. Mencken could always track her down when Sara H. was in need, she said later in an interview. "It was the one time in my life when Henry failed to find me."

The letter Henry wrote Sara a few days after the death expressed numbness and bewilderment. Sitting in her hotel room in New York City, she read his letter. He thanked Sara for her condolences, and for all she had done for her friend over the years, then recounted the last sad weeks: "Down to two weeks ago, though she was plaining [sic] going downhill, there was no reason for alarm. But then came meningitis, and in a few hours it was hopeless. It was dreadful to see her suffer, but in a few days she came to peace and ease, and I think she died without any pain." He was having trouble working and was thinking of going abroad for a time with his brother. He wrote, "We must meet when I get back, and talk of her. The place seems filled with her, and so I have hardly begun to miss her. But I hate to think of the months ahead." He planned, when he was able to work again, to put together a collection of Sara Haardt's stories, to be called *Southern Album*.

Sara grieved all the more keenly for not having been there at the end. Henry had told her that she could choose something from Sara H.'s things to remember her by, and after a trip out west with her mother and aunt, she arrived in Baltimore in September, her and Henry's birthday month. The two stood together at Sara's grave "in the autumn sunshine, desolate and silent."[3] Although she had intended to ask Henry for a favorite ring of Sara's, a gold scarab ring that had a compartment which Sara H. liked to say was for poison, the ring had already been given to Mencken's goddaughter, Sara Anne Duffy, who was named for Sara H. Instead, Sara took a pin box to remind her of her friend.

Unable yet to talk about the loss of Sara H., Henry and Sara M. spoke instead of the Fitzgeralds. As it happened, Scott and she were both staying at the Stafford Hotel in Baltimore, and by Sara's account, Scott called her room and asked her to come to his room for a drink. Sara's reply was: "Sorry, but that's out of bounds for me, Scott." She described how he entreated her to come up, as he needed someone to talk to. Sara resisted, not feeling so wonderful herself. Scott then tried to charm her, saying: "I've always said that you had the most beautiful voice I've ever heard—not exactly Southern, not exactly English, but something wonderful in between," but Sara was uncharmable, and sad besides, and went to bed.[4]

After her visit to Baltimore, Sara returned to Tuscaloosa, where she saw family and friends and helped her mother with the house and social engagements. Her mother's life was characterized by needlework and bridge and United Daughters of the Confederacy meetings, by the Sunday "women's section" of the paper, filled with reports on meetings of the various women's "study clubs"—Qui Vive and Twentieth Century Club and Talisman among them—describing how the hostess decorated and what refreshments she served. Sara's heart responded more warmly to intellectual discussions held at the home of older friends who kept a kind of salon that met in their home. She later described it in a letter as having "a little family living room overlooking the lily pool, where there was a large collection of records, including a recording of the Fifth Symphony, so worn that it was only a faint echo of the struggle of human beings with human nature and human destiny. On Saturday and Sunday evenings, more likely than not, old and young gathered there for beer and Beethoven." But social engagements and family travel were considered more appropriate than salons for a young(ish) woman and her family teased her "unmercifully" for her highbrow interests. To a neighbor of the Mayfields, Sara's mother was "an eccentric old lady who had outlived the era, . . . a delicate, old world, sweet little lady." In contrast, Sara seemed "adventurous, daring, masculine, matter of fact." Sara described Zelda's mother, Minnie Sayre, as "reared in the tradition in which Southern ladies accepted the wing of the chicken along with the double standard and found consolation for it in religion if they could," and her own mother was not so different from Zelda's.[5] The two did not live easily together in the same house, but they remained close, in their way, until Susie's death. When an unexpected family tragedy occurred in 1937, it was Sara who wrote her mother with the news. Her brother, Jim, had married Elizabeth "Betty" Mason of Laurel, Mississippi, in 1934. Betty was the daughter of William H. Mason, who patented the hardboard compound he named Masonite. Betty became pregnant, but in the winter of 1937 had a stillborn child. Sara wrote her mother, then visiting family in Panama, "It is very hard to have to write you that Jim's baby, a little girl, was born dead on February 21. . . . They buried it that afternoon in a simple white casket at the foot of Grandmother Mayfield's grave. . . . Dr. Watson read a short service, and that was the end of all our hopes and expectations. Brother and Betts were wonderfully brave about it, and are already planning to have another baby at once."

Professionally and personally at sea and looking for sources of guidance, something to indicate which way her life should go, Sara more than once consulted an astrologist. She had a lifelong interest in the esoteric, and had considered doing a thesis at the University of London on the writer Thomas Lovell Beddoes, who had initially studied medicine because he was "motivated by his hope of discovering physical evidence of a human spirit which survives the death of the body."[6] Sara wrote several times of a mystical experience she had in 1935 on Dauphin Island, a barrier island off the Gulf Coast of Alabama. In a dream, "a woman crowned with light appeared to rise from the sea, urged me to fulfill the destiny to which she had appointed me, and [g]ave me directions for doing so. There followed an inexplainable series of dreams which had such a profound effect upon me that it might be called a conversion."[7] She came to refer to the woman in this vision as Our Lady of Light. Fearful, however, that in a conservative Christian state such as Alabama, a mystical experience could be misinterpreted as mental illness, Sara wrote and spoke of her experiences sparingly, and only to those she thought would understand. (Sara herself was not religious in any conventional sense. As a child, she had regularly attended an Episcopal church with her family, and her father required her to learn Greek in order to read the New Testament in its original language. As an adult, however, she considered herself more pagan than anything else: "I am probably devoutly religious in that I believe in the strength of the sun, the power of the sea, the love of the earth and the blessedness of growing things. I love the Episcopal service and appreciate the aesthetic value of the ritual, but I have never had any formal religion, nor felt the need of it."[8])

One of the astrologers Sara consulted was called Madame Lorol, of the Southern Astrological School in Fruithurst, Alabama. The school had been in existence for at least two decades and in addition to offering readings sold occult books. Madame Lorol prepared for Sara two typed horoscopes (fifteen pages for 1937–38 and ten pages for 1940–41) and in one comment displayed a striking prescience: "The presence of the Sun in your 12th house does not mean anything at all serious. It simply means that perhaps a third of your life will be spent in comparative seclusion, not in a sense of repression or obscurity, but more likely you will have some one to look out for your affairs and not come prominently before the public. It most assuredly does not indicate suicide or insanity." Sara would in fact be hospitalized for insanity, but Madame Lorol was right about one thing: in being hospitalized at Bryce, Sara would spend about a third of her adult life "in comparative seclusion" and with others looking out for her affairs.

Another horoscope mailed to her from an astrologer in Texas from around 1937 must have picked up on Sara's unsettledness as well, advising her that because of the influence of Neptune on her chart, Sara should "refuse to become involved, too enthusiastic or too antagonistic, against anything. For issues are inclined to become confused, distorted, and your imagination talks, rather than reason. The desire for the new, beautiful, untried and strange experiences of life cause[s] all repressed emotions or desire to come to the surface. Under such a vibration, deception, intrigue and self-undoing can occur, if one is living on the plane to attract these conditions." The astrologer's advice was sound, but, given the intensity of Sara's personality, difficult for her to follow, and the coming years would find her suspecting deception and intrigue in ways that could lead to "self-undoing."

The Texas astrologer also gave advice on an unnamed romantic interest Sara had asked about. As an astrologer, she of course asked for the person's birth date: September 12, 1880—H. L. Mencken's birthday. Sara Haardt had died in 1935, and the horoscope was compiled for 1937–38, so Sara was at least considering whether a relationship with Mencken was possible or advisable. The astrologer advised that the man in question was not whom she would marry, even though they were compatible, astrologically speaking. Sara never publicly admitted to considering a relationship of that sort with Henry, saying of him that, after her father died in 1927, "Mencken stepped into my father's shoes and from that day forward stood *in loco parentis* to me."[9] After Sara H.'s death, they had stayed in touch, fondly and often playfully. She addressed him with various humorous endearments, including "Palm of Learning" and "Commander of the Faithful."

Whatever thoughts she might have had about Henry, their correspondence and friendship were a bright spot in her life. On September 11, 1936, the day after Sara M.'s birthday and the day before his, Mencken wrote, "It was grand to see you in New York. Another meeting soon!" They had celebrated their birthdays with lunch at the Plaza and dinner at Lüchow's German restaurant. Afterward they went to the theater with writer and fellow *Smart Set* and *American Mercury* editor George Jean Nathan and actress Lillian Gish. Henry encouraged Sara's writing ("Your orders are to spit on your lovely paws and resume work on the book"), thanked her for getting *his* astrological chart done ("I am delighted to discover by it that I'll die rich"), and chided her on romances ("I suspect that you have fallen in love with some magnificent specimen of Southern manhood").

Despite limited success, Sara did think of herself as a writer. Once, riding alone by the Black Warrior River near Tuscaloosa, the bank caved in and she and the horse fell into the river shallows. She was dragged by the panicked horse and nearly died, but what she was thinking of, in what could have been the last moments of her life, was writing. She described the experience in an undated fragment: "As I began to regain consciousness, that sublime universe of universals—of form with[out] shape, light without color, music without sound, being without existence—faded into a state in which life danced the cancan in a charnelhouse. And the tune the pipers played was that 'Muss ess sein?' 'Ess muss sein?' from Beethoven's last quartet—'Must I live and try to write? You must live and try to write.'"

Perhaps because of Mencken's continuing encouragement, Sara rallied herself to work on her writing projects. She'd certainly had enough experience to fill several books. Moreover, she had a literary agent, Adrienne Morrison of New York City. Morrison had been a successful stage actress who married Eric Pinker, the son of a successful London literary agent; the two of them set up an agency in New York, Pinker and Morrison. Rusticated in Tuscaloosa though she may have been, Sara had connections with a capital *C* in the larger literary world. She existed. And, while not works of genius, most of her writing was solidly good, competently crafted, sometimes even lyrical, though occasionally crossing the line into the flowery. Sara's prose reflected her personality: dramatic, driven by high ideals, and tending to view human nature with absolute ethical clarity rather than nuanced judgments. She often enlisted her brother's secretaries in typing her manuscripts and seems to have made them feel a part of her literary team. One of the secretaries, Escoe Connell, wrote her in the midst of one project that "We are both anxious to help you, all we can. . . . I enjoy your letters so much and am so sorry that I have been hindered in handling everything for you."

One of her projects, the autobiographical novel she titled "Strange Possession," was rejected by Knopf in 1936; the rejection letter read in part, "we aren't very enthusiastic. . . . The book seems to waver between either being a novel pure and simple or a picture of Alabama under the New Deal." Based on her experiences with her unemployment colony on her family's farm, the novel details the rise and fall of her project, along with a snapshot of Tuscaloosa life in the early 1930s. She worked and reworked drafts of the book under other titles, "The Unbalanced Virgin" and "Angels of Earth." Also in a southern vein was her play *Earth Takes Its Toll*, which she deliberately wrote as a melodrama and described as "a tragedy deriving its central conflict from the clash of ante-bellum pride and prejudice with present day progress in the South." With a murderous stepmother, quarreling brother and sister, embezzlement of funds by a minister, a secret marriage, a poisoning, and a beating, it is packed with emotion and action, tonally similar to Tennessee Williams's *Cat on a Hot Tin Roof* (1935). It takes place in the heat of midsummer and is set in 1934 at the antebellum Black Belt mansion called Thorn Hedge, "in the Deep South behind the Doric façade of a Confederate family which symbolizes the broken-down aristocracy of the South." She worked to get the play on Broadway, pitching it to an actress friend, Sally Bates, husband to filmmaker Pare Lorentz, but some kind of misunderstanding occurred. Sara called Sally and asked her to return her letters and the manuscript of her play. Sally slammed the phone down, perhaps with good reason. The fallout, leading to what Sara labelled "personal antipathy," had been building for at least a year and a half, and in Sara's mind was linked to her difficulties at National Distillers as well as the theater. Although Sara claimed to have written the play with Sally in mind, in fact she already had tried to interest actress Katherine Cornell in it. Cornell's assistant wrote Sara that the play was not right for Miss Cornell, and offered a critique as well: "If you will permit me to make a criticism of your script, I felt that the explanation of the murders was a decided let-down. I felt that it became a tame ending to learn that all the noble shielding and heroics had been in behalf of the old colored servant, who had not aroused any particular feeling or interest up to that time."

Deciding to stage *Earth Takes Its Toll* in Tuscaloosa, likely hoping to generate interest for it, finally, in New York City, Sara was able to use the university theater for a four-night run beginning October 29, 1937, on Homecoming Weekend. In preparation, she made up extensive files of sketches, color wheels, and photos cut out from magazines to illustrate various expressions, "types," and "gestures"—presumably to help the student actors. As often happened with Sara, drama was not limited to the stage. As she described it a few years later in a letter, the dean banned her play "'as representing a side of the South we do not care to have advertised.' I sent the manuscript down to be mimeographed and sold as 'the play Dean Barnwell banned.' The ban was revoked in double quick time and the show went on." Awakened at night by another series of "phoney calls," she was "warned, from obviously academic quarters, that the Ku Klux was going to wait on me after the opening." Not to be deterred, she got a block of tickets to the play "and sent them to every Klansman I ever heard of . . . opened the house wide and asked them to a party after the performance. I also invited the dean. The Klansmen came, in tuxedos and without rope and faggot, and we spent a hilarious evening together waiting for the dean to appear." Sara disdained the Klan as low-class, once writing in her journal that she had dressed for a Mardi Gras Ball "as a Klanswoman from the Order of the White Camellia" because "no more perfect disguise for a Mayfield ever existed." Caring more about what she perceived as class than about issues of race, and more about defeating the powers that be than anything, she was apparently oblivious to the symbolism of welcoming violent racists into her home; in making them her guests rather than her adversaries she had defeated the dean and simply preened in her victory.

After each performance, audience response forms were handed out, following the precedent of a professor at Harvard who had employed the technique to improve the plays performed under his direction. Audience members could fill out the form right away or return it to Sara care of UA's Blackfriars theater group. The general character of the responses was that the play was not a great success. Comments included, from one patron who saw the play twice, "There was very little empathy on the part of the audience, which was . . . the main trouble throughout the play." From another: "There were too many elaborate phrases and expressions. If you took away the proverbs and Bible quotations you wouldn't have much of a play left. To me it sounded like O'Neill." Theater chair Marian Galloway wrote Sara a short note to accompany her critique, saying "I hope my review of your play is not too blunt. It never seems to me worthwhile to soft-soap someone who is working seriously. And I certainly have great respect for your idea and for your ability to write." Sara seems to have taken these comments in stride; she saw herself as a professional and throughout her life sought out criticism that would improve her work.

Sara had written just about everyone she knew in Alabama to invite them to the play, and afterward wrote masses of thank-you notes to those who had come and to everyone who had helped with the play, including the actors. With the play ended, the thank-you notes completed, life in Tuscaloosa seemed dull, and she wrote a college friend that "my love life is as pure and uninteresting as Ivory Soap and confined to being the inevitable dinner partner for the visiting literatuses and gubernatorial candidates." Looking for more, Sara hoped to find work writing for the movies. From Tuscaloosa, she wrote to United Artists in Hollywood, looking for work as a scenario writer. She went to California for the Rose Bowl game on New Year's Day, 1938, to watch UA face off against the California Golden Bears.

In California, she ran into Scott Fitzgerald at a party given by an Alabama friend. She had seen Zelda recently in Montgomery, looking, she thought, "far healthier and happier than she had in Baltimore." Scott, about to leave for Hollywood, had wanted Zelda to go to Highlands, the sanitarium in North Carolina, while he was there, but this made no sense to Sara: "Her manner was easy and gracious. There was nothing even slightly offbeat in what she said and did." Suddenly she understood his unwillingness to have Zelda come to California with him. He was with "a beautiful blonde . . . who looked enough like Zelda to be mistaken for her at a distance." Another day, she went to the MGM commissary with actress Margaret "Peg" Sullavan, a friend from her theater days in New York, and at the commissary met Clark Gable. Scott was at the commissary too, again with the beautiful blonde, Sheilah Graham, and after Gable left he chided Sara for not talking more to the film star. But, said Sara, she just wasn't excited about seeing him, having had plenty of experience with actors in her work as a casting director in New York. To Sara, who had hoped for better, Hollywood was "one great sideshow," just a "gold-plated clip joint."[10]

In Hollywood, Sara was asked—or at least thought she was asked—to try out for the part of Scarlett O'Hara in the upcoming film of the hit novel *Gone with the Wind*. She had worn a "crimson suit" (the university's color) to a party in Hollywood and that "gave the college boys the idea that I was a natural for Scarlett," as she later wrote to *GWTW* author Margaret Mitchell, asking for an interview.[11] Still hoping to get hired as a scenario writer, she wrote to the director of research at Selznick International Pictures, "I would appreciate it if you would be so good as to keep me in mind when you start to work on *Gone with the Wind*. For as our mutual friend, Mr. Richards, will tell you, I am much better qualified to work on the script than to play Scarlett O'Hara. I may live to be an old and respectable citizen, but I doubt that I will live the Scarlett legend down." In the end it was not Sara but Scott Fitzgerald who would end up as one of the writers on the film, doing revisions in his last weeks under contract at MGM.[12]

Although she tended to write in a very serious vein, Sara did have a sense of humor, and one of her projects in the thirties was a comic play titled "If You Kiss a Rogue." Using real people as characters, including writer friends Jim Tully and H. L. Mencken, playwright Wilson Mizner and his brother, architect Addison Mizner (the two are described as "the boys from Benicia, who live by their wits"), and actresses Lillie Langtry and Lillian Russell, she set the play in New York, Florida, and Hollywood between 1906 and 1933, the year Wilson and Addison Mizner both died of heart attacks, Addison in February and Wilson in April. (The play wasn't produced, but Sara's instincts about the material were sound, and as often happened with her, ahead of her time: in the early 1950s, Irving Berlin wrote an unproduced musical about the Mizner brothers titled *Wise Guy*, and Stephen Sondheim, much later, wrote a musical about them, variously titled *Wise Guys*, *Road Show*, and *Bounce*, first produced in 1999 and then again in 2003 and 2008.)

Sara kept trying out different projects in different genres to see if she could make some headway. Using material from her time on her plantation, she wrote another play titled "Mojo," based on the songs she had collected from her tenants. She wrote to NBC about making her "negro play" into a radio play: "Some of the music came from so deep in the swamps that the director of the Tuskegee Choir once told me that he had never heard anything like it this side of Africa." The records she had made of the songs would be made available to the producer of her play. Although NBC showed no interest in staging it as a radio play, Sara did have an offer from the Federal Theatre Project to produce it, if she was willing to do some revisions. But she ran into bad luck: the FTP lost its funding and was canceled in June 1939, so the play was not produced. The full title, "Ol' Son Uv Time (Mojo, Natch'el Bohn Eastman)," suggests the tone of the play. H. L. Mencken wrote to her: "I think you have captured the character of the . . . blackamoors much more successfully than any of the other Confederate dramatists, and don't bar even the swellest of them." Never to be produced, heavy on dialect and caricature, condescending at best and simply racist in many ways, the play was described by Sara as "an attempt to derive a folk drama from the negro's primitive culture."

Ever since Leslie Howard had encouraged her in London to write about Leonardo da Vinci, Sara had been working and reworking that material into a play that focused on the subject of his most famous painting and was, not surprisingly, titled "Mona Lisa." Years after that initial meeting, Sara wrote to Howard offering him the play and describing how she had invented a meter she called "flowing verse," which "rolls along suiting the meter to the speaker and the speech to the occasion." Every character was "assigned a typical metrical line" and she had "scored every scene . . . with a tempo." While working on the play, excited about her progress, Sara talked about it with those friends in Tuscaloosa who held the gatherings of "beer and Beethoven" at their genteel home, which somehow resulted in a falling out with them. Reading between the lines of Sara's letters, the break was most likely over the question of Leonardo's bisexuality. Discussions of bisexuality may have been fine in London or New York City, but they were off limits in the conservative, religious South, including among these intellectual but conventional people. Sara had felt so at home with those "white-haired, blue-blooded aristocratic friends of mine, who used to call themselves my 'Other Mothers'" that she kept her music at their house and was "like an *enfant de la maison* there." They were the only ones in Tuscaloosa she trusted enough to allow herself to be seen without her "debonaire mask." But they behaved with what she described as "abstract maniacal cruelty." In addition to being dismayed by their rejection of her work, Sara must also—although she would not admit it to them or anyone else—have felt dismayed that her trusted friends could never understand her own sexuality. This pattern of complete trust in one or two people, then feeling betrayed by them, then (generally) taking an attitude of gracious forgiveness, happened with these friends, with Sally Bates and Pare Lorentz, and with others throughout her life. She even fell out briefly with her new agent, Lurton Blassingame (whom she had engaged when Adrienne Morrison died), over his comments on her autobiographical novel. Blassingame wrote her that "reading this portion of your novel on the train coming up, I saw Idlewyld again and you in it. Not that I tried to read you into the story, but the portrait of a vigorous and questioning mind within a house built for a way of life few can know today naturally made me think of you." Although Sara herself had written that "none of the happenings in this book are imaginary," she must have responded to his letter with a sharp rebuttal, as Lurton wrote back, "Dear Sara: I must have phrased myself badly: I certainly did not intend to say your heroine bore a resemblance to you. I meant that reading of a restless mind in an ante-bellum home made me think of you, but not you as the character portrayed. There's a difference." Despite her general willingness to revise her work, Sara could be prickly when she felt she'd been misunderstood.

Chapter 6

"A Bit of Choice Inside Information"

With War in the Air, Sara shuttles between the New York Theater and Fort Hancock. Experiments in the New Field of Plastics. Freelance Reporting and a Plan to defeat Hitler.

THE MOST AMORPHOUS DECADE OF SARA'S LIFE CAME TO A CLOSE AS the late nineteen-thirties saw the rise of Nazi Germany and the buildup of Hitler's war machine. Having worked hard at her writing but experienced minimal success, she allowed her literary efforts to be sidetracked by world events, finding an external source of focus that satisfied her sense of drama and destiny. Sara's aunt Fredrika (whom she called Aunt Honey or Aunt Hun) was married to Forrest Williford, a World War I veteran and commanding general of the 2nd Coast Artillery District, stationed at Fort Hancock, New Jersey, on a barrier spit called Sandy Hook, part of the coastal defense system for New York Harbor. Having once again returned to New York for theater work, Sara stayed with her aunt and uncle at Fort Hancock off and on during 1939. There she heard frequent talk of the growing national concerns about whether the United States was to be drawn into yet another war.

Shuttling between New York and Fort Hancock, working in theater but also keeping track of war preparations, Sara invented her first plastic, which she called Plastex, and which she hoped to go into business producing on the home plantation with her brother, Jim. The whole plastics business, as she described it, had come about by accident that summer when she was working in New York, staying with the Willifords, and trying to make set pieces for the theater. She shredded some insulation board and sent her Uncle Williford's butler out for a "binder." By mistake he brought back "something I had never heard of, but I dumped it in, and found, to my amazement that I had a fiber plastic." The binder was casein, a milk protein. "We have had great excitement over the invention of the plastic, even Uncle Forrest is enthusiastic about it," she wrote her mother. Trying to be supportive of her daughter's efforts, even if she didn't exactly understand them, Sara's mother offered to sell an antique to raise the money to produce the plastic commercially, but Aunt Honey offered to loan Sara the money instead. By the time Sara had put in a patent application for Plastex, the improvement on a dry plastic formula, dated September 29, 1939, she had decided it had uses beyond the making of theater sets, describing it as "a high explosive composition" that would replace "ordinary guncotton" and could be made from "any wood or woody fiber to be used in making ammunition . . . where cotton is unobtainable." One of the signed witnesses to the patent application was her uncle Forrest Williford. The patent application form uses "he," "his," and "him," throughout: Sara, being both precise with language and unwilling to cede her status as a female inventor, carefully typed over each of these as "she," "hers," and "her."

From Fort Hancock, Sara wrote Mencken in late August with news of British cruisers at Sandy Hook "waiting to give chase to the *Bremen*" (a German ocean liner ordered back to Germany from New York in advance of Germany's anticipated invasion of Poland). Asking him to come up to gather news and to celebrate their birthdays, she uncharacteristically pleaded, "Please come—I ask you like a lady." Imagining that she would go abroad as either a war correspondent or a volunteer, she was full of dire predictions for the future. "My hunch is that I'll never come back. . . . Will you try to come up so that you and I can celebrate our mutual birthday in September, the eleventh. I have an idea that that [*sic*] it will be the last one—and a gala one."

At Fort Hancock, on August 24, Sara witnessed the arrival at Sandy Hook of President Roosevelt on the ship *Tuscaloosa* (what a coincidence, perhaps even a sign, she must have thought). She wrote Mencken a description of the event, with a rare insider's view: "The President came into the harbor on the cruiser Tuskaloosa, transferred to a destroyer and was met at our dock by a guard of honor and the band. . . . As I was with Mrs. Williford, I was within three feet of the President. He had to disembark by means of a special gangplank. Even with two aides, he had a hard time making the grade. His face was contorted with pain, his body shaking from the strain, and his hands trembling like a man with palsy. He had great difficulty in standing at attention while they gave him twenty-one guns and played the Star Spangled banner. His car was drawn up to the edge of the gangplank, a special step let down, and he was half-lifted, half-slid into the car—and carefully protected from the newspapermen and the newsreel people until he was safely in the car. Then the flashbulbs went off and the Roosevelt smile went on." Describing him to Mencken as "a mountainous wreck of a man," Sara nevertheless felt, seeing him, that "one can not help but admire the will that has triumphed over such infirmities. . . . He has courage, if nothing else; and does evoke sympathy. His press is an eternal tribute to the human kindness of the Fourth Estate." Believing that the president wanted the US to enter the imminent war in order to "save the face of his administration" and win a third term, and sure that the US was not militarily prepared to do so, Sara implored Mencken to write against US involvement: "Oh, Ma[e]stro, use your pen." Although she didn't write to Mencken about it, Sara also harbored the belief that a secret group of advisers meant to use entry into the war to invoke an Industrial Mobilization Plan that would mobilize resources for war, with the aim of placing the country under a dictatorship and keeping journalists from investigating what she believed was a Fascist plot occurring at both state and federal levels.

On September 1, 1939, Adolf Hitler's troops invaded Poland. It was a momentous day in world history, and it altered the course of Sara Mayfield's life, as well. When the invasion occurred, President Roosevelt was notified by telephone and made a note at 3:05 a.m. that he had "directed that all Navy ships and Army commands be notified by radio at once" of the invasion.[1] The *New York Times* that day ran a banner headline on the front page: "GERMAN ARMY ATTACKS POLAND; CITIES BOMBED, PORT BLOCKADED; DANZIG IS ACCEPTED INTO REICH."

England declared war on Nazi Germany on September 3, 1939. Sara had attended a reception at West Point the day before and drove through New York City on her way back to Fort Hancock, "through the bread lines of the Bronx and the grubbiness of the Jersey Flats," as she described it in a letter to Mencken. That evening, back with her aunt and uncle, she went to a cocktail party, "where all the silk hats and swallowtail coats, all the brass hats, gold braid, and bombast that could be mustered in the metropolis were being pressed into service to glorify economic starvation and legalized murder." Call it noblesse oblige or a social conscience, it pained her to be at a swanky gathering when people were in the streets not too many miles away going hungry.

When Sara was a little girl, the newspaper article about children of the Alabama judiciary had noted that "she is in line for membership in the colonial Dames, the D.A.R.'s, the U.D.C.'s, and other patriotic orders to which her mother belongs. When she goes up to the Capitol and walks into the Department of Archives and History, she sees several of her ancestors on the walls along with the great ones of the State's history." From childhood, she was supposed to do something, to be someone, and now her desire to succeed, and to be part of something bigger than herself, was further fueled by the news she heard and read. Perhaps she could go abroad: she talked to her old flame Joseph "Beck" Phillips, now working for *Newsweek*, about a possible foreign correspondent's job. She wrote her mother with war news: the sinking of the British transatlantic passenger ship *Athenia* by the Germans, with two of the Mayfields' acquaintances among the dead; the question of whether and when the US would be drawn into the war; and how she stayed up late at night with her Uncle Forrest, "with maps, charts, statistics, and speculations." She also looked for government employment, and even wrote to the FBI about a job with that agency, receiving a reply from J. Edgar Hoover himself that "only male applicants are eligible to apply" for the position of special agent, and that there were no plans at the present to expand the agency's investigative personnel beyond that.

In the fall of 1939 Sara applied to work as a reporter for Transradio, an innovative news service that sold stories to radio stations nationwide. Partly so that she could investigate what she saw as Roosevelt's overeagerness to go to war and partly to learn about conspiracies she was sure were abroad in the southern states, she wrote to Herbert Moore, head of Transradio, about working for his service in the US or abroad. Moore wrote back that while her qualifications were "impressive" he did not currently have any staff positions open and was only hiring freelancers. He politely asked her to drop by the offices the next time she was in New York City. She took him up quickly on his offer, they met, and she immediately began sending so many stories that only a month later he wrote that "you have literally snowed us under with material." It was, however, material that he could use. Moore was especially interested in insider reporting from Fort Hancock ("safe and sound information regarding military affairs can always be used"). He also thought that as a southerner she might provide "a bit of choice inside information regarding what the Ku Klux Klan is doing in the south now, if anything." Her first check from Transradio was for $12.50: $2.50 for a story regarding Charles Lindbergh's visit to Fort Hancock, and $5.00 each for stories on "various new weapons" and "troop arrivals at Ft. Benning in preparation for the winter manouvers [*sic*]." You could get a loaf of bread for about a dime then, so $12.50 was a decent amount for three small stories.

The mixture of having family members in the military and being a free-lance reporter, however, created problems. When, as part of the story on "new weapons," sent to Transradio and broadcast by popular radio announcer Arthur Hale, Sara reported that her aunt and uncle's son-in-law, a colonel in the US Army, had a patent for an explosive that could help combat the Nazi arsenal, the son-in-law, William McPherson, was furious. Sara wrote a pile of apologies to try to clear up what she felt was a misunderstanding of her motives. To Aunt Honey, she pleaded, "What I told Mr. Moore was innocuous enough and designed solely to see that Mac was given credit for something very wonderful and protected against any suspicion of having discussed military affairs."

Herbert Moore supported Sara's reporting, correcting her only in saying that she need not have revealed to anyone her connection to the story, which he assessed as "perfectly sound and reasonable." He wrote to her, however, of his concern that the War Department "might scalp" her if they thought she was responsible for other stories as well. In the meantime, he asked her to "let us know what transpires from your contact with the indignant Captain [*sic*] and his mother-in-law and sit tight hereafter." Transradio would invite McPherson to correct any inaccuracies, but if he could not, "we won't be concerned with the matter at all, because we have no consideration whatsoever for his private or personal emotions."

Despite being generally supportive, Moore regularly had to rein Sara in. He asked her not to undertake any trips to gather news, as the expense would not be justified by the story, and to consider the brevity of the typical radio story, 200 to 500 words, which was not suited to the "bulky material" she tended to send him. In December 1939, back in the South and using Tuscaloosa as her home base for reporting, she wrote to him about her investigations into political corruption in Louisiana, and he responded that although "most everyone would like to see it exposed," it would be foolish of him or any other press service to break the story, due to the certainty of being sued for libel and having his news service put out of operation. "So you see, this is not a question of integrity or morals or of courage—it is solely a question of sound business." Even though he had known Sara for only a few months, Moore could sense the idealism, the high-flown motives, and her tendency to overreach at times. He wrote, "it is apparent to me that you are operating at an altitude that is substantially over the head of any press service known to me." Nearing thirty-five, as Sara increasingly thought about and reported on issues related to the war in Europe, she may have felt a growing sense of purpose. But, as Moore sensed, she also created stresses for herself that threatened her psychological equilibrium.

When in Tuscaloosa, Sara took to holding informal salons for young people on Sunday evenings, engaging UA students, she wrote to Moore, "with what I perversely insist are the elements of liberal education: good books, good music, good food, open discussion, and open minded reading." When not talking with students or writing letters or helping her mother, Sara read as many newspapers and magazines as she could get her hands on, cutting and pasting articles onto blank paper to create files on the Middle and Far East, Syria, Turkey, Palestine, Iraq, Afghanistan, India, Nepal, Bhutan, China, Tibet, Japan, and the Philippines—all places she imagined she might be posted as a foreign correspondent. She made up a folder on world history, with maps of various nations and notes having to do with World War II, including Sara's own handwritten key of Soviet, British, French, Italian, and American naval bases in Asia and a "War Map of Europe" from the *New York Times* of Sunday, March 3, 1940. Sara was schooling herself in war, hoping to go abroad, just as intensely as she had embarked on graduate studies in English literature or explored inventions using cotton by-products and creating new plastics.

She regularly reported to Herbert Moore, and, as much as Moore appreciated Sara's insider status with the military via the Willifords and her political connections, he may have begun to wonder about her interpretation of events when she wrote him of her suspicion that Mexican radio stations were jamming American stations when the Dies Committee was mentioned. (The House Committee on Un-American Activities, often called HUAC, was also known as the Dies Committee after its chair, Martin Dies Jr.) He wrote to her, mildly, that though it was "always possible," it would be an ineffective tactic since not all stations could be jammed.

Sara visited Fort Benning, Georgia, to investigate poor conditions and troop morale and sent the story to Moore. She tried to assuage his concerns about reporting the story by saying, "As far as the War Department goes, we are, I believe, well within our rights." She tried to reassure him of her sources, as well: "You doubtless wonder how I come by my information. When I was a young girl, my father was called the 'Kingmaker.' As legal advisor to a series of Alabama governors, he had [a] desk in the capitol in Montgomery, which as the Cradle of the Confederacy had remained the political headquarters of the Deep South. In order to keep me out of trouble, he made me work in his office there in the afternoons. Consequently, I've known most of the politicos in this part of the world ever since I was a child."

Looking for story material beyond the military, she wrote to Margaret Mitchell asking for an interview prior to the film premiere of *Gone with the Wind* at Loew's Grand Theatre in Atlanta on December 15, 1939, and retold the story of being asked to try out for the part of Scarlett O'Hara. Because she didn't earn enough from her freelance writing, she looked for other sources of steady income, consulting a local geologist and friend, Edgar "Jerry" Bowles, about investigating the commercial properties of her land, including the mineral rights for brown ore, graphite, mica, manganese, bauxite, and gold. Bowles frequently did forays around the countryside, and Sara wrote a tongue-in-cheek poem to him, "To Jerry, Going to the Field (with no end of apologies to Mr. Lovelace)." It begins:

> Must I tell you you're most unkind?
> Leaving me the nunnery
> Of a dull desk and quiet mind
> To rocks and tests you fly.

Living at home with her mother at Idlewyld, she also conducted scientific experiments unrelated to the previous work with plastics, taking graduate classes in 1940 in biology and endocrinology and submitting a bibliography to her professor titled "The Effect of Suggestion on Oxygen Consumption, Metabolism, and Endocrine Balance." What was she up to? One of her research folders contains a citation from a 1938 study on homosexuals regarding endocrine imbalance, based on urine tests of estrogen in males. Sara's own notes on personality regarding masculinity and femininity cover determination of gender in the womb, hermaphroditism, and theories of bisexuality, with reference to Freudian and Jungian ideas. One note ends with the conclusion, "Q.E.D. . . . that the degrees of attraction between any two human beings . . . arise in direct proportion to the square root of the index of similarity in members of the same sex; and in inverse proportion to the square root of the index of similarity in members of the opposite sex." This conclusion is based on her "psychosomatic assumptions" that such attractions can be measured by computation and the idea that "every particle of matter in the universe, according to Newton's theory of gravity, attracts every other particle with a force directly proportionate to the product of the two masses, and inversely proportionate to the square of the distance between them." In Sara's rationally phrased but ultimately nonsensical formulas, she seems to have been trying to work out scientific principles that would explain why certain people, including certain people of the same sex, might be attracted to one another. Emotions were messy; sexual attraction was confusing. Perhaps it could all be explained in equations, tidy and certain, and, if so explained, perhaps variations in diet could prevent the occurrence of the less acceptable manifestations of desire.

At some point in her research and thinking, questions of sexuality began to become intertwined with questions of mental health. An undated type-script in the same set of files titled "Notes on a System of Psychosomatic Therapy and Its Effect Upon Metabolism: The Neuro-Endocrine Balance and the Total Personality Adjustment" describes a complex system of approaches using individual and group therapy and physical and spiritual wellness tech-niques, based on recent findings in neurology, psychiatry, endocrinology, and psychoanalysis, to achieve "readaptation of the individual" and "total person-ality adjustment." Such adjustment would be based on the patient learning to "see the connection between his unhappiness and his symptoms and to realize that he must assume the responsibility for such changes in his tech-niques or his environment." Pondering these things, she often stayed up late, wondering about the relationship between metabolism and mental states, and the effect of various bodily functions such as blood pressure and menstrua-tion on mania and melancholia. She meant to use her mind, the power she trusted, and science, which she also trusted, to overcome or perhaps better understand what might have seemed a sexual or personality "maladjustment." But what if she couldn't? What if what she was expected to be and what she was were in irresolvable conflict?

A rambling narrative she wrote in the spring and summer of 1940 in-corporates the multiple and intertwined strands of her life then: family matters—often confusing and complicated—personal relationships, news writing, and scientific research. She wrote of a cruise on the Gulf Coast with her brother, James, his wife, Betty, and Betty's family, the Masons, who owned a yacht: "James and I amused ourselves by plotting a mystery story laid on a fabulous island near Mobile and incorporating the incident of Treseder's attempt to play on my fear of insanity and convince me that I was crazy, plus a family aversion to being locked in into an episode—a psychological murder by repeated suggestion of insanity to a victim with the same sort of fears, who was eventually driven mad, locked up and died of shock. It was too cold and horrible an idea for the kind of mystery I wanted to write so I cut it out of the synopsis of what eventually became a who-dun-it called The Riddle of the Sphinx. However, Betty, who was a voracious reader of detective stories and fancied herself as an amateur detective, never forgot it."

Another section of the narrative describes more family conflict, with Betty's sister, Jean: At a social gathering, Sara was dancing with the young geology professor Jerry Bowles. Bowles called out to her brother, "Did you know I'm going to marry this girl?" As Sara described it, James broke in on them and warned her off Bowles, saying that he was "earmarked" for Jean. "James then wanted to know if I were interested in Sumner Thomas, a Birmingham banker, a widower with two children whom the Partlows had introduced to me. I told him that I was very fond of the children and that Sonny, the boy had been working with me trying to make a model of a plastic plane by spraying a certain type of plastic on a rubber form. James said that Mr. Mason had told him that it would be a good idea for me to 'stop trying to be a feminine Leonardo da Vinci and stick to my writing.'"

Despite discouragement from her family, Sara continued to pursue her scientific work, even asking her brother to help her in obtaining patents for inventions having to do with aviation and her work with plastics and on entering into negotiations with an attorney at the Bendix Corporation about her inventions. A dry plastic mix called Poltex, made with cottonseed meal, she named after Polly, one of the children of Sumner Thomas, her new love interest, because they had built a "little plastic skyscraper" together from the material. She sent Polly a letter enclosing the formula, which Sara advised Polly to have her father put in a strong box at the bank, although she let it be known that she felt "honor bound" to make the initial offer for production to her in-laws, the Masons, as the new plastic "might have serious repercussions on the Masonite patents." She consulted with a local engineer she knew about a cotton harvester/ginner she had invented, planning to use the cotton byproducts for wallboard, visiting him at home, and laying out the blueprints on the floor; afterward, he confided to his family that he did not believe the contraption would work.

In the early summer of 1940, Sara's old Goucher professor Marjorie Hope Nicolson, who, like Sara, was interested in the intersections of literature and science, came to Alabama to speak to the Sigma Xi scientific research society at UA. Her subject was Mad Madge, more properly known as Margaret Cavendish, the seventeenth-century Duchess of Cavendish, a prolific writer and thinker who was the first woman to visit the Royal Society of London. The parallels between Sara and Margaret Cavendish were abundant: upper-class women who rejected boundaries and fences of all sorts and were frequently judged for their failure to behave appropriately. Sara embraced that identification. She wrote to a friend that Nicholson had been "somewhat amazed at the way the men teased me about a synthetic rubber I'd made from vegetable oil." Leaving the meeting, Marjorie said to her, "If these people are sane you and I are crazy." Sara wrote later, jokingly, to Marjorie, "If they put me in the booby-hatch, please come to see me next time Dean Harris drags you out to the University—it's just across the line."

In the winter and spring of 1940, Sara was still thinking about what had happened in her job at National Distillers in 1933–34 and entered into a correspondence with the assistant district attorney of Manhattan, Frank Severance. Thomas Dewey, the district attorney, was running for the Republican nomination for president. Somewhat opaquely, she wished them her best "both in the campaign and in the investigation," and enclosed a telegram regarding her National Distillers papers, including "one my Mother sent me after my apartment had been broken into by someone looking for these papers which fortunately she had hidden just before she left for Alabama." She offered to testify in any case brought against National Distillers, but told him, "I want to be very cautious, for if I was subpoenaed in the investigation, under the circumstances, it would mean that my sanity would be tried in court—not that I have any doubt about it, but it isn't exactly a pleasant prospect." In June she sent Severance her deposition about the episode, having told him in December 1939 that in addition to the deposition she made at the time, "I have documents which might constitute admissible evidence in regard to falsification of the financial statements, and deliberate sabotage by one faction in order to force the other factions out. . . . If there can be such a thing as a crucifixion of a mind, those estimable Distillers put me through it in what a Wall Street analyst who checked the records for me called [the] damnedest attempt at psychological murder he had ever heard of."

Given the connection to Dewey and the urgency, in Sara's mind, of bringing her National Distillers material to light in 1940, she likely believed that chief funders of incumbent Franklin Delano Roosevelt, who were linked to National Distillers (among them Joseph P. Kennedy, father of the future president), could be charged with fraud and corruption in a way that would reflect badly on Roosevelt's 1932 election to the presidency and his subsequent repeal of Prohibition, and would thus help Dewey defeat Roosevelt for President.[2] Sara's renewed interest in what she saw as a conspiracy with multiple interwoven strands, in the context of the heightened political climate of a presidential primary, seems to have been a signal of increasing imbalance in her mind. Writing to family members in April 1940 to thank them for sending her a gift of perfume at Christmas, she apologized: "Please forgive me for not having written sooner, but I have been busier than I ever was in my life." While Sara was writing to Severance, researching news articles, and continuing to work on science projects, she was also expected to help her mother get the house and yard in shape because the state garden club, of which Mrs. Mayfield was a prominent member, was coming to Tuscaloosa for their annual convention. The local newspaper covered the meeting: "Garden Federation Visitors Honored with Luncheon," describing the event at the Tuscaloosa Country Club: "Mrs. James J. Mayfield, president of the Tuscaloosa Garden Club, and a speaker without a peer, presided at the luncheon, and her welcome rang true. There was a bit of humor interwoven with deep sincerity in Mrs. Mayfield's talk, which met a responsive chord in the hearts of her hearers."[3]

Eager to get out of Tuscaloosa and away from garden clubs and society news, Sara applied for jobs in the American Field Service (a volunteer ambulance service), the Canadian Red Cross, and various news outlets for foreign correspondent work. She corresponded with Transradio's Herbert Moore about running a story in a radio spot titled "Confidentially Yours" about her "proposed invention regarding plastic material." By July she was working with Moore for the general release of her story on the invention of a new plastic for a mystery weapon and writing to a friend with news connections, asking her for help "to break it in as many ways as possible, omitting anything that might give alien agents a clue. I want to avoid any personal notoriety." She also wrote to her friend Jim Tully asking for help breaking the story, telling him of her work with the plastics that "the scientists provoked me until I was ready to shoot the works. It is not easy for anyone who lived ten years under the fear of post-encephalitis to pull such a Mad-Madge stunt. It is fast getting my nerve. I wish you were here to reassure me."

The release of the story on a mystery weapon was part of what she termed the "V-Campaign" (the V stood for Victory, among other things, including the *V* of Beethoven's Fifth Symphony). Although no evidence survives to prove it, she believed that the Transradio job was a cover for her work in psychological warfare, and, while reporting on war stories, she created the twenty-two-page "Outline for a New Type of Aerial Warfare: V-Plan." The V-Plan had its inception in a conversation with an officer at Fort Hancock who mentioned that the US did not have an agency directed at countering Hitler's psychological propaganda. As she wrote in an early draft of her book on the Menckens, "At his request, I promised to outline a plan of counter-measures for him. A week later he returned and asked me if I would take a cover job with a newspaper and work with the M.I." The V-Plan asserts the need for a worldwide strategy to combat Hitler's aggressions and the importance of US involvement in the war in Europe. Although she believes America will eventually end up physically fighting the Nazis, Sara advocates for a psychological campaign to begin immediately, a series of signs, symbols, and musical compositions, disseminated through the media: "Ideas can overturn empires; air waves can invade and conquer."

In a discussion of mass paranoia, she writes in "Outline": "In an individual, schizophrenia, the modern term of the dread *dementia praecox*, is marked by a splitting of the personality. In war, . . . a social schizophrenia, or splitting of the body politic, takes place. . . . Withdrawal, isolation, suspicion, fear, and regression into juvenile attitudes of dependence, are symptoms of a schizoid state, whether they occur in an individual or a nation." Hitler's "War of Nerves" has a greater chance of success "due to the speed-up, cut-throat competition, economic warfare, wars and rumors of wars," the result of which is that "the nerves of modern man are wearing thin." Psychological armaments along with good mental hygiene are needed, she asserts.

For Sara, the war without and the war within were a series of infinitely reflecting mirrors, and the battle against Hitler was in significant ways no different from the battle against her own neuroses. Her discussion of the "dread *dementia praecox*," written prior to her first commitment, is an almost literary foreshadowing of the "paranoid precox" diagnosis she was given at her commitment, with paranoid precox being a subtype of the general "dementia precox" category. (The diagnosis of dementia praecox gave way to that of schizophrenia, introduced by psychiatrist Eugen Bleuler, and the term "dementia praecox" was no longer used after the *Diagnostic and Statistical Manual of Mental Disorders* was published in 1952.[4])

Trying to find any grounding in truth in Sara's story is tricky. There *was* an official V-Campaign, making use of the letter *V* for victory in Europe and England, augmented by the Morse code for *V*, three dots and a dash, the same rhythm as the opening bars of Beethoven's Fifth Symphony. The index and middle fingers held up, palm out, a gesture popularized by Winston Churchill, also reinforced the idea of victory. Using the alias Colonel Britton to protect his identity, Douglas Ritchie, an assistant news editor at the BBC, broadcast instructions across Europe that helped inform the resistance. Secret codes, false identities, underground subterfuge, and sabotage—had the nation not been at war, such ideas might well have seemed over the top. But that was the common perspective of the time, and Sara's use of such language about her war work is consistent with the tone of other reports, thus difficult at the time, and even in retrospect, to write off as completely unfounded.

In addition to her earlier attribution of its origins, Sara also wrote of the V-Plan that it "began . . . in New York in 1935, as a not too serious 'conspiracy to end war' among a group of English-speaking people in the press, radio, and theater. As one of them was writing a scenario on Beethoven at the time, the Fate Motif became a kind of signal. Translated into the Morse Code, the da-da-da-Da of the Fate Motif became the three dots and a dash of the V, which was subsequently adopted because it is the first letter in the call of the short wave stations in the Anglo-Saxon outposts in America, Asia, and Australia." (The "one of them" who was writing the Beethoven scenario was, not surprisingly, Sara, who shared with H. L. Mencken a "reverence . . . close to worship" for the composer.[5])

It seems possible that Sara may actually have contributed to the formation of the idea of using *V* as a tool of resistance. After her London days, she had remained friends with Leslie Howard, who became involved in the British war effort as an actor and producer, including that of a 1942 film released as *Mr. V* in the US. In the movie, an archaeologist, using a dig for Aryan artifacts as cover, smuggles people safely out of Nazi Germany. Howard would die in 1943 when a civilian airplane in which he was traveling was shot down by the Luftwaffe. Questions still remain about why the plane was targeted, and Sara, for once, was not alone in suspecting skullduggery when she said that he "died somewhere between London and Lisbon, playing *Mr. V* in actuality better than he had played it on the screen," as she wrote in a letter to her friend Liz Thigpen Hill.

Sara also wrote to Liz about the V-Campaign, but Liz wrote back that she "couldn't understand" Sara's letter. She went on, "The V Campaign etc. are too intricate for me to comprehend. I just forget it. I am off to sign some papers with TJ & Edward. Hope I can get to Tuscaloosa sometime after that." Liz was now a wife and mother, busy with her life in Montgomery; it sometimes felt to her like "so many things, circumstances & people to bind me to the rock," but it was the life she had chosen, and it was very different from Sara's. The role of the "traditional wife" was described by Charlestonian and famed gardener Emily Whaley, a contemporary of Sara and Liz's, as being "a woman who puts down whatever she is doing to go to the place she is needed. *Then* you can go back and entertain yourself."[6]

Sara wrote to Herbert Moore in mid-July that she was ready to escape back to the Gulf Coast barrier island she so loved: "For the past six weeks I've been so balled up, stuck up, and burned up with plastic, stifled with acid fumes, and half dead from lack of sleep, I would like to run away to Dauphin Island and never come back." As soon as they break the mystery weapons story of mass-produced plastic planes carrying explosives, she asserts, "You can run very close to saying 'Stop the war.'" In thinking that one propagandistic news story could stop a world war, Sara was at best being very optimistic, but was more likely—despite continuing to manage other aspects of her life—in a kind of solipsistic state, believing that the fate of the world could be in her and her friends' hands. It was exciting, but exhausting: the different areas of her life all seemed to need so much attention, and however little she slept, there just wasn't enough of her to go around.

Chapter 7

"My Heart if Not My Nerve Is Broken, and My Time Is Short"

Giving an Account of Sara's Removal to the Sheppard Pratt, her Return to Tuscaloosa, and her Resumption of Scientific Experiments and Reporting Work.

G IVEN SARA'S OVERACTIVITY, HER LACK OF SLEEP, AND HER TEN- dency to see conspiracies in the world around her, her mother and brother became concerned about her well-being while she was living at home and interacting closely with them. In the summer of 1940 Sara's mother arranged for her commitment to a mental institution, the Sheppard Pratt in Baltimore, for a rest cure. Sara did not want to go to a hospital, and in fact felt she had been tricked into it, which she had.

An argument with her mother may have precipitated the commitment. In the course of the argument, Sara apparently became violent. A handwritten list she later made, "Questions Involving My Family," asked: "1. If Mother did report that I made a 'homicidal attack' on her the night before I was taken to Sheppard-Pratt, which I doubt, to whom did she make the report? And why?" Always the author of her own narrative, though sometimes an unreliable one, Sara wrote up a description of the events leading up to her hospitalization: She had quarreled with her brother, first at his office and then by telephone, over family matters. Her mother had admonished her for speaking harshly to her brother, and they fought, though not, by her recollection, physically.

The next morning, her brother came by, apparently to make up, and proposed that they take a trip to Washington, DC, together, as he had business there. Sara wrote, "I accepted gladly and began sorting the papers that I wanted to take to patent lawyers, those that I wanted to take to Steve Early, Robert Sherwood, & Lister Hill about psychological warfare and the V Campaign, and the stories and affidavits about the Fascist activities in the South and some notes of mine on the psychology of suggestion and psychological warfare that I wanted to take on to New York to discuss with Herbert Moore. Meanwhile, Mother and my secretary packed my clothes. As she was closing the suitcase, Mother asked me if I wanted the bottle of whiskey put in. I said, 'No, thanks. I can't drink corn.'" In this unpublished narrative, Sara mentions "corn whiskey" several times and how she doesn't drink it, but the mention of alcohol suggests that drinking was at least, in part, involved in the family's decision.

When Sara and James arrived in Washington, he told her that he needed to go to Baltimore to try a case there and suggested she accompany him and see her friends there. Sara's mother and brother, had, of course, planned everything out, and when they arrived in Baltimore they were met by people that James introduced as his clients but who were in fact from the Sheppard Pratt Hospital. When they got to the hospital, with its barred windows, Sara suddenly realized what was happening.

Her account continues, describing how she turned to her brother, asking: "'Do you know where you've brought me? This is a nuthatch, Jim. You'll wreck my life and ruin your career. You can't do this.'

'Yes, I can,' he said. 'You've been working too hard. You're going to stay here and have a complete check-up.'" Then the nurses each took one of her arms and moved her firmly towards the asylum.

Far from being restful, the hospital, from Sara's perspective, was "a sinister-looking sanitarium with enclosed passageways joining its buildings, barred windows, locked doors, and dismal rooms that appeared to have been done by a decorator with a depressive psychosis." She found the food nearly inedible. Sara decided to try to use humor to relieve the sense of absurdity she felt and did a drawing titled "State Slimming—1940 model." To her mother, however, she bemoaned losing weight despite eating everything she could stomach. She had a cold, and complained that when she tried to stay in bed to get better, an attendant told her to "Get the hell out of there, floozie, before I break your neck."

From the Sheppard Pratt, she wrote to Henry Mencken, "There is nothing wrong [with] me in mind or body and never had been since I landed [here]." She worked to keep her temper and her self-control, realizing that it would be better for her to present a calm demeanor. Zelda had been at the Sheppard Pratt six years earlier, and Sara wrote in an early draft of her book on the Menckens of how the nurses spoke of Zelda, telling Sara "how brilliant and talented she was. On hearing from them what she had to endure, and how bravely, even gaily, she had faced the ordeal there, my admiration for her increased day by day."

In her letters, though, she wrote angrily to her mother of her brother's "charges that I was addicted to barbiturics [*sic*], to drunkenness, and to ungovernable tempers." In denying her own behavior, Sara could have been both truthful and wrong: she didn't remember any instance of losing her temper, even if it had occurred. Sara's mother wrote back that "the doctors said you must have complete rest for a while." She continued, "You had told me several times that you thought you should go to a hospital for treatment that you were on the verge of a nervous breakdown—Sheppard Enoch Pratt is the finest hospital in the US for nervous troubles. There you get the most up-to-date treatments and the best scientific help in the world. We did what we thought was best for you." To save Sara's pride, and perhaps their own, they had taken her out of state so no one would know she had been committed.

It seemed like a nightmare, the stuff of dreams, yet somehow Sara's horror of being in a mental institution had come to life. Sara decided she had been committed by her brother for what he called her "wackie idea" about plastic planes but that she felt was based on sound scientific research. All the materials for her propaganda campaign involving the "robot bomber plane" were in the briefcase she had been carrying. If she sued for release, the Sheppard Pratt officials, she believed, had threatened to expose the contents of her suitcase, and she could not take the chance on having the details of the V-Campaign released prematurely. Sara believed that she and H. L. Mencken were working on the V-Campaign together, and that, although he was accused of being pro-German and she pro-British, he "was doing everything he could to help me. . . . neither one of us had any political connections with either one. We were both very much attached to Beethoven's Fifth Symphony. . . . His garden wall had a cast of the Fate Motif and a bust of Beethoven set in."[1] Mencken wrote to Sara expressing his sympathy and concern. Naively, or perhaps jokingly, in one letter he asks, "What are the rules about alcoholic refreshments? If you are allowed anything of the sort, let me know and I'll bring you a flagon."

From the beginning of her commitment, she had been writing letters and sending telegrams to anyone who might be able to get her out: to her aunt

Honey Williford ("am desperately anxious"); to her brother, Jim ("Mother heartbroken"); to her young friend Sonny Thomas ("my heart if not my nerve is broken, and my time is short"); to her doctor at Sheppard Pratt ("as my problems are not mental, physical or emotional, but economic, I feel that it would be much more wholesome for me to busy myself in trying to get a job"). Thinking that her family believed she "might get loose in the East and go to the F.B.I.," she wrote to J. Edgar Hoover saying that she had been "abducted across Maryland state lines" while on her way to Washington "about a fortnight ago to confer with the Civil Aeronautics Authority at the suggestion of Mrs. Roosevelt." Believing herself fully sane, she wrote, "Needless to tell you, I realize that any communication of this sort, coming as it does from the inside of a mental institution, is highly dubious" but assures him that the UA chemistry professors she is working with on her plastics experiments take her work seriously. To her mother, she lamented the loss of time to work on her experiments and apply for patents and the attendant loss of secrecy about her projects as well, "in that I have been forced to talk about them a good deal here in order to convince the doctors that they were the product of my brain and not a figment of my imagination." In a way, her assertions were true: some things *were* the product of her brain, but, sadly, her brain also sent messages in error, and it could be very difficult for Sara to see when a thought was the result of her brain taking a wrong turn and not a rationally deduced conclusion.

What might be thought of as the reasonable state of suspicion in war preparations nationally and internationally—the possibility of infiltration by foreign spies, the existence of conspiracies, the need for secrecy—made for a strangely congruent atmosphere in which Sara's own suspicions and theories thrived. For example, one historian has written how, in March 1942, Sara's brother, James, would contact military intelligence with the claim that Black people in Tuscaloosa "were 'being subjected to alien propaganda' that encouraged them to side with the Axis powers," and that the nature of the propaganda was that the Japanese were "colored people" as well and that they would have a better situation if Hitler won. The agent assigned to investigate Mayfield's claim concluded that "'the situation is sufficiently grave to warrant close attention.'"[2]

From the Sheppard Pratt, Sara wrote to friends that she had been put in a room with Frances Jackson Reynolds, daughter of North Carolina senator Robert Rice Reynolds, an isolationist and nationalist with, some thought, Fascist leanings, dubbed "the Tar Heel Fuhrer." Frances confided in her about her father's Fascist connections, and Sara felt she had received credible information about an "Internal Axis" power. She vowed to do all she could to get the story to US military intelligence and the FBI.

Improved, but not considered well enough to be released, Sara was transferred back to Tuscaloosa for several months at Bryce Hospital—presumably to be closer to family—and admitted there as an indigent, patient number 39158, on September 28, 1940, having turned thirty-five while at the hospital in Baltimore. Her mother arranged for a Mr. and Mrs. Davis to bring her

FIGURE 12. Bryce Hospital's main administration building

Bryce Hospital opened in 1861 as part of a movement to reform care for the mentally ill, but by the time Sara was there, it was underfunded and overcrowded. (Alabama Department of Archives and History)

back to Tuscaloosa, and asked Sara, "Please be as considerate of them as possible, as I know you will be." Meanwhile, Sara believed that she had had herself "remanded" to Bryce for further evaluation. At Bryce, the doctor's notes in her "Family and Personal History" noted that "attack came on gradually; lasted about four years; she is not addicted to alcoholics; not easily managed at home; has delusions of persecution, visual hallucinations; resists, will not cooperate; is destructive of property; does not do her work well; first cousin, Dixon Mayfield, is now a patient in B.H."

Sara had begun her commitment in Baltimore, her college town, the home of her friend Henry Mencken, of Sara Haardt Mencken, now five years gone, and of professors she idolized from English classes at Goucher, locked up in the town of her young womanhood, of so much promise. Now, returning to Tuscaloosa, coming home but not home, she was driven past the stout pillars at the entrance to the hospital, down the long straight alley of trees that culminated in a circular drive by the main administration building. At the center of the drive was a statue of a woman, Hebe, the goddess of youth, holding a pitcher from which water poured.

When it opened in 1861, with Peter Bryce as its first superintendent, the Alabama Insane Hospital was a model mental health setting. Reformer Dorothea Dix traveled the South, advocating for better care for the mentally ill, and, with the help of the governor and other state politicians, convinced the Alabama legislature to appropriate funds for the hospital in 1852. It was built on the Kirkbride Plan devised by psychiatrist Thomas Kirkbride and designed by architect Samuel Sloan, with a central building and wings coming out from it on both sides, men on the west side, women on the east.

The central, three-story building is topped by a dome, the whole building painted white, shimmering on summer days, stark and snowy-looking in the winter. Four columns and a portico with arched windows suggest a classical structure, a temple to mental health. Initially, with the light and space of the Kirkbride Plan and the therapeutic innovations of "moral treatment," based on treating patients respectfully, without restraints, and returning them to their communities when possible, the hospital represented rational, informed progress in the treatment of mental illness. It was thought that useful employment would help in a patient's recovery, so patients did work at the hospital, including farming and sewing. But by the time Sara was there, it was sprawling, overcrowded, understaffed, and sadly underfunded. Beyond the therapeutic use of work, produce grown on the Bryce farm was needed to supplement the limited budget established by the legislature.

Before being shown her room, Sara was taken to the admissions building for processing. Such a far cry from the admissions offices at Goucher, or London, and Chicago! And what a comedown to be brought back to her hometown like a prisoner and placed in the worst sort of hotel, one with poor beds, bad food, strange companions, odd smells, and an unpredictable length of stay, privacy only a memory. She was given a physical as well as a mental examination: "Hair gray; eyes blue." She was tall and slim: 5'9", 108 pounds. After about ten days, she was examined by the medical staff, who asked her to explain her "violent and ungovernable behavior" and her hallucinations. Sara denied having a temper and explained away what her mother had described as hallucinations about bats: "Well, we have an old house and bats will sometimes come in the house, my mother was supposed to have had the attic screened but I came to find out that it wasn't, anyway a bat did come into my room. I merely said to my mother, 'I wonder if that bat could have brought parasites into the house.' You know they do have parasites on them; so I wanted some investigation made. The parasites turned out to be crabs. I told my mother and said that I had better call Burdette [her cousin, a physician at Bryce]. She said 'You are not going to call Burdette, I would not have him know that you had that for anything in the world.' That was reported and turned into an hallucination."[3] After the meeting, the doctors debated among themselves whether she was psychotic, and whether paranoid precox, paranoid schizophrenia, or paranoia was the correct diagnosis. They settled on paranoid precox, the "precox" indicating the early onset of mental disorder.

Despite the diagnosis, Sara was capable of clear-eyed observation of those around her. In a letter to her doctor in November, she wrote eloquently: "It is probably impossible for anyone who has never been locked in an asylum to imagine how the patients feel—how desperate they are, how discouraged and hopeless, sunk in their own misery, terrified by their prison and by the outside world, sick from illness, from tedium, and from the tragedies that surround them, isolated and lonely with a loneliness that is worse than pain, devoid of faith, hope, and courage, tortured not only by the stern realities of their plight but by the distorted nightmares of their imaginations. Death has no tragedy beside the fate of the unburied dead in the ward of a mental hospital, however fine the hospital and the staff may be." Given the way she felt, it was especially heartening to hear from her agent, Lurton Blassingame. Blassingame was a contemporary of Sara's, raised in Auburn, Alabama, and married to a Montgomery girl. Not having heard from Sara in some time, he asked how her work was going and hoped she hadn't been ill. Whether he'd heard of her commitment through the Alabama grapevine and meant to be encouraging, or was simply checking in, her isolation was eased by knowing that she was missed by friends in the literary world.

Scott Fitzgerald died on December 21, 1940, while Sara was confined in Bryce Hospital. Writing to a friend about his death, Sara recalled how "when I was a young girl whenever he and Zelda came to Montgomery they were wined, dined, and toasted from the time they arrived until they were poured on the train. He was the idol of the jellies and the flappers, the laureate of the Jazz Age, the White Hope of the Sat. Post. It is impossible to think of him lying alone in a third rate mortuary, and Zelda withering behind the bars of a mental hospital." Sara felt bleak, but she was allowed a visit home the day after New Year's 1941, and as she was listening to the radio heard the "Fate Motif"—the famous opening bars of Beethoven's Fifth. Hearing the music that she connected with her V-Campaign plans, she shed tears of relief, believing the broadcast was a sign that the plan was being implemented, that the various threads of her life made a meaningful pattern. As she wrote in an early draft of her Mencken book, while she was being driven back to the hospital, she wrote on a visiting card, "So pocht das Schicksal an die Pforte! Op. V" (Thus Fate knocks at the door). Back at the hospital, she "slipped it into an envelope and mailed it to Mencken. A few days later I was released from the hospital and began making preparations to turn the V-Campaign over to the government."

Sara was released from Bryce in early 1941, and by that summer she was able to view—or at least report on—her commitment in a lighter vein, writing to her former professor Marjorie Nicolson: "Fortunately, I could see that there was no little humor in the arch rebel of the University being under observation in the psychiatric clinic here, next door to the lunatic asylum; in a Bourbon reduced to scrubbing floors and cleaning toilets in a psychopathic ward, side by side with redneck defectives, syphilitics, and prostitutes." She was known to tell people, half-humorously, in Tuscaloosa that she and another person who had been discharged about the same time were "the only two sane people in Tuscaloosa," proved so by the fact that doctors at Bryce had judged them so in releasing them.

Furloughed into the care of her mother, Sara was described by her doctors at the time of leaving Bryce as "getting along pleasantly and quietly, had become more cooperative, had quit protesting to a large extent. She gave evidence throughout her stay in the hospital of being a markedly paranoid personality, inclining toward much self-justification but as time went on suppressed many of her undesirable traits. At the time of leaving she was in much better health than formerly and was quite eager in making promises to conform with the wishes of others on the outside." She had also gained weight, weighing 125 pounds when she left, compared to the 108 on arrival. The diagnosis she left with was "Paranoid Condition with an acute episode of confusion, irrationality and over-activity [in] connection with drugs." Sara's interpretation of her situation was in marked contrast to her diagnosis: she believed that she had been observed and found *not* to have paranoia, and wrote to H. L. Mencken, almost breezily, "Suffice it to say that I was freed and cleared in short order, and my brother made to apologize, but it was a ghastly business."

After she was released from Bryce, her Transradio boss, Herbert Moore, wrote: "We are glad to know that you are back home from your rest trip and that you are well enough to resume writing." Presumably, Moore was being polite in using euphemistic language to refer to her commitment, but Sara wrote in a note she attached to the letter, "i.e. to Sheppard Pratt. However I was not sick as he assumed." They continued to correspond, and Moore wrote her in March, clearly wanting to be understanding and not press her in any way. "Fortunately, we are flooded with good material and can give you a long, long time to formulate your thoughts to prepare any contributions which you may wish to submit." He went on, "You ought to try conscientiously to be normal for a long while, because that, by paradox, is what the minority will soon be doing, now that the majority of peoples everywhere are definitely rushing headlong into the thickets of derangement." In June, Sara wrote Moore, "Incidentally, I have converted the psychiatrist who had me under observation in the psychiatric clinic here to our way of thinking on the question of propaganda and mass hysteria and persuaded him to do a story for us." Moore clearly liked Sara but had become concerned for her mental well-being; he was beginning to realize that the meaning she made from his comments was not necessarily what he'd intended.

Sara, in making sense of having been in a mental hospital, created a narrative for herself: the commitment to Sheppard Pratt had come as a result of her work in Military Intelligence, as a civilian employee in what she referred to as the "Counter-Espionage and Counter-Propaganda Section of the U.S. War Department." Feeling that her work was essential to saving the world from Hitler, Sara saw her own behavior in relation to the V-Campaign—that is, not folding under the pressure of being committed to a mental hospital— as sacrificial, successful, and, implicitly, heroic, "a calculated risk, a terrific chance to take" but worth it. As she wrote in what she called a "Proposed Interrogatory," "no sacrifice by any one individual is too great to avoid the Armageddon that looms just around the corner." Sara's paranoia, which others could see clearly as illness but which she could not, made life so much more exciting, intense, and meaningful for her: she wasn't a writer manque who'd been institutionalized, she was a spy, always under observation and sometimes under attack.

Once home at Idlewyld, and feeling she had lost precious time while hospitalized, during the first six months of 1941 Sara increased her laboratory experiments to help with the war effort. She kept detailed records, noting the uses and combinations of different chemicals and compounds, including urea, formaldehyde, casein, hydrochloric acid, nitric acid, and sulfuric acid, as well as cotton stalks and fiber. While other women her age were trading recipe cards for cakes and casseroles, perhaps planting a victory garden or knitting scarves for soldiers, she was making up recipes for explosives. One was made of Masonite fiber, water, nitric acid, and sulfuric acid, and among her notes on her experiments are the phrases "try this" and, of a plastic explosive, "This did not work at all." She wrote patent application letters and had them notarized, for a rubber substitute (January 16), a "dry plastic composition" (January 26), "improvement in organic glass" (February 7), "improvement in inexpensive plastic composition" (March 1), "improvement in anti-fouling compound" for ships (April 1), "method of pulping fiber" (May 3), "method of extracting casein" (May 19), "possible anti-aircraft defense" using static electricity (June 13), and the use of plastic prop tanks and fake cemetery headstones to provide camouflage for soldiers (June 13). In her letter to a patent researcher in June, she wrote, "I have quite a sum of money due to me. As soon as it is paid, I will forward it to you to cover the filing of the other patents."

Working with explosive compounds, recently released from the hospital, and perhaps a bit disheveled to boot, Sara could seem a little frightening to the neighbors. She could be functional in many ways, charming and intelligent—and yet difficult to deal with, almost more confusing for her family and friends than if she had been clearly "mad" all the time. To the neighbor who grew up next door, Sara was something of a mystery: a forward-thinking, strong-minded female. Many years later the neighbor reflected that "she was ahead of her time in many ways," but "her eccentricities were not accepted at all during that era." "Eccentricities" could cover all manner of deviation from expected norms, from how one dressed to whom one was attracted to, a polite word for someone who didn't behave the way she was expected to and, worse, didn't care. The shift from being thought of as eccentric to being deemed insane could mean the difference between freedom and incarceration. It was a common enough occurrence to become a trope in Alabama literature, featured most notably in William Bradford Huie's autobiographical first novel *Mud on the Stars* (1942) and Harriett Hassell's *Rachel's Children* (1938). In *Mud on the Stars* Huie's protagonist, Peter Garth Lafavor, a student at the university, is taken to Bryce Hospital with his psychology class, where patient #4864, a delusional old man with syphilis and alcoholism, is brought out for the amusement and edification of the tittering undergraduates. It is Lafavor's grandfather. Garth knew he was insane but did not know he had been committed by the family, "in the hope that something might be done for him."[4] After initially freezing up with uncertainty and dismay, Lafavor chooses to do the honorable thing, acknowledging that the man is his grandfather, taking his hand, and leading him back to his cell. In *Rachel's Children*, two of Rachel Isbell's sons, thinking they can get the land she has deeded to their brother, Jahn, scheme to have her declared insane and finally hector her into a confusion that allows them to have her admitted to Marston's, as the hospital is called in the novel. The brothers, Henric and James, arrive at Marston's with their mother: "From the narrow barred windows high on the third story pale distorted faces looked downward upon the great stone circle where the driveway ended. The late afternoon sun cast glimmers of shadow and light over the English turrets and over the secret, dark stone of the walls. The front door stood open. The corridor was vast, vaulted, stretching to the wide oak staircase, with frets of white marble railing the domed glass in the center of the ceiling. Through it the sunlight glanced downward in bars and circles of opalescent and milky luminance, and lay across the door into the waiting room."[5] Rachel deteriorates swiftly and dies not long after her admission, her quarreling family around her bed, her beloved Jahn there as well to comfort her as she dies.

In the summer of 1941, after her first commitment, Sara finally got to Washington, DC, to meet with Stephen Early and Robert Sherwood, both of whom worked for President Roosevelt, about her plans for psychological warfare, afterward writing Early that she had been "awed" by their meeting and thanking him for his "courtesy and kindness." Although Sara very likely initiated the meeting, she wrote to her patent lawyer that she had been summoned to the president's executive offices to meet with the two men, and that they believed her plans "should be taken over by the government and made official without delay." Early was FDR's press secretary from 1933 to

1945, and Sherwood, a playwright, worked for FDR as a speechwriter during the war. It's quite possible Sara knew Sherwood from literary life—he knew Zelda and Scott as well—and from the theater world in New York City, and that he would have agreed to a meeting based on their personal connection.

Although she stayed in touch with Herbert Moore, his letters in the summer of 1941 continue to encourage her not to overdo. When she writes of plans to get use of a military fort on Dauphin Island to use as a center for mental healing and well-being, he responds, "be sure to practice what you preach about relaxation." When she writes of her persistence in working on science projects related to dry plastics to be used in aircraft fuselages, despite facing resistance and rejection, he advises, "If I were you, I would not attempt very strenuously to solve this kind of problem in the face of so many discouragements." He hopes that "[you will] turn your superior efforts to creative writing from which you can derive direct pleasure and satisfaction."

Sara did not take Moore's advice. Expecting US entry into the war, she wrote to him about plans for M-Day, or mobilization day, for US troops. She suggested how to approach their news coverage, and asserted that there was little time to waste: "If the idea appeals to you, I think we'd better move swiftly, because come M-Day there ain't gonna be no news except from GHQ." That fall, having employed Sara off and on for two years, Herbert Moore began to pull back from their frequent correspondence, telling her in September that new responsibilities would keep him from being able to write as extensively to her as he had been. A letter in October from his colleague, Dixon Stewart, further discouraged her from sending any military secrets to Transradio, urging Sara to "avoid the kind of sleuthing and snooping which would easily be misunderstood." With war on the horizon, Moore wrote again to Sara, advising her to keep her mind on "long-term objectives" and to avoid "militant attitudes"; above all, she mustn't discuss anything learned from military family members, even in letters to friends, as "nothing is private these days."

When Pearl Harbor was bombed, December 7, 1941, Sara and her mother were on an extended visit to the Willifords, Sara's Uncle Forrest and Aunt Honey, in Hampton, Virginia, by the Hampton Roads naval base, which had been preparing for war since the Germans invaded Poland in September 1939. She wrote to Herbert Moore, "We live between the alert and the all clear. Planes drone overhead, day and night. Long eerie shafts of blue-white light begin to rake the skies as soon as darkness comes. By dawn, the coast guns are pounding, pounding, pounding. The windows rattle, the foundations of the house tremble." The day after the Pearl Harbor attack, Moore gently broke the news that Sara's work would no longer be needed: "I am afraid that the outbreak of war will make it very difficult for us to use much material of the sort that you have previously sent. Obviously, everything is now changed and one cannot be critical or exploratory. . . . So it looks like there will be a temporary finis to our pleasant relationship as far as news coverage is concerned." In response, Sara sent a formal letter of resignation to Moore, and he in return offered to serve as a reference for her and encouraged her to "associate yourself with some branch of defense because you have fine qualifications to do valuable work in these crucial days." And, like many at the time, he anticipated that they would be able to work together again soon, as "Hitler is already licked" and that the war would only go on for "another year or even 18 months."

Chapter 8

"Trying to Do One's Bit"

The War Years pass with Much Frustration. Extensive Correspondence and Investigation regarding Homegrown Fascists. At long last, the Opportunity to report on Postwar Conferences.

WHILE IN VIRGINIA, SARA'S MOTHER HAD WHAT SARA DESCRIBED in a letter to a family member as a "very severe heart attack." They returned to Alabama, where much of the duty of caring for her fell to Sara. Sara chafed at domestic life, writing to her old friend Liz Thigpen Hill in Montgomery for Liz's birthday that "the routine at home always gets me down and I always break loose in some completely unexpected manner. This time I've amused myself by building a biological Noah's Ark—with bees to pollenize a garden that feeds chickens, rabbits, and a calf, which in turn fertilize the garden—and incidentally attract the flies to feed the frogs I've put in the fountain." She says that she has "learned to grow plants an inch high in a week from the time the seed[s] were planted, double the rate of growth in the chickens by feeding them anterior pituitary, and force metamorphosis in tadpoles in five days with thyroxin."

As Susie recovered, the Mayfields took in boarders during the war to help with expenses, and Sara believed that one man, a flight instructor at the Alabama Institute of Aeronautics in Tuscaloosa, was a Communist agent who was trying to recruit her to go to Russia. Getting the word out in case anything happened to her, she wrote to both the FBI and Herbert Moore about this development. Sara reported to Moore that two samples from her plastics experiments were missing from a drawer, and that as a result of her suspicions she had "fed" some incorrect information to the mysterious "Mr. K.," as she referred to him.

Eager to get away from both the tedium and the tension of home, and determined to contribute to the war effort in some way, Sara applied to join the War Department; the Office of the Coordinator of Information in Washington, DC; the WAAC (the Women's Auxiliary Army Corps); and the US Navy, either in recruitment or in Women Accepted for Volunteer Emergency Service, commonly known as the WAVES, the naval branch of women's auxiliary service. Knowing that her time in a mental hospital could prejudice her efforts, she convinced both her brother and her mother to write letters on her behalf. Sara asked her brother, by then a lieutenant with the 19th Bombardment Group of the US Army Air Corps, to write to her doctor at Sheppard Pratt to ask for Sara's diagnosis from her 1940 commitment to be changed "so that her civilian work would not be obstructed thereby." In the letter, he wrote that "The physicaians [*sic*] who subsequently examined her do not agree with your digonosis [*sic*]," suggesting that the chemicals she had been working with in her experiments might have brought on her problems. He also writes that he had "conveyed" Sara to the hospital in 1940 "out of fear that [his] sister was working herself into a nervous breakdown" by "working on various plastic and chemical experiments . . . loosing [*sic*] weight and sleep rapidly and her physician had prescribed barbiturics [*sic*]." With her relative lack of scientific expertise, Sara could possibly have suffered from handling chemicals carelessly, as her brother suggests. One of her scientific papers describes the results of her experiments on promoting artificial photosynthesis using "activated formaldehyde," and she once wrote to Thomas R. Taylor of the National Inventors Council that she had suffered from "formaldehyde poisoning" and bronchitis.

Despite her brother's assertion that the doctors at Bryce had changed her diagnosis, when the Navy contacted W. D. Partlow, the superintendent of Bryce Hospital, he stated that he writes "under pressure" and because the Mayfields are family friends (Sara addressed letters to him "Dear Part"). Sara Mayfield, he says, is a "fine person" but he is "sorry that I have to state that Miss Mayfield is a neurotic individual or a paranoid." Sara, a prodigious writer of letters, did not give up, and a letter from the psychiatrist at the Armed Forces Entrance and Examination Station in New Orleans practically begs Sara to stop writing about an appointment: "Since you were examined at this station, a tremendous amount of correspondence concerning your case has been sent to me, and further correspondence was attached to your letter of 9 July 43. I am directed to advise you . . . that your case has been closed and that it will not be necessary for you to send us further certificates."

Although she was turned down for military work in New Orleans, Sara did find employment there, with the Office of Censorship, District Postal Censor. A letter from that office confirms that Sara was offered a job; it was, said the recruiter, at a salary less than what she has said would be acceptable, but asks whether she is interested, based on attending training school and "satisfactory character investigation and a medical examination." This clerical position, to Sara, was the perfect place for her to observe what she believed to be a Fascist conspiracy between the mayor of New Orleans—part of the Internal Axis—and Italian Fascists. She even disguised herself in old clothes, the better to seem like "a country-school teacher, meek, humble, and dumber than they really come," as she wrote to a friend. Working in New Orleans, she found the evidence of conspiracy she was looking for and, hoping to get the story out, she pitched it to Frederick Lewis Allen at *Harper's Magazine* with the following assertions, gleaned from her work at a "certain government agency" in New Orleans:

"The situation in New Orleans is an engraved invitation to something vastly worse than a Pearl Harbor. The [Mayor] Maestri machine, which has been operating hand in glove with the Unione Italiane, a fascist propaganda organization, has not only been giving out propaganda and strategic information through the OSD, but broadcasting the movement of troop ships via the drivers of a taxi company owned by them, and we have excellent reason to believe, by the drummer in an orchestra at the Roosevelt Hotel, who drummed out the messages in morse code." Allen did not accept the story.

Sara had expected a coup by pro-German forces in the South in September 1942, writing up her suspicions and findings in "Rebel Report on the South." These "Star-Spangled Fascists . . . planned to instigate trouble, racial or labor, I suppose, call out the State Guard and take over." No such coup occurred, but Sara's ideas were grounded in some reality: there *were* concerns about an Internal Axis in Latin America, fomented by Nazi agents there, and the Emergency Advisory Committee for Political Defense was established in January 1942 to expose and fight it.[1] Her concern with homegrown Fascists also led her to write a letter to William Mitch of the Committee for Industrial Organization in Birmingham, proposing an alliance of "labor, women, and the Old Guard down here" that "could be united into a Confederate party that would break the democratic hegemony that has put us in the power of the Star-Spangled Fascists, who by raising the issues of White Supremacy, States Rights, and the right to strike, are deliberately fanning the fires of another Civil War." In this proposal, while still implicitly embracing a white power structure that would maintain order and avoid societal upheaval, Sara sought to redefine the term "Confederate" and "Lost Cause" away from association with allegiance to the Confederate States of America and toward what she saw as some deeper allegiance to the democratic foundations of the US. She refers to "Confederates" as those whose "ruling passion is what they call the Lost Cause, i.e. the Constitution, the Bill of Rights, the Declaration of Independence, the New Testament, and any common book of etiquette."

Apart from the job with the postal censor, there is no evidence that Sara had any position in counterintelligence. The National Personnel Records Center in St. Louis, Missouri, a branch of the National Archives, having conducted a thorough search of federal civilian personnel records, has no record of her employment whatsoever. This doesn't mean that she absolutely did not work for the government. She could have been working without pay, or she could, conceivably, have worked for a government contractor. Additionally—although no correspondence survives to confirm this—she could have been involved with an entity called the Writers' War Board, an organization founded in early 1942, shortly after the US entered the war. Initially called the Writers' War Committee and organized in response to a US Treasury Department request for writers to help promote the sale of war bonds, the WWB was a private organization that received government funds. Serving as a liaison between the Office of War Information and writers in the private sector, it eventually expanded, promoting propaganda campaigns on multiple fronts with the efforts of more than four thousand writers.[2] Sara definitely knew writers who were involved with the board. Her friend Jim Tully corresponded with the Writers' War Board in July 1943. Her friend Carl Carmer was one of the members of the inaugural board of the WWB, and the advisory council included director Marc Connelly, for whom she had worked in theater in the 1930s, as well as many other writers with whom she likely had at least a "passing-a-cocktail" acquaintance.

With the war on the European front coming, finally, to a close with the D-Day landings at Normandy on June 6, 1944, Sara had not been sent abroad as a reporter, as she'd hoped, but she did feel that she had helped quell the Internal Axis at home. Her own summary of the war years, in a letter to a family member, gives the best flavor of how she experienced that period of her life: "D-Day found me with two tokens cash to my name, too far underweight and blood count too low to take the State Department appointment when they said take it or leave it, and too disillusioned with all idealistic and patriotic endeavors from five years in the silences, undercover, underground . . . in short, too fed up to have but one thought in mind, i.e. making the money to mend my fortunes. . . . Between that and getting in and out a nuthatch, in and out Maestri's spiderweb, and in and out a hearse—inadvertently, I assure you, helping to give F.D.R. a life term and making Europe safe for Comrade Joe—I don't know which is worse. If there is a Golden Mean between the two extremes, I'm all for finding it." In theory, Sara may have wished to find a golden mean, but in actuality she always had trouble with balance. It was intensity that made her feel alive, not calm stability. She was driven to create mammoth projects for herself and then, exhausted, was desirous of complete escape. Simultaneously wanting to work for the good of humanity and do nothing but slip off to Dauphin Island and stare at the ocean horizon, she wrote to Herbert Moore that "I had rather live off shrimp and fish in peace than to eat caviar in turmoil. The only reason for trying to do one's bit, is so that one can retire to the eternal verities with a clear conscience." To Sara, those eternal verities were to be found in nature: "the power of the sun, the strength of the sea, the force of the wind, the beauty of the earth, and the everlasting life of growing things."

The opportunity for travel reporting came belatedly, with the opportunity to report on the Inter-American Conference on Problems of War and Peace in Mexico City, a meeting of twenty Latin American countries gathered to discuss proposed elements of the United Nations Charter. Representatives from these twenty countries met from February 21 to March 8, 1945. Readers of the *Tuscaloosa News* would have seen the announcement, on March 4, 1945, that "Miss Sara Mayfield, only daughter of Mrs. James J. Mayfield[,] and a brilliant writer, is attending the Pan-American Conference in Mexico for a well-known syndicate. She will spend some weeks in Mexico and plans to visit centers in South American [*sic*] before returning home."

She had continued her chemistry experiments, and before leaving she signed an Agreement of Agency with a partner, Garrett R. Lane, regarding profits from patents licensing and authorizing him to manufacture several formulas and designs including paint remover, wood cleaner, and dry plastic. Her mind was ever-busy with multiple projects: the day before, she had written a patent application for a "domestic service station," a truck equipped "for the servicing of homes and yards and the delivery of ready to serve meals [to] aid in the solution of the domestic labor problem"; the application was accompanied by drawings of how the mobile "service station" would be organized and stocked. She also sketched out and wrote up a patent application for hollow plastic building blocks for prefabricated houses and a "glazed plastic tile" to cover the blocks. In a third patent application letter, also dated February 19, 1945, she described "an improvement in an electric rotor for use in kitchen, club, and hotel" that would enable the rotor to be used for mixing and beating but also, through the use of various attachments, "sanding, sharpening, scouring, polishing, buffing, polishing shoes, cutting, slicing, carving, mixing drinks, use as a fan, bottle brush, or dishwasher." Her letters were accompanied by detailed diagrams.

She prepared for her trip abroad as well, corresponding with Pan American Airways on her itinerary, packing, and getting the necessary vaccinations for her trip south of the border. Of the shots, she wrote to Herbert Moore, "I doubt if they can make me feel any worse than I do from acid burns and formaldehyde fumes." Although still in touch with Moore and Transradio, Sara received her press credentials from the *Birmingham News*, which was to pay her five cents a word, for a minimum of a thousand words a week (that's at least fifty dollars a week), and her own byline.

She took a copy of *Timeless Mexico*, a travel book by her friend Hudson Strode, to read on the train, but encountered so many characters telling so many outlandish stories, not to mention having a cascade of travel mishaps, that she had little time to read. A far cry from Tuscaloosa, Mexico City was a metropolis of wide avenues packed with cars, buses, and motorcycles: in the morning filled with children in uniforms going to school, shoppers heading to the market, workers heading to the office or factory; in the evening people crowding the streets, some headed home while others went out to one of the many nightclubs. Finally, Sara was somewhere interesting.

Sara's press credentials came in a small booklet bound in dark green linen, and she worked hard to earn her five cents a word. She collected draft proposals and resolutions from various South American countries and the United States, press releases and news digests from the conference proceedings, pamphlets of addresses to the conference, and various related documents, including President Roosevelt's speech to the US Congress on March 1, 1945, after the Yalta Conference in Crimea. She went to a show of caricatures of the major figures at the conference by Mexican artist Matias Santoyo and snagged as mementos some original sketches by Santoyo, a few of them signed by their subjects: Nelson Rockefeller, who had organized the conference, for one. She attended a charity costume ball and a dinner for foreign correspondents at the restaurant Sans Souci. One article Sara filed, published in the *Birmingham News* under the headline "Spirit of Sincere Faith Pervades Conference Air," reported that "an unofficial poll in the corridors and courts of the Alcazar revealed a marked feeling of hope, confidence and enthusiasm among the Latin-American nations represented here."

In addition to artists Frida Kahlo and Diego Rivera, she rubbed shoulders with screen stars Errol Flynn, Orson Welles, and Rita Hayworth, as well as a number of lesser-known actors, both American and Mexican. They drank at Giro's nightclub, owned by A. C. Blumenthal, a real estate developer and the-atrical promoter Sara may have known from her theater days; he was soon to be divorced from his wife, the former Peggy Fears, a former Ziegfeld Follies girl. Using a French euphemism to refer to Blumenthal's involvement with the prostitution trade, Sara described him as "backer of Ciro's and its most glamorous *poules des luxe*." Wanting to do everything and not waste a mo-ment, Sara squeezed in some tourist activities, visiting Lake Xochimilco with its floating gardens, outside Mexico City. She even took a burro ride, wearing a floral shirtwaist dress, chic straw hat, and earrings, with her clutch purse tucked under her arm. She wasn't in her regular riding attire, but she was comfortable on horse-, or in this case burro-, back.

When the conference ended, she traveled by train from Mexico City to California, stopping in Los Angeles on her way to the United Nations Con-ference on International Organization (UNCIO) in San Francisco, where fifty nations would gather in April 1945 to create the United Nations Char-ter. Sara was filing stories for Transradio again; Herbert Moore asked her to look into "negro settlements . . . developing overnight" in LA and other stories relating to social and economic changes in California during the war, reassuring her that he was not asking her to write "Hollywood trivia." In Los Angeles Sara stayed at the elegant Biltmore Hotel, with its art deco style and chic customers. She wrote a number of articles with titles such as "Roman Holiday in a Rumor Mill," "Hollywood Residents 'All Mixed Up,'" and "Ber-serk at the Beverly Wilshire Bar" and talked and drank with other journalists and delegates on their way to San Francisco. She sent a telegram to Nelson Rockefeller, then Assistant Secretary of State for American Republic Affairs at the State Department, whom she'd just seen in Mexico, telling him about a story she had uncovered of an "intensive effort to sabotage Pan-American unity and undermine San Francisco conference." She asked him for advice on releasing the story, thinking it would help the US in "winning the peace" but believing the government, rather than an individual, should release it.

When President Roosevelt died, on April 12, 1945, she found herself reflecting on the contrast between the high life in LA and the soldier's lot, and was moved to write a satirical political poem, not her usual form of

FIGURE 13. Sara Mayfield riding a burro in Mexico City

In 1945 Sara went as a freelance reporter to cover the Inter-American Conference on Problems of War and Peace in Mexico City. In addition to reporting on the leaders of Latin American countries as they discussed the United Nations Charter, she met famous artists and actors in Mexico City's nightclubs and squeezed in some tourist activities, including a ride on a burro. (University of Alabama Libraries Special Collections)

expression. On Biltmore Hotel stationery, she typed "Berserk at the Beverly Wilshire Bar," which begins:

> The Commander-in-chief has gone down the long road.
> They brought his body back in state this morning.
> "So what? Another old-fashioned. Make mine a Martini,
>   please."
> At dawn an airborne division landed behind the lines
> On the outskirts of Leipzig; by noon, they were blood and
>   guts.
> "Say, if I thought about this war it would drive me nuts.
> Another round and let's forget it. V-Day and Spree Day."
> Yesterday a detachment of Marines hacked their way across
> Okinawa through jungles, fevers, mosquitoes, and a rain of
>   fire.
> "Talk about sunburn, pal, I got mine at Palm Springs last
>   week.
> My damn back was so sore, I just didn't go back to work."

Sara's prose style and sensibility are exemplified in "All Mixed Up," datelined April 17, 1945. The article begins, "Here in the heart of Moronia, the film capital of Phoneyland, where all that is worst in America is raised to the Nth and multiplied by the worst that can be imported from four continents, conversations begin in divers ways—and end with the monotonous refrain, 'I'm all mixed up.'" She goes on: "What once passed for democracy in this platinum-plated clip-joint has been turned into high comedy by the pressure of war, the flood of defense workers, the internecine strife between right and left, capital and labor, Fascist and Communist. . . . Nobody wants to talk out here in the land of the freak and the home of [the] knave these days, particularly about politics." Instead of political or business leaders, Sara sought out the unemployed, the alcoholic "has beens" of Hollywood, and the careless, cynical rich. Repeating the phrase "all mixed up" throughout her piece for humorous effect, she describes "the overstrained, overcrowded Los Angeles area" and the stress of the war years on the city's inhabitants. She tells of going "into a downtown bank to cash a fifty dollar check. The bank clerk's face was tense and drawn under a deep coat of tan. One arm was stiff and his hands trembled as he fumbled with the bills. He had to count them twice. 'Sorry,' [he] apologized, 'but I'm just back from the army and I get all mixed up.'"

She tried to visit the LA offices of Transradio to report on her activities, and what should have been a simple trip became a memorable adventure. "On my way out to the Transradio office in Hollywood that afternoon, I took a ride that ranks high among the wild rides that I have taken by plane, train, ferryboat, and burro back. The big red buss [*sic*] was manned by a blonde cutie whose heavily mascaraed eyes were everywhere but on the traffic. We veered and reeled down Hill Street until we sideswiped a car." Starting back up, the bus "reeled, jerked, and tore through the suburbs of Los Angeles." Eventually the bus driver decided to join her fellow drivers on strike: "At the next corner, she said, as [she] left the buss again, 'I gotta make a telephone call. I'm all mixed up.'" Sara's narrative continues: "At that point, I took a taxi, and together the driver and I spent the afternoon exploring Southern California. If I was a babe in Hollywood's mazes, he was worse. He knew Chicago like a book he said but he'd only been in Los Angeles a few weeks and *he* was all mixed up. . . . When the driver handed me the meter check, I told him I'd just go on and buy the taxi outright. 'Honest,' he grinned, 'I didn't mean to take you for a ride, lady, I just got . . .'

"Without waiting to hear that again, I paid the bill and hurried [to] find out from the Housing Authority what was going on in Little Tokyo. . . . When the Japanese had been moved out of the Western Defense area, the negroes, Mexicans, and Phillipinos [*sic*] had crowded in. . . . Now the Japanese were beginning to return from the relocation areas but the invaders refused to evacuate Little Tokyo and things were *all* mixed up there."

When she got to San Francisco, her stories were more serious in tone. She filed an article on peace with Germany and Japan; another on the invasion of Honduras ("Central American fief of the United Fruit Company") by armed Honduran exiles from Guatemala; one titled "British Women Delegates Want to Be Regarded as Party Leaders Not Women"; a very positive description of the training center for WAVES on Treasure Island in San Francisco Bay; and one titled "Victory in Europe," a piece in which Sara describes how "the contrast between the celebrations in Times Square and the sane, sober V-E Day that this correspondent spent with the Navy in San Francisco's Bay Area indicates the shift in the center of gravity of the United States' war effort from the east coast to the west." Among the press corps was a young John F. Kennedy, there during his short stint as a reporter. He was just another young journalist, albeit one who was a wealthy war hero.[3] Said one friend, "She didn't like him; he was, of course, a Yankee and a snob. She sort of pitted him in the same category as Scott Fitzgerald."[4] Sara may also still have harbored resentment against JFK based on her assessment of his father's involvement with National Distillers and Franklin Roosevelt. In Sara's mind, there were no coincidences, and she doubtless wondered if he was there with a "cover job" as a reporter.

So far from home, she was delighted to have a reunion with her brother, serving in the US Army Air Forces in the Pacific. In January 1943, he had survived a plane crash in Guadalcanal after being shot down while the US was fighting the Japanese for control of the Solomon Islands. On his forehead was what Sara described as "a great V-scar on his face," just one more indication, as she saw it, that that the V-Campaign was real and he had been wrong to have her committed. In San Francisco, there was near hysteria over Japanese balloon bombs. The US press, however, was asked by the government not to report on the bombs so as not to let the Japanese know their degree of success. Possibly as many as six thousand such bombs were launched by the Japanese military to explode on the West Coast of the US. Sara and her journalist friends tried to keep the story from brother James as they entertained him, but later learned he'd been sent to San Francisco as part of an effort to shoot the balloons down.

Sara's press kit included her San Francisco press credentials and a registration packet with an incongruous mix of information: telegraph and cable how-tos, a list of movies, including Walt Disney shorts, for delegates to the conference, a pamphlet on San Francisco's tourist sites and another titled "War Housing in the United States"; a special edition of *California Farmer*, and an invitation to the Pan American Grand Ball. She also received stacks of press releases and pamphlets from the various countries participating in the conference—among them Australia, France, China, Korea, and India. A letter from Georgia Lloyd, head of the Campaign for World Government, an organization promoting a single political authority for the entire world, was included, as was a letter on the "fight for total peace" to UNCIO's American Delegation from Ely Culbertson, an expert on contract bridge who decided to devote himself to the cause of world peace, to be achieved "by means of an international policing organization."[5]

Also in town for the conference was Rev. Gerald L. K. Smith, described by Sara as the "rabble-rousing revivalist and one-time henchman of Huey Long, now National Director of the America First Organization," who denounced the UN conference on behalf of US nationalists. Although Sara did not agree with Smith, she supported his right to speak—she invoked the saying attributed to Voltaire: "I disapprove of what you say, but I will defend to the death your right to say it"—and was angered by the conference's refusal to credential him and then by his being arrested for speaking publicly. Herbert Moore refused to run what he saw as an article overly sympathetic to Smith after explicitly asking Sara not to report on him. He explained in a letter to Sara that "we cannot run the risk of having this man suddenly announce to the American people that we are on his side. We are not on his side and don't intend to be on his side and don't want anyone representing us pretending to involve us on his side. . . . This man is a desperate kind of demagogue and will make the most of your innocence in newsgathering activities."

In response, Sara abruptly resigned from reporting for Transradio and asked Moore whether rumors that the service had been bought by the Russian news service TASS were true. Unlike the time she sent in her letter of resignation to Moore after Pearl Harbor, she was now firm in her determination to leave the news service for good. Standing on principle, Sara liked the idea of self-sacrifice for a noble cause, a higher purpose. Sara and Moore then exchanged a series of letters, each cordial but firm. Sara wrote that working for Moore "has been, I admit, excellent training and the association with you has been a long and pleasant one, but, in the last analysis, it's getting [me] nowhere fast." He responded forcefully to her letter, defending himself and saying perhaps it was best that their association ended: "It is to be regretted that we have reached this point, but maybe it was unavoidable." Apparently in response to something she had told him, he wrote that he did not "know anything about the antics of people with strange voices who might have called you on the phone," but "it is too fantastic and too cockeyed to have any part in our busy existence." Finally, he wrote, "In conclusion, if shying away from the alleged news releases of Gerald L. K. Smith is a gag on news reporting, give us more gags of that kind or give us death."

A week later, Moore had cooled down, partly in response to another letter from Sara, and assured her that it had been "a pleasant association." He wrapped up matters of any remaining stories and any money due her, said he was sorry that her reporting for Transradio had not been "a sufficient livelihood" for her, and promised to send a general letter of recommendation for her to use in looking for other reporting work. Their letters continued for several years, as she occasionally sent in a story idea or he requested information on a contact she might have. Their last correspondence was in January 1948, when he wished her the best on her plastics and cotton projects.

She had imagined that in San Francisco, things would be less muddled than in LA but instead she found "the 'Tragedy of San Fiasco.' . . . Money and power speaking; right and justice gagged. Muddling mendacity, moral turpitude glossed over with smooth phrases and slick publicity." She wrote to H. L. Mencken that covering the two conferences was an experience "which I should have hated to miss but which I would never want to repeat again." Ever idealistic, Sara had hoped for a postwar "world democracy, based upon a community of ideas, rather than upon race, class, territory, or conquest." Education would be the means to achieving such a world, and at one point, she considered organizing an Institute for Education in World Democracy at the University of Alabama. But the US State Department and the delegates to both conferences were, she wrote to Mencken, "cynical, stupid, and cowardly" and gave up too much to the USSR. Disillusioned, she was ready to move on.

She would, however, have to say goodbye to a new love, a friend of a friend, a man visiting the city but stationed in India as a vice president of an oil company. This romance repeated the pattern of many of her earlier love affairs. Although she liked him "very much," she wasn't going to be swept off her feet, and wrote to friends, "He's coming east to meet my family in a few weeks and try to persuade me to marry him and go back to India. Perhaps, someday, but not yet." The man, Victor Brown, was in the process of getting a "Reno divorce" and wanted her to marry him as soon as he was free. Sara, meanwhile, went to Blacksburg, Virginia, to wait for passport clearance, hoping to travel as a news correspondent in what she saw as a cover job for the State Department. Vic wrote in the throes of love: "I wish I could tell you how I feel about you—nothing has happened like that to me before—You were wonderful and I wanted to be close to you as soon as I saw you. . . . Last nite was *very* bad without you—and so is now—I'd give a lot to be where we were two nites ago. I hope you're happy right now and wonder if you're also thinking about two nites ago." Sara, leery of losing her independence, was still not interested in marrying. She and Vic moved on from their brief romance.

When the reporting trip abroad failed to materialize after the UNCIO meeting, Sara returned home to Tuscaloosa and resumed her chemistry work on various projects. Although a September 29, 1945, letter from Robert Boehm, director of research at the Masonite Corporation, expressed his "brutally frank" opinion that "there is nothing in this disclosure which would permit the Patent Office to grant you a patent," Sara believed she was protecting her in-laws' business interests in informing them of her work. Although some of Sara's theories have the ring of textbook paranoia, occasionally something that sounds unlikely does turn out to be true. After all her experiments and applications, she would, finally, receive a patent, number 2517906, granted August 8, 1950, for "dry plastic composition, containing urea-formaldehyde, plaster of paris, wheat flour, and veneer dust"—and this while she was a patient at Bryce. Surely she was the only patient in the history of Bryce, and a rarity in the history of mental patients anywhere, to receive a letter from the US Patent Office, adorned with a blue ribbon and a red seal, stating, "We take pleasure in handing you herewith Original Letters of Patent." She worked with UA chemistry professors S. J. Lloyd and A. M. Kennedy and chemical engineering professor Kenneth Coons in her efforts to extract useful products from cotton stalks. And it's a testament to Sara's relative functionality and likeability that that she had colleagues who were willing to work with her and to take her work seriously and that she had so many friends who enjoyed spending time with her. She was generally good company. Cigarette in one hand, "bourbon and branch water" in the other, she told great stories, and she'd throw her head back and laugh at your stories as well.

Sara hoped one of her patents would bring in money, but without the intensity of the war effort her activities lacked fizz. A bit at loose ends, Sara visited H. L. Mencken in Baltimore in the fall of 1945, where she found him "rotund, bouncy, full of steam and 'malicious magnetism.'" They went to lunch at Schellhase's Restaurant, ate soft shell crabs, drank beer, and talked about the just-ended war, war correspondents, and the UN Conference. Puffing a cigar, Mencken leaned back and opined that "there were no stupider men than diplomats, nor any more antisocial. Their dishonesty, he added, was so deep-seated that most of them were quite as unconscious of it as a Georgia Cracker is unconscious of his hookworms and his fleas."[6]

On a visit to Montgomery, she went by the Sayres' house to see Zelda. It had been five years since they'd seen each other, almost five years since Scott's death, and when Sara got there, Zelda was taking a disabled neighbor child for a walk with her, as she did every day. Sara was touched by how Zelda treated the girl "with a tenderness and compassion that reminded me of Zelda's care for me some thirty-odd years before on that same Sayre Street hill."[7] By 1945 both Sara and Zelda had experienced stays in mental hospitals. Did they confide in each other, or simply choose, as southern women will, to talk of more pleasant things—plants, clothes, books, shared acquaintances? The language of Zelda's friend Livye Hart Ridgeway, in a remembrance of Zelda, gives an indication of how a southern lady might soften the story: "Zelda was in and out of several rest homes (the poor darling was not always just normal)."

Sara still thought of herself as a writer, albeit one who had recently been immersed in journalistic rather than literary writing. She needed a postwar writing plan for herself and decided to apply for a Guggenheim fellowship to collect and write about Black folklore and music. Her project was already half done—she had collected a number of songs during her days on the family plantation in the late twenties and early thirties—and the prestige of a Guggenheim would help with other publishing projects. The money would be welcome, as well. Describing her process in a biographical statement that may have been written for the application, she wrote "While I was out on the plantation I collected some 300 negro songs from the swamps and organized an orchestra among my negroes. Their music is like nothing you ever heard in Harlem or on Broadway. In fact, if it were on the air it might create a new style in music that would replace swing." Her use of the possessive in the phrase "my negroes" reflects so many things: a legacy of ownership, a sense of both superiority and concomitant responsibility rooted in the idea that she should be what she referred to as a "good master" (as when she wrote to the parole officer at the El Reno, Oklahoma, prison on behalf of a prisoner there, describing him as "an old family servant . . . [who] has been with us ever since he was a child"), and a lack of awareness of racial injustice. Sara was not chosen to receive a fellowship, despite a letter of support from Lester Raines, director of dramatics at UA, stating that Sara's "attitude toward the whole racial problem is sound and in accordance with Northern ideals," and that she "is sympathetic to their [the Blacks'] problems." His additional assertion that "by birth and culture she is a daughter of the South and understands how to get and encourage the colored folk in the backward sections of this region to give her their native songs," combined with Sara's quasi-anthropological approach to gathering raw material from the "folk," must have seemed culturally out of step with what the selection committee was looking for. That same year they awarded a fellowship to a young African American painter named Jacob Lawrence who would tell the story of his own people through his work, rather than having a white person, however sympathetic, tell it for them.

Chapter 9

"A Season in Tuscaloosa"

Considerations of Sexual Attraction and Love. A Period of Extraordinary Activity with Experiments, Plans for a Newspaper and a Blue Book, and Family Duties. An Account of being forcibly taken to Bryce Hospital and left there.

SARA SITS IN HER FOUR-POSTER BED, A FAMILY HEIRLOOM, IN THE upstairs room at Idlewyld, writing letters to friends, windows open to spring air. Jonquils bloom in the yard, their yellow echoed by the forsythia bushes' sprays. Last week there were crocuses. Next week there will be the sudden purpling of redbuds, white spiraea, and then cherry, dogwood, and irises coming up in time for Easter. She sees all this, and the beauty moves her, but she is turned inward. In 1945, the war ended, and she turned forty. She has returned to Alabama, but for how long, and for what purposes? Will she always be alone? She thinks, and then she moves to her desk and types, a sheaf of single-spaced pages over a five-day period, from Friday, March 22, to Tuesday, March 26, 1946.

The entries are heady, intellectual, abstract, masking the details of whatever individual crisis she was going through, but clearly she was struggling with a personal crisis. On March 22 she alludes to bisexuality, desire, and love: "When I was very young, a great actress told me that 'Man is a bisexual animal and must have friends and lovers, too." She writes of Liz, and of their mothers, "Suze and Daze." Feeling herself separated from her best friend and their shared history by fate, she nevertheless had "yielded to the temptation to carry on for Suze and Daze by sending Daze a birthday card." As much as she wanted to find a way to reconnect on an essential level with Liz, to reenter what she called, throughout their lives, "The House of Thee-and-I," she knew it was but the "nightmarish ghost of Thee-and-I": "If the pattern of life is a spiral, I came a full circle on the upgrade between detaching myself from it physically twenty years ago and detaching myself from it, emotionally and spiritually, a few weeks ago."

On Sunday the twenty-fourth she lay outside on the porch playing a record of Beethoven's *Ode to Joy* over and over again and looking up at the purple clumps of fragrant wisteria blossoms. She went to bed "convinced that the knowledge of Western science is as the babbling of children as compared to the Wisdom of the East."

On March 25, still sorting through the crisis, she writes, "Thee-and-I was a great illusion, a magnificent obsession. In the beginning, it was a figment of Daze's imagination that took form and being . . . a carefully conditioned sense of attachment, which was neither physical, mental, or emotional, but spiritual—a trellis on which we grew. . . . Now . . . it is merely a jealous, possessive, cruel demon crying out for the Golden Age, going through the grotesque motions of carrying on an irretrievable past into an unpredictable future, driving Liz into seclusion and melancholia and me into the Absolute by some infernal remembrance of things past."

She thought about the past and the present, and how to reconcile them: "After twenty years in Montgomery and ten among the International Society of Juvenile Delinquents across three continents, I'd seen all I ever want to see of the sad satiety that comes from fumbling in the flesh for a certainty that isn't there. If that's love and romance, give me beer and music." Instead, she chooses "work without attachment—eighteen hours a day of it, chemistry, psychological warfare, journalism, declining all kudos and rewards that could politely be declined." The next day she writes of her hope "to make Liz realize that this day only is ours and in it we carry on, not for the sake of those who went before us or for those who are to come after us" but, implicitly, for themselves. Always a spiritual seeker, destined as such to be an outsider in "the land of the Doric façade," Sara concluded that "to be a lady is to be mistress of one's self and servant of all; to be a Yogini, to be mistress of one's heart and mind; to be an Enlightened Spirit, to be mistress of one's illusions and one's relation to time."

Sara wrote herself through the crisis, at least for the time being, and returned to "work without attachment" on a variety of projects, including plans to start a second daily newspaper in Tuscaloosa (with a plant in town to produce newsprint from cottonstalks). She wrote many, many letters in pursuit of both the newspaper and the paper plant, and engaged in correspondence, bid seeking, and list making as she considered publishing a revised version of *The Alabama Bluebook and Social Register*. In addition to a paper plant in Tuscaloosa, she planned to set up a plant to produce plastics in Childersburg, Alabama. She camped out there with partners on the project, "with no refrigeration, no hot water, no green vegetables, not much help, a bed in the midst of bales of acetates," and, she wrote Aunt Honey and Uncle Forrest, "after two weeks of eighteen hours work a day . . . [I] came home feeling fine."

For the next two years, while Susie pursued her garden and social club activities, and James worked in his law practice, Sara made drawings of various inventions, including a "continuous process Drier and Seive [*sic*] for Laboratory use," "plastic ceramic tools," a "Tropical Chippendale coffee table to be moulded from plastic with ceramic tile top," and different units to aid in the collection of sawdust from sawmills. She made up and labeled samples of paper and cardstock with different ratios of cotton fiber to wood pulp. In late 1947 and early 1948 Sara was hard at work on articles of incorporation for the "Plasticast Corporation." Her partners were Kenneth Coons, a UA professor in chemical engineering, and S. E. Harless. She developed radio advertising spots and a sample letter regarding how Plasticast worked: when water was added to the dry cellulose mixture made from cotton byproducts, it hardened into a durable material. She changed the articles of incorporation of the Mayfield Cotton Corporation to the Southern Cellulose Corporation, to aid in the promotion of the "Cotton Harvester Combine" and to form an organization for the promotion of Plasticast. To keep up with her various projects and holdings, Sara hand-drew a corporate family tree under the heading "The Alston V. Temple Foundation," subtitled "100% Directors/ Welfare, Research, Music, Communications, Fellowship." (Alston V. Temple was a pseudonym she had occasionally used for reporting.) In this work, Sara was up with the times. In fact, a Plasticast company already existed, with offices in Chicago and Palo Alto, California, and it was advertising its product in *Popular Mechanics* as early as August 1947. An ad in the November 1947 issue claimed "Magic Liquid Casts Plastics." Sara saw the ads, but thought perhaps her in-laws, the Masons, had something to do with undermining her company, and she wanted the FBI to investigate the matter.[1] She also saved correspondence with the Camden (Arkansas) Furniture Company, who wrote her definitively that they were unaware of the Chicago company but that *they* held the trademark for the name Plasticast for furniture, although they would be interested in selling her that trademark if she wanted to use the name for furniture as well as other uses.[2]

She experimented on her family home with different uses for her casein-based plastics, and over the course of several years used it to replace plaster arabesques damaged by a burst pipe, as well as to fill in cracks in a marble mantel and between boards in the wood floors. The plastic was working so well that she decided to do over an upstairs bathroom with walls and floors of veneer plywood painted with plastic and even a shower curtain made of chintz and sprayed with the plastic mixture. From there she moved on to spraying the garden furniture with the plastic spray and then painting the kitchen with it as well, postulating that she could hose the walls down in the absence of domestic help. Although she wrote in a sample draft letter that her company has "samples showing no deterioration after eight years and four rooms, two baths and two kitchens done over in 'Plasticast' which have been used daily for four years and a half," one Tuscaloosa resident recalled that the Plasticast in a bathroom in Idlewyld had run down the walls after only one day. What her mother thought of these experiments can be readily imagined—but Sara was very hard to dissuade, once she got an idea in her head.

Indefatigable, she wrote more letters (always keeping a carbon) regarding Plasticast and her other products to companies and institutions in Alabama and all over the US, including Marshall Field and Company, Auburn University, the *Tuscaloosa News*, Alabama Power Company, the Southeastern Research Institute, Reichhold Chemical Company, the Alabama Bottlers Association, Schwartz Toy Store in New York City, Nolin Brothers Refrigerator Company, World Die Caster, Avondale Mills, and Union Carbide. She wrote letters asking questions about patents, letters trying to straighten out her right to the name "Plasticast," and letters to old friends about her new pursuits.

While keeping track of established projects, Sara drove herself to work on a series of new experiments on plastics and cotton byproducts. In early 1948 she took detailed notes on experiments conducted in two sequences, January 5, 6, 8, 9, 10, 12, 13, 18 and February 10, 11, 13, 14, 15, 25. She began another set on March 21. When Sara had a goal and a mission, she reveled in hardship. Was there a manic element to this, or more a determination to avoid any difficult emotional engagement by exhausting herself with work? Whichever it was, or both, her eighteen hours a day of frantic work eventually became too much for her, too intense a pace, and one she could not keep up forever.

Adding to her stress was the horrible news of Zelda Fitzgerald's death in a fire, trapped in a locked ward with chains on the windows, at the Highland

Hospital in Asheville, North Carolina, on March 10, 1948. The *Mobile Press Register* reported her death on March 11, with the headline, "Mrs. F. Scott Fitzgerald, Widow of Author, among Those Killed." The article described the "holocaust of fire" and gave details of the burning buildings, how patients scattered into the woods, and how the community helped to comfort them, concluding with a paragraph on how Mrs. Fitzgerald was "a writer in her own right." Zelda's funeral was held on March 17 and *Time* magazine reported the death on Monday, March 22: "Died: Zelda Sayre Fitzgerald, 48, invalid wife of Jazz Age Novelist F. Scott Fitzgerald; in a fire which destroyed a building of the Highland Hospital (for mental and nervous diseases); in Asheville, N.C."

At Idlewyld, Sara's behavior became worrisome enough that her mother began to consider having her committed once again. One of the stories that floats around Sara is that she chased her mother with a butcher knife one night. There are other stories of sharp objects in southern literary life: the first time Scott Fitzgerald had dinner at the Sayres' home in Montgomery, Zelda's father supposedly chased her with a carving knife after she provoked him with teasing.[3] When Boo Radley stabs his father in the leg with scissors in *To Kill a Mockingbird*, the ease of sending him to Bryce must be resisted: "Miss Stephanie said old Mr. Radley said no Radley was going to any asylum when it was suggested that a season in Tuscaloosa might be helpful to Boo. Boo wasn't crazy, he was high-strung at times."[4]

The details of Sara's behavior in early March are unclear, but the day came when Susie Mayfield decided that her daughter should be committed again, and she exercised her power as Sara's mother to make that happen. March 23, 1948, was a slightly chilly, drizzly day, easing into morning rather than announcing it. Sara was in her sitting room upstairs at Idlewyld, when suddenly four men—sheriff's deputies, she thought—broke the lock on the door, told her to come with them, and took her down the stairs, out to a waiting car (were neighbors observing the scene through their curtains? she wondered), and off through town to Bryce Hospital. Sara, feeling fear and dismay as she watched familiar downtown streets and the university campus pass by, requested that they allow her "legal or psychiatric counsel" but was refused. Powerless, she was taken to the Women's Receiving Building, once more down that green alley, once more to answer the questions of men in suits, with clipboards and pleasant, unreadable expressions.

Her initial admission notes state that the "attack came on gradually, and has lasted eight years; has been insane before and a patient in B.H.; is not easily managed at home; methods used for restraint were not any good; she is delusional, [illegible], feels persecuted; attends ordinary work poorly." The next day, psychiatrist Sam Darden interviewed her, asking why she thought she was there. Sara responded, "Either for observation or for protection. My mother has been so hounded to have me put here that she was on the verge of a nervous breakdown herself." Sara went on to say that her brother's marriage was in trouble, and his wife, wanting a divorce, custody of their son, and the Mayfield house, was trying to impugn the sanity of Sara and her brother. Dr. Darden's notes concluded, "Practically the entire interview is taken up by the patient's telling me about how her sister-in-law has been trying to undermind [*sic*] her and Jimmie, the patient's brother. The patient is rather tense and resentful. No hallucinations were elicited. Her judgment is poor and her insight is nil." That same day, Sara attempted to run away, to the home of Dr. Partlow, on the Bryce campus, but a nurse caught her and brought her back.

Two weeks later, she was brought before the medical staff of five doctors, plus a transcriptionist to record the entire interview: six against one, as Sara saw it. When Sara was asked if any of her family had been to visit, she replied "no," then leaned back in her chair and turned her eyes away. Asked why she came to the hospital, she responded, "I don't know, Dr. Darden. I think I know actually what happened but as to the whys, I am not at all certain." Afterward, the five doctors agreed on a diagnosis of "paranoid condition." Sara started a journal and recorded her own notes about her admission, writing that a doctor had told her early on that if she wanted to leave Bryce, she "would have to be more conciliatory towards" James because James was afraid that Sara, if released, "might try to 'annoy and embarrass him.'" It is not possible to know whether a doctor said this to Sara, but, given the law at the time, it certainly was possible for families to lock up a relative they deemed inconvenient or embarrassing. A childhood playmate of Sara's who also knew her as an adult in Tuscaloosa, interviewed at age 103, said that she had heard at the time that Mrs. Mayfield and Dr. Partlow, the head of Bryce, were good friends, and that Dr. Partlow had told Susie Mayfield that Sara was "never getting out of there." That was how things were then, she said; if someone had influence they could have you put away, and gave as an example her uncle, who was—she asked what those men were who liked other men and was prompted with "homosexual?"—a homosexual, and her father had him put into Bryce and he was there for the rest of his life. You could do that then, she said: it just took a judge, and it was very easy to get someone in and hard to get out.[5]

Chester Walker, the probate judge of Tuscaloosa County who, just a little over a year before, had signed the papers of incorporation for the newspaper Sara hoped to set up, and whom she addressed as "Dear Ches" in a letter about county tax exemptions for new businesses, now signed the Letters of Guardianship appointing Sara's mother as her legal guardian. After Sara's name appear the letters NCM: non compos mentis. This sad little document, dated May 21, 1948, itemizes the cost of each aspect of the proceedings:

appointing Guardian	6.25
Declaration unsound mind	16.00
Sheriff Notice & summoning Jury	6.50
Guardian ad Litem	7.50

The total came to $36.25 and was paid on May 26. Court documents show that a jury of "six disinterested persons" met on May 17, 1948, and concluded that "Sarah Martin Mayfield is a person of unsound mind." The order of the probate judge to the sheriff regarding those proceedings, using traditional legal language, states, "You are hereby required to take the body of the said Sarah Martin Mayfield, and, if consistent with the health or ability, have her in Court to be present at the place of trial." Sara presumably was not deemed well enough to appear in court. It was this absence of "taking the body" to court, the legal principle of habeas corpus, that Sara would later attempt to argue as grounds for being released.

Since at least the late nineteenth century, it had been all too easy to have someone committed to a mental hospital. Although some reforms had been enacted, intended to safeguard the rights of those potentially being committed, the shift from medical determination to a judge's determination made it possible for a family member and an agreeable probate judge to commit a person against his or her will, after which few criteria regarding treatment or length of stay had to be met, and patients had little recourse to the courts. At the time Sara was committed, state hospitals provided most public mental health care, and inpatient care predominated, with a peak, in 1955, of 560,000 patients in the United States.[6]

It does seem that at least part of the reason for having Sara committed came from her family's being bothered by her frenetic activities and skeptical about her ability to invent something of worth. Sara may in fact have needed treatment, but the commitment also got her out of their hair. When Sara's mother and brother were interviewed in May as part of the commitment process, the doctor recorded their complaint that "she is constantly making some plans to do something," including inventing a cotton picker on the model of a steam shovel and working to put new plastics on the market, which her brother dismissed as impractical. In early 1948 Sara had been planning to work with the Bryce Hospital farm on one of her inventions and had written a letter about her plastics work in which she said that "we are contemplating embarking on the pilot plant operations with the cottonstalks next fall. A large farm implement manufacturer has become interested in developing the necessary harvesting and concentration machinery, Dr. Partlow has offered us the use of the cotton lands on the State Farms here for experimental purposes and Dr. Coons has acquired sufficient equipment in the Chemical Engineering Department of the U. of A. to take care of the pulping and bleaching." By March 1948, Sara was a patient at Bryce, not, as she had intended, a partner with the hospital in her research.

Trying to understand her situation, Sara sat in her room with a notebook, making out a list of "Questions Involving My Family." Question number ten on the list is, "A number of little things that Mother said and did incline me to think that arrangements to have me committed had been made some time prior to March 23, 1948, [and] as she must have known that the deputies were coming that morning to take me to the hospital, why did she offer me sedatives?" Under the heading "QUESTION: Did patent rights have anything to do with commitment?" she also drew up notes on similarities between her commitment in 1940 and that of 1948, starting with "about to file patents for plastics" under 1940 and "about to file patents for cotton project" under 1948. Sara could see the similarities between what she was doing in 1940 and 1948, but she could not recognize that, however legitimate her scientific investigations might have been, erratic, overactive behavior preceded both commitments.

Sara wrote of her first weeks at Bryce: "To the tedium of those days of forced labor, helplessness, and silence, was added the shock and grief of Zelda Fitzgerald's death." Although she didn't need to be reminded, Sara saw a "terse, tragic notice" of Zelda's death in print when she picked up a copy of *Time* magazine that someone had left lying around in the ward. Zelda had been in the hospital and had died in a fire. Now Sara was in the hospital— what would happen to her? Zelda had gone ahead of her, and, instead of teaching Sara how to fly fast down a steep hill, she had perished. Sara would worry about fires the rest of the time she was at Bryce.

Just three weeks after Sara's commitment to the mental hospital, her mother was down in Mobile for a Colonial Dames tea to commemorate the fiftieth anniversary of the charter group of organizers, which had first met at the Grand Hotel in Point Clear, Alabama, in 1898. The *Mobile Register* described the event: "The house was attractively decorated throughout with arrangements of Spring flowers. . . . The tea table was exquisite with an arrangement of yellow tulips, roses and jonquils in a silver epergne, flanked on either side by silver candelabra. At either end of the table were massive silver services."[7] As the ladies paid tribute to Mrs. Mayfield, "the only living charter member," how many of them knew that her daughter had, once again, been committed to what Alabamians referred to as "Bryce's"? Did they whisper in another room, did friends offer a supportive glance or pat? Did someone say, pityingly, "bless her heart"? In 1893 Susie Fitts Martin gave her high school's valedictory speech. She chose as her epigraph lines from Shakespeare's *All's Well That Ends Well*: "The web of our life is of a mingled yarn, good and ill together." Perhaps she thought of those lines during the commemorative tea. An article on the gathering a few days later called Mrs. Mayfield "one of the most beloved matrons of this city."

That same month, Susie Mayfield made her will, just over a page long. She left everything to her son, Jim, and named him as her executor. She signed her name beneath these words, "I have full faith and confidence that my beloved son, James J. Mayfield, Jr., will adequately support and maintain my beloved daughter, Sarah [*sic*] Martin Mayfield, who is now non compos mentis, should she survive me. If by some miracle, or the mercy of God, my said daughter should be permanently restored to her sanity, I have implicit confidence that my said son will deal justly and fairly with her concerning my property."

On September 9, 1948, the day before Sara's forty-third birthday, the first since she had been committed the past spring, her mother and brother came to visit, bringing a birthday cake and presents for Sara. It was not a happy visit, though, as they quarreled about the night before she was taken away to Bryce, with Sara writing afterward that her brother had said "he was not there on the night that I was reported to be 'chasing Mother.' Mother said she knew nothing about any such reports."

Later that fall, Sara's doctor wrote that she complained to other patients that "the doctors had turned the observation back on her and that it was making her shoulders hurt." A week later, Sara was again brought before the medical staff, who reaffirmed their initial diagnosis of paranoid condition. To Sara, it made sense to conclude that her Sheppard Pratt/Bryce commitment of 1940, her 1948 commitment, her patents, and her brother's divorce from Betty Mason Mayfield, daughter of engineer and inventor William H. Mason, the owner of the Masonite company, must all be connected in some way, and further must be related to the custody battle for their son, William Mason Mayfield, called Mason. Writing her brother from Bryce in those first months, Sara was worried about Mason: "In view of the fact that Mother told me that Betty and Jean had taken Mason to an asthma clinic in Mississippi I want the reassurance of knowing that he was taken there with your consent and Burdett[e]'s and that you are both satisfied as to his whereabouts and safety." Sara adored the little boy, having once described him in a letter to H. L. Mencken as "the rosiest, sturdiest, sweetest little fellow with the most amazing scientific bent." (She was bereft, when, the next year, Mason was caught in the polio epidemic and died, several years before polio vaccines became widely available.)

As she described the family's situation in a letter to her patent lawyer, her sister-in-law "attempted to force me to testify against my brother. . . . If I would agree to do so, Betty argued, the commitments would be removed and the Mason Corporation would protect the patent rights which would, on my death, revert to Mason," once her brother was declared unfit and Sara was made the boy's guardian. Sara made a list of Betty's "fears" and "obsessions" that could provide possible motives for having Sara committed. Writing to her lawyer of her worries about the effect of her absence on her plastics business and her patents, Sara surmises that the Masons' nefarious schemes must be responsible for her commitment and concludes that her own family's "unaccountable attitude is due to misinformation, alienation, duress or blackmail." She did not believe that there were sufficient grounds for her family having had her committed and, well before the law was solidified on the question of commitment hinging on someone being a danger to self or others, wrote one of her business partners that she hoped to seek damages against the Mason family, but it depended "upon the decision of the doctors as to whether I was lawfully committed i.e. actually dangerous to myself or society."[8]

In her journal Sara made lists of other reasons why her brother, sister-in-law, Bryce officials, trustees of the First National Bank, and others might have wanted her committed; beyond the plastics patents and the trouble with the Masons, perhaps it had to do with the 840 acres she owned that she believed had been cut for timber in 1932 without her permission, or perhaps it was her attempt to start up a rival newspaper in Tuscaloosa. She decided to write press releases to activate a campaign for her being discharged from the hospital, and to do so she took on the persona of Roberta Bruce (a feminized version of the fourteenth-century Scottish hero Robert the Bruce, known as Braveheart, who successfully opposed the English in wars for Scottish independence). Sara/Roberta wrote, "After a group of local newspeople had organized a newspaper to compete with the *Tuskaloosa* [*sic*] *News*, one of them, a former correspondent for Transradio Press, was railroaded into Bryce Hospital without a hearing and is still being held without legal or psychiatric counsel or trial." As Roberta Bruce, Sara also wrote of the "unholy alliance" of superintendents of Bryce and Partlow hospitals, politicians, bankers, and businessmen, titling one press release–style statement, "Fascist Rule Threatens White as Well as Black in Alabama." She wrote, "The embattled liberals and baffled aristocrats in Alabama are no longer sure that 'It Can't Happen Here.' For the hillbilly Hitlers have formed an Unholy Alliance with the 'Big Mules,' the financial oligarchy, which, with the help of the Black Belt politicos, the Ku Klux Klan, and the self-perpetuating boards of trustees of the University of Alabama and the Alabama State Hospitals, maintains a fascistic stronghold on the administrative machinery of the State of Alabama." Part of Sara's fury in being committed derived from the realization that being a white woman from a prominent family did her no good when it came to seeking release from the mental hospital. The extensive web of connections she took for granted, the easy trading of favors among the powerful she had grown accustomed to, seemed, in fact, to be working against her. When she could, she tried to cement alliances, writing to her cousin, Peabody Burdette Mayfield, who was on the Bryce medical staff, as "Dearest Birdie," and asking for his assistance in being released. She ends the letter, "You certainly have a great many friends and admirers here. It makes me proud of you."[9]

Sara's worries were fed by the fact that her brother had become involved in Alabama politics. Somewhat progressive by the definition of those days, as a prominent attorney in Alabama he had successfully argued a prolabor case in the US Supreme Court in 1940, establishing the right to picket in Alabama. In 1948, the year Sara was committed, he stood up to southern separatist Democrats in the 1948 Dixiecrat revolt. Some southern electors wanted to be allowed to vote for Strom Thurmond as presidential candidate rather than President Truman because of their vehement disagreement with Truman's civil rights program. As a result of his lack of fidelity to the southern cause, he was unfairly accused in 1948 of conspiring, with "Governor James E. Folsom and some of his associates" to have "entered into a 'conspiracy' to keep for themselves money raised for the fight over Alabama's electoral votes." James spoke on the witness stand, accusing states-righter Horace Wilkinson of being behind the suit: "This motion has the same stamp and smell of that individual who cares not for the Democratic Party of the South but only for his personal aggrandizement, notoriety, and benefit. Once before, he attempted to disrupt the Democratic Party by using as his firebrand our Catholic citizens, and now he is attempting to use as his firebrand his hatred for our negro population."[10]

Despite her voluminous writings on the various possible causes for her commitment, Sara never wrote anything about her sexuality or sexual behavior, but, given the times she lived in, that is hardly surprising. If she did have homosexual or bisexual feelings, as seems likely, it's no wonder she would be reluctant to admit to them in any form that others might read. Starting in the late nineteenth century, as attitudes changed, overt admission of same-sex attraction had become dangerous. The authors of *Intimate Matters* cite the case of a woman who "passed" as a man in the 1850s, even writing a memoir about being "the female hunter." In the 1880s, she was committed to a mental hospital for "sexual perversion . . . a 'Lesbian' . . . [with] 'paroxysmal attacks of erotomania.'"[11] In Alabama in the 1930s, Bryce's Dr. Partlow had led an effort to authorize the superintendents of mental hospitals to enforce wide-ranging compulsory sterilization, upon discharge, of "sexual perverts, homosexuals, sodomists, rapists, the mentally deficient, and those 'habitually and constantly dependent upon public relief or support of charity.'" A compulsory sterilization law was actually passed in 1935 by the Alabama legislature but finally vetoed by the governor.[12] Other attempts were made in 1939, 1943, and 1945, but failed.[13] Across the country, homosexuals were regularly committed to mental hospitals by their families to be "cured," and were even subjected to transorbital lobotomies.[14]

Sara had a precursor of sorts in a woman with the traditionally male name of Andrew—Andrew M. Sheffield, committed against her will in 1890 by her half-brother and father, when she was about forty years old. Conveniently, her half-brother was a probate judge: a family member and the law in one person. John S. Hughes, in the introduction to *The Letters of a Victorian Madwoman*, his annotated collection of Andrew Sheffield's letters, begins Andrew's story as she sits in a jail cell in Guntersville, Alabama: "She was addicted to chloral hydrate, an opiate commonly used to induce sleep, and had become involved in an abusive and sexual relationship with the doctor who supplied her the drug. Most immediately, she had attempted to burn down the house of a neighbor who was feuding with the doctor. So, embarrassed and concerned, the men of her family decided that she must be forcibly confined. Facing the grim and nearly certain prospect of Andrew's prison term for arson, her brother and father grasped at the less stigmatizing alternative of her hospitalization for madness." Notes describing her case include the phrase that it was "impossible for her friends to control her." As with Sara, a complicated mix of culturally inappropriate and mentally unwell behavior characterized Andrew's situation. Hughes writes that early mental health reformers were able to "succeed in bringing madness partially under medical control, and they did relieve countless families of the burden of managing the aged, the deranged, the eccentric, and the dangerous." Control, however, is the key word: "To the asylum superintendents and trustees, the needs of humanity and the imperative to control were in no way exclusive. To them, distinctions between deviance and disease (which they termed 'depravity' and 'insanity') seemed blurred at best." In Andrew's case, the control took the form of removing her from her home, taking away her freedoms, even placing her on the "demented ward," part of the "back wards" where, wrote then superintendent Searcy, "she could not find patients to disaffect with her abuse of the officials . . . and where she could not frighten others with her horrible tales."[15]

Andrew always insisted on her sanity, even asking to be tried for the arson as a sane person rather than be left to languish in Bryce. Her father, who shot and killed the doctor after Andrew was arrested, was tried and acquitted, and kept his freedom.[16] Sheffield died in Bryce in 1920.

Sara likewise continued to proclaim her sanity, demanding a habeas corpus hearing for herself and also keeping up with her press releases and letter-writing campaigns. But as time passed and she was still at Bryce, she began to understand that this commitment was different from the first. Slowly, steadily, the routines of her life "inside" sidled in and took the place of her life "outside." She had responsibilities, but they were mandated by others; ward attendants and nurses determined the course of her day. Institutional life became, simply, life.

Chapter 10

"Inside Insanity"

Further Particulars relating to a Diagnosis of Paranoia and the Administration of Shock Treatments. Socializing with Other Patients and sending Presents to her Family. Sara investigates Conditions at the Hospital and finds them lacking.

WITH LITTLE TIME TO CALL HER OWN AND LITTLE PRIVACY, SARA had ample opportunities to misunderstand her interactions with others. She believed that the conspiracy to keep her at the hospital was widespread, and she was always on the lookout for traps laid by the staff, believing, as she wrote in a statement about her commitment, that she "was alternately held incommunicado, under an almost intolerable inquisition, then allowed to go about freely in the hope that I would attempt to run away."

The doctors, as was common at the time, prescribed electroshock treatments for many of the patients. First used to induce seizures in mental patients in Italy in the 1930s, electroconvulsive therapy, or ECT, could be successful in treating a number of mental illnesses, including psychosis and depression. The author of a history of ECT has written that the treatment, and even the threat of it, however, were also used to control difficult patients, and Sara may well have been one of those patients.[1]

Sara was given a course of treatments and later described them in horrific detail in a section of her unpublished autobiographical novel (this version is in the first person, but in another draft Sara referred to her character by the number Sara herself had been assigned at Bryce, 488). In one scene, the Sara character, who assisted in preparing patients who were to be administered electroshock therapy, one day finds that the patient being called in for shock therapy by the nurse is, in fact, herself. The scene continues:

"'Next for shock treatments?' I echoed her incredulously.

'Yes, take off your shoes.' There was a catch in her voice. The R.N.'s face was as white as her uniform; the doctor's mouth was set in a thin tight line. Whatever had happened, they were not responsible for the decision to give me the shock treatments, of that I was sure, so I steeled myself to take it as stoically as I could. I kicked off my shoes and climbed on the carriage.

'What's this for?' I asked. The R.N.'s hand was like ice as she brushed back my hair and rubbed the compound on my temples. Neither she nor the doctor answered. They both knew the story. While on government business during the war, I had been shanghaied into a private hospital, across several state lines in violation of the Lindbergh Law. The hospital staff had tried to exculpate themselves for holding me by trying to sweat me into admitting that I was 'mentally ill' when I was brought there. Then seven years later when I asked to have the commitment contested, four deputies had suddenly picked me up and brought me to the state hospital, where the superintendent's family were relatives of the sister-in-law who, to the best of my knowledge was responsible for both commitments and friends of the superintendent of the private hospital where I had been held. Even so, it was a well-known fact that I had incurred a well-conditioned respect for mental health as the result of a mistaken diagnosis of what turned out to be typhus and it was also well-known that I had once used a similar situation in a story I was writing and cut it out because it was too cold, terrifying and psychologically brutal for a whodunit. But here I was, lying on the carriage with the electrodes of the shock therapy apparatus being clamped to my temples. Luckily I had better sense than to try to talk but cold perspiration was pouring from under my arms and there were goose pimples over them. I was still wondering if they would actually give shock treatments when there was a flash of light under my lids, a dull stab through my chest, then nothing . . . nothing."

Whatever the therapeutic value may have been to some patients, to Sara the experience was one of rank injustice. She wrote that "the retrograde amnesia which is one of the results of shock treatment lingers for months, plunging the patient into the icy abyss of terror that opens when he or she tries to recall some name or event that has been 'shocked out.' Those patients who apparently improve under shock treatment are in the minority—and very probably they would have improved as much with rest and routine alone, had the shock treatments not been given. Those who break under shock treatment join the army of deteriorated patients on the back wards who are never seen by the public and whose sole purpose in life is to provide state institutions with more appropriations where appropriations are made on a per diem per patient basis [for] maintenance funds which more often than not are diverted to buildings and salaries."

Sara had personal experience of the "back wards," which she referred to as the "Black Hole of the Bryce." Although she perceived that she was "suddenly removed to the disturbed ward on the pretext that I had made a 'sarcastic remark' to a patient," her doctor wrote in his patient notes for October 7, 1949, "This patient is an increasing source of disturbance in the hospital. She is a constant troublemaker. Hardly a day passes that she does not decide that some certain patient is spying on her and is here merely for the purpose of spying on her. She constantly reveals to people as 'needling' her and frequently says that she is tired of 'needle soup.' She has an unlimited number of ideas of reference and it seems that she manages to develop several new ones each day." The doctor's annoyance comes through in his notes, actually supporting to some degree Sara's assertions about shock treatments and patient control. With a high patient load, managing patients and keeping the peace was a significant concern, and having a "troublemaker" under his care meant that any trouble Sara caused tended to be magnified, as she created disturbances among people who were already disturbed. But Sara never meant to cause trouble; she acted on what she believed to be the facts, seeing herself as a truth-teller rather than a trouble-maker—and her doctor, of all people, should have known that being mentally ill was not the same as being intentionally difficult. After nine shock treatments in the course of a month, physician Sam Darden wrote of her on December 2, 1949: "Her general behavior is better. However, she is extremely delusional, paranoid, unreasonable, and impractical. She has no insight."

Other women may have been less traumatized by the treatments. At Bryce, patients and medical students sometimes played bridge together; a medical student might help with shock treatments in the morning and play bridge with the women in the afternoon, where they would tease him that he, not having been shocked, had an unfair advantage on them. Most of the female residents at Bryce were in the east wards, numbered 1 through 9, the original Kirkbride-design wards. Several—4, 5, and 6—had porches. The 1920s-era Ladies Receiving Building (sometimes referred to as the Women's Receiving Building) also held some patients, but its primary function was admissions. After Sara's course of electroshock therapy, Dr. Darden reassigned her from one ward to another "because she has developed so much antagonism toward some of the patients in the new building because she feels they are carrying on some private investigation of her case." However, he continued, "In spite of her paranoid thinking, she is usually cheerful, has a feeling of humor about the situation and should adjust satisfactorily on a better ward." In the next four years she was moved four times, ending up in Ward D, in the separate Ladies Receiving Building. She complained to her mother, who wrote her the day after Sara turned forty-five: "Sara Darling: I went to see Dr. Tarwater. He said that you were back on 25 & that putting you in the old ladies ward was a mistake—that it was done by Dr. B[illegible]. Billy Partlow went with me & was wonderful help. *Please* don't talk about anybody." The superintendent's wife had held a birthday party for Sara and, Sara's mother wrote, had reported that Sara was "a charming hostess, so poised & cordial."

Sara wrote to her mother at least once a week—typed, dense missives, the language often taut with anger and frustration at the conspiracy and at the situation in which she finds herself, trying "to live, much less write a letter, with three patients in the little room you saw, the systematic interruptions and the systematic inquisition in full swing." She could alternate easily between comments on how she was being observed and a discussion of social visits, clothes, and the health of mutual friends. To her they were equal parts of her reality. In every letter, she urged her mother to get her out, making a feminist as well as a legal argument: "No woman's work or time is of any importance to men outside that in connection with *kinder, kirche, kuche*, but I wish you would please be so kind as to take me out of here and not let whoever is responsible for keeping me here waste any more of mine in what is just as illegal, unethical, stupid and cruel as a medieval trial by ordeal." For Sara's mother, every letter reinforced the knowledge that her child's mind had become skewed, that from being a bright, strong-willed, adventuresome little girl she had developed into an adult who believed that those who loved her most were subjecting her to misery, and whose intelligence and will were now directed toward resisting advice and treatment. Perhaps she should have taken Sara out once she was stable again, found a way to help her manage and have a productive life. But perhaps it was just too hard, too much, and she made a deal with herself to do all she could for her daughter without subjecting herself to more than she could handle. She was seventy-two when she had Sara committed, an old lady by the standards and life expectancy of the day, and she may not have expected to live much longer.[2]

She would have had some encouragement in believing Sara was better off at Bryce from Sara herself, who suggested in the first month of the new decade, what poet Robert Lowell referred to as "the tranquillized fifties," that she was accommodating herself to life in Bryce. She wrote to her mother, "In view of all that has happened since I've been here . . . I shall proceed to make my self as happy and comfortable here as possible, do just what I want to do, and have wanted to do for some time, work on my sculpting, and get Mrs. Hubbard to give me a quiet place to write so I can turn the *Mona Lisa* into a novel. However, don't let them [the Masons] forget that to the rest of the damages, corporate, patent, personal, professional, etc., I am adding for every hour I stay here, just exactly what the *Observer* and the *Southern Cellulose* paid me, i.e. five dollars per hour." As though she were away at college writing to her mother to "Send food!" she went on, "Since I decided to settle down as comfortably as possible and do the things I want to do on the Mason's [*sic*] time, I asked Betty [Simms] to let me use part of her food locker, so I'm enclosing a list of the things we like and can prepare. Please send as much as you can, for we have a great many friends. Coffee and mayonnaise are the prime essentials." She considered other ways to adapt to institutional life, including producing scenes from her "negro play," "Mojo," and wrote to Bryce recreation director Virginia Dobbins, "I think that Act I, Scene 3, laid in the washyard, would probably be easiest to adapt and stage." She attached a full copy of the play for Miss Dobbins to read.

Six months later, she embarked on a somewhat different tack, writing to her mother that she was "sorry not to have seen you when we came out to West End to play baseball. I asked to go in that all that could be done to embarrass my family or me was done when I was ridden through the streets with a uniformed nurse on each side of me when I was here before. Now, the more I'm seen in public, calm and coherent, the sooner public indignation will force the hospital to allow me to be brought to court." It is touching to imagine Sara thinking that there will be "public indignation" that will force the authorities to release her.

With chores, meals, recreation, chapel, meetings, and occasional free time, the days, months, and even years passed in the routine of institutional life. On March 23, 1952, Sara noted an unwelcome anniversary in her journal: "Four years ago, I arrived here at the psychiatric building, thinking that within a few days the commitments would be reversed and I would be clear, free to marry and go on with my work!" (It's unclear whom she was thinking of marrying.) Her mind rarely rested while she tried to make sense of her situation, often in writing but also through art. She made watercolor drawings of an inside hallway and of the center circular drive at Bryce to accompany a

FIGURE 14. Sketch by Sara Mayfield titled "Inside Insanity"

This political cartoon–style sketch was one of many Sara did depicting injustices in the mental health system. This one, from November 1952, portrays mental patients as victims of various entities, all part of an "Unholy Alliance." (University of Alabama Libraries Special Collections)

description of life at Bryce, of how easy it is to have someone committed and how ignorant and fearful the general public is about mental illness. When she overheard a doctor talking with patients in the yard outside their ward, she noted how he "answers as best he can the eternal question 'when can I go home'" and observed that "matters in a psychiatric hospital are arranged for the convenience and comfort of everybody but the patients."

For the most part, she focused her anger on J. S. Tarwater, superintendent of the hospital beginning in 1950, although she at times believed Dr. Darden was also involved in the conspiracy. Her patient records from her time at Bryce, many of them dictated by Dr. Darden, indicate that she was almost always well-behaved, polite, civil—but that she had the persistent delusion that she was being persecuted and that the patients around her were "stooges" sent to spy on her. Sara, like the eggs she dyed for Easter, "some . . . half-silver, half-colored, others half-gold and half-colored," was of mixed parts, half-ill, half-sane, half-in, half-out, half-deluded, half-aware. Always colorful. Apart from her beliefs about stooges and conspiracies, she behaved in a way that most would consider normal. She had a weekly order from Sam Jackson's grocery store on nearby University Boulevard delivered to her at the mental hospital, as well as occasional items from other stores—Jean Naté bath lotion, books on yoga, sheet music, guitar strings. (She kept careful track of the orders; on one occasion writing, "As far as I can see both Sam Jackson's order and H&W's are correct—a rare occurrence.") From H&W drugstore, a typical order included stamps ("12 4c stamps"), stationery ("a box of air mail stationery, not too thin"), Luden's cough drops, eye makeup, and platinum rinse for her gray hair. From Sam Jackson's, a large can of V-8 juice, a six-ounce jar of Sanka, Carnation Instant Chocolate Milk, "lunch tongue" meat, anchovies, pressed ham or chicken (depending on what was available), and Durkee's dressing. Sara gave birthday parties for and small gifts to the other female patients. She joined the Sesame Study and Bridge Club at Bryce, complete with membership card, just as though she were a lady about town in one of the study clubs. At the same time she was writing forcefully worded letters seeking to obtain her release, she was also keeping up what might be thought of as proper southern–lady correspondence, including birthday cards, seasonal gifts such as Easter candy, get-well notes often signed "with a heart full of love," and thank-you notes to friends and family who had taken her to lunch or the movies or shopping or brought her magazines. In addition to being mannerly, with each letter she sought to strengthen the invisible filaments between herself and others, ties that had existed before she was sent to Bryce and that she needed as reminders that she did exist outside of this absurd situation. Being in Bryce was ridiculous, and at times it may have felt like something to be ashamed of, but to be forgotten would be worse.

Susie Mayfield's club and social life continued in a parallel universe to Sara's. Her home, Idlewyld, was featured in the 1950 Tuscaloosa pilgrimage of homes. A Chamber of Commerce brochure relates the early history of the house, from its beginning in 1820, just one year after statehood, and goes on: "It is completely appropriate to identify this house with its present owner, Mrs. James Mayfield, for she is in every way the gracious embodiment of the character of the lovely house."[3] Sara's brother, James, remarried in June 1951; Sara was hurt not to be invited to the wedding. She cut out and pasted into her journal a newspaper clipping about the wedding of Janette Smith Gibson and James J. Mayfield Jr. and a few days later cut out another one from the Sunday newspaper: "Chic Chignon—Mrs. James Mayfield's choice is the low coiled chignon." The wedding also reignited earlier concerns. At several points in her journal for June she notes "psychological assaults" designed to get her to testify that James had not been a fit guardian for Mason, the son from his previous marriage who had died two years ago. What she perceived as assaults continued in July, when she wrote of entering her room and finding a copy of the *Saturday Evening Post* on her bed, open to an article titled "Trial by Terror," concerning an American reporter subjected to physical and psychological torture in cold-war Hungary. Meanwhile, Sara's brother continued to share responsibility for her with their mother. One summer, while her mother was visiting family in Virginia, Sara wrote to James about her grocery order, and he responded that he had immediately called the grocer, Sam Jackson, to expedite it. He continued, "It will be a great pleasure for me to come to see you just any time if you will let me know when you want me to come." In another letter, he wrote Dr. Darden about money he had deposited in her hospital account, continuing, "Of course, I do not want Sara to want for anything and would deeply appreciate your personal kindness in advising me from time to time as to her needs."

When she was in a particularly bad stretch, everything that happened in the hospital was connected to the conspiracy—someone showed her a cartoon about a monkey and then someone else offered her a banana, and she was sure the two things were related. An infestation of bugs was designed to echo one of the charges against her when she was sent to Sheppard Pratt. One of the most extended, complicated plots Sara perceived involved small cakes given to her as gifts. Throughout her journal of this period, crinkly or flat paper wrappings with ragged edges are stapled or taped to the day's entry like warning flags. She had been concerned for some time about food-related conspiracies. After reading *The Lute Player: A Novel of Richard the Lionhearted*, by Norah Lofts, she became very conscious of cakes. One of the characters tells the others that he has mysteriously "received a . . . quite sizeable cake." A discussion of the Old Man of the Mountain, a Persian leader also known as the Prince of the Assassins, takes place, and we learn that "the cake by your bed means The Old Man of the Mountain is after you! I believe it is a fact . . . that men have died of fright upon receiving one of his cakes."[4]

Sara interpreted this passage as a message to her, which was then reinforced by her persecutors sending numerous little cakes. "Their" game was to frighten her into reacting to the possibility of being killed, and her game was to eat the cake as though she hadn't a care in the world. She complained to her journal one day, attaching a "Mocha Malt" label to the page, that this was "the eleventh" cake episode in three weeks. The little cakes persecution could also expand to include fruit and cookies. In one incident, a patient named Jean brought some fruit to Sara, "But she was so disappointed when I went up and took a handful of grapes that she waited until I went in the little sitting room, then she took out a box of chocolate covered graham crackers, added it to the fruit and brought in and passed it to me. I ate the chocolate cover[ed] graham cracker as if I were wholly unaware of the uses to which chocolate and crackers have been put during the inquisition and made no comment and no complaint." So concerned was Sara that agent provocateurs were trying to discredit her (the reasons varied over time but all involved making her into an unreliable witness in some situation in which she might be called to testify) that she stopped writing about the inquisition for a time. On January 28, 1953, for instance, she wrote, "Omitted keeping a day by day account for two months to try by indirections to find directions out. Apparently, the inquisition proceeds whether I record it or whether I don't." That summer, she was moved to the disturbed ward again, because, wrote her doctor, Sam Darden, on August 12, 1953, "this patient has been quite a problem for the last two or three weeks. She is an extremely delusional and paranoid individual without any insight. She is constantly referring to 'Stooges' and to a psychiatric observation which she feels is going on and revolving about her. She feels that the other patients here in many incidences are not actually patients at all, but merely people sent here to observe and watch her. She has made it quite unpleasant for the other patients on the ward and patients on other wards in the hospital. It finally got to the point where we had to move her for the benefit of the other patients involved."

In what must have been puzzling for those who loved or worked with her, Sara could be quite logical about other things, reporting calmly on conditions in the cafeteria, for instance. She complains in her journal of patients having to wait so that "all the silver—Bryce flat, rather—is taken up and counted," and that the food is less plentiful than before: "In short we have been sitting longer and longer for less and less." On Saturday night, they have an unappetizing meal of "weiners, kraut, prunes, bread and milk." She notes that "conscies"—conscientious objectors to the war in Korea—have been put to work at Bryce, to the consternation of union employees, and wonders whether their consciences would allow them to intervene if "one patient was about to conk another over the head with a Coca-Cola bottle." When nurses used to dine with the patients, "There was peace and quiet and dignity in the dining room. While now, anything can happen at meals and frequently does. More often than not, the radio attachment on the television is blaring at one end of the room and at the other, patients are banging out discords [sic] on the piano, smashing dishes or having, or pretending to have convulsions while the rest shout, cry, bang the silver and disregard the nurses [who] try vainly to enforce 'Quiet, ladies!'"

She also observed general conditions in the hospital, providing an articulate insider's view: "The stairs have not been scrubbed nor the table cloths changed since I noted it last. And if the untidy patients on #23 and 24 are being stooled every two hours, it is hard to know why the stench is so bad we frequently have to put our windows down and hold our noses to keep from gagging on our way to the yard. The snuff-dipping and gum chewing in the auditorium which was supposed to be stopped, go straight on. There is no pretense of stopping it in the dining room, nor of stopping the snuff dippers from spitting in the sinks and drains. Nor is there any pretense of any other kind of sanitation in the dining room. The bread, which is always stale, although the bakery adjoins the dining hall is brought in in dish pans and dealt out by the arm-full by patients whose hands and clothes never look too clean and who sleep on the floor between meals and relieve themselves in the corners or just outside the door."

As part of her self-appointed mission to study and report on hospital conditions, she took extensive notes on not only the dining room and food but also the state of the various wards and the nurses' hours and wages. She also did research into the average amounts spent per patient and the number

Figure 15. Women's dining room at Bryce Hospital

The women's dining room, Bryce Hospital, in the 1940s. Sara took notes on hospital conditions and wrote of the disorder, noise, and lack of sanitation she observed there. For her part, Sara wrote of bringing something extra from her own food supplies to share with her table and of practicing foreign languages with any patient who spoke one. (Alabama Department of Archives and History)

of people with nervous disorders who were or would be hospitalized in the United States. Along with the larger concerns of staffing, funding, and general lack of cleanliness are the small but significant daily indignities: not enough toilets or washbasins on the ward (three toilets and two washbasins for the eighty women on Ward 25, for instance); having to wait outside, even in the rain or cold, to enter the cafeteria; the difficulty of doing laundry and keeping one's clothes cleaned and ironed; the presence of spit from snuff on floors and walls and in sinks; and the smells, always the smells. She tried to find the humor in the madness: writing one day in her journal of poor living conditions in the Old Building at Bryce, she refers to her ward with a pun, as the "walled-off Astoria."

Sara had to endure the same general conditions of the hospital as others did, but because of her family connections and some family money, she at least had a better chance of supplementing her food supplies, getting new clothes, and acquiring personal items, than did most patients at the time. In Alabama, mentally ill people who needed treatment faced overcrowding, underfunding, and difficulty being seen as full citizens deserving of full rights. One university professor speaking to the Tuscaloosa Rotary Club in 1952 told the assembled Rotarians that, in Bryce, which had bed space for 2,048 patients, there were currently 4,688. Nationally, hospitals spent $2.04 per patient, but at Bryce only $1.58 was allocated.[5] As early as 1920, the hospital had changed from progressive institution to warehouse. One scholar wrote that the hospital had undergone "a transition from the self-conscious gentleness of Kirkbride's therapeutic era to a less optimistic acceptance of crowding and the primary demands of custodial care. Moral treatment in those years totally disappeared from the institutional vocabulary."[6] Sara argued that Bryce could be run more efficiently, with more money per patient, and no need to build new wards, if, as she wrote in her journal, "there were laws passed to prevent unlawful and unjust commitment and put a stop to having the hospital used for an old age home, a flop house for indigent sluggards, a reformatory for erring husbands and wives, a soft spot for beating legal raps and a dixiecrat concentration camp."

Still a reporter, Sara used her journal observations as background notes for newspaper articles. As cofounder, with recreation director Virginia Dobbins, of the *Bryce News*, beginning in 1951, Sara spoke the patients' truth to the hospital's power. Subtitled "Of the Patients, By the Patients, For the Patients," the newsletter included contributions from patients, with jokes, stories, and cartoons, as well as editorials and news items. One scholar who studied the paper observed that the *Bryce News* "contained surprisingly direct criticism of the institution, or at least those funding it," concluding that "the great legacy of *The Bryce News* is the light it sheds on life as a patient."[7] Articles often commented on staff-patient ratios, health and safety issues in the hospital, and on other concerns such as the question of habeas corpus. While such criticism may seem to be unwelcome, it might actually have served the interests of the hospital to have appeals for more funding, which they would have wished for as much as patients did. In this work, Sara anticipated the patient (consumer) rights movements of the 1960s and 1970s and, to some degree, the antipsychiatry movement of the 1960s, which held that mainstream psychiatry often does more harm than good and that the power structure of doctor/patient is coercive and oppressive. Critiquing the poor conditions at the hospital, she also anticipated a landmark lawsuit, *Wyatt v. Stickney* (1970), which began at Bryce and resulted in the development of nationwide standards for "what would constitute minimally adequate mental treatment at a state psychiatric institution."[8]

As poorly funded as Bryce was in Sara's time, things got worse there in 1970 when a cigarette tax earmarked for Bryce funding was cut, and nearly one hundred employees, including twenty professional staff, were fired. The firings initiated the case of *Wyatt v. Stickney* with employees adding a young patient, Ricky Wyatt, as a plaintiff to assert that patient care would suffer as a result of the layoffs. Federal District Court Judge Frank M. Johnson Jr. determined that a federal suit could not be brought based only on the layoffs but agreed to hear the case on the grounds of patient rights, and the case became forever associated with Ricky Wyatt.[9]

Though federal civil rights legislation would include more rights for mental patients as well as bar discrimination on the basis of race, the mental hospital system in Alabama was at a low point in the late 1960s. In a 2008 interview, Ricky Wyatt described Bryce in 1968, when he was committed as a fourteen-year-old boy whose family did not know how to handle his getting in trouble at school: "The back ward employees were often very cruel and callous. . . . The nurses and aides and sometimes even the supervisors would make people fight so they could bet on the winners. Or they might just lock us all up so they could have a good card game without being disturbed. To get us up in the morning they might come in there and poke us with a broom, or throw hot water on us. Of course to me the worst thing was that I knew there was nothing wrong with me. They couldn't tell; they just assumed I was sick. But I knew."[10] At that time, "Alabama was 50th out of 50 states for expenditures for the care of people with mental illness or mental retardation in public institutions . . . [and] allotted 50 cents per day per patient in funding the physical plant, clothing and food budgets for those facilities."[11]

An attorney in the *Wyatt* case confirmed Sara's earlier assessment, recalling that "anybody who was unwanted was put in Bryce. . . . Bryce had become a mere dumping ground for socially undesirables, for severely mentally ill, profoundly mentally ill people, and for geriatrics."[12] Judge Johnson ruled on March 12, 1971, that "there can be no legal (or moral) justification for the State of Alabama's failing to afford treatment—and adequate treatment from a mental standpoint—to the several thousand patients who have been civilly committed to Bryce for treatment purposes. To deprive any citizen of his or her liberty upon the altruistic theory that the confinement is for humane therapeutic reasons and then fail to provide adequate treatment violates the very fundamentals of due process."[13] Despite the efforts of some doctors and other professional staff to provide good treatment for patients, investigations into conditions at Bryce (and at Partlow State School for Deficients) uncovered multiple cases of abuse, neglect, and cruelty, as well as horrible filth. A major overhaul of the system was called for.

In early 1972 Judge Johnson ordered all the parties in the case to meet and develop standards for that "minimally adequate mental treatment." Treatment would be measured not in outcomes but by the numbers: not only psychiatrist/patient ratios but the number of other staff and even how often linen would be changed and at what temperature dishes would be washed. Judge Johnson's decision, when appealed, was upheld in circuit court, and when the state still failed to meet his requirements, in 1977 a federal court officer was assigned to assess state compliance, oversight that was not lifted until 2003. Judge Johnson also presided in the 1971 case *Lynch v. Baxley*, which, in upholding the provisions of due process in involuntary commitment, "set standards that would profoundly and almost immediately affect the lives of hundreds of thousands of politically powerless Americans." Another landmark case, *O'Connor v. Donaldson*, in 1975, resulted in the US Supreme Court establishing what is generally known as the "danger to self or others" standard, after Kenneth Donaldson sued for release from a state hospital where he had been held for fifteen years, based on a diagnosis of paranoid schizophrenia.[14]

Sara, a patient in a mental hospital in the 1950s, was two decades ahead of her time in calling for massive reform of the system in Alabama. Though born of frustration, her efforts in researching injustice and then hammering out articles and editorials on her old typewriter connected Sara to the life she had before institutionalization. One editorial from 1952, titled "United We Stand: Patients' Recommendation," emphasized the need for the patients, staff, doctors, and the public to work together to improve the hospital and encouraged investigations to increase funding and raise standards of care. "Bryce Hospital and the other hospitals that make up the Ala. State Hospitals . . . need more help than censure. Of course, there are many, many things that need correcting. They will never be attended to unless brought out into the open." Although the staff and doctors are dedicated, she wrote, they are stretched thin, and it is up to the patients to assist in their own recovery: these "'residents' who did not ask for admittance in the most part, yet who must call the institution home, also have a great responsibility in making the hospital a better place to live. . . . Part of the 'cure' is learning to associate with other people, to adjust, to assist, to share."

To that end, Sara made plans for a "Patients' Committee on Psychosomatic Hygiene," which would function alongside a "Citizens' Committee on Psychosomatic Hygiene," and she drew up a series of stated objectives for both. Objectives of the patients' committee included the study of hospital conditions and patient needs, legislative funding, and promotion of better conditions in hospitals, support for "psychosomatic hygiene"—a term suggesting patients' responsibility for maintaining mental health—and finally, "to endeavor to remove as much of the stigma from mental illness as possible and to urge the hospital planner to cooperate by removing the distinction between general hospitals and mental hospitals in as far as is practical." Her objectives for the citizens' committee parallel those of the patients' committee, but her closing objective reveals that her earlier concerns about national and international psychological warfare, as well as psychological attacks on her personally, were still present: "To propose to the American Red Cross that it establish units and train personnel to administer first aid and prophylaxis in an effort to combat the psychosomatic effects of psychological campaigns and cold wars."

Sara's campaign for mental health hygiene on behalf of all patients allowed her to practice daily routines, positive thinking, and concern for others that helped her cope with hospital life. From an old *Reader's Digest* she cut out an article titled "How to Gain Emotional Poise": "1. Get the right mental picture of your life. 2. Scale down demands you are making on other people. 3. At any cost in effort, keep your world from growing small." Sara even came up with a contest that she advertised in the *Bryce News*, with a prize of two and a half dollars (the *News* cost two cents). Patients were to submit a three-hundred-word essay on "ways and means of securing the release and providing for the rehabilitation of patients without the needed family help, the financial means or the training and skill necessary to get a job and reestablish themselves on the outside."

As the scholar who studied the *Bryce News* points out, she also alerted patients to the possibility that their mail was being read: "Persistent rumors are circulated among the patients in regard to the way in which the hospital handles their incoming and outgoing mail. Last week one of our inquiring reporters asked about these things at the Post Office. According to the postal regulations it is permissible for the hospital authorities to open both incoming and outgoing mail, even sealed and stamped letters sent by the patients to their relatives." The idea of losing the freedom to communicate as well as all the other freedoms was especially painful to Sara. She composed messages to the outside world as though they could be folded up and squeezed into pill bottles, tossed out the window, and set adrift on a current that flowed to powerful men who could, if they only would, free her.

The legal principle of habeas corpus, in Latin "you have the body," makes it possible for an imprisoned person to petition to be brought before a judge so that a determination can be made as to whether they are being held lawfully; it can also be used for someone who has been involuntarily committed to a mental institution. On March 13, 1952, Sara wrote in her journal, "There has been great excitement at the Old Building over Joyce Goode's application for a writ of habeas corpus. Walter Gus Woods has offered to get her out and to help those patients who will testify for her." So many strands of Sara's story seem to lead to yet another convoluted tale of illness combined with injustice, and Joyce Goode's is one of those. The beautiful young woman who was "senior queen" of Murphy High School in Mobile, Alabama, in 1937 and worked as a fashion model in New York was committed to Bryce on April 13, 1948 (less than a month after Sara was committed) after she "flew home from New York to her Mobile home and chased her parents from the house with a knife," the *Atlanta Constitution* reported.[15] A year later she escaped from her third-floor room in Bryce by shinnying down a rope left by a repairman. She was recaptured near Mobile after stories about the "beautiful but dangerous" escapee ran in state papers. In April 1952, during the hearing for her release that had Sara and other patients so excited, the *Chicago Defender* and *Jet* magazine (both publications with a primarily Black audience) published items not carried in other sources. As *Jet* put it under the heading "Legal Explanation of the Week," "A person is insane if he (or she) believes in racial equality, attorneys for the Bryce Hospital in Tuscaloosa, Ala., insinuated. Seeking to foil ex-cover girl Joyce Goode's attempt to gain release from the hospital, where she has been confined since 1948 for insanity, they partially blamed her alleged insanity on a belief in racial equality. One of the attorneys, C. M. A. Rogers, said in a hearing on the case that Miss Goode admitted to him that she would not mind if her daughter married a Negro." The *Chicago Defender*'s story ran on its front page: "Called Crazy for Racial Beliefs."[16] Somewhat surprisingly, after that testimony, an all-white, all-male jury judged Goode to be competent, and she was released. A letter she had written at the time of her commitment and made public when she was released read in part: "I can only see this horrible asylum life of torture and torment, beginning in hell, being in hell, and ending nowhere except in a blackout. There's no way to escape. Insanity d e s c e n d s uninvited upon people. They deserve humane treatment while ill and freedom while well."[17]

Goode's return to freedom would, however, end tragically. The next year, 1953, Joyce married a Black postal worker in Chicago.[18] She had a son with him, but the couple became estranged, and she began taking drugs. As "a registered dope addict," she had a pending court appearance to determine whether she would be allowed to keep custody of her son, and, just three years after the court battle in February 1952 that secured her release from Bryce, she leapt to her death from a seventh-story hotel room in Chicago. *Jet* magazine ran the headline "White Model Wife of Chicago Negro Leaps to Death," noting that "not even her husband, Charles, appeared at the inquest." The *Chicago Daily Tribune* announced, "Model Leaves Baby in Room, Leaps to Death," and wrote that she had pinned a note to her coat sleeve, 'Please take care of my baby in room 708.'"[19]

After Joyce had won her release, obtaining a writ of habeas corpus and winning her own freedom became Sara's main focus but also a source of suspicion. Whenever Sara had hopes of getting a writ of habeas corpus or heard that the grand jury was in session, she sensed an intensifying of activities against her. A typical entry describes attempts to confuse, trick, and disappoint her with a "shell game" in which her family makes plans with her and then changes them, "attempting to make me suspicious of them or issue invitations to me to serialize delusions that might mitigate what the defendants have done."

On May 23, 1952, Sara wrote in her journal about her plans for getting released. She had been talking with a patient named Kay about Kay's and her possible release, using either Sara's lawyer, Gus Woods, or another attorney as their advocate. She made plans to have some stock converted to pay the lawyer to work on Kay's release first, then hers, and "suggested that someone get the union or Gus Woods to put an add [*sic*] in the paper advocating Civil Rights for patients." It must have seemed as though her freedom was within reach. Four long years had passed, but now she had a legal advocate and a strategy for release. Intrigue and resistance were everywhere, however. In September 1952, having just turned forty-seven, she described various other patients who had promised "they were going to get a lawyer to get me out" but failed "to keep their word." When she saw her doctor and asked him about being brought before a grand jury, his response, as she recorded it, was "Oh, we don't want anything to do with the old grand jury." She recalled that she had been told that "Dr. Darden said 'We can't let Sara Mayfield be brought before the Grand Jury. She knows too much about us.'"

Part of being released, she understood, was "behaving"—conforming to expectations that were as much a part of the larger culture as of the hospital culture, and not giving those who conspired against her any extra ammunition. She tried to participate in all activities, to "be a lady," and "return good for ill," as she wrote in her journal. Her plan was not simply to conform, though; she believed herself to be waging a guerilla war of good behavior. On September 18, 1952, she spent the day scraping floors by hand, although she knew it made more sense for a paid employee to be doing the work with an electric scraper. That night, she wrote in her journal: "I realize that part of the attempt to break me has been an unconcealed attempt to drive a square peg in a round hole, to take a highly trained, highly specialized person, who could have worked in a lab or an office, and make them do the kind of drudgery that I have been forced to do in the kitchen, in the pottery shop, on the scrubbing squad." She had decided, however, "to take the hard labor as a joke, do it cheerfully, and laugh it off." To live in a world in which signs fall around you like hailstones, to be battered and bruised but not defeated—such was the script by which Sara lived in Bryce Hospital in the 1950s.

Chapter 11

"A Very St. George for Courage"

More Losses. The Sustaining Power of Writing, Art, Music, and Yoga. The Odd Permeability of the Border between Town and (Hospital) Gown.

A S A MATTER OF DISCIPLINE, AND FOR THE RECORD SHE WAS KEEP-ing of her incarceration, Sara continued to keep up her journal writing, but, like her life at the hospital, the entries tended to be repetitive, almost as though she were bored with writing them. She wrote of the details of her day and the various irritations she experienced, and she continued to report on the "stooges" pretending to be patients who hounded her. She could, at times, be lyrical, as when she wrote, one early April day, "The full tide of spring has rolled over the land. There are a hundred shades of green in the trees about the lawn and a half dozen of pink in the peach trees that blanket the hill below the old water tower. At no other time is it so cruel to be caged." But such entries are rare.

The hospital routine was occasionally broken up by chaperoned visits out, for lunch or to run errands with her mother or another relative. The Bryce campus was built on a hill above the river, right next to the University of Alabama campus. Heading west on University Boulevard from Bryce, you pass the university, and, if you keep going through one of the older neighborhoods and past the University Club, end up downtown. On the other side of downtown is Capitol Park, where the state capitol building once stood, and beyond that Sara's home, Idlewyld, and the country club.

The closeness to both town and gown made it easy, for patients who were deemed able, to leave the hospital on short visits out, often just for lunch or a holiday celebration but sometimes for an overnight or weekend trip. Visits "outside" were meant to help patients heal by giving them small doses of life beyond the hospital, with the hope they could eventually live on their own—and yet, for Sara, the terrible feeling of being a walking ghost in one's own life could be more painful than simply being stuck "inside." On one visit home, she discovered that her sister-in-law-to-be had taken over her sitting room as though Sara were never coming back: "[Janette] took me around [after lunch] to show me what she had done to the upstairs . . . she and Jim had taken my room 'for theirs' and were using my porch for a dining room and the back room for a kitchen." However hurt she was, though, Sara said nothing, believing that it would only reflect badly on her case to show her disappointment and anger.

Everyone she might run into in town knew, of course, that she was a mental patient, so when she was checked out for the day, picked up by a relative and driven away from the hospital, through campus, and on to downtown—to lunch at the McLester Hotel, to shop at Lustig's Bookstore for books or small gifts and chat with the maiden-lady Lustig sisters, Esther and Maxine, or to pick up some small item like sunglasses for another patient at Woolworth's, on University Boulevard—she would have been aware of people's eyes upon her, and she was ever-conscious of the need to behave sanely. Her journal entries highlight the absurd experience of being committed *by* your mother but being sane enough to go to lunch *with* her, of being an ill person with whom nothing is visibly wrong. No matter what she did, it was as though she could always, like a marionette, feel the slight tug in her shoulders, on the tops of her hands and feet, in the middle of her back, in all the places where the invisible strings were attached. The doctors always had the legal right to recall her, to tug on those strings to make her feet move back toward the hospital, or to take her by force if necessary, bundling her up and returning her folded body to the ward. Sara exercised all her willpower to hold her head up and pretend she didn't care. After a visit from her longtime friend Liz Thigpen Hill, who often sent letters and small gifts from Montgomery, Liz wrote Sara, "I can't tell you how I loved being with you yesterday. It was like turning back a page in my life's book to that sweet & happy past when we were young & gay before so many shadows fell across our paths. . . . Anyway I loved seeing you and although I'm not given to openings of the secret places of the heart and handing out compliments I'll have to say you've got the guts & when you alighted from the car to go back in you did it as if you were going into the Ritz—a very St. George for courage."

Beyond Sara's institutionalization, which she saw as unjust and unwarranted, further isolating her in this period was the loss of her main lifelines to the outside world, first her mother, who died on July 29, 1954, and then her brother, at age forty-five, in 1956. She also lost her great friend Henry Mencken who died on January 29, 1956. In a way, she had already lost him, as he had been unable to keep up a correspondence with her in Bryce after suffering a stroke in November 1948, the first year of her commitment, ending their jolly comradeship of letters. Strangely, there is no note in Sara's patient files about her reaction to the death of her mother, or even that her mother has died. Her brother handled their mother's estate and had guardianship of Sara transferred to him, becoming fully responsible for handling Sara's finances, expenses being primarily to Lustig's Bookstore, Sam Jackson's grocery, H&W Drugs, Pizitz Department Store, and her personal account at Bryce, for a standard allowance of twenty-five dollars held by the steward of Bryce. As he took on her accounts, he learned of payments to a life insurance policy and for taxes on land she still owned in Tuscaloosa, Chilton, and Elmore Counties. Income included dividends from stock in the Curtiss-Wright Corporation, the United Corporation, General Baking Company, and US Steel, deposits totaling about twelve hundred dollars for 1955, against disbursements of a little over nine hundred.

When Susie Mayfield died, James had just been elected to the state Supreme Court; widowed now for twenty-seven years, Susie must have been proud to see him follow in his father's footsteps. An article in the *Atlanta Constitution* from June 6, 1954, titled "Folsom's Success Story Grows as Three Candidates Sweep In," led with the statement, "the James E. Folsom success story in Alabama politics grew bigger this week as Folsom-backed candidates swept to lopsided victories in three of four statewide races" and ended, "the incoming governor, who served his first term from 1947 to 1951 and whose proposals for legislative reapportionment, sharp tax increases, and $50 monthly old-age pensions were blocked by the legislature, added: 'These elections just concluded verify one thing and one thing alone: The people themselves are going to have the program which I have preached down through the years.'"[1] But Folsom lost popularity in the summer of 1955 when he resisted a bill, ultimately passed by the legislature, meant to be an end run around *Brown v. Board of Education*. Mary Stanton writes in her biography of white civil rights activist Juliette Hampton Morgan, a Montgomery librarian, "By the end of September, Governor Folsom no longer had the support of rural whites, who had once comprised his largest constituency. They could not afford to privately educate their children, and they interpreted his unwillingness to fight against integrating the public schools as a betrayal of their trust." It was a time of such resistance to integration, writes Stanton, that "even Montgomery's most reputable citizens were not exempt from being called subversives."[2] Juliette Morgan herself, as a result of the terrible ostracism she endured from many in the white community in response to her courageous actions against segregation, would kill herself at the age of forty-three in the summer of 1957. Even whites much closer to the middle on race could be affected by the pressure to declare allegiance to a segregated South.

About a year and a half after their mother died, Sara's brother died in his apartment in Montgomery. James, now divorced for the second time, having buried two children, lived alone and was found by his maid when she came to work. The radio was playing, the phone was off the hook, and he was lying in his bed, propped on two pillows, a bullet hole through the right side of his head. The biggest headline in the *Anniston (AL) Star* that day was "Tornado Series Rips Path through 11 States; 41 Die." Below that was the simple notice of a more personal disaster, "J. Mayfield Fatally Shot." The subhead: "Justice's Death Called 'Obviously Suicide.'"[3]

The next day, Sara's cousins came to deliver the sad news. Her doctor wrote in his progress notes, "The patient did not seem particularly perturbed by this news, though she did cry quietly for a time." Friends got in touch immediately. Liz Hill sent a telegram: "THINKING OF YOU WITH DEEPEST LOVE AND TENDEREST SYMPATHY." Another friend, Ruby Folsom, Gov. Jim Folsom's sister, said, "AM THINKING OF YOU IN YOUR TRAGIC SORROW. MAY GODS RICHEST BLESSINGS BE YOURS. WITH ALL MY LOVE, RUBY." The Alabama State Senate rapidly passed a resolution honoring James, and state senator E. W. Skidmore sent it to Dr. Tarwater with the request that he have a member of staff present it to Sara. He wrote, "I will appreciate it, if, when the resolution is presented to her, my personal condolences and sympathy be extended to her."

Although Sara at first was disbelieving that her brother had died, seeing it as part of a campaign to distress her, she soon absorbed the news into her own interpretation of events and told her doctor that she didn't believe her brother had committed suicide, despite the existence of a suicide note. She believed that Jim, with his knowledge of guns, would not have shot himself with a .22 caliber pistol, the small caliber being more likely to cripple than kill him. Finally, she decided that if he did kill himself, it was because of unnamed forces that drove him "to desperate measures, whatever those measures were." Perhaps her mother, too, had been killed by "a stroke of apo-plexy" due to techniques of intimidation used on both her and Sara.

Sara's delusions about her brother's death were almost certainly just that, but she was correct in perceiving that his suicide was due to more than per-sonal concerns. The African American woman who worked as a maid for James Mayfield, Lorine Lewis, was quoted in numerous accounts saying that "the justice had told her Monday he was having 'a devil of a time' over segre-gation and that someone was trying to get his job away from him."[4] Another article stated, "Friends said he had worried in recent days about his campaign for re-election in the May 1 Democratic primary and about his health."[5] His suicide note, delivered by a friend to the *Tuscaloosa News*, helped illuminate his state of mind and the crushing conflicts and pressures he felt as he pre-pared for the May 1 elections. In the letter, written on Alabama Supreme Court stationery, he wrote: "My health is such that I should not have under-taken a campaign (for re-election). I regret that I cannot continue. I send my love to all my family." He continued, "Every decision I have ever made has been honest and non-partisan. While some may criticize my economic be-liefs, none can say I have not honestly tried to do my duty. I have been true to the Heritage of my grandfather, a Confederate cavalryman, and to my father, a justice of this court."[6] Although he invokes a Confederate heritage, James was under pressure in the campaign to be much more outspoken about main-taining racial segregation in contemporary Alabama.

The climate in which Judge Mayfield died was charged with racial ten-sion, especially in Montgomery, where the bus boycott was underway, hav-ing started the previous December after the arrest of Rosa Parks; it would continue through December 20, 1956. (Juvenile Court Judge Wiley C. Hill Jr., Elisabeth Thigpen Hill's husband, had heard the Claudette Colvin case in March 1955, in which a fifteen-year-old girl was arrested and convicted for refusing to yield her seat to a white person on a bus in Montgomery, nine months before Rosa Parks's refusal.[7]) Perhaps Lorine Lewis herself had walked or gotten a ride to work through the Montgomery Improvement As-sociation car pool instead of riding the bus, the morning she found her em-ployer dead. A scholar of the period wrote that James Mayfield's challenger in the primaries, state senator James Samuel Coleman Jr., was "a conservative and leader of the White Citizens Council movement." The White Citizens' Council in Montgomery, which had been formed in October 1955, meant, like other citizens' councils, to apply crushing economic and social pressure to whites to enforce segregation, despite the recent *Brown v. Board of Education*

FIGURE 16. Alabama Supreme Court with James Mayfield Jr.

Sara's younger brother, James (*front row, far right*), was, like his father, an Alabama Supreme Court justice. (Alabama Department of Archives and History)

ruling, and, in Tuscaloosa, a judge's decision in the summer of 1955 that Autherine Lucy should be allowed to enroll at the University of Alabama. (Lucy attempted to enroll at the university in February 1956, sparking riots that occurred only blocks from Sara's room in a ward at Bryce.) Senator Coleman, wrote the scholar, in his "campaign made a point of injecting race into the election. . . . The race . . . left the strong impression that by 1956 segregation was the primary issue to the state judiciary."[8] Coleman became the default Democratic nominee for the position after Mayfield's death and was elected to serve as an associate justice of the state supreme court.

This was Sara's loneliest period at Bryce. Her closest family gone, beset on all sides by stooges, how did she keep going? Institutional life worked as a kind of life support system that breathed for her. Food, shelter, the basics of life were provided. The structure of the day moved her through the meals, activities, and leisure time. But she craved agency and could not simply turn her body and mind over to the system: she observed, she advised, she interfered, she demanded. A solitary silhouette against an overcast sky, she wrote letter after letter to public officials and doctors and family acquaintances, desperate to communicate with the outside world, however imperfectly or wrongheadedly she may have done so. Read as a metaphor, the letters can be seen as a message from the psyche: something has gone terribly wrong here. Things aren't as they should be. The familiar is strange and ominous, the smiling faces are false, I am being tested on a daily basis to see if I will crack. Unable to understand what was happening to her, she searched for logical sequences and found them everywhere, spinning the threads of her life into patterns only she could see.

After James's death, Sara became the ward of her cousin, Peabody Burdette Mayfield, a physician. Burdette and Henry Mayfield, the executors of James's will, made a final accounting of his expenditures on Sara's behalf. Idlewyld was kept for some time by relatives, and many items were moved from the house to their homes, though some were sold by James's ex-wife, Janette. A large trunk of Sara's papers was removed from the house and, although Sara's alma mater, Goucher College, was interested in the collection, Stanley Hoole, director of the University of Alabama library since 1944, lobbied her to donate her literary papers to the Alabama Collection of the university's library. Waters Paul, a psychologist who had befriended Sara at Bryce, and whose wife, Sue, worked at the library, encouraged Sara as well, and a plan was made. With a worker from the hospital carrying the large trunk of letters and various other writings, Dr. Paul and Sara delivered her papers to Dr. Hoole. Mrs. Paul, who would help to sort through and catalog the collection, remembered that "Sara accompanied the papers, and Waters accompanied Sara." These papers would sit for some years after their initial organizing by the library staff, but, like a seed waiting for the right conditions to germinate, the idea of working with those papers to create a book would eventually give Sara a project, and a purpose, to launch her out of the hospital.

For now, Sara dealt with her grief in the old way—through writing and research. She studied French art, and prepared a forty-four-page typescript titled "Study Guide for Modern French Painting" dividing French painting into two periods, 1855–95 and 1896–1956, and offering an overview of movements and individual artists in clean, straightforward prose. She painted, as well, and sat in her room, or on the porch, or in the occupational therapy

FIGURE 17. Sketch by Sara Mayfield of Bryce Hospital's main administration building

Throughout her years in Bryce, Sara sketched, painted, and sculpted. This sketch of the main administration building at Bryce includes a fountain with a statue of the Greek goddess Hebe, which Sara referred to as "the unbalanced virgin." (University of Alabama Libraries Special Collections)

room, and took extensive notes on watercolor and oil painting, working with pastels, the use of perspective, and color theory. She sketched and painted what was around her—other patients, nurses, the buildings and grounds—but also what she imagined, such as the heads of marionettes for a "tone poem" titled "Death and Transfiguration." She drew, in pastels, a picture of "the corner of the hydrotherapy where I work and keep my paints, easel, etc. The wall is not so pink nor the tiles in the wainscoting so green, but the trouble with the colored pencils which I used is that it is difficult to get the exact colors." It was the mental hospital equivalent of an artist's atelier.

She also renewed her interest in chemistry and plastics, ordering such publications from the US Patent and Trademark Office as "Improvement in Cementing Materials for Ornamental Compounds" (mixing milk curd, lime, and fibers to simulate veneer, wood, and stone) and "Improved Composition for Mouldings," a process developed in 1869 by brothers Joseph and Wilhelm Thiem. Wanting to preserve scholarly decorum, she wrote a note to herself to "give Brothers credit for plasticizing protein." And she invented things, based on her own needs as an artist. On June 18, 1956, she took out some drafting paper and sketched a "Painters Palette and Pan" to go with a patent application, writing of her invention, "the unique feature of the painters palette and pan is that it provides a speedy and efficient method of preserving the colors and the nature of colors on a painters palette from one sitting to another and a clean and convenient way of conserving the palette used by painters, whether occasional or professional."

Perhaps she was having trouble sleeping with clips in her waved hair, because on June 25, 1956, she drew a sketch of her "sleep-easy wave clip" designed to "provide a more flexible, more comfortable wave clip which can be worn at night." Throughout the late 1950s and up until 1961, Sara worked on a design for an "autocopter," "a light vehicle that could be used for transporting passengers or cargo by land, water, or air." In her drawing, the contraption looks like an old VW bus with retractable rotors on top of it. Like her conspiracy theories, Sara's inventions tended toward the all-inclusive: a single vehicle that would work on land, water, or air; a mobile service station that could provide a range of services; a dry plastic that when mixed with water could make objects that would camouflage soldiers, provide the building blocks for houses, or be molded for ornamental use, all while taking advantage of cotton byproducts.

Despite Sara's being generally well-behaved, her paranoia was persistent and her insight poor, prompting her doctors to continue looking for ways to treat her illness. By the fall of 1956, they had access to a new drug, chlor-promazine, known by the trade name Thorazine. Described as "instrumental in the development of neuropsychopharmacology, a new discipline dedicated to the study of mental pathology with the employment of centrally acting drugs," Thorazine helped some of the least responsive patients at state in-stitutions in the US and seemed at first like a miracle drug.[9] Originally in use as an antihistamine, then tried experimentally by a French surgeon who was looking for ways to lessen the effects of surgical shock on patients, the drug seemed to calm patients and ease their anxiety about surgery. Another surgeon, aware of its effects, told his psychiatrist brother-in-law, and chlor-promazine was "discovered" as an antipsychotic drug. Approved for use by the US Food and Drug Administration in 1954, Thorazine was initially used in state institutions, when pharmaceutical company Smith Kline convinced state governments it could save them money by providing the means to easily control difficult patients.

Sara was one of those patients in one of those institutions. According to her patient note for November 20, 1956, Sara was started on "100 mg. of Thorazine twice a day," with the dosage to be "gradually increased until she does receive maximum benefit from the medication." The doctors decided to try her on this new medication because, as one note read, "For the past few weeks this patient has not been getting along well. She has been rather fussy and she has been quite a problem in the Art Class. She is argumentative in her attitude toward the Art Instructor. The patient tends to take over and teach the other patients in Art. She is rather argumentive [*sic*] with the other patients and has created disturbances on several occasions." Even though she was on the drug for over a year, her condition did not improve. On Janu-ary 14, 1958, her doctor noted, "This patient has shown no particular change during the time that she has been on Thorazine, and we are going to dis-continue the medication by lowering the dosage gradually over a period of several days. She remains rather delusional and paranoid in her thinking." Sara had her own version of why she was given the new drug. As she wrote in a statement titled "To Whom It May Concern": "When friends made an attempt to secure my release in the fall of 1956, I was given lethal doses of thorazine—800 milligrams a day over a period of fourteen months, every milligram of which I saved and asked to have turned over to a federal grand jury." Could she possibly have avoided taking the medication? That could ac-count for its lack of effectiveness. Or perhaps she does not change because her "condition" is not one treatable by mental health practitioners.

The doctors also experimented with letting Sara go to the university campus just next door to Bryce, although there were some occasional mix-ups. One day, Sara ran into the daughter of family friends at the campus café, called the Little Bo, short for Little Bohemia, after the artsy types who hung out there, in the Art Department building. After talking for a long time, the young woman offered to help Sara run errands and then took her to her house for coffee so that her parents could visit with her. When they asked Sara when she needed to be back, she said it didn't matter, but when they eventually drove her back to the hospital, the staff were out on the grounds looking for her. Sara had decided it was better to be "in trouble" at Bryce than to admit to old family friends that she was less free than she presented herself as being.

As Sara's days unfolded, she occasionally found something amusing to report in her journal, as when she went to a dance for patients and was proposed to by a man who offered "as an inducement 1500 head of hogs. I've had some prize offers during my psychiatric career but that tops them all." She went to music classes, where she learned to play the guitar, and she studied photography. In art class, she took lessons on the pottery wheel—"I turned a small bowl and brought a cylinder up to about nine inches, which is doing pretty well for a beginner"—but something must have happened, because the next day she was taken away from the wheel, and she couldn't understand why "when I want to learn . . I'm not allowed to do so." With the other patients she watched a movie, *Partners of the Plains*: "It must have been made for asylum consumption for no one who was not locked in would sit through it." They also watched a film called *The Gentle Warrior*—"a narrative of the life of Dorothea Lynd[e] Dix who, as Rev. Blakeney pointed out was directly responsible 'for founding Bryce Hospital and taking the mentally ill out of jail.'" As part of the goal of integrating patients back into regular activities, they were sometimes allowed to go to church away from the hospital. Sara often went to services at Bryce and occasionally went to Canterbury Chapel, the Episcopal church on the UA campus, within walking distance of Bryce. One Sunday, she wrote that several patients had gotten together to go to church and take communion, but then had not been able to go after all. "The idea of using the sacrament of communion as the trap door in a psychiatric maze doesn't shock these people here as it does Episcopalians, I suppose."

Sara liked to record her banter with doctors, as though they were part of a stage play. She and Dr. Darden, who playfully called each other "cousin," were frequent banterers. One time, she was wearing a new dress she had made herself when she ran into Dr. Darden and another patient. She reported on the encounter: "'We'll domesticate her yet,' he said.

'Not a chance.' Then I told him, 'There are two ways that anyone can take any experience, Dr. Darden, constructively and destructively. Since I've been here, I've written a book which a number of patients have found very helpful and I'd like to go to the library and [do] the necessary research that it will take to finish it.'" After one encounter with Dr. Darden, she recorded her retort: "I'm just a misplaced newsgirl, thrown into captivity and domesticated by force." In her narration of events, so many of their encounters have a kind of Hepburn and Tracy spark, the cool, wise-cracking man and the passionate, smart, clever woman. By seeing herself as the heroine of her own story, Sara was able to create a narrative of fierce endurance and spunky determination in which she ultimately would prevail. She would write, for herself, a happy ending.

In June 1958 she wrote of a fellow patient bringing in a cantaloupe, ham, and V-8 to share with Sara and the other patients, but, significantly, recorded no paranoid suspicions about the fruit. That same summer, she noted an instance of cafeteria humor: A new patient "who has not yet become accustomed to the Bryce routine of weiners three times a day" made up "The Bryce Song: 'Weiners in the morning, weiners in the evening, weiners at suppertime, be my little weiner, and love me all the time.' The patients roared and the doctors joined in." Sara, unlike many other patients, was able to afford extra food and have it delivered from outside. She always shared what she had. One day, as she was walking toward the cafeteria with a stack of glasses and a pitcher of tomato juice, she was asked by another patient if "'she's going to try to serve everybody.' 'As far as it will go,' I assured her with a smile, 'I've never yet learned to eat in front of people without sharing whatever I have.'" Sara gained strength from seeing herself as a helper, even when she felt annoyed by others' behavior.

When she was feeling relaxed and unworried, Sara could display near-maternal kindness, trying to "tempt" a new patient to eat sherbet and cantaloupe and bringing malted milk to a teenage patient she had befriended. It bothered her, however, that her simple kindness could be misinterpreted at times: "When May came out of the visitor's room apparently she'd been crying. So at supper I fixed some aspic and took it to her. Afterward when she came up to thank me she told me how much she appreciated the aspic and added 'This shows that you love me and that's very important now.' She was certainly jumping at conclusions."

After a decade in Bryce, Sara was accustomed to if not wholly comfortable with life in an institution. One night she did laundry and read a book instead of going to a "community sing." Another night she went to a cooking class and then got ready to go to a Bryce dance being held across town at the Veterans Administration Hospital. She described her preparations: "I shampooed my hair, bathed, put on a fresh pink linen dress that had just come from the cleaners." When she stepped outside, she ran into an acquaintance from town, who remarked, "Why Sara, you look perfectly beautiful—like a lovely pink rose." Sara, still adept at the pleasant sophistry of southern ladies, replied, "You haven't changed a bit, Elizabeth," and then "we exchanged compliments for several minutes."

Doctors often wrote of Sara that she had little or no "insight." The problem of poor insight, or denial of one's condition—called, clinically, anosognosia, from Greek words meaning "without," "disease," and "knowledge"—has been described as "essentially social: the extent to which a person agrees with her doctor's interpretation." But letting go of your belief in the truth of what others may see as delusions carries a cost. As one writer observed: "If a person goes from being a political martyr to a mental patient in just a few days—the sign of a successful hospital stay, by most standards—her life may begin to feel banal and useless. Insight is correlated with fewer hospital readmissions, better performance at work, and more social contacts, but it is also linked with lower self-esteem and depression."[10] While Sara's distorted perspective may have made enduring life in the hospital more of a crusade, a cause for bravery, than if she had merely accepted her diagnosis, she was, increasingly, simply less invested in hospital life. Some slow shift was occurring, hard to pinpoint, but perceptible.

Nearing the end of the nineteen-fifties, Sara began to practice yoga alone in her room, first thing in the morning. Writing in her journal about watching a calisthenics class, with patients wearing white pants and rolling on the floor, she practically cackles, "When I thought of what I'd been put thru for exercising in pajamas on the floor here in the privacy of my own room, I had to laugh." She endured the comments and kept doing the yoga. It must have helped. Yoga had been brought to the US by Indian teachers in the late nineteenth and early twentieth centuries, so Sara might have learned of it then. The forties and fifties saw a great expansion of practice in the US, with books by yogis making yoga both popular and accessible. In addition to her yoga practice, Sara attempted to regulate her schedule in order to improve her well-being, writing in her journal, "I try to vary my activities. I exercise and study Russian before breakfast, practice on my guitar and do my laundry afterwards, then sculpt or paint or write.'"

Despite being kept from a normal life, Sara tried to keep her mind and imagination alive, nor would she feel that she had been forgotten by those on the outside: the carbons of her thank-you notes, for example, attest to a bounty of Christmas presents in 1959, mostly from family members—books, a robe, Christmas jewelry, shoes, soap, lotion, holiday lunches, and, from Christ Episcopal Church, candy. She began all her notes with endearments: Dearest B, Honey Darling, Dearest Nidi and Tom, Dearest Mark, Dearest Aunt Narnie, Dear Mary Em, Dear Mary Lou, Dearest Mabe, Dear Luke and Tiny, Dear Freddie and Richard, Dearest Luch and Herbert, My dear Aunt Judy, Dear Rev. Cook, Dear Andrea and Wilburn, My precious Judy, Dearest Edith, Dearest Mary, Dear Camie, My precious Larry and Brenda, Dear Camilla, Dear Fred and Anna, My sweet Pat and Mike, Dearest Ruth, Dearest Virginia, Dear Ruth, Joe, and Aunt Willie, Dear Carmel and Carmen, Dearest Janette, Larry, Don, Jeff, and George Jr., Dear Sonny and Bessy, My dear sweet Campions, Dearest Henry and Lois, Dearest Larry.

Sara wrote to her former sister-in-law, Janette, and her children on Christmas Day: "Many, many thanks for the Yardley's bath powder and soap. I loved the fresh clean smell of the lavender so I rose early this morning, took a bath instead of a shower and luxuriated in it. The proper accompaniment was a parody of one of Mary Martin's songs from South Pacific, 'I'm going to wash this Bryce right out of my hair.' For, as usual, they have celebrated the birth of Our Lord with a sadistic saturnalia in which they have pulled out all the stops, cruelty, alienation, effrontery, obscenity, perversity, crudity, deceit, errorism, disappointment routine, *Nutcracker Suite*, coconut cake, frustration, etc. which amuses me when I think of the bill of goods the Masons, the McQueens, the Partlows, the Lawrences, the First National Bank and the Tuskaloosa News, not to mention the Sheppard-Pratt have deliberately bought for themselves and each other. Hope the children had a wonderful Christmas as well as you, Jette, Earl, and Big Don." In that note, particularly, her tone veers from courteous matron to conspiracy theorist and back again.

What were the family conversations like as the thank-you notes came in, with their mixture of the proper and the paranoid? What would it mean to take her on in your household? What were their responsibilities to her? Perhaps in part to salve their consciences, they remembered her on holidays, took her to lunch and shopping, enjoyed her company, most of the time, but they mistrusted her ladylike mien, imagining the wayward thoughts going

FIGURE 18. Christmas season at Bryce Hospital

A hallway in one of the women's wards at Bryce Hospital, decorated for Christmas, from the 1940s. Holidays were especially difficult for Sara and other patients, and Sara repeatedly referred to what she saw as a "sadistic saturnalia" conspiracy by hospital staff to make her miserable and confused around Christmas. (Alabama Department of Archives and History)

on in her head, wondering just how crazy they were. When she spoke to a cousin about wanting to leave the hospital, the cousin asked, "But where would you go and what would you do?" No one was eager to take her on, to take personal responsibility for her. Further, despite her apparent ability to take care of herself, even with her delusions of persecution, there was as yet no law that mandated a patient's release after a certain amount of time or set uniform standards for improvement that would lead to release. Sara remained a patient by default, doing the best she could in circumstances that she had grown used to, but would never accept.

Chapter 12

"If They Call Me, All Right; if They Don't, I'm Happy"

Showing Sara's Increasing Engagement with Writing and Life beyond the Hospital. Two New Friendships give her Hope. Beginning to work on her Papers at the University Library.

WHEN 1960 DAWNED, SARA WAS STILL AT BRYCE. THE DAILY ROUND of life now included sculpting, a cooking club, a stagecraft class, occasional dances, bridge, and other amusements. Although her suspicions about doctors, patients, and powerful people in town and around the state continued to crop up in journal entries and notes, some slow change was taking place, and the doctors and other staff seem to perceive it as well. Heading out to an art exhibit on the UA campus, she met the Bryce chaplain, Reverend Allen, who told her, "You look like a million dollars." At the exhibit, she was more impressed with the photographs on display than with the paintings and sculpture, but mostly she was just happy to be out and about. "It was a fine day, more like spring than spring some time is." She sought out art everywhere she could find it, in town and on campus, remarking in her journal of one lithography exhibit that "much of it was interesting but too advanced for my taste. There was a Picasso, a Chagall, & a Henry Moore among the lithographs." Visiting Paris and London in the 1920s, Sara could have seen original early works by Picasso, Chagall, and Moore, perhaps even met the artists themselves, and here were their works, and here was she, feeding herself with art as she had done all her life.

It is hard to pin down exactly what shifted in Sara. Although turning points can be distinct and dramatic—a conversation, an event, a book—more often they take the shape of an internal thawing beneath a seemingly solid surface, and suddenly spring breaks out in greenings and blooms. Maybe it was a new decade, or a growing circle of friends outside the hospital, or turning fifty-five that helped propel Sara towards the rest of her life. Whatever it was, she was shifting along with the zeitgeist.

Her focus on writing and art was giving her more purpose; she decided "not to waste any more time trying to get to the recreational and religious activities. If they call me, all right; if they don't, I'm happy." She felt a renewed determination to finish the long-planned "Mona Lisa" as a novel: on January 7, 1960, she wrote in her journal, "If I can get by with it, I don't intend to go to but one activity a day until I finish re-writing the *Mona Lisa*." She persisted, although "the rewriting goes very slow." She was struggling with imagery for the towns of the novel and requested a book titled *Medieval Cities* from Lustig's bookstore. She kept up her artwork as well, drawing portraits of other patients. Sara took her work seriously enough to write scornfully of another patient, an artist manqué who dressed all in black, wore dark sunglasses, put her hair in a bun, and wanted everyone to look at her work: "She's about one-tenth art and nine-tenths exhibitionism." With the goal of being able to read European literature in the original languages, she continued her language studies, which were extensive; she wrote in her journal that "having learned Greek, Latin, Gothic, Anglo-Saxon, and Middle English, as well [as] French, Spanish, Italian, Portuguese, and German, I did not think I would find Russian very difficult. But the Cyrillic alphabet, the lack of articles, the declensions of nouns, adjectives, pronouns, and numerals with six cases to a declension make it rough going, not to mention the vagaries of pronunciation and spelling." While studying Russian, she tried to keep up her other languages, practicing with anyone at Bryce who spoke another language. In the cafeteria, when her usual lunch companions were out with their families: "I ate with Fraulein Hildegarde and talked German with her." In earlier years, she had worked to learn sign language so that she could communicate with deaf patients she had observed, concluding from her observations that "the isolation of insanity is different from the isolation caused by physical affliction and more difficult to overcome," adding "I want to think about this some more."

Sara kept busy, but she never stopped lobbying to be released. With her lengthy time in Bryce and all her letter-writing to officials, she became the asylum equivalent of a jailhouse lawyer, advising other patients on lawyers and writs of habeas corpus. She described in her journal how she counseled,

"Don't ever worry about anything here until it happens . . . then don't take it seriously—or they'll tag you with an anxiety complex." Her advice was not always sage, however, as when she advised a Roman Catholic woman committed for alcoholism to send her letter requesting an investigation not to the Civil Rights Council but directly to US attorney general Robert Kennedy because he was a Catholic, too. She took the possibility of repercussions against herself and patients she helped seriously but forged on anyway. When she helped another patient write a letter to attorney Gus Woods, the patient asked, "What will Dr. Darden say if he finds out you helped me? Will he give you a shock treatment?" Sara responded, "He'll know the moment he reads it that I dictated it, and you can't tell what they'll do here but he knows that I've gotten at least a dozen people out the same way." When yet another patient worried about being accused of being "sick" and getting shock treatments herself if she contacted a lawyer, Sara was roused to say, "What do you care. If standing on your constitutional rights is being 'sick,' there are a great many sick people in this country." Once, when a patient's relative advised the patient not to pursue a lawsuit, Sara concluded that the relative must have been threatened. "Blackmail is one of the most common and effective means of stopping writs of habeas corpus." However misguided or deluded in her interpretation of events, Sara was brave, willing to risk the horror of repeated shock treatments and to rally the troops to risk it along with her to defend their rights—even when a patient told her people were saying "Sara Mayfield is sick and getting sicker."

She continued, occasionally, to worry about issues of sexuality, and believed she was being baited by another patient who asked to read the first two chapters of "Mona Lisa" then initiated a conversation with Sara about a staff psychiatrist writing a book on schizophrenia, saying that "the general consensus of opinion was that schizophrenia was the result of an escape reaction from homosexual tendencies." Sara recorded her response: "It's difficult to define what you mean by homosexual tendencies. It has always struck me as absurd to pillory Leonardo da Vinci on the basis of anonymous accusations in an age in which bi-sexuality was in full flower." Her worries about a "smear campaign" related to homosexual behavior resurfaced when Sara suspected a nurse of "issuing an invitation to see who would try for the last three months" and wondered about "all the unwarranted affection" when another female patient kissed her on the cheek. When a discussion of the smear campaign came up at lunch, she counseled a young patient to work on "turning yourself into a young lady and staying out of the way of women with mustaches." One patient, Kitty, was a friend but also an irritant and a worry. When Kitty sat on the end of Sara's bed and a nurse came by, Kitty asked, "Do you suppose she saw me?" and Sara responded, "Why shouldn't she?" The next day a patient told of one female patient getting in bed with another, and then told dirty jokes, which Sara found distasteful.

After twelve years as a patient at Bryce, Sara still suffered from delusions and paranoia, and she continued to perceive plots and campaigns against her. How could she bear up under the inquisition? What would save her? Order, focus, and writing. In April 1960 she wrote of razor blades being left around to encourage her to commit suicide but ended her entry triumphantly: "I finished the second draft of the Mona Lisa." She was rightly proud of her self-discipline, writing to her former sister-in-law that the work proceeded, but slowly, "with few or no correct reference books, my knee for a desk, and two or three people talking to me while the work was in progress—and attempting to bone up on all the languages I ever studied simultaneously, plus the regular hospital chores." Deep in work on her Mona Lisa book, she studied the life of Caterina Sforza, an Italian noblewoman and warrior "celebrated for her courage," and found her a fit model.

In the spring of 1960, when a patient in her ward was moved to a new ward, Sara asked if she could move into the single room, by herself, and was given permission by the nurse. A room of her own, after all those years! Another patient helped her move, and she rigged up a lamp from her camera tripod and a floodlight. Now she could read and write in her room and not have to take her materials to the hydrotherapy or occupational therapy rooms, where she was constantly interrupted. She found some Rembrandt reproductions to put on her walls, put her books and musical instruments where they were easy to get to, and had friends in to study Spanish together or just visit. Dr. Darden came by, and found the atmosphere "beatnik and boho."

Although Sara continued to use her journals to work things out, to record daily life, and to compile evidence of the inquisition against her—perhaps for the record, perhaps even expecting that the doctors were surreptitiously reading her words, she began to write fewer entries. On June 30, 1960, she wrote, "At this point, it occurs that a large part of this journal could be subsumed under 'I don't know.' I am very tired of posting it every day, particularly as I don't think anyone ever reads it." The tone of her journal entries began to change as well, as when she wrote, "Friday's [sic], my days off when I'm not too busy to take them, are wonderful. This morning, did a little shopping at Sam Jacksons, browsed in the Ala. Book Store and in the stacks. Read Chas.

Fenton's The Apprenticeship of Ernest Hemingway and Gertrude Stein's 'How Writing Is Written.' Was not impressed by the latter."

With the "Mona Lisa" draft finished, she decided to spend some time working on an exposé about what she called the Unholy Alliance in her town and state. She sat by the dense, aromatic arborvitae in her dress and silk stockings, seeking a little coolness and privacy in its shade as she charted the unseen warp and weft of connections between bankers, legislators, doctors, journalists, and lawyers, "behind our own iron curtain." Her thoughts continued to run to conspiracy. Reading of a new book criticizing US foreign affairs, she wrote that "someone should write on U.S. psychological warfare . . . how it could have been so thoroughly bungled I don't see—though one of the most effective ways to do that is to lock up the one U.S. citizen who's been more signally successful in that field than anyone else and deny her a lawyer, or trial, or even a hearing."

Whatever was on her mind, by hospital standards she was behaving herself and not being disruptive—unlike in previous years—and her doctors began allowing her to go out more with friends, with requests approved by her guardian, Henry Mayfield. In the summer of 1960, she made a new friend at Bryce, Mildred Rosenbaum, of Florence, Alabama, who lived in a house designed by Frank Lloyd Wright, the only one in the state. They were simpatico, and every night would listen to one or two of the Beethoven quartets Mildred's husband, Stanley, had brought for her when he visited.

Right before Christmas, she went to the library but "there was too much holiday spirit abroad in the library for any great amount of work to be done. I finished my shopping and got Janette's box with her things and the children's to her. Classes were out at noon and [by] two p.m. the U of A was deserted. There is nothing on earth as lonely as a university without students." Christmas came and went with no mention by Sara of any "sadistic Saturnalias," and in 1961 on New Year's Day, she wrote on the first page of a new notebook that she "spent the hours before church today in an examination of conscience, moral, intellectual, and artistic, in preparation for making New Year's resolutions. Alas, to quote the Episcopal prayer book, 'I have done those things which I ought not to have done and left undone those things which I ought to have done.' Among the many New Year's resolutions to remedy my sins of omission and commission was one to be more painstaking and conscientious about keeping the Journal than I have been recently." She did keep up with it daily for a little while, but because she had more going on outside the hospital than before, the entries became less frequent, a sign of her increasing turn toward the outside world.

Every once in a while, she was triggered by some of her old concerns. Just after New Year's, a patient named Louise went out to lunch with her parents and returned with a cake to share with the ward. Afterward, Sara recorded that "as she handed me a piece of it, she said, 'We went by your house and it has a "for sale" sign on it.' And so another one of Dr. Kay's patients has been roped in[to] 'the assassins with the little cakes' game. . . . It is certainly tedious." Instead of being outraged, however, she affected—and perhaps even felt—only a mild annoyance and did not write about it anymore.

On one of her approved "sleeping out" trips in the fall of 1960, Sara had made a short visit to the Rosenbaums, and on January 17, 1961, Mildred, now released, and Stanley picked her up at Bryce and drove her back to Florence for a two-week vacation with them. She enjoyed the social life, the family atmosphere, and the modern "Usonian"-style home, designed by Wright for the Rosenbaums when they were a young married couple. Situated overlooking the Tennessee River, the house was a haven to Sara, with its abundant natural light and clean lines. In January, it also was cozy to be in her own guest suite with a heating system built into the concrete floors, and positively luxurious to be in a quiet room with no threat of interruptions. She even had her very own bathroom. Mildred's piano and Stanley's books, music and literature and witty conversation—all this felt like heaven after so many years in Bryce.

Perhaps it was time to leave the heaviness of Black Belt plantation country and family history behind and settle in the hills of north Alabama. Sara seriously considered moving to Florence: people were kind to her, she fit in with the cultural life of the town, and the Rosenbaums were there to sponsor her socially as guides and friends. Added to that was the amusement of living in a town called Florence, as Leonardo da Vinci had. She retained a lawyer, was offered a job as producer of a daily morning show with a television station in Florence, to be titled *Vanity Fair*, and was ready to be gone. Stanley's parents, the Louis Rosenbaums, offered to let her stay in the studio apartment that went with their house, right across the street from Mildred and Stanley.

On January 31, 1961, when the Rosenbaums took her back to the Ladies Receiving Building at Bryce, she asked for her belongings and requested a discharge. The staff member on duty that night called Dr. Darden, who spoke with Sara by telephone, and explained, as he wrote in his notes, "she could take her belongings but that we could not give her a discharge. I explained to her that she was on furlough and that she would be discharged six months from the date of her furlough. I told [her] that she could remain out of the hospital as Mr. Henry Mayfield had agreed to her staying out and not coming back at the end of the two weeks, which had previously been planned. She would not agree to this, however. She said that if we would not give her a discharge she demanded that we take her back in the hospital until at such time she could obtain a 'quiet writ of habeas corpus' or a discharge from us. She was, therefore, returned from furlough at her own insistence. She talked at some length about a Federal Grand Jury investigation and various other things she has talked about for many years." Three days after she returned, two FBI agents showed up at Bryce and informed Dr. Darden that she had contacted the Florence office while she was on furlough, and that the Birmingham office had requested that they visit her, which they did, "briefly."

The hospital was legally bound to follow the transitional furlough/discharge sequence, but Sara was unwilling to accept their explanation and asked her doctor, as he wrote in his notes, "'Who is holding me here? Who is not willing to close the business up and give me a clean sheet? Is it Dr. Tarwater, Dr. Smith, or who? What in the dickens was I put here for? I want to see the medical interlocutory. I want to see what they did allege.'" In one entry to her patient records, physician Sam Darden wrote: "[Although] we do not feel that her mental condition has shown any significant change . . . we have felt that she might possibly be able to adjust outside the hospital. . . . However, this patient has declined to accept the furlough." We'll let you go on furlough, they say. I won't go without a discharge, she says. We can't discharge you unless you go on furlough, they say. Then I won't go, she says. And so they go round and round in a battle of wills, and for a long time she is the more stubborn. The Rosenbaums' generosity and support, though, had shifted something within, and, however slow the trajectory, Sara was now on her way to imagining a life beyond Bryce, and how to get there.

In explaining their reluctance to declare Sara restored to sanity and simply discharge her, her doctors struggled to explain to others how she might appear at first meeting. In a letter to a staffer for Alabama senator Lister Hill inquiring about Sara's situation (Sara's old friend Liz Thigpen Hill was married to Senator Hill's cousin), her doctor briefly recounted Sara's initial commitment in 1940, how it had been "necessary for her mother and other relatives, on competent medical advice" to return her to Bryce in 1948, and how, thirteen years later, "Miss Sara, unfortunately, has not recovered. . . . She is a very intelligent, indeed, cultured person, who in ordinary conversation and letter-writing may show little indication of abnormal thinking. Here in the hospital we are able to see evidence that she is not mentally well. She yet

holds and expresses delusional thinking, which has prevented us from rec-
ommending discharge." One of the tragedies of Sara's enforced confinement
in Bryce is that her "delusional thinking" was considered, at that time, to be
sufficient cause to deprive her of her liberty for almost seventeen years, more
than six thousand days and nights. However well-meaning her doctors and
family may have been, that she and many others had insufficient recourse
to law or to better treatment, and endured unacceptable living conditions,
makes clear the need for such reforms as *Wyatt v. Stickney* brought about.

Sara's undergraduate studies in English literature likely provided some
specific as well as general consolation for her plight. As a student at Goucher
she had read Byron's "Prisoner of Chillon" and written a paper about it: "Byron liked to imagine himself as being persecuted, and therefore the poem becomes a sort of imaginative autobiography. In it he also displays his hatred of
tyranny and his passionate soul." Of Byron's prisoner, the young Sara wrote,
"He gradually learns to love despair, and has made friends with the rats and
spiders about him. Finally, his friends come into power and rescue him, but it
is with great reluctance that he leaves, so resigned has he become to his fate."
Sara, the "Prisoner of Bryce," never became resigned to her fate, but for her
own reasons she was reluctant to leave, determined to be declared sane, once
and for all, so that she could not simply be recommitted. In addition to feeling she was in the right, she also had one very practical reason for demanding
a full discharge: as long as she was on furlough, she would be under the care
of her guardian and thus unable to be in charge of her own finances or in
other ways to have legal agency.

Having decided to stay at Bryce for the time being, she wrote letters
to thank everyone in Florence for their hospitality: to Mr. and Mrs. Louis
Rosenbaum, Stanley's parents, and to the Rosenbaum family, Mildred, Stanley, sons Michael and Alvin, and their friends: "Mildred's wonderful food and
delightful parties make the return to plain living quite an abrupt change. For
all the high life we enjoyed, I found nothing more pleasant than the quiet
evenings at home, talking to Stanley and Mildred, discussing photography
with Michael and Alvin and singing folk songs with Gould, Diane, Bill, and
Kitty." In addition, she wrote a number of bread-and-butter notes to people
she had met and visited with. To a woman named Roberta, she wrote, "I can't
go down the list of those that entertained me in Florence without wanting to
thank you again for your thoughtfulness and kindness in having us over for a
cup of coffee. It was a pleasure to be in your home and see all your attractive
things and meet your charming friends."

Sara decided to try to be productive for however much longer she was in Bryce, and in February 1961, she was given permission by her doctors and by Stanley Hoole to go to the university library, sit with her papers, and annotate and take notes on them for a possible book. With the encouragement of Dr. Hoole, she was planning a memoir about her life and her literary friendships, especially with the Menckens and the Fitzgeralds. Sara Haardt Mencken had died in 1935; Zelda had died in the fire in 1948, eight years after Scott's death in 1940; and Henry Mencken had suffered a stroke in the fall of 1948, sharply curtailing his writing and reading life, and died in 1956.

Working at the library, sitting at a big wooden desk with a typewriter in front of her, papers around her, and shelves of books on walls in the corner behind her, Sara began to establish more of a life of her own away from the hospital. Having taken up photography, she was allowed to develop photographs in the art department's darkroom, and she often made plans to have lunch with friends she made on campus. Now middle-aged, if she and John Sellers had stayed married and had had a child, Sara could easily have been a society matron by then, labeled and sorted and doting on a grandchild or two. But she most certainly wasn't, and not just because she lived in a mental hospital. She saw herself, more than ever, as intellectually alive and socially active, thinking about a future that might just include independence.

Sara continued her daily work at the library without any difficulties arising. In the spring of 1961 she was allowed to visit her old haven, Dauphin Island, for a week. She was released into the care of Carolyn A. Hager, who ran the Story Apartments, where Sara stayed. Afterward, Mrs. Hager wrote Sara, "Will be anxious to hear more about the story of Dauphin Island and want you to know we certainly enjoyed your visit with us." But the trip was in some ways a disappointment; although, wrote Sara, "it was once a lovely, lonely, peaceful island . . ." it was now "full of clubs, casinos, motels, tourist camps, and littered with paper cups, flatboys, and beer cans. No more refuge there."

Her routine now was to walk from the Bryce campus to the UA campus, and as the months passed she met more people in the library and began to make new friends "outside." In mid-December she walked over to campus on a frigid day "with a rain that was liquid sleet" and arrived at the library drenched and shivering. "About the time I thawed out Jim and Bill insisted on going to lunch. Hartwig, a young law student, joined us and the talk turned on the reorganization of the State Dept. and our foreign policy or lack of it." Bill was Bill McMinn, a philosophy professor and friend of Sara's. Sara wrote in her journal the next day that "Jim Fowler loaned me Mark Schorer's

Sinclair Lewis, which makes Lewis vastly more interesting than he was." Being on campus was good for Sara; young people energized her, and she recorded in her journal one day, "One never knows what one will see here on campus. Last week there was a double decker bed out in front of Graves Hall with a sign exhorting the students to get out of bed and vote for some candidate or other; a baby elephant in the Union Building plastered over with another candidate's signs; and a black and white cocker spaniel in Little Bo which had its white areas [dyed] purple."

In the summer of 1962 Sara came close to getting a job at UA's Audio Visual Department, having become acquainted with its head, James Nesbit. Nesbit needed someone to help take and develop photographs, and Sara had taught herself the skills required for the job. She was interested in the opportunity to earn some money, writing in her journal, "Photography is an expensive hobby. It cost me $8.00 to have my light meter fixed." Initially, Nesbit spoke with her about the position, having checked with his head photographer that he was willing to work with a woman in his department. As the paperwork for the job made its way through different administrative levels at the university, however, it was turned down due to "budget constraints," and when Nesbit told Sara the news, she said, according to her patient notes, that "she could accept the reasons, but made the statement that she knew something would happen to keep her from being hired." A week later, her patient notes recorded the news that audio visual had decided a man would be better for the job, given that "the department was downstairs on a concrete floor in the dark room." Between the two designations that might have kept her from getting the job, being a woman, apparently, was worse than being a mental patient. Perhaps Sara took this in stride, as she did not comment on it in her journals. As Sara's thick notebooks give way to loose-leaf pages, ruminations on stooges give way to notes on etymologies and Shakespeare's language, and cranial measurements of Borden and Babs Deal, writer friends of whom she planned to make busts. A photo credited to Sara appeared with a review of Borden Deal's book *The Loser* in the *New York Times* in March 1964, under the title "Political Drama Way Down South."

On another page in Sara's notebook, she made a list:

> Talk to Sidney about:
> articles for Yale Rev.
> biography of Southhampton
> Travel Club

_____ [illegible] on Shakespeare
_____ [illegible] of Mona Lisa
Fork and Spoon Club
Driver's License
Biography of Kit Marloe [*sic*]
Contest?
Chess
Theta Chi House
Reading party
House boat
Clay for head.

She also wrote down the Latin phrase "non norunt, haec monumenta mori," from the Roman poet Martial. Comparing literary works with ruined tombs, the phrase asserts that books alone are the only "monuments" to immortality that do not die.

The Sidney to talk to on her list was Sidney J. Landman, a young man who had finished an MA at Vanderbilt in 1958 and who would go on to receive his PhD from Vanderbilt in 1967, specializing in Shakespeare and Renaissance literature. Presumably he was teaching at UA in the interim, while he looked for a permanent position. Sidney loved architecture and antiques, cared about the finer things of home decor, from furniture to silver to china, and enjoyed the opera, classical music, and theater. He was very much a kindred spirit, and Sara enjoyed encouraging the development of cultural awareness in this young man and took pleasure, as well, in his attention. From what was likely an initial meeting with mutual friends on campus, he seems simply to have befriended her, writing her notes and letters in beautiful calligraphic handwriting, reading her manuscripts, picking her up to go to lunch or run an errand or visit with his mother, Kathlyn, with whom he lived. Playfully, he addressed a card to her "For the Duchess of Idlewyld from Lady Kathlyn and Sir Sidney." Sidney and his mother's generosity and friendship began to give Sara the feeling that she was not alone and boosted her confidence about leaving the hospital. When the Landmans bought a house in 1963, they offered it as a home to Sara as well; she wrote in her journal, "He says they have a room for me and will testify for me, take the responsibility for me, talk to the doctors or do anything else to get me out."

Chapter 13

"Only an Imaginary Line"

"Sleeping out" with Friends and Family and going to the UA Campus to write.
Arguments with the Doctors over a Furlough versus a Discharge. An Inward Shift.

A S THE EARLY SIXTIES CONTINUED, SARA WAS ALLOWED MORE AND
more freedoms. The doctors observed that she could handle being away
from the hospital for the day, and for longer visits to stay with friends, without incident, and came to trust her on her own. Sara once wrote to a friend,
"There is only an imaginary line here between the university and the asylum" and, increasingly, she spent more time on the university side than on
the asylum side. She worked hard to present a "normal" front to staff at the
hospital and to friends outside of it. One of Sara's doctors wrote, "Frankly, I
think Sara is as well mentally now as she was when she was released from the
hospital several years ago after her first admission." (The "several years" was a
period of more than two decades, but the sentiment holds.)

. On one occasion, she asked a theater professor, T. Earle Johnson, to take
her to a reception at the university president's mansion, a white Greek Revival structure facing the green expanse of the university's main quad and the
bell tower known as Denny Chimes, after the UA president who had spoken
at the installation of the monument to Sara's father, back in 1928. Professor
Johnson picked her up at the hospital and drove her the short distance to the
reception. As he described it, "She was very calm and seemed very normal
and behaved herself in a perfectly discreet and genteel manner. No one could
find anything wrong—no one could find any fault there. Of course, people
knew where she was, so they were eyeing her; I could tell that, and I imagine she could, too. After the party was over, I took her back to Bryce. She

thanked me, turned and kissed me goodnight, and I left."[1] Sara was practicing being outside, and doing well.

Much of her time now was spent at her old Corona typewriter, which she had nicknamed "Calvin Coolidge," after the American president, because it "does not choose to run." She worked in her hospital room and in the library, but sometimes also lugged the typewriter over to the audio visual lab in Woods Hall, where she was allowed to sit and write. On cold, wet days she wore her "Cossack boots" to tromp across the Bryce lawn and through the university campus to its historic heart, choosing either the library or Woods Hall, seeing friends both places. In addition to her work at the library on her papers, she spent time putting together an application for a grant from the Bollingen Foundation to complete a final draft of her book on Mona Lisa. She revised her mystery novel, "The Question of the Sphinx"; generated ideas for newspaper and magazine articles that she pitched to *Atlantic Monthly* and *Life*; and in early 1963 she wrote to the publisher Alfred A. Knopf that she had completed a first draft of her literary memoir, based on the work she had done with her papers at the library; she was calling the book "The Constant Circle."

Although she made light of it to friends, working on her literary memoirs created in Sara a great sense of loss. As she wrote to her old college friend Dorothy de Santillana (whom she called Tilton), now an editor at Houghton Mifflin, on March 23, 1963, the fifteenth anniversary of her commitment to Bryce, "This comes under the head of ventilation, not correspondence. . . . But every time I look at the Mencken letters, I could pull a Tom Wolfe: 'O lost, Sal, ashes under a cold slab in Loudon Park! And Henry, O lost forever lost, dragging at the anchors against oblivion somewhere in the starry spaces, grieved by the interstellar winds. O Tilton, strayed behind the façade of H-M's senior editor, O lost in the jungles of contemporary lit. O Zelda, buried in the alien earth of Maryland. My Maryland, drowned in the wine of sour grapes: O lost, lost, lost. O Mayfield, rebel-ghost-[of-a]-rebel-ghost, gray and pale with prison pallor, silenced in a green-barred hell. O lost, forever lost! O where, O when, O why?'" Dorothy, for her part, encouraged Sara but wrote of her with concern in a letter to Elise Sanguinetti, an Alabama novelist: "She is gifted and some of her correspondence is quite brilliant. Suddenly it breaks and goes quite off. I am sure it is extremely important to her to believe herself still connected with the world of letters in which she was so passionately involved when she was young."

Dorothy expressed interest in "The Constant Circle," but, in her capacity as editor rather than friend, would eventually reject the Mencken manuscript, writing to Elise Sanguinetti, "I had the difficult task of writing Sara we couldn't publish her mss although parts of it are *very* good—but today it is minor, half-forgotten literary history—but it shines for her as it did 30 yrs ago—because it was when she last really lived. I felt *very* badly." Dorothy was mistaken in her assessment of Sara as living in the past, but she was a good friend who kept up her side of the correspondence and cared about Sara's well-being, writing to Elise that she hoped for any news of Sara she could send and that she hoped Sara was "happy and comfortable. She had so many devoted friends in the past and moved around in so wide a geographical circle as well that it saddens me to think of her so long cloistered."

Now less and less cloistered, Sara sometimes met her friends Borden and Babs Deal for coffee at the university, and the Deals would sometimes come by and take her out to eat at a restaurant on University Boulevard only a few blocks from Bryce. A young writer who had become friends with the Deals, Wayne Greenhaw, sometimes accompanied them, and the four would sit back and entertain each other with stories and talk of writers and writing. To show her affection for the Deals, Sara, now fairly accomplished at sculpting, finished the clay busts of their heads she had been planning as gifts to them; the busts are now held in the Borden Deal Collection at Boston University. Feeling and acting more and more like a working writer, she simply didn't have time for the Bryce version of office politics.

In March 1963 she began corresponding with Dorothy de Santillana about a possible visit from writer Clancy Sigal, a friend of Dorothy's who had written to Sara about visiting her to talk about the South for an article he planned to write. Sara was now using a post office box, no. 3435, on the UA campus, safe from the hospital steward's prying eyes. In advance of Sigal's trip, Dorothy sent Sara his book *Going Away: A Report, a Memoir*, the story of a radical young man on a road trip in 1950s America, but the package arrived "with both ends of the carton ripped open and the back torn loose from the wrapping." Although Sara, as usual, suspected the damage had to do with the ongoing inquisition against her, the package might well have been opened due to Sigal having been blacklisted in 1950s Hollywood as a Communist in the McCarthy era and being under surveillance by the FBI. Planning for Sigal's visit, Sara wrote Dorothy that she had asked her friends the Zoellners (Dick was an art professor, Ruth editor of the *Alumni News*) "to take him about and ply him with liquid refreshment." Her reason? "Alas, my circuit is limited and worse, I am a dry cell, not so much as a glass of beer in fifteen years, for fourteen of which I didn't smoke." What's wonderful about her note is the idea that it's her decision not to drink, not her institutionalization, that would hamper properly entertaining Clancy Sigal. Many years later, Sigal remembered Sara as "a total and wonderful charmer."[2] Meeting one another, they trailed their pasts behind them like streamers. Sara had her journalism and her travel, her plantation and her "unemployment colony," her family history and her Bryce history. Sigal was a radical, an antiwar and civil rights activist, an early advocate of rights for mental patients, an experimenter with LSD, and—along with psychiatrist R. D. Laing in London—a proponent of a radical approach to schizophrenia, treating patients as being in an equal relationship with the therapist. His obituary (he lived to the age of ninety) described him as a "novelist whose life was a tale in itself."[3] Sara and Clancy were from different backgrounds— plantation Alabama and Chicago labor activism—but both of them were natural rebels and questioners. Sara, having recounted to Dorothy what she told Sigal, wrote, "It might be wise for you to warn Mr. Sigal that while I'm Confederate to the bone, my view of the South today is somewhat biased by my hard homemade experience in it." After Sigal's visit to Sara, Dorothy de Santillana wrote to Elise Sanguinetti that he was "deeply impressed by her but found her situation *tragic*."

Sara began to inch closer and closer to leaving. She was still demanding a habeas corpus hearing, which she saw as the best way to clear her name and establish her sanity, and did not want to be merely furloughed. With friends Dick and Ruth Zoellner, she went out to the property she owned, where she had tried her unemployment colony in the thirties, and considered a move to the woods. After all, she wrote Dorothy, "I remember that I have been just as fed up with the avant garde in Paris, London, New York, and San Francisco as I am with the rear garde in Alabama today and the only means of getting away from what strikes me as just as much mass madness on one side of the bars as another, is to have a mile on posted land around you and a river in front and a few handpicked neighbors—with a Walden Pond outside, a Henry James interior, and St. Theresa of Avila sleeping quarters."

The big question for Sara's doctors, now, was how she would manage completely on her own. At Bryce, she followed the routine of the hospital, was given permission to go to campus, and in her free time read, painted, wrote, and listened to music. Even when she was in "the midst of one of those maelstroms of many things into which I seem to have a talent for immersing myself," having some externally imposed structure enhanced her emotional stability. In May 1963 she was allowed to go to Virginia for two weeks to visit her aunt, completely on her own. When she returned, her doctor wrote: "Her condition is considerably improved over what it was when she entered the hospital, although she is still inclined to some paranoid ideation. We would like to see her remain out of the hospital, but for reasons of her own, she refuses to leave without an outright discharge." There is no explanation of why they don't just *make* her leave, but perhaps they were reluctant, after all this time, to simply kick her out into the world on her own. She had become "Miss Sara" to them, well-known and generally well-liked, and they wanted what was best for her and hoped she would come around to their way of thinking. Her guardian, her cousin Henry Mayfield, also wrote a letter attesting his wish that she be released.

While things were beginning to open up for Sara, they had been hard on her dear friend Liz, who had experienced the deaths of all the close male relatives in her life over the course of just a few years: her father in 1958, her brother in 1961, her husband in June 1963, and her father-in-law six months after that, January 1, 1964, a New Year's Day death, like Sara's father. Like Sara's brother, Liz's husband, Wiley, had taken his own life with a gun. Liz had found him early one Sunday morning.[4] Liz wrote to Sara just after New Year's in 1964 that she had gone to Milwaukee to visit relatives just after Christmas, her first without Wiley. And now, "I have just had the news that Wiley's father has just died, . . . one more link with the past. Soon there won't be anyone who remembers *anything* but you and me—." In 1958, when Liz's father had died, she had written to Sara, on the back of the engraved card from the family, "My heart is full of love & gratitude for you but it is bruised & broken & the words won't come. Thank you for your letter & the book. I am lost without my best friend & companion, my strong wall of protection—the curtain has fallen, & there will never be another drama such as we have known—I am grateful that Father died as he lived, simply & with dignity & nobility, & that he did not have to endure the indignities of age & illness."[5] Being Dr. Thigpen's daughter in Montgomery was a source of pride and identity for Liz, and she would have been constantly reminded of his absence after so long a life in one town. A 1950 feature article on Dr. Thigpen in the *Montgomery Advertiser*, as he was about to turn eighty-five, having practiced medicine for fifty-eight years, praised his contribution to Montgomery and to his patients: "The world's greatest physicians sparingly use the word 'great.' Yet they have lavished it upon both the skill and humanity of Charles Alston

Thigpen."[6] Sara was among the few left who could understand what all those losses meant to Liz.

For the rest of 1963, Sara continued to do work at the UA library—an intense, alive creature walking briskly across the invisible line from the hospital grounds onto campus, clad in her trench coat on chilly or damp days. She "slept out" (in the hospital's parlance) with friends or family several nights, and on Christmas Eve 1963 was released into the custody of Sidney Landman and came back to the hospital on Christmas Day. She must have written of Sidney to Liz Hill, because a note in the margin of a letter from Liz to Sara queries "*Who is Sidney?* I think I like him." She even began to contemplate going abroad when she left the hospital, requesting a passport application in March 1964.

She was mostly too busy to "post" her journal, as she called it, but in mid-June 1964 she dated a page "Ward 33, Bryce Hospital, May 25, 1964." Under that, she wrote down a quotation from a recent article in the *Times Literary Supplement*: "Talk to yourself, and people begin to grow concerned. But commune with yourself in writing, and it is quite natural and above suspicion." This she finds quite amusing "in view of the above address." She often had lunch on campus with Sidney and other friends, and enjoyed recalling their dialogue. One day in late spring she wrote, "Had lunch today with Frank Crosby. He and Sidney are so much like men should be—and usually aren't—that I have great affection for them. I told Frank I wished that I had known him twenty years. He said, 'Watch out. There are some wines that age to a peak and then swiftly deteriorate.'" Another day she "said to an English professor friend . . . that with all [Henry] James' insistence on the virtues of gentlemanliness, when you analyze his male characters, they all appear to be a bit caddish. 'I was not aware that there were any real male characters in Henry James,' he said." Those gatherings may not have been the Algonquin Round Table, but they were a far cry from the Bryce cafeteria. Sara's journals more and more became a true record of her days, rather than of her grievances, and on May 30, with a lightness beginning to show up in her entries, she wrote, "Sidney and I had a holiday as the library's closed on Saturday between semesters. So he came for me early this morning and we set off to Sharpe's to get some lobsters for a celebration tomorrow before he goes back to work on his thesis and I go back to *Mona Lisa*." Instead of writing in her room on either the latest revision of "Mona Lisa" or her "Constant Circle" literary memoir, she read a biography of Catherine the Great in the afternoon, and then went to the Landmans', where she broiled the lobsters and Mrs. Landman prepared broccoli, tomato salad, hot rolls, and strawberry shortcake. A feast.

Sara sent news of her writing life to the *Goucher Alumnae Quarterly*. Appearing in the summer 1964 issue, which made no mention of where she lived, was the note, "At the U. of Alabama, *Sara Mayfield* is editing the letters of Sara and Henry Mencken that were among her papers when the librarian at the university asked her to give them to the manuscript room there. As soon as she has finished this work, Sara hopes to get away to England to continue some research there." There's so much hope in that "hopes." Sara's agent, Lurton Blassingame, wrote in the spring of 1964 about possible projects she was working on, with the understanding that she was about to be discharged: "I am glad to learn about your impending release from Bryce. You write very well and I hope that freedom will enable you to develop the career for which you have such real talent." Throughout his correspondence with Sara, Blassingame treated her work seriously, praising what worked and critiquing what didn't, making plans for approaching journals and publishing houses with her work.

Sara thought of herself, always, as a writer, and studied the books she read for what she could learn from them. On the last day of May, she was reading Henry James's preface to *The Princess Casamassima* and thinking about her own writing: "James says . . . 'that clearness and concreteness constantly depend, for any pictorial whole, on some individual notation of them.' . . . That is, I suppose, upon a 'point of view,' an organizing of sensations, events, etc., around a foreground observer." Another day she was reading James's prefaces to the New York edition of his works, and commented that they "are not easy to read; there are barren stretches and thickets of overemphasis . . . but here and there one finds splendid things that give a writer pause such as; in the preface to The Awkward Age: 'Remember,' they say to the dramatist, 'That you have to be, supremely, three things: you have to be true to your form, you have to be interesting, you have to be clear.'"

Lurton Blassingame had written encouragingly of her "Constant Circle" manuscript that he believed it should be published, with a focus on Mencken and a major reduction of material about her own life, and saving the material on the Fitzgeralds for another book, and she had taken his comments to heart and worked hard on cutting the manuscript to a manageable, publishable size. In June 1964, she received permission to take a trip to the Humanities Research Center at the University of Texas in Austin to use materials there related to "The Constant Circle." She went to Austin by herself to work on her book and was there long enough to receive mail. Sidney Landman wrote, "The library staff members miss you and have inquired of your doings." She returned to Bryce with more plans for research travel; Dr. Darden, after receiving a note from the social services department at the hospital requesting his permission for Sara to make a trip to Princeton, Yale, and Cornell, typed a succinct note in return: "Attention is called to my current note of Aug. 11, 1964. It certainly is all right for Sarah to go on the trip, and I wish she would stay. But she won't."

Although Sara clearly was better, she still was prone to mistaken interpretations of what people said and did, in ways that were hard to put into words. In the fall of 1963 Dr. Hoole wrote her that she would need to move from the room she was using in the library and work in a different room. A year later, as Dr. Darden's progress note from December 21, 1964, describes it: "For about four years Sarah has been going over to the Library at the University and doing some work on organizing some letters on H. L. Mencken that she had. She has in the mean time gotten into various other projects over there which were not associated with her original one. The original plan was for her to spend three months over there and this was arranged with the agreement of Dr. Hoole. Dr. Hoole called me recently and discussed the situation with me. He was somewhat concerned because Sarah has gotten into various other projects during these four years, and he felt that she was interfering to some extent with the functioning of the personnel, etc. at the Library. He said that Sarah would stop him rather frequently and tell him that she was working on a certain project that he had asked her to do, whereas Dr. Hoole said that he did not ask her to do any project. He said that Sarah had simply branched out into various other things and that it had gotten so complicated it was difficult to put one's finger on any one thing. He said that Sara was not actually causing any trouble at all but that she simply 'usurped.' He said that she would move into space that had been reserved for faculty or other personnel and then she would just more or less take over certain things and certain areas. He asked that, if possible we terminate this arrangement without hurting Sarah's feelings. He had told Sarah a couple of weeks ago that he was concerned about being somewhat of a 'guardian' over her as she worked over there, so I approached it from that angle. I told Sarah of Dr. Hoole's concern, that he was considered somewhat her 'guardian.' Sarah was quite gracious about it, as she is everything else, and wrote me a letter dated December 12, which I have placed on file. He permitted Sarah to spend a few days winding up what she had to do over there and she is now staying on the ward and following the routine of all the other patients. We have terminated this arrangement for her to go over to the library." The affection that both men felt for Sara shows in their reluctance to hurt her feelings and their agreement to come up with a plausible excuse for her removal.

On December 14 Sara wrote Dr. Hoole that she would stop going to the library now that she had finished her work, primarily so that she would not put him in a difficult position by making him vulnerable to harassment by her enemies. But after four years of going to the library and feeling the sense of freedom that being on a college campus can bring, going back to the routine of the hospital was confining. It felt like a step backward, when she had been so convinced she was moving forward. Taking encouragement, however, from the acceptance of an excerpt from her book on Mencken for the 1965–66 *Fitzgerald Newsletter*, Sara persisted in her work, even though she felt, as she wrote to Norman Moon, a lawyer she had contacted, that "the inquisition has been turned on full blast for some weeks now."[7] Dr. Darden's December 22, 1964, entry gives some idea of the way information that entered Sara's mind could take some detours and come out somewhere entirely different. Darden writes that he is enclosing a letter of Sara's in the files, one of the many he receives from her, because it gives "a pretty good idea of just what her present mental state is." He continues, "In the first part of the second paragraph it is interesting to note the comments she makes about my letter of October 28, 1964, to Mr. Moon. Mr. Moon had sent her a copy of it. From our letter to Mr. Moon, Sarah has the opinion that we think she is of sane mind, sound body, that she has violated no laws and that she has done nothing for which she could be committed to this hospital either before or since she was committed. It is interesting that Sarah gets this interpretation of my letter as none of these things are commented on in the letter. . . . She [also] makes the comment that she is inclined to think the bar association must be investigating the situation in some way. . . . These things and other comments she makes give a pretty good idea of her interpretations of various things."[8]

Christmas and New Year's passed, and in February 1965 she was still working away on "The Constant Circle" on a rickety wooden table next to her bed, papers and books spread all around her. She did find time to go to a group therapy class, where they discussed taking responsibility for one's emotions and managing one's thoughts. She noted in her journal that the discussion was remarkably sensible, "more practical and helpful to anyone with emotional problems than the year of psychoanalysis that I had . . . at the University of London and I told Dr. Darden to tell Mrs. Meighan so." In the next class, Sara took notes on the ways in which self- and world-perception affect actions and emotions, essentially a cognitive-behavioral approach to mental health, summarizing that "the nut of what Mrs. Meighan advocates, I take it is constructive introspection."

Pondering her situation, inching closer to accommodating herself to leaving the hospital for good, even if it was on their terms, she attended two special events: a concert by Carlos Montoya ("a gnome of a man and a flamenco wizard") and a lecture by Eudora Welty on "fiction-writing in the South." Before Welty's lecture, Sidney took her to the University Club, a big white antebellum, Greek Revival building about a mile from the UA campus. She reflected on being away from the hospital: "It was very odd and very gay to [be] sitting in a bar again, even if I could only have a seven-up while Sidney had bourbon and branch water. But there was a cherry in the 7-up and popcorn on the table and plenty of literary and academic gossip to compensate for lack of other stimulants."

On February 17 she went to another therapy lecture, summing it up with the teacher's words: "Thinking is just talking to yourself. . . . We want to impress upon you that you *can* do something about your problems. But only you can do it." Even though she seemed to admit that some of what was said by the therapists could be useful, she scorned their lack of knowledge, from the inside, of what it means to be a psychiatric patient: "They don't know what they're talking about. They have no conception of the fear and anger aroused by sudden commitment. They are paid by the hospital and their efforts are devoted to trying to brainwash the patients [into] accepting the hospital's point of view and they have no desire to see the patient's point of view and no remote conception of it." The last words in that journal entry, February 17, 1965, would be the last entry ever in her Bryce journals: "no one should be allowed to practice psychiatry or psychology who has not been suddenly committed or subjected to the same restrictions and inquisition to which patients are subjected."

On February 18 she wrote a fairly mundane letter to Sidney Landman, thanking him for dropping by a copy of the *Saturday Evening Post* and some of his mother's peanut brittle, asking him to pick up a new typewriter ribbon for her, telling him about her schedule of discussion group, music study, and sewing, and complaining about Bryce, from the food: "cold oatmeal, half-baked potatoes, and God save the mark: french fried carrots," to the lack of heating: "it's so cold here that my fingers are too numb to hit the keys—or at least the right keys." She said nothing about leaving. But then, on the night of February 24, less than a month short of her seventeenth anniversary in Bryce, she carefully folded her clothes, packed them and her books, papers, and camera equipment into her two suitcases, tucked keepsakes and artwork and photos into the nooks and crannies, set her two guitars beside her, and waited.

In her patient note for February 25, 1965, her doctor wrote: "When I made rounds yesterday morning, I found Sarah with her bags and things by her bed. She said that she was ready to leave. I was quite surprised as we have been trying to get Sarah to leave the hospital for years, but she had steadfastly refused to do so unless released on a discharge basis." He goes on to write that a friend of Sara's—almost certainly Sidney—had recently asked him about her status and then had spoken with Sara; apparently Sidney managed to convince her to leave the hospital and worry about clearing her record afterward. If any one great moment of revelation or alteration of thought came to Sara, it went unrecorded. Instead, it seems that a combination of factors—friendships, with the Rosenbaums, professors and students, and Sidney and his mother; the encouragement of Dr. Hoole and the intellectual engagement she felt in working on her papers, reviewing her own life and what she had been through, along with the hope of publishing a book; and some inward shift toward the present and the future, the feeling, in the year she would turn sixty, of it being time, past time, to live whatever years she had left on her own terms—caused her to decide to leave. If it had been necessary for Sara to accept "the hospital's point of view," she never would have been released. But the psychiatrists—even knowing that she might never relinquish her belief in a conspiracy—thought she would be all right on the outside.

The rest of the doctor's note reads, "Released on trial visit from Ward 33 to her own custody. She plans to go to . . . Princeton where she will continue her research on the Mencken papers and the various other things that she has under way." Sara had work to do, and friends, and she summoned her good sense and her courage and took her final drive down the long alley of oaks, away from what had functioned as her home for seventeen years.

Chapter 14

"Free, Clean, and Clear after All These Years"

*Relating the Establishment of a New Life, and Sundry Travels to complete
her Book on the Menckens. Sara resumes Control of her Finances and Living
Arrangements but not the Close Connection she craves with an Old Friend.*

H AVING AT LONG LAST LEFT HER LIFE IN BRYCE BEHIND, SARA LET
it be known around town in Tuscaloosa that, a few weeks after her
commitment in 1948, the doctors had determined that she was perfectly
sane, and that she had basically only *slept* at Bryce during her seventeen-year
stay there, being free to do as she pleased during the day. Although letters to
close friends, and even some unpublished written material, refer to her years
in Bryce, one letter to Betty Adler of the Enoch Pratt Free Library in Baltimore, written shortly after her release, included a brief biographical note
stating that she had been involved in "research in contemporary literature,
1948–1965." (It's unclear exactly at what point in their correspondence Betty
learned she was at Bryce; Sara wrote her about her Mencken research as early
as 1961, with the return address of her PO box at the university, and one letter from Betty asked, "Do you teach?")

Another story of Sara's release that circulated was that she had written
John F. Kennedy after he was elected president and that, three days later, with
the final word coming from the newly elected governor, George Wallace, she
was out of Bryce. The chronology is off (Kennedy was elected in 1960 and as-
sassinated in 1963, and Wallace became governor in 1963, whereas Sara left
the hospital in 1965), but Sara's spin is evident—and she *did* write to Wallace
about getting a habeas corpus hearing. Kennedy's signing of the Community
Mental Health Act in 1963 may have connected him in her mind to the idea

of patients being released into the community, and Sara *had* met the young Jack Kennedy years ago in San Francisco.

Upon leaving the hospital, Sara was determined to hit the ground running. After the trip to Princeton, where she visited in the library with Carlos Baker, the Hemingway biographer, she went to Baltimore for the summer to read through the Mencken collection at the Pratt Library. She found an apartment in the Rochambeau Building, built the year of her birth, 1905, which she described in a letter as "old and Baltimorish—but so am I—it's [*sic*] chief virtue is that it's only a block from the library. . . . I'm now in the process of having the woodwork washed and the venetian blinds cleaned—apparently the first time it's been done since General Rochambeau camped there in 1782." In Baltimore she finally met librarian Betty Adler, whose *HLM: The Mencken Bibliography*, had come out in 1961. An undated letter from Betty exclaims, "Thanks for a delightful afternoon! You were just as I had pictured—vivacious, charming & so intelligent! Do come back soon again."

Princeton. Baltimore. Not, ever again, Bryce. An apartment to which only she had the keys, control over what she ate, whom she saw, when she went out and when she came in. The simple act of making a piece of toast and a cup of coffee in her own kitchen felt like freedom. Nor does there seem to have been any Rip Van Winkle effect: while in Bryce, she had kept up with what was going on in the world, and she had been "out" on visits to friends and family. Most importantly, she had never stopped being Sara, even in the worst days when her paranoia and delusions rattled her to the point of fury. She was always herself; now she was more able to set aside the thoughts of persecution in favor of living in the present. In December 1965, with a contract for "The Constant Circle" in hand, Sara declared to her agent, Lurton Blassingame, "You are marvelous! And I can never tell you how much I appreciate your sticking by me through this long, dark, unprofitable valley. What *do* you mean 'the best terms' you could get? Just between us, they are three times my wildest expectation."

As a young girl, an adult, and even throughout the years in Bryce, Sara had paid careful attention to her finances, never losing the ability to keep detailed accounts of her incoming and outgoing funds. Released from Bryce, she meant to live on what she had, primarily income from investments, and in March 1965 she wrote her cousin and guardian Henry via his secretary, Barbara, requesting that they send her a cashier's check for $350.00 each month, as that amount "is about the minimum on which I can get by with for room, food, supplies, photostats, stationary [*sic*], cosmetics, transportation, etc.—and far from the lap of luxury at that." From Baltimore, she wrote them with an update on her life there: "Between the heat and the work, I feel like a cross between a potato in a steamer and an orange in a reamer."

She pushed herself to work hard, but not too hard, writing to a friend, "There is little to report here. I train like an athlete, live like a Christian, and work like a fiend." From her room, she pondered not only the biography she was finishing but the nature of reality and truth, writing that there is nothing "so conducive to cold, hard realistic thinking as the four bare walls of a hotel apartment." She continued in a philosophical vein: "'What is truth?' Old Dr. Williams used to say the historical variety was constituted by any fact attested to by two independent witnesses. This seems a facile definition applied to biography. But then what is the truth of any human life?" Shifting to a more humorous vein, she noted that her sitting room in the hotel overlooked "the Cardinal's residence. . . . On Mondays, when I look out and see the good sisters hanging the Cardinal's blue and white striped—well, it would seem irreverent to be more specific—out on the line, I am reminded that not only is this a man's world but there are alarming indications that the next is also likewise arranged."

Sara fell back into some of the old patterns of her Goucher days, socializing with visiting literati and then reporting to friends on her encounters. In a letter sizzling with Dorothy Parker wit, she wrote to her old friend Dorothy de Santillana, "We had a visit from Allen Tate last month. I'd never met him before—and wish I never had; he was so drained, bloodless, emaciated, and mousy, mentally and physically, that if he is the voice of the South, what the South needs is Geritol and lots of it." When the annual open day for the Mencken Room at the Enoch Pratt Library came, on September 11 (as it happened, Mencken's and Sara's "shared" birthday), Sara was there, chatting with Betty Adler and others, "a small woman with white hair and wide, quick smile," as a journalist described her. He noted that she has "done her best to get other initiates to think of H. L. Mencken neither as a disturber of the peace nor as irreverent (among usual labels) but as a setter and preserver of standards—an Old Defender."[1] The night before, Betty had given her a birthday dinner, which Sara deemed "a rare treat and each course . . . a culinary marvel." The day after the Mencken celebration, she reached a milestone, finishing her rewrite of "The Constant Circle" "just before midnight on September 12." It left her, she said, "more dead than alive" from the strain of writing about people she cared for so much, "reaming it out from so close to the heart." Betty Adler, who had seen Carl Bode at work at the Enoch Pratt on *his* Mencken biography, cheered her on in the race to finish first: "Bode and I don't communicate, so I do not know what is being done on Olympus. Far too lowly to be told."

With work on "The Constant Circle" nearing completion, Sara turned to her other job, an essential one as she saw it: to clear her name. In late September she wrote to her cousin Henry: "When I left, you told me that the

FIGURE 19. H. L. (Henry Louis) and Sara Haardt Mencken

H. L. (Henry Louis) and Sara Haardt Mencken in a December 1933 photograph taken for use in their passports prior to a 1934 Mediterranean cruise. Sara Mencken died in 1935, leaving her husband and her old friend Sara Mayfield bereft. In 1968 Sara published her literary memoir of the two, *The Constant Circle*. (Courtesy of Enoch Pratt Free Library, Maryland's State Library Resource Center)

outcome was up to me. Now that I've lived over six months on the outside, accomplished what I set out to do and more, stuck to what the Episcopalians call 'a sober righteous and godly life,' avoided entangling alliances, medication of any type, strong waters, driving a car, going out unescorted in the evening, radical groups, dissentions [*sic*], or anything that might cause trouble or criticism, lived within my allowance and saved about $600.00 of it, let's begin to figure out the next step." She dreaded going back to Tuscaloosa, though, and told her friends so. When she got back home, she found a note that the thoughtful Betty Adler had mailed before Sara even left Baltimore: "Hello Sara! You are still in town, but as your home coming sounded unjoyous, wanted at least one welcome note to greet you."

She hired a lawyer to have the Letters of Guardianship revoked, and in December 1965 her doctors submitted letters to the probate judge of Tuscaloosa County. One is signed by the doctor she saw as her old nemesis, J. S. Tarwater, the superintendent of Bryce, and states, "This is to certify that Sara Martin Mayfield of the County of Tuscaloosa, State of Alabama, was released from the Bryce Hospital, Tuscaloosa, Alabama, February 25, 1965, having been restored to sanity." When the good news came through, Sara practically shouted it from the rooftops. On March 4, 1966, she wrote two of her longtime friends, *Baltimore Sun* journalist R. P. (Robin) Harriss and his wife, Margery. They had been wonderfully supportive, even offering to get her a job teaching at the school at which Margery was principal. Sara cheered: "To borrow an old cliché, 'I want you to be the first to know': my lawyer has just called to say that the lunacy proceedings have been revoked, the inquisition and the guardianship lifted, and my disabilities completely removed. And I can never tell you how much I appreciate your loyalty, friendship, and encouragement in the long, hard fight to have it done." Sara dedicated *The Constant Circle* to Robin and Margery, "most constant of the constant circle," in gratitude. She also wrote to Betty in Baltimore, and to her agent, Lurton Blassingame, with the same information, adding, "Imagine being free, clean, and clear after all these years—with no time to celebrate on anything but the typewriter and Buffalo Rock." On March 8, 1966, Blassingame wrote back, saying, "Certainly I'm pleased to hear the good news you got from your lawyer. If you were here I'd treat you to a glass of champagne in celebration." With her name, and the question of her sanity, cleared, Sara felt free to work, travel, give parties, make friends—to enjoy all the pleasures of an unencumbered existence. The Lustig sisters, who owned the bookstore she often ordered from while in Bryce, had been her friends for many years, and in a thank-you note for a birthday present, Maxine wrote, "Words cannot tell how proud I am of you and how wonderful I hope your future will be. Your genius is equalled only by your beautiful spirit and sweetness. I will enjoy my lovely red wool scarf for a long time to come. I have enjoyed your love and friendship most of my life—Thank you for so much."

In Tuscaloosa, Sara first rented a small house at 605 Fifteenth Avenue, across the street from her cousin-in-law, Cannie Mayfield, and about a block south of University Boulevard, near the UA campus, so that she could walk wherever she needed to go. Not certain that she would stay in Tuscaloosa, she meant initially to tie up some loose ends, writing to a relative that she had "taken a small apartment here to try to collect my scattered effects and un-snarl my tangled affairs." To Robin and Margery, who had advised against her staying in Tuscaloosa, she explained, "The only thing to be gained by it is the control of my property and the knowledge that I had the visceral fortitude to come back and run the gauntlet."

A friend from those days described her apartment as "clean and nice"; it was cozy as well, with gas space heaters to keep off the chill. She endured "the infernal paperhangers" in order to have nice wallpaper put up, and for decoration she set out sculptures she had made at Bryce, including one of a white swan. Maxine Lustig wrote Sara, "I feel so good about you when I think of you in your lovely apartment and surrounded by your devoted friends who love you and safe now. Isn't it wonderful?" As a gesture of hope-fulness, Sara planted a dogwood tree in her front yard. She looked out on it from her study in the front bedroom.

The family home, Idlewyld, had been sold around 1963, with James's for-mer wife, Janette, and James's executor, Burdette Mayfield, asserting that a buyer had been found who would purchase the house for $11,000, considered a fair price in that, as their legal language expressed the case: "the house lo-cated thereon is old and in a bad state of repair and that the best interests of the beneficiaries under said last will and testament of James J. Mayfield, Jr. would be best served by converting said real estate into the aforesaid amount of cash."[2] On the mistaken assumption that, after fifteen years at Bryce, Sara was a permanent patient, items in the house had been given away or sold as well. When she surprised everyone by leaving Bryce, Sara did her best to recover what family items she could. She wrote one relative, "I'd appreciate it if you would return my silver pitcher and the family portraits that Honey took to Virginia." This must be the most awkward letter a southern lady could imagine writing: *Please return my belongings you purchased/took/were given while*

I was in the mental hospital. An American Empire sofa, a sideboard, a decorative Coromandel lacquer screen, and her mother's silver and crystal were among the items that she retrieved.

In Sara's version of what happened with Idlewyld, "When public sentiment began to press for my release, they [the First National Bank], had the furniture, rugs, drapes, linens, etc. in Idlewyld, my mother's home sold, despite the fact that they were heirlooms and irreplaceable [*sic*] for the most part, and belonged to me personally, not my mother. They then tore down a brick cottage we owned brick by brick, left Idlewyld open to be looted and sacked, and refused to release me 'because I had no place to go.'" Among the lost items was a compact on which Zelda had painted the capitol in Montgomery; Sara had been "advised to keep [it] in a bank vault" but didn't. Sara always tried to keep a sense of humor, and when Sidney Landman wrote her in the summer of 1965 that a beauty parlor had been opened up in Idlewyld, Sara wrote back that "what you have to say . . . amused me very much. At that, it's better than having it turned into a mortuary chapel."

Sara had tried to stay on good terms with her former sister-in-law, Janette, writing her a chatty letter from Baltimore about her research in the summer of 1965. That fall, the tone of things changed. Sara wrote her in late 1965 that she hoped they could reach a settlement and avoid going to court, but she eventually retained a lawyer to communicate with Janette when no settlement was reached. By the end of the year Sara was writing to ask that her daybed be returned "at once" and referring to "a list of things of mine missing from Idlewyld" that she would be turning over to the lawyers. A letter to her attorney in 1966 refers to items "for which Janette should be held responsible." In October 1967 another lawyer in the same firm wrote to Janette requesting that they meet to discuss "an accounting concerning certain property belonging to Miss Mayfield which was removed from the house at Idlewyld during the period of her incompetency . . . and perhaps avoid the necessity for any legal action." By February 1968, three years down the road and beginning to enter *Bleak House* territory, she had her lawyer file a lawsuit to recover Sara's property, and eventually the parties agreed to settle. On March 12, 1971, her lawyer wrote to Sara: "The Circuit Clerk has released to us the $500.00 deposit made by Janette and the First National Bank in payment of our recent consent judgment." He closed by saying that "it was a delight to work with you on this case."

Lawsuits between family members are never pretty, and Sara wished to avoid any such wrangling after her own death. After her disagreement with

Janette, Sara requested of cousins that, should a "fatal accident" befall her, they clear out her apartment and store her belongings before notifying anyone, "so there will be no argument" over her estate. With her sanity declared, Sara also did what a person "of sound mind" is allowed to do: make a will, so that her wishes would be known. Dated September 1, 1966, just before her sixty-first birthday, the will covers bequests of money (a thousand dollars each to four friends and a cousin); family treasures—portraits, silver, furniture; and literary rights, mineral rights, and real estate, with her cousin Henry Mayfield receiving the bulk of the estate. To her young nephew, Jeff—James Jefferson Mayfield IV—she left "the sum of one dollar in hand and one silver mustard spoon belonging to my mother, Susie Fitts Martin Mayfield, and the portrait of James Jefferson Mayfield."

Out of long habit and even friendship, she kept in touch with Bryce's Dr. Darden. In one letter sent from Princeton, she let him know that she had changed addresses to a more affordable hotel. She continued, "You can't know how wonderful it is to be free, to be back in one's own world, and to be among old friends. All goes well with me and I hope with you." In January 1966 she sent him a letter with an article about her work on the Mencken book. He responded, "Dear Cousin Sara," (continuing their old joke), "Your recent letter was much appreciated" and closed with the hope that she should feel free to call on him if he could ever be of "any further help." He had enjoyed reading the article and reflected that "as a result of our 'association' over the past years, I felt that I had somewhat of a part in this. And I must add that I feel that as a result of my association with you over these years, I feel that I have a much better rounded 'education.' My friendship with you has certainly been most rewarding to me and most pleasant." Sara wanted Sam Darden to know that she was doing well, and he was at pains to let her know that he recognized that and admired it.

With a sense of starting afresh, Sara hoped for a closer relationship with the one constant in her life, the friend Sara valued more than any other, Elisabeth Thigpen Hill. Through everything, from their youthful travels through Europe with Miss Margaret Booth, Sara's father's death, her various jobs and travels, from her first commitment and through World War II, and then all through the long seventeen years at Bryce, Sara had remained friends with Elisabeth, whom she addressed as "Liz," "B," and "Seraphim." Liz, for her part, was a stalwart friend to Sara, even with Liz's many familial and social commitments in Montgomery—a life Sara might have led if she had stayed in the capital city: marrying, having children, serving on the altar guild at church, joining the various clubs expected of a woman of her station. The friendship survived thanks to a mutual commitment to their shared history, their mothers' friendship, and the way, as Sara described it, their mothers "knotted our heartstrings together."

Sometime in the mid- to late sixties, Sara wrote Liz after a visit to Montgomery for Liz's birthday: "Standing there on the porch at 1412, I knew that I had come a full circle. The spark that ultimately led to the Light, the gleam that I had to follow until I found the Grail were kindled in the House of Thee-and-I but I had to spend almost forty years in the Wilderness searching before I was 'free' to turn back." To Sara, her friendship with Liz was a refuge, "the House of Thee-and-I" in which she could rest and feel secure, and securely loved for who she truly was. This letter was significant in its assertion that "with each succeeding year, . . . I love you more," but it was far from singular; from January of 1966 through to the end of the year, Sara wrote a series of intimate letters to her old friend. In part, Sara wanted to come to the rescue of Liz in her melancholy state, as she grieved the deaths of family members in recent years, and she wrote Liz urging her to come to Tuscaloosa for a visit and stay with her: "If you want to come here and hole up in splendid isolation upstairs, why don't you do it? I'll lay in a stock of books and records for you, send up your meals, and you won't have to come out of the silences until your mind changes." Her apartment, she says, is "a simple place" and she lives "a simple academic life"; she doesn't know whether a visit would be "a relief and refuge from the complexities of your menage and the complications of your life" but she urges Liz to at least try a change of locale to lift her spirits. As she wrote the letter, Sidney was there as well, working away on revising his dissertation, interrupting her with questions which she humorously parodied for Liz. She was still typing on Calvin Coolidge, the ancient Corona. In February, Liz was still blue, and Sara encouraged her: "You have everything in the world to live for and there are too many people who love you and need you for you to sink into despair, 'the Sickness unto Death,' as Kierkegaard calls it." Sara had learned to wear a mask to cover her troubles, but she was not sure she'd advise Liz to: "The sheer physical effort of pretending to be blythe [sic] and amiable while I run the gauntlet here leaves me so limp and exhausted that I fall asleep over the first paragraph of Aristotle at bedtime."

Over the winter, Liz planned to come up with Rosalind, Zelda's sister, but warned Sara, who was now working on the book about the Fitzgeralds with material culled from the original manuscript of her literary memoir,

"She doesn't think she can agree to another book as that wretched Nancy Milford has almost driven her nuts." (Sara had learned in the last year that Milford was writing a book on Zelda.) Liz herself didn't want to agree to much: "I don't mean to be uncooperative about the 20s—I just want to remain anonymous and stay in the recluse role as it's easier that way." For Sara the biographer, using old friends as sources was a tricky business, balancing the need for information and timely communication with the old ties of emotion and history that bound them.

In March she once again invited Liz to visit: "If the silver is not polished, the place is littered with books and papers, and I'm working in a sweater and old slacks, you can forgive and forget in view of the fact that I love you and want to see you too much to stand on ceremony—after some fifty-seven years with you all the way from Roma to Napoli, not to mention the tin tub in the pension in Firenze." A check for fifty dollars, "a belated Xmas present," accompanied one of Liz's letters, with the imperative, "If you want to please me *use* it." But Sara left the check uncashed.

For several years, as she worked on her books, in various stages, Sara continued to worry about Liz, to Liz herself and to their mutual friend Dorothy de Santillana. Sara wrote Dorothy in July 1966 that "Thigpen" and her brother had traveled to Boston for his Harvard class reunion, of which Sara wrote she could "think of nothing more depressing . . . and not exactly what the doctor ordered for E.T.H., who, after a series of major tragedies, is not far from becoming an emotional basket case as it is." The letters continued off and on, but by September 1966 took a very different tone. Sara took umbrage at one of Liz's responses and typed a tragic epitaph to their friendship: "We've come a long way together. After almost sixty years, it's hard to realize that we've come to the end of the road and the parting of the ways. . . . My first and great mistake was ever to have come back to Alabama; and my second was to try to salvage, at least, the spirit of the Buried Life; but obviously it, too, is dead and buried under the wreckage of—well that, likewise, was doubtless, as you see it now, a 'fictitious memory,' and so, I take it, was all in which the letters I wrote you in that vain salvage attempt were rooted." She asked Liz to burn her letters, and instead of her usual, "Thine," she signs off "Adieu." Liz wrote back that they had *not* come to "a parting of the ways" but that she must attend to her many family responsibilities: "I do the best I can. I forget nothing of what has been but if I didn't put the pedestrian in between me & that I would go insane—the bonds between you & me are the same as always. I remember all the little high moments of Daisy &

Susie—I remember most of what you do—but I cannot live that past every hour of my life."

A week later, Sara wrote back apologizing for her dramatics, insisting that she had signed off "A Dieu," and that she would always be there for Liz, but if "A Dieu" "is too similar to adieu, *vaya con Dios*." By way of explanation, Sara wrote that she understood Liz was "toting a weary load, on a rough road, in a troubled time," and that Sara herself was in "an extremely trying, crucial time, in which, Alger-fashion, I have to do or die." Trying to get Liz to revisit their happy past or re-create a happy present only creates the "heartsickness of hope deferred." She reminded Liz, "Remember that for over half a century I've given you absolute love, loyalty, and devotion of a kind that I never gave anyone else, and I doubt that anyone outside your immediate family ever gave you. And I'm too old to change, even if I wanted to, which I don't."

After that, she continued writing Liz with affection and, sometimes, longing. In 1966, Sara went to Montgomery at Christmastime and saw her, and writing afterward was filled with joy at the recollection: "Just in the moment, as you came in the door, there was an epiphany of something that has gone out of life, a brief, bright glow of happiness unalloyed, pure, sheer joy. The sight of your beloved face, the sound of your voice, the touch of your hand dispelled something that I don't know how to describe except as an idleness of the heart—a state in which one simply goes through the motions, living and loving, working and playing, but not really caring." As the spring of 1967 came, she daydreamed, "I wish that I were stretched out on the earth beside you under a pine tree, with the warm spring sun on my back, the aromatic smell of the needles in the air, and not a sound except the song of the river from the spillway and a mockingbird in the distance." At 4:30 in the morning on New Year's Day, 1968, she wrote Liz that she was living a "Spartan life" but found it "much happier than living on the kind of whirligig I did last fall. I had done with the Romeos a long time ago and last year I had done with the razzledazzle, the rat race, the jet set, and a great many other things, including the wanderlust. All in the world that I really want to do is live in peace and quiet and be with you. For, in the course of the shucking-off process, I realized how much you mean to me since you're the only person now living who knows and loves the things that I know and love and who is part of that inner life. So, bright and early, I begin the New Year right by putting the first things first and writing you." Liz, Sara wrote, was "the one person left who can speak my patois." A year later she wrote after seeing Elisabeth and going to a movie together that "I loved the evening with you 'thee and

I alone.' It was like the good gone times, and the balm of Gilead to my harried soul. *Lion in Winter* was fine, and I enjoyed it almost as much as I did sitting in silence beside you." (Perhaps inadvertently, perhaps intentionally, Sara echoed a phrase of Scott and Zelda's—"the good gone times," from their jointly credited story "Show Mr. and Mrs. F to Number—.")

In June 1969 she summarized their friendship: "You are always in my thoughts and prayers. You and I will always keep keeping on come whatever catastrophes may befall us." Two years later she struck a similar note, continuing to worry over their closeness like picking at a loose thread on a dress: "Since Aunt Lyda's and Lucia's deaths, you mean more to me than anyone ever can or will, so I hope 'there's nothing wrong with our friendship,' as you say." That November, she said more plainly than ever before how she felt about Liz: "Do you remember when in this paper hurricane which swirls around me I put a carbon of a letter to you about burning my letters, keeping the House of Thee-and-I sacrosanct, etc. in a letter to Dorothy Tilton. It was the only [time] I have ever referred to it to anyone but [you] who wasn't part of it and that was inadvertant [*sic*]. Tilton called me from Boston to tell me what had happened. Then she said 'My God, Mayfield, I've known you for fifty years and this is the first time I've ever had any inkling of what was behind that stone wall inside of you.' It's just one of those things I feel too deeply and too intensely about to put the feeling into words. I can't even explain it; I only know that it's very real; and that, as ever, I'm very muchly Thine."

It may have been exhilarating, but it also must have been exhausting, to be loved so utterly and emphatically by Sara. She let so few people see her real self, and when she dropped "the mask" she was naked in her love. Elisabeth could not possibly have responded with the force Sara wished for.

Chapter 15

"A Hardworking Scrivener"

Treats primarily of Sara's Literary Life and Work. The Constant Circle *is
published to Good Reviews. A Trip to Europe for Research and Pleasure.*

I N THE ABSENCE OF THE INTENSE EMOTIONAL CONNECTION SHE SOUGHT
with Liz, Sara, as always, had resorted to work. Describing herself as "a
hardworking scrivener," she would publish the book about the Menckens,
The Constant Circle, in 1968. *Exiles from Paradise*, on the Fitzgeralds, would
come out in 1971, and *Mona Lisa: The Woman in the Portrait*, in 1974. Her
books were meticulously researched, extensively revised, and given to numerous readers for their comments before publication. The last to come out, the
Mona Lisa novel, was the one she had worked on the longest. Indeed, before *The Constant Circle* came out, Sara had actually hoped to have a novel as
her debut book, worrying to her editor that "I'd rather pull myself out of the
wreckage by my own bootstraps than by the coattails of people I once knew."

She had originally intended a single comprehensive literary memoir, but
in consultation with her agent decided to focus on the Menckens in one
book, the Fitzgeralds in another, and take much of her own personal history
out of both, except as it related to her main subject. They both agreed the
Mencken book had a better chance of being accepted, so she worked to bring
it to completion first. When she wrote to a friend in the spring of 1966 to
thank him for reading the manuscript, she described how she was beyond
ready to be finished: "I've labored over it so long, and am so sick of it that
I turn green at the sight of it, having just been through it twice, cutting out
my personal history, everywhere I could—the inventions, the Sheppard-Pratt,
the V-Campaign, the mystery weapons, the Chapultepec and San Francisco

conferences, etc. . . . . It struck me as irrevalent [*sic*], immaterial, and deterent [*sic*] to the unity of the book, so I asked permission to cut it all out and I feel that the C.C. is a far better book without it and in much better taste. My agent suggests making another book of it. But not for all the gold in Golconda!" She both loved and tormented herself over her work, writing to friends that "there is just one dirtier word in the English language than 'write,' that is 'rewrite.'"

In May 1966, as part of the process leading up to the publication of *The Constant Circle*, Sara's editor at Delacorte, Richard Kennedy, came to Tuscaloosa for several days, and he and Sara cut some 150 pages from the manuscript to make it less academic and more of a book for a general readership. It was difficult work, but Sara warmed to Kennedy, writing her agent that "I liked him so much, both professionally and personally—and learned a great deal from him." She saw that he was properly hosted, having cocktails and dinner with her philosophy professor friend Bill McMinn and his wife; a luncheon with English professor Thomas Rountree; tea at the elegant, Swedish-style home of Hudson and Therese Strode; and a sightseeing tour of the town with young poet John Finlay.

It wasn't always easy to balance her writing life with her life life, as she wrote to a friend while she was completing *The Constant Circle*: "It never fails that when anyone is trying to make a deadline, everything that can happen does. In the midst of trying to get the C.C. off to the publishers, we had a blizzard, the typist, the proof-readers and I were all snowbound. The thaw brought a succession of plumbers, painters, and carpenters, whose activities and mine were complicated by a procession of visitors. Then we had an Arts Festival, then we had Mrs. [Lyndon B.] Johnson, now my aunt is coming, my typist is ill, felled by the flu epidemic—in short, since the day my agent wired me he'd sold the book, there's been a serialized production of Hellzapoppin going on here."

With her friendships in the English Department and in town, Sara was often included in local literary events. She met and visited with Robert Penn Warren when he spoke at the university, but she found both his discussion of his poetry and his conversation at the party afterward "tedious." She wrote Liz Hill about the cake someone had ordered for the occasion, describing it as "a culinary monstrosity in the form of a great book, one page of which were the titles of his novels and on the other his name, writ bold in box car letters." Although she enjoyed being a part of things, she at least sometimes felt she would rather be around "well-bred" people than the "beatnik intellectuals" of academia.

Sara corresponded with literary critic Matthew Bruccoli concerning her book about Mencken, and he read the manuscript carefully, offering both line by line and more global editing suggestions and writing her that it was "a useful and readable job. It must be published." Reading the book sparked a revival of his interest in Mencken's work, and he told Sara that he was now planning to teach Mencken's work in a seminar. Not knowing that Sara was considering a separate book on the Fitzgeralds, he encouraged her to add more about them: "You know things that nobody else knows, and we all need this material. . . . This material is not merely interesting gossip or even scandal: it will help us to form a correct or balanced view of the Fitz marriage. . . . Since your picture of Zelda is unlike any other I have encountered, I would like to see you fill in all the details."

August Mencken, Henry's brother, was harsh in his response to a draft of the manuscript when Sara shared it with him in May 1966. "You have silly or gross errors on almost every page and such signs of carelessness do not help the book." Sara responded, "Weeding the errors out of it is not the easiest thing to do, since not only do the authorities conflict but as often as not the sources." Throughout the preparation of the Mencken book, she had struggled to get permissions to quote from a number of sources. She wrote to a Princeton librarian with whom she'd been corresponding about Mencken's letters that she planned to secure permissions in advance for quotations she meant to use in her Fitzgerald book.

Somehow, though, the book crept forward to completion, and sitting in her wingback chair, working on pages on a lap desk, Sara did the last edits on what would become her first book, published when she was sixty-three. She sent the final draft off to the press, and when she told her friends in Baltimore, she received another effusive letter about her news from Betty Adler: "Really, we are all so elated! You could not picture a happier rooting section. Our champ made it!!!"

With the Mencken book off to the press, it was time to shift her focus back to the Fitzgerald book. Before she did so, she decided that, after all these years, she was ready to travel abroad again. The excuse was that she needed to do some last bits of research for "Mona Lisa," her historical novel about Leonardo da Vinci. Sara's passport picture looks almost deliberately plain: simple, waved, short white hair, no earrings or other jewelry, a white shirt open at the collar, little make-up, if any, and no lipstick. Sara, unadorned. In the summer of 1967, having made all her arrangements to be away for some time, she went abroad with the idea of retracing the steps of

Leonardo in towns all over Italy. She fell in love with the town of Bologna, with its university, square, fountains, and cafes filled with "il dotte e grasso," (the learned and fat). In Florence, she settled in to work on "Mona Lisa" at a pensione along the Arno, the Pensione Quisisana, where, many years later, *A Room with a View* would be filmed. She doesn't mention whether she had a view, but, thrifty as always, she might well have taken one of the less scenic rooms. She worked on writing and research in the morning, and in the afternoon relaxed with shopping and sightseeing.

While she was abroad, her cousin Henry's secretary, Barbara Stubben, who helped with financial arrangements back in Tuscaloosa though Sara was now in charge of her own money, carefully accounted for all of Sara's incoming and outgoing financial transactions, and, woman to woman, encouraged Sara to "go ahead and get yourself some clothes, but not *too* subdued, you're not eighty yet!" She filled Sara in on the health of a family member, said she'd talked to Sara's landlord (Sara sublet her apartment while she was gone), and told of a trip "Judge and the Mrs." took to San Francisco. "Judge was sweet enough to bring me a souvenir back (he always does)." A note from Henry is written on the last page, praising Sara's letters and urging her to enjoy herself.

Returning from her trip, Sara contemplated her long-term finances. She had not worked for money since the 1940s. Now, two decades later, not knowing how much she would be able to earn with her pen or whether her investments would hold up, she decided to seek full-time work. In the fall of 1967, she applied for a position as an assistant editor at the University of Alabama Press. In considering her application, the press director, Morgan Walters, decided to consult Dr. Tarwater at Bryce, writing: "Miss Mayfield . . . is obviously a brilliant woman, but appears to be at least slightly eccentric. I would greatly appreciate an opinion from you or a member of your staff who knows her best as to her suitability for the meticulous and demanding work of an editor of scholarly books." Dr. Tarwater's response is not included in her files but he must have replied at least somewhat affirmatively. Sara was hired.

Sara's writing background and her proficiency with languages were assets to her as an editor, and as a member of the Press editorial staff, Sara copyedited manuscripts and suggested subjects for book acquisition. In her editorial notes for one book she worked on, *Letters from Alabama, 1817–1822* by Anne Newport Royall, Sara wrote of Royall, a noted and sometimes notorious journalist, that she was "a full hundred years ahead of her time," and that instead of winning a Pulitzer, as she would if she had lived in the twentieth century, "her sharp-tongued crusades against corrupt politics, organized religion, temperance movements, social injustice, poverty, and war earned her the name of the 'virago errant' and won her the distinction of being the only woman in the history of the United States to be tried and convicted as a 'common scold.'" Anne, clearly, was a woman after Sara's own heart.

Sara herself wrote numerous and often pointed memoranda to the chief editor, Francis P. Squibb, on how she should manage her time at work. She also wrote letters to director Morgan Walters about what she saw as Francis Squibb's difficult behavior. In one memo headed "Confidential" and dated "5 a.m., Tuesday morning," suggesting a sleepless night, she complained of "corrections in red ink that suddenly appeared the latter part of last week" and implied that Francis had been interfering with the manuscripts she was in charge of. With good reason, Sara worried that, in the carefully staged process of editing manuscripts, Francis's not following procedure would introduce errors into the final product. Working in close quarters in a converted bungalow on the UA campus would only have exacerbated any frictions between staff members.

She found the work exacting and exhausting. Sara described her job to a friend: "Not only do I have to edit, copyedit, translate and check translations in French, German, Spanish, Italian, . . . do character counts, and write publicity releases, not to mention working alternately and sometimes simultaneously for the director, the editor, and the science editor. . . . I have not written a line of my own since I went to work there." She longed to create but found herself with little time or energy after work to do so. Writing to a family member, she bemoaned not having "a spare moment to write, sculpt, paint, or do any kind of creative work that might make some money."

Sara was much better on her own than working as part of a team, and in August of 1968, she met with Morgan Walters to let him know that she just didn't think the job was working out and she planned to leave the Press. Not ten minutes after she had left Walters's office, she later wrote him, the dastardly Francis Squibb "came in and wanted the German dictionary, which happens to be one I bought to replace the one that belonged to the office. I told him that I'd be glad to let him have it as soon as I finished the *Mitteilung*, he thereupon demanded that I do the translation for him in direct violation of your instructions to him and to me." Squibb's behavior cemented her decision to leave, but, although she meant for her resignation to be effective September 1 and looked into other jobs—teaching at the Montgomery, Alabama, campus of Auburn University, or possibly moving to Baltimore for editorial work—for the time being she remained at the Press. Walters had asked her to stay on until he could find a replacement.

With *The Constant Circle* about to come out in the fall of 1968, including an introduction by literary critical giant Edmund Wilson, Sara—instead of the "anticipatory goose pimples" Betty Adler predicted over her book's publication—kept having sties. When the book arrived in the mail, however, she was thrilled. But she now had the publicity tours to do. She wrote to a friend that she hoped she would have familiar faces at events in New York City and Baltimore, for "publishers functions terrify me, and I shall badly need moral support." Sara's press tour of New York City, September third through the twelfth, included reading from her book on WNYC's *Spoken Word*, doing several interviews for print, radio, and television; and lunching at the Algonquin Hotel. On her birthday she was on the WMAR show *Woman's Angle*, which, the Delacorte Press publicity schedule noted, was "color TV." After New York, she was happy to go to Baltimore for a publication party hosted by her old friends the Harrisses, with, she crowed to her cousin, "two hundred people, an orchestra, a champagne bar and an open bar, wonderful flowers, and buffet fifty feet long." Back in Tuscaloosa, she celebrated the publication of her book at an afternoon gathering at Lustig's bookstore, along with her friends the Lustig sisters and writers Elise Sanguinetti and Hudson Strode, both of whom she'd known for years, before Bryce and during. Also present at this eclectic book-signing were a young Lee Smith, whose first book, *The Last Day the Dogbushes Bloomed*, had just come out, and football player and coach Steve Sloan, author of *Calling Life's Signals*. In north Alabama, she gave a presentation to the American Association of University Women, where she signed a book for her friends and encouragers in Florence, the Rosenbaums: "For Mildred and Stanley, who lived through it from beginning to end. With my love, Sara."

Sara was more nervous about public appearances than about reviews; when the book was done, it was done. Still, the literary world always has had its share of intrigue and backstabbing, as a letter forwarded to her by Betty Adler attests. Carl Dolmetsch, an English professor at the College of William and Mary and author of a 1966 book on Mencken's *Smart Set* magazine, wrote Adler in regard to her query about some Mencken letters, then proceeded to lambaste Sara based on an advance copy of her book he had been sent: "The material relevant to the S.S. is all cabbaged from my work. . . . I wish she had been a bit freer with ascriptions of sources—even though she hands me a bouquet (or nosegay, at least) at the end. What is original in the work is pure gossip and who in hell is interested in gossip about a man who's been dead more than a decade and who was, in effect, a passed hand even when he died? . . . Still, I'm surprised she got it finished and out, at long last. It must have been at least 10 yrs. since we first started corresponding about it. I'll have to review it and I'll probably perjure myself, as usual." The loyal Betty wrote at the bottom of Dolmetsch's letter, "With such friends who needs enemies?" She also passed along, as balance and consolation, the news that an editor at the *Evening and Sunday Bulletin* in Philadelphia had written to her declaring Sara "a modern Pepys."

In addition to writing an introduction to Sara's book, Edmund Wilson, in a long essay-review in the *New Yorker* that covered several books on Mencken, wrote that Sara's portrayal of Mencken "brings us closer to his personality than any other has yet done" and her description of his marriage to Sara Haardt "brings out Mencken's considerate and sensitive side in a relationship which seems to have been unique to him." All in all, he finds it "a well done and a valuable document. It is a good thing that someone has survived to write it." Sara wrote to thank him for the review: "Such a review from the dean of American critics makes me feel that it should be framed and hung rather than pasted in a scrapbook."

On a personal note, Edmund Wilson described in his review how Sara's recollections of Montgomery with Sara H., Tallulah, and Zelda, made him reminisce about his own encounters with those Montgomery belles. "In New York, they gave the impression of young barbarian princesses from a country where they were free to do anything." He recalled how he "recognized the type in bud when I once came up from the South on the train, sitting across from a pretty blond belle in rolled stockings with her feet on the opposite seat, who played jazz on a phonograph all the way." Wilson may have enjoyed Sara's descriptions of those belles, but some Montgomerians did not. Sara wrote to the senior editor at her publisher that there had been "uproars" from some of Sara H.'s family and from people who had never even read the book. Thinking of her next book project, and of possible responses to it, she continued: "But, fortunately, I can see that however deeply the knives in the back may have cut, they cut me free to publish the Fitzgerald material, if and when I choose to do so."

Generally speaking, reviewers of the book were interested in Sara's friendship with the Menckens and in the insights that resulted from that closeness, but were critical of other aspects. One reviewer assessed the book as "a generous appreciation . . . rich with anecdotes" but found the biographer "too good and too decorous a friend to make a good biography" even though, or perhaps because, "her good manners and enthusiasm are everywhere evident."

In January 1969, Sara's agent, Lurton Blassingame, sent her first royalty check for *The Constant Circle*, and urged her to "do the best you can" to promote it. "If this book has a good press and a good sale, we will be in a much better position to exploit . . . your next book on the Fitzgeralds." "The Fabled Fitzgeralds," as they were then calling the book, could ride on the coattails of the Mencken book's success. Sara hoped for good sales, and in the summer of 1969 she wrote to Blassingame that the $1,750.00 she had received in royalties so far seemed very low to her, given that the book had already gone into its fourth printing. (Of course, the royalties would depend on the print run, the total number of books printed, not the number of times it had been reprinted.)

Whether the book brought Sara much in royalties, it did bring her some acclaim: in 1970 the Alabama Library Association would award *The Constant Circle* their annual prize. Friends Stanley Hoole, Hudson Strode, and both Babs and Borden Deal were previous winners. From her old friend and library mentor Hoole, Sara received congratulations on the book's publication. He was the first person thanked in Sara's acknowledgments, and, having watched the manuscript develop from the very beginning, he wrote, "I know you are relieved. And I am pleased to have played even a small role in your successful accomplishment." Letters from the general public arrived as well, with one from a local admirer heaping praise on the book and declaring "You, indeed, dear lady, have given us a work that cannot but live—and managed it without bussing the posterior extremities of yankee literary critics, as with the run of southern novelists."

In the spring of 1969, still working at the UA Press, Sara was invited to speak at LaGrange College, in LaGrange, Georgia, on Mencken and Fitzgerald. Arriving at the college, she learned that she was to speak not in a lecture hall but in the chapel, and, feeling that the change of venue made parts of the talk unacceptable, performed "the fastest censoring ever done" on her planned lecture, "Mencken, the Baltimore Antichrist, and Fitzgerald, the Jazz Age Laureate." During her visit, Sara stayed with a friend at the college, English professor Murial Brittain Williams. Dr. Williams, born in 1923, had grown up in Tuscaloosa and received her BA, MA, and PhD from the university. One of Murial's sisters, Thelma, was a nurse at Bryce Hospital who had befriended Sara, and another sister was mother to two children Sara had been allowed to visit with and give presents to while in Bryce. It was a small, small southern world.

In the summer of 1969, she returned to Baltimore in triumph as a literary celebrity at her alma mater, the invited guest speaker at the annual banquet for Goucher's Seventy-seventh Alumnae Reunion, where she delivered remarks on the Menckens. For the occasion, she wore a summer dress and a large corsage, and her novelist friend Jim Cain sent a sheaf of white orchids for her room, to mark the occasion, which, she wrote him, "made me feel as if I were sixteen again." She reconnected with her old friend from the twenties, the woman she had written passionate letters to, Anne Hackman, who, very much out of touch, had written Sara after reading *The Constant Circle*: "I've often wondered where you were and what you were doing. The last I knew of your plans you were engaged to Tee. Did you marry him or anyone else? . . . I note that you are still living in Tuscaloosa, but wonder if your home is still Idlewyld." Anne herself had married and had one child and three granddaughters. In that forty-year gap in communications, so much had happened, but being at Goucher made them feel like girls again, and they were soon calling each other "Hack" and "Mayfield." Sara and Anne would stay in sporadic touch after that, but, like Liz, Anne had a different life from Sara's, as Anne herself recognized: "My life is so different from yours—grandchildren, housekeeping, gardening and the winter job as fund representative for 1929 and the Goucher Alumnae fund."

In addition to catching up with old friends, Sara had a busy weekend full of scheduled activities, and she enjoyed it so much and was so unwilling to miss a moment that she wore herself out. When she returned to Tuscaloosa, she experienced heart troubles that landed her in the intensive care unit of Tuscaloosa's Druid City Hospital (Tuscaloosa was nicknamed the Druid City for its oaks, not its oak-worshippers), "having learned the hard way," she wrote to a friend, "that my spirit is younger than my cardiovascular system." After each workday at the Press, she came home, undressed, and changed into pajamas. In August she revised her will, although she wrote to Liz Hill that she didn't really think she was dying. Still, she wanted Liz to know what she was leaving her, including a small amount "to throw a champaign [*sic*] celebration the day I depart this world of woe."

The heart trouble was enough to make her decide it was truly time to leave the Press, and she wrote a brief note to Morgan Walters that her mind was made up. Sara left the Press in late September 1969, shortly after her sixty-fourth birthday. A memorandum from Morgan Walters to the staff announced her resignation "for reasons of health" and noted that she would continue with freelance work for the editorial department.

Chapter 16

"Zelda Has Been a Villainess for Long Enough"

Further Literary Efforts, this Time in writing about the Fitzgeralds, resulting in Conflict and Strife. Another Trip to Europe involving Certain Calamities. Exiles from Paradise is published to Mixed Reviews, but Life goes on.

WITH THE TURN OF ANOTHER DECADE APPROACHING AND THE confidence she had gained from the good reception of her Mencken book, Sara pushed forward with her second literary biography, this time on Zelda and Scott Fitzgerald. Both books had come out of the unwieldy and overlarge literary memoir she had written after going through her papers at the library while still in Bryce. With the help of her agent, she had reshaped her ideas about the material, cutting most of the purely autobiographical, and decided to go with the Mencken book first. In 1969, with the first full-length biography of Zelda about to come out in the next year, a book written not by Zelda's old friend Sara but by a young woman named Nancy Milford, Sara was wondering if they had done the right thing.

Sara had published some short pieces on the Fitzgeralds, wanting to lay claim to the material as a biographer. The Winter 1965 issue of the UA student journal *Comment: The University of Alabama Review* included an essay by her titled "The F. Scott Fitzgeralds in Paris: Reminiscences." She had just left Bryce when it was published. That same year she had tried for national publication in *Horizon* magazine, but her proposal was rejected with a note saying that the editors felt that "the whole crew, and their life in Paris, has been done to death." Sara had a different sense of rising interest in the Fitzgeralds as a result of being around college students; she saw a parallel between the twenties and the sixties, and when she went to pick up her mail on campus she was sometimes stopped by students interested in her friendship with the Fitzgeralds. While working on the Mencken book, she kept the Fitzgerald material alive, publishing another piece in *Comment* in 1968, "Memoirs of Paris with the F. Scott Fitzgeralds and Ernest Hemingway." At that point, her biographical note stated that the article was an excerpt from her work in progress on the Fitzgeralds, which she was now calling "Exiles from Paradise." (The editor of *Comment*, Howell Raines, then a graduate student, who would go on to become executive editor of the *New York Times*, later recalled Sara as "a lovely, eccentric Southern blossom."[1])

Sara's instincts were right: interest in the Fitzgeralds was indeed on the rise. Nancy Milford, whose thesis on Zelda for her 1964 master's degree from Columbia had gained a publishing contract for a full-fledged trade book on the basis of that interest, placed "The Golden Dreams of Zelda Fitzgerald" in the January 1969 issue of *Harper's Magazine*, in advance of her book's publication. That same month, Sara's agent wrote of her Fitzgerald book, "My one nagging regret is that you did not begin working on the book over a year ago, so that we could then have had a contract and announced it then and so [done] something to tuck down on Milford."

The stage then, was set, for authorial battle. Milford versus Mayfield. A Yankee and a self-described Confederate. A fan and a friend. When the *Harper's* article came out, Sara wrote to Zelda's sister Rosalind about her own writing plans, making the best of being second to publish: "Mrs. Milford's article jarred me, so I know how you must feel about it. Perhaps it may be some solace to you to know how many indignant letters have been written to me about it. I shall most assuredly let her have her say first and then answer her if I can. But I want to have my material in shape so that when her book comes out I'll know what to add and what to cut to avoid repetition." She had been speaking disparagingly of Milford for years, writing to her agent in 1966: "Elizabeth [Thigpen Hill] tells me that Nancy Milford has almost driven Rosalind wild with queries, etc." She even told UA librarian Stanley Hoole that it was her "express wish" that her papers be "restricted to the use of mature scholars approved by you," presumably to keep the young Milford away from her material.

Sara, however, had already given an interview (one she would come to regret) to Milford on March 16, 1965, less than a month after she had left Bryce for good, almost seventeen years to the day after Zelda's death. Milford was just short of her twenty-seventh birthday, Sara headed toward her sixtieth; Milford was born in Michigan and educated at the University of

Michigan and Columbia, a Midwesterner and then a New Yorker, and Sara was a lifelong Alabamian who, despite forays into the larger world, had not broken free of her state's gravitational force. But despite their differences in age and upbringing, relations were initially agreeable, with Sara taking on the role of the older woman mentoring a young writer. Two days after meeting Milford, Sara wrote her a letter from the Peacock Inn in Princeton, New Jersey, where she was reading the Fitzgerald and Mencken materials, which concludes, "As I think you know, no one is quite as keen about seeing you bring off the book on ZSF as I am. Best luck and my heartfelt good wishes. It was, let me add, indeed, a pleasure to have met you, and I enjoyed the lunch, the tea, and you." She later, however, wrote to a friend that Milford had "told me that Scottie had turned over to her Scott and Zelda's letters in which they bandied somewhat dubious charges against each other. Whereupon, I simply clammed up, told her a few anecdotes about Zelda's childhood, and let it go at that, not knowing whether Scottie had actually turned the letters over to her or whether she was simply trying to draw me out about the ones to me I'd burned." She gave Milford permission to use descriptions of a couple of incidents from her and Zelda's Montgomery childhood, but by March 1966 she had "clammed up" completely in relation to "Miss Milford," writing disingenuously, in response to a letter from Milford: "My journals, diaries, and so forth are in the vault. I haven't looked inside those for the Paris years in so long that I haven't the remotest idea what's in them." In a postscript, she added, "The article you asked about appeared in December, 1965 in *Comment*, a little magazine published here at the University, edited by John Martin Findlay [*sic*]. It was so full of printer's errors that I think the pressmen must have been celebrating Christmas. As I don't have a copy of it, I can't give you the volume, number, etc." A lifelong packrat of papers, she did, of course, have a copy.

In early 1970 Sara received galleys of Milford's *Zelda* for review, presumably because her Mencken book included some material on the Fitzgeralds, as it would have been an odd choice for the publisher to send galleys to a "rival" biographer. Sara read the book, then wrote to her editor at Delacorte: "The further I read in the galleys of Miss Milford's book, my jaw dropped. She has simply taken material which I gave her and which I told her I was going to use and used it almost verbatim." She fumed, then wrote to Milford, addressing her as "Dear Nancy." The letter, couched in reasonable language but holding a barely veiled threat of legal action, was returned to Sara. She then wrote forcefully to the assistant general counsel at Milford's publisher,

Harper and Row, that they had been "gravely misinformed" about a number of elements related to her contact with Nancy Milford, but despite Sara's bluster, she was, unhappily, in the position of being able to do very little about Milford's use of her quotations or stories, having given her permission already. Letters went back and forth between Sara and Milford's publisher and Sara and her own publisher, Delacorte, whose counsel concluded, "Although I certainly appreciate and sympathize with your sentiments . . . I do not believe that, as a matter of law, there exists actionable copyright infringement or other redressable legal wrong. Also, Harper maintains that Miss Milford has a letter from you which if interpreted liberally would tend to give permission to Miss Milford for the use of certain material and information appearing in ZELDA." There the matter rested, at least as "a matter of law." It was the kind of situation Sara had found herself in all her life, a mixture of misunderstanding, hurt feelings, and a sense of injustice at how she had been treated.

Bolstering Sara's sense of righteousness was the fact that Nancy Milford and Scottie Fitzgerald Smith, Zelda and Scott's daughter, had also come into conflict. Milford, a doctoral student at Barnard, was "discovered" by Harper and Row editor Genevieve "Gene" Young, who had read a piece in the *New Yorker* on expatriates Gerald and Sara Murphy and their friends the Fitzgeralds and then happened to hear about Milford's project. As a history of New York publishing described the editing process, Milford's first draft was "basically a collage of letters from Scott to Zelda" and the editors asked for numerous changes; more revisions followed, and "after seven years, Nancy Milford had skillfully pieced the letters together, and Gene edited them." According to this version of events, Scottie had intended to help a graduate student and was dismayed when a thesis became a potential New York publishing sensation. The editor sent the copyedited manuscript to Scottie, who asked scholar Matthew Bruccoli to read it for her, and his report on the manuscript so upset her that she "immediately called Gene Young. 'I'm not going to sue you,' she said, 'but how would you like it if I came in and slit my throat in your reception room?'"[2] Lawyers became involved. Edits were made.

When she read the advance copy of Nancy Milford's book and launched into her crusade against the inclusion of "her" stories, Sara was in the midst of preparations for a trip to Europe, and the flurry of letters over the following months would crisscross the Atlantic. After resting from her heart troubles for a few months, and perhaps concerned that she wouldn't have as many opportunities to travel if her health deteriorated, Sara had decided to take a months-long trip with UA philosophy professor J. B. "Bill" McMinn, now

divorced, and his girlfriend Caroline Plath, who would later own an eccentri-
cally run bookstore on University Boulevard, adjacent to the UA campus. On
the eve of the trip, Sara was interviewed by the managing editor of the *Tus-*
caloosa News, who described her as "tall, lean, white-haired and as aristocratic
as any ante-bellum planter aspired to be." Still journalistically minded, and
hoping to recoup some of the costs of the trip through selling articles, Sara
said that she planned to write about European night life, since her traveling
companions were "night people."

In February 1970, Bill, Caroline, and Sara boarded a commercial freighter
in Jacksonville, Florida, and, after a stop in Savannah, the ship sailed for Europe. Bill bought an old Volvo in Amsterdam and they drove around Holland, then headed south, to France, dealing with periodic car breakdowns and
often driving on winding roads in rain and dark before finding a hotel for the
night. Sara described the beginnings of the trip to her editor at Delacorte,
Dick Kennedy: "Sad to say, Bill bought a joke book called *Europe on Five*
Dollars a Day. Despite my telling him that 'Europe on Twenty-Five Dollars
a Day' was a more accurate title for such a guide, he insisted that hotels were
plentiful and cheap here and that there was no sense in bothering to make
reservations—even during the Easter holidays. Consequently, we waded
around in the slush until 1 A.M. trying to find a vacancy in one of the flea
bags recommended in his joke book. He and Caroline had come off without raincoats or overcoats; they caught cold in Holland, and I caught it from
them." After yet another disastrous night, "it occurred to me that there is just
a hairline between a good sport and a damn fool and that I was courting
pneumonia, so I insisted on coming here to the Lutetia for the night. Next
day I spent twelve hours chasing around in the sleet and rain with Caroline
and Bill on the same kind of fool's errand before I decided to hole up here
and stay until I'd done my work." In fact, Sara, who was beginning to have
a good income from the sales of coal and gravel mining on her land, often
stayed in nicer hotels—including some she remembered from the twenties—
than Caroline and Bill could afford, and she visited Ritz bars wherever they
popped up, thinking to write a travel article about them. For the most part,
however, she did not investigate night life as she had planned, being tired out
at the end of the day.

Staying at the elegant Hotel Lutetia in Saint-Germain-des-Prés on Paris'
Left Bank in Paris, while her companions went to England and Scotland,
Sara did some last bits of research for the Fitzgerald book and made a point
of interviewing some of the same people Milford had interviewed: Edouard

Jozan, the French aviator with whom Zelda may or may not have had an affair, and one of Zelda's psychiatrists, Oscar Forel. After interviewing Jozan in Paris, she wrote to Fitzgerald scholar Matthew Bruccoli—aggressively making her case against Milford—that Jozan had been reluctant to meet with her "because he had had such a terrible time with Milford. He said that she arrived 'full of wild ideas about Zelda' and that she seemed to be 'raving mad.'" A French friend and scholar was with her and was able "to smooth things out for me. After he had reassured Jozan, the admiral opened up and talked for two hours about Zelda and himself. His account of their friendship tallied . . . exactly with mine." She described Jozan to her editor, Dick Kennedy, as "still very handsome and charming and it is not hard to see why Zelda was attracted to him."

Sara also was able to interview Zelda's former doctor Oscar Forel, who, she wrote Bruccoli, "was very reluctant to talk to me over the phone because, he said, 'I have had infinite trouble with another American writer,'" meaning Milford. He did, however, agree to meet with Sara in person, and she later wrote him a thank-you note for the interview. In one strange, fantastical scene that occurred before she met and decided she liked Forel, Sara wrote Dick Kennedy that, one night in Paris, "I had fallen into conversation with a painter who happened to be sitting beside me in a restaurant. After I told her what my errand was here, she confided to me that she had been under treatment by Forel and gave me an address through which he could be located. She said that he was a 'despicable character, an unethical doctor, and a mean man.' I asked her whether she thought he had actually given Nancy Zelda's records from Prangins. She replied, 'Probably, if she was young and pretty and did not object to an old man's advances.'" It's as though Sara had summoned the ghost of Zelda, and then believed in her own summoning.

Although she was working on the final draft of the Fitzgerald book, and hoped to write freelance pieces as well, Sara still intended to enjoy herself. Shopping, however, was not to be among the list of pleasures: she wrote friends from Paris: "The fashions here are horrible. Today's keynote is that anything goes, from long, unbelted shifts, leather jackets, fringed à la Buffalo Bill, worn with turtlenecks and striped slacks to thigh-high minis with knee-high boots. And this in places where one used to see the most elegantly dressed women in the world. . . . I confined my shopping to the purchase of one washcloth at Au Bon Marché."

In Spain, as Bill, Caroline, and Sara reunited, the trip went from irritation to crisis. Staying on the island of Ibiza, Sara hurt her leg when she slipped on a wet tiled terrace going from the hotel to the beach. Instead of going to Greece with Bill and Caroline, she stayed on at the hotel, where she rested and made her final additions to "Exiles from Paradise." since her publisher was becoming anxious about getting the book to publication. While recuperating, she wrote a friend, she could "do little more than limp to the beach to oil and broil, roast and baste." Given the choice between the beach and a hospital bed, however, she much preferred to lie on the beach "and watch the human race amuse itself" than to lie in a hospital bed, "reading detective stories and looking at the ceiling." On Sara's birthday the hotel staff and owners, not wanting her to celebrate alone, gave her a dinner with "hors d'oeuvres, filet mignon, a birthday cake, and crêpe suzettes" followed by champagne and a concert by the hotel band.

She liked the people and the beauty of Es Caná, Ibiza, so much that she actually contemplated moving there permanently and setting up a health spa, an echo of her old desire to set up a mental health retreat on Dauphin Island. After several months in residence, now well enough to travel, she left the hotel at dawn on a chilly, gray day. Someone was up to give her hot coffee and say goodbye. Getting home by "train, plane, and wheel chair" was not easy, but, finally, she made it. It was good to be home, and gratifying to see at the train station, family and friends there to greet her; they "had parked their cars parallel to the railroad tracks so that one or the other of them would be near where the Pullman stopped. Three strapping cousins boarded the train and put me and a mountain of luggage in the nearest car. Ten minutes later I was in the Druid City Hospital."

By December Sara was out of the hospital and back in her apartment, wearing a brace on her leg but able to walk and to drive her car. Several years after being released from Bryce, she had gotten a driver's license. To do so she was required to get a form filled out by Dr. Tarwater stating that she had had an "Emotional Disorder" but was "Now Recovered." Friends dubbed her big white Buick the "Queen Mary" and held their breath when they rode with her. She considered stop signs merely a suggestion and generally just slowed briefly, tooted her horn several times, and proceeded forward. Her friend Alex Sartwell said that "Sara was the terror of the streets. Her whole attitude toward life showed up in her driving."[3] Driving around town, going here and there, paying her bills in person instead of spending money on stamps, Sara, not surprisingly, had a number of minor accidents. One day she came out of the post office downtown and found the Queen Mary on fire, she knew not why, but soon had it repaired and back on the road.

Milford's *Zelda* came out in 1970, and, Sara's agent, Lurton Blassingame, doing his best to ride the wave of Zelda interest, worked to place parts of Sara's forthcoming book in magazines. He forwarded to Sara a letter from the associate editor of *Good Housekeeping*, who seemed to see Sara's work as a positive step in restoring Zelda's reputation: "Zelda has been a villainess for long enough, and it's a good thing somebody is trying to tell her side of things." Blassingame was able to place an excerpt from "Exiles" in *Atlanta Magazine* in January 1970, and in July 1971 an excerpt appeared in *McCall's* (coincidentally, the same magazine that had featured, in its October 1923 issue, an article titled "What Became of Our Flappers and Sheiks?" with a byline by both Fitzgeralds). By then, though, Milford's *Zelda: A Biography* was a Book-of-the-Month Club and a Literary Guild selection, and it came out in paperback from Avon in 1971, boasting on the cover "The 6 Month Hardcover Bestseller—Over 1,000,000 Copies in Print."

With the publishers preparing promotional materials for her book, Sara had hoped that Scottie would allow her to use as an endorsement a complimentary statement Scottie had made privately in a letter to her. Sara wrote, "I don't want to pressure you, but I would like to point out again that it would do more than any one thing to refute Milford's book." But Scottie declined.[4] In the letter Sara wished to quote from, Scottie had written, "Obviously, I can't say I enjoyed reading it, because for Heaven's sake, who could possibly enjoy reading such a documentation of arrogance, insanity, and waste about one's own parents, but I do think it's the best thing written yet on the subject." Now, Scottie implored Sara, "*Please* don't use that statement in any blurb or publicity. I really mean it and I want you to know it, but I never have and never want to be associated with any sort of promotion of *anything* about my parents, good or bad. There's something uggsy about it to me—maybe it's my Confederate background." Sara, she says, takes the "'Montgomery' point of view" that Scott destroyed Zelda, but Scottie has decided—"I *think* I think . . . that if people are not crazy, they get themselves out of crazy situations"; unfortunately, the absence of any definitive answer as to why her parents were mutually self-destructive "is the conundrum that keeps the legend going."[5] Having read the final draft, Scottie reassured Sara, "I want to tell you again how good I think it is—and believe me, when I can read anything at all about my parents without getting a bad case of hives—I am so tired of their drunken episodes I could SCREAM—it's got to be good."

Sara was hopeful about her book, but with the publication, on March 30, 1971, of *Exiles from Paradise* came further conflict with Milford. The very first line of Milford's *Zelda*, published the year before, is "If there was a confederate establishment in the Deep South, Zelda Sayre came from it." Turning to the notes section in the back of *Zelda*, one finds Milford's acknowledgment that she had begun her book with a paraphrase of someone else's statement: "If there was a confederate . . . : Sara Mayfield to NM, interview, March 16, 1965." Milford did not use "superscript" numbers at the end of a sentence to send readers to endnotes—a system most people who have written a term paper would be familiar with—but instead, in the notes section in the back of the book, gave brief quotes from the page referred to and the source of that phrase. This system creates a less academic, more readable style and is common in books intended for a general readership, but it also requires that readers go to the notes section if they are to know which statements in a book are from other sources. Although Milford had properly cited her source, not many people read endnotes, and when Sara stubbornly decided to use her own words on page four of her book, "If there is a Confederate Establishment in the Deep South, Zelda came from the heart of it," Mayfield looked as though she'd borrowed from Milford, not the other way around. Knowing that it was in Milford's book, Sara could have chosen not to use that line, but she felt it belonged to her and was loathe to lose it. One reviewer noted the repetition but somehow missed Milford's attribution, writing, "It is hard to determine just how much Miss Mayfield owes to the homework done by Mrs. Milford," adding "The question is made even more perplexing" by the two very similar sentences.[6] He essentially implied that Sara had committed plagiarism, a charge she found infuriating.

Additionally, *Exiles from Paradise* was strongly criticized by reviewers for its lack of documentation. In manuscript, the book contains one draft with extensive footnotes, at the bottom of the page, and another with endnotes in the back, but at some point in the editing, despite Sara's protests, those notes came out, in order to present the book for general readership rather than as a scholarly publication. Sara had a feeling it was a bad idea, and in the fall of 1970 wrote to a professor at the Sorbonne with an interest in Fitzgerald, "To my chagrin the editors have decided to cut the notes from 'Exiles' in that *Zelda* has frequently been criticized as pedantic. . . . I could weep over having them cut from the published version, but tears are of no avail with publishers." Sara did her best to show that the book had been thoroughly researched, despite the lack of endnotes, writing in the first paragraph of her acknowledgments, "*Exiles from Paradise* is based in part upon unpublished letters, diaries, notes and clippings, as well as upon available published sources for which permission has been obtained." She noted that a "heavily documented and bibliographed manuscript of the book" was filed in her papers at the UA library for scholars who wished to check her sources. In that annotated manuscript, the notes cite all the sources listed in her bibliography in the published book as well as personal letters and "verbal communications," mostly between 1968 and 1970, with a number of different people, Montgomery natives who would have known Zelda growing up and writers and others who knew Zelda in her life with Scott. Since, by her own account, Sara had destroyed her letters from Scott and Zelda as well as letters from others about the Fitzgeralds, and her own diary entries about them, prior to writing the book, she would have had to rely on memory for any information contained in them. (Apart from the letters from Scottie, the one piece of undestroyed Fitzgeraldiana in Sara's papers is a scrawled note Scott wrote at a party in Montgomery, which she quotes in *Exiles*. Asked to write something for his hostess, Mary McCall Henderson, he wrote at the top, "SKOT FISGUREL by Merry Mac-caul" and below: "I have never scene Skot Fisgurel sobre but he is a grate freind of mind. He has offen toled me about his methods. He begins in the mawning with 3 (three) strong whiskeys and from then on for years and years he seldem stops. I myself am a danscer and kan skarkely write my own name." Although he tossed the crumpled fragment into a wastebasket, Mrs. Henderson retrieved it, saved it, and later sent it to Sara.)[7]

Sara's letter burning was intended to protect Zelda's reputation, most likely to do with sex. When Milford's book was being published, Sara had written to a Montgomery friend that she had hoped Rosalind wouldn't read *Zelda*: "I told E.T.H. years ago to try to keep it from Rosalind if she could, but Scottie let the cat out of the bag—and the Milford claws are sharp—and I don't wonder that Rosalind is perturbed about it." The "it" was likely accusations of homosexuality hurled back and forth between Zelda and Scott, but Sara will not even mention it by name. Whatever she might have said in the company of those she trusted, Sara tended in her writing to either deny or make light of homosexuality, in herself and others. In one letter to Liz Hill (the E.T.H. mentioned above), she recalled their youthful travels in Europe, wishing they could go back to "the places we went together when we were really young [and] gay—and gay still had its original meaning."

Rather than trade on what she saw as gossip, Sara hoped to supply aspects of Zelda's early biography that few people were aware of, including how she was writing before she ever met Scott; one prize-winning story, titled "The Iceberg," was published in Sidney Lanier High School's literary journal in

1918. Though a dedicated researcher and disciplined writer, Sara relied on her own personal experience in creating a portrait of her friend, wanting her to be remembered for her energy and kindness, not her sadness or sickness. She wrote to a novelist friend in 1969 that "Zelda's wit was astringent and her idiom salty; she was far from being a saccharine Southerner. In her prime she was one of the most brilliant and beautiful creatures I ever knew and far more attractive than Scott ever was. But life with him, to put it delicately, was more than any woman could cope with and within a few years of her marriage to him, she was broken, dispirited. I wish you had known her before she cracked-up."

Unlike Nancy Milford, who wrote of Zelda as a young bride, "Zelda's taste in clothes had definitely improved from her earlier days in New York. . . . Her Southern accent was very much in control," Sara Mayfield was the ultimate southern insider.[8] As such, she was attuned to the subtleties of southern belle behavior and the circumlocutions of southern speech, as well as defensive about the South in a way Milford could not have easily understood. Her hackles were raised by the cultural snub implied in saying that Zelda's

FIGURE 20. F. Scott and Zelda Sayre Fitzgerald

F. Scott and Zelda Sayre Fitzgerald in 1920, shortly after their marriage. Sara remembered the youthful, happier Zelda and hoped in her book on the Fitzgeralds to fill in a side of her childhood friend that had been missed by other biographers. (Library of Congress, Prints and Photographs Division, LC-USZ62-111780)

fashion sense needed improving or that she needed to have her southern accent "in control."

Despite her obvious affection for Zelda, however, in *Exiles from Paradise* Sara points out Zelda's capacity to be "ominously self-destructive"; she assesses the Fitzgeralds' marriage as it fell apart as a "relentless feud" and recounts numerous incidents of their joint misbehavior. She is most negative toward Scott in regard to his drinking: "More than any man I ever knew, Scott wanted to be good, kind, noble, and lovable; and when he was not drinking, he came very close to being all these things, but when he was drunk, he was sometimes the antithesis of them."[9] Already disinclined to like Hemingway from her acquaintanceship with him in the twenties (she once told a friend in Tuscaloosa that Hemingway "wore a sweatshirt and made his wife walk behind him like a squaw"), Sara blamed Hemingway as well as Scott for Zelda's initial commitment to Malmaison in 1930: After a "violent quarrel" in which Zelda "threatened to leave him and air her complaints in the divorce court . . . Scott realized that she had to be silenced. Hemingway already had indicated how it could be done."[10]

To Sara, Zelda was trying to establish not only an identity but also a means of supporting herself with her dancing, writing, and painting, desperate to leave a marriage that had become a trap, a husband who had become an alcoholic. She writes, "Zelda's frantic efforts to make a career for herself . . . were not motivated by an obsessive illness but by a clear-eyed realization of the financial uncertainties of her life with Scott and, perhaps, also by her unhappiness over their marital difficulties." There are so many echoes of Sara's own life in her descriptions of Zelda: her own unhappy marriage to a handsome man who drank too much and had affairs; her determination, after their divorce, to support herself without relying on a man; and her unexpressed and unacknowledged insight into mental illness and commitment to an institution.

Sara's book was ostensibly about both Fitzgeralds but, because it grew out of Sara's childhood friendship with Zelda, emphasized the Zelda side of the literary equation. Sometimes chatty, sometimes catty, colorful, personal, and readable, the book received numerous reviews, mostly mixed-to-poor, and has a reputation among scholars of being the least objective of the Fitzgerald biographies. The *New Orleans Post-Crescent* reviewer saw *Exiles* in a positive light: Pooh-poohing "the zealots of the current Fitzgerald cult," he writes, "for simple credibility about the legendary Fitzgeralds of the Jazz Age, this is the book. It should leave anyone with any personal recollection of their era feeling that at last he knows what made F. Scott Fitzgerald tick." A reviewer in the more staid *Library Journal* wrote, "*Exiles from Paradise* is a bitter, poorly written book that rehashes events with which everyone is already familiar, especially after Nancy Milford's excellent *Zelda*." Also comparing the two books was the *Washington Post*, whose reviewer wrote that Mayfield "is clearly in her girlhood friend's camp, even more so than Nancy Milford, who wrote the bestselling *Zelda*." He decides, however, that the book's "reason for being," that "Sara *knew* Zelda . . . is reason enough," providing "intimacy and authority no one else can equal." The *New York Review of Books* complained that "Miss Mayfield's *Exiles from Paradise* breathes down the neck of Miss Milford's recent biography of Zelda . . . [and] is the most depressing of the current set of Fitzgerald studies." The reviewer goes on: "Her writing taps a vein of pure, cloying cliché, deviating frequently into slur and innuendo." Although a paperback edition of *Exiles* came out three years after the original publication, it was not reissued after that.

Sara was aware of the reviews. But when asked by a reporter "if it infuriated her that critics should doubt her biography," responded "I don't care. . . . You've done the best job you could. You've told the truth, not the whole truth, but the truth and from there on out it's the next book."[11] Although some critics doubted her ability to recount conversations from many years ago, a friend in Tuscaloosa said that "she never forgot a conversation she ever had— even in her last years, her memory was very good."[12] The reviews, though not very positive, must have helped sales; in August 1971 Sara wrote her agent that her editor had told her the book had sold over 10,000 copies already, not anywhere as good as Milford's, but respectable.

Sara's book on the Menckens had brought her to the attention of aspiring writers, and she enjoyed serving as an informal writing mentor to several, among them a student from Demopolis, Alabama, named Johnny Greene. Greene was gay, as were several of Sara's friends, some more openly than others in that conservative environment. The son of cattle farmers, Johnny sought Sara out as a sympathetic presence when he was an undergraduate at the University of Alabama. As he would write in a remembrance of her, "Sara was a writer's writer, and the business of writing as Sara knew it . . . had nothing to do with the romantic notions others frequently imposed on writers and writing."[13] Sara called him "Lad" and taught him that "writing is work" and that revision is "an inescapable requirement of the craft." Talking over coffee "'hot as hell and black as midnight'" or a couple of beers, Greene wrote, the two enjoyed "good conversation and lots of laughs. . . . On the afternoons we wandered over to a restaurant near the University Club for drinks. On the trips we made to Montgomery for cocktail parties with Black Belt eccentrics. On the quiet afternoons we sat in her apartment near the campus, and she worked on my manuscripts while I took notes on hers."[14]

To celebrate publication of *Exiles*, Johnny, now in New York City, sent roses to Sara for a party in Tuscaloosa, at which his parents were in attendance. He also wrote a review, which he gave to Sara, intended for the *New Republic* but apparently never published. Far from a puff piece but definitely written from a southern sensibility, Greene's review describes the book as using "an impressive array of first hand information and scenes" to prove Sara's theory "that Scott's own weaknesses complicated their lives to such a degree that Zelda became his scapegoat." Not all readers may be convinced, he says, but "that Miss Mayfield's theory is tenuous to some is only more evidence to those in the Black Belt who daily protect their Zeldas that theirs were lucky not to get caught."

After all she had put into her work on the book, and the difficulties with Milford during the publication process of *Zelda*, Sara was ready to be done with public discussion of her friend. But when *Exiles* came out, she did her authorial duty and sat for a number of interviews as well as a round of other publicity events. It was necessary, and at times exciting, but tiring. Sara, sixty-five when the book was published, wrote to a friend, "Between trying to keep my nose powdered, my clothes pressed, and my white gloves clean, I began to think that the hippies might have something." In one interview, Sara admitted that "Zelda was the exhibitionist, and I was the inhibitionist. . . . I have always had a grand aversion to the literary life or to the theatrical life or whatever it is that people go in for."[15]

When Sara visited Montgomery doing research for *Exiles*, Wayne Greenhaw, a young writer whom she'd known as a friend of Borden and Babs Deal back in her Bryce days, described her in his "Chitlins and Caviar" column for a Montgomery paper as "still a beautiful Southern belle." In July 1971 she was back in Montgomery with her completed book, presiding at the dedication of Fitzgerald Park in Montgomery, giving a seminar on the Fitzgeralds at Huntingdon College, and doing a couple of local television appearances about the book. She visited the state archives to look at the Bankhead family letters for a biography of Tallulah's early years that she was planning, and archives director Milo Howard had her over for cocktails in the evening. In the fall of 1971 she was invited to be the guest of the Birmingham Centennial Committee on Cultural Events on New Year's Eve at the Calico Ball,

crimson-white

vol. 81 - no. 5 - july 19, 1971 - university

The Literary World's
Sara Mayfield

By DESPINA VODANTIS
Editor

Tucked away on a quiet street in Tuscaloosa is the home of Sara Mayfield, perhaps one of today's only living historians of an era that is not likely to occur again.

Miss Mayfield, the biographer of Zelda Fitzgerald, friend of Tallulah Bankhead, and companion to the Menkens, is a most charming woman, one who has globe-trotted with the world's intellectuals.

Her recent book, Exiles In Paradise, is under review, criticism, and praise as another addition to the long list of biographies on the Fitzgeralds, considered the most precious couple of the Jazz Age.

This couple of paradise is seen under a different eye, the eye of Miss Mayfield who lived and matured with Zelda Fitzgerald, and knew Scott equally well.

She acted as a buffer between them in their years of marital turmoil and always remained the true friend of Zelda, whom, as she points out in her book, suffered the jealousies of Fitzgerald because she herself possessed superior artistic abilities.

In common, Miss Mayfield and Zelda had Montgomery and mutual friends; in retrospect, Miss Mayfield holds the memories of Zelda and has pointed them out to prove that it was Zelda who really was the great Fitzgerald.

Miss Mayfield's biography is the talk of the literary Fitzgerald circle. Newsweek and The Times have reviewed it with doubt, McCall's ran excerpts in their latest issue. Miss Mayfield has offered to the reading public a picture of the Jazz Age couple never before imagined.

"I don't care," Miss Mayfield said when asked if it infuriated her that critics should doubt her biography.

"You've done the best job you could. You've told the truth, not the whole truth, but the truth

and from there on out it's the next book."

The next book Miss Mayfield is writing is about Tallulah Bankhead, a relative by marriage to the Mayfield family. When Tallulah came home to visit, Miss Mayfield said, "The cry would go around the neighborhood, lock up the piano, here comes Tallulah."

Of the Fitzgeralds, Miss Mayfield contends that Zelda was the more vivid of the two

and the most memorable. Due to Miss Mayfield's infuriation that Fitzgerald and his friends should discredit Zelda, she wrote the ... draft of ... in Paradise in six weeks.

"Zelda was the exhibitionist and I was the inhibitionist. Zelda could put out and put over." And, it was because of this charm Zelda had, that Scott began to discredit her. Miss

Mayfield added that the Jazz Age effected her ch... well.

The book enti... written by Nancy M... dissection of ... friend of Miss ... in a letter, and d... view Zelda as a "real and vibrant person."

The friendship between Zelda and Miss Mayfield had been maintained over the years by occasional meetings over the globe between the friends, and

was constantly being reinforced by these continual reunions.

Miss Mayfield admits there were many letters from the Fitzgeralds to her which she burned. At the time they were written, the Fitzgeralds were having marital difficulties and they were in Europe. Miss Mayfield felt she was a link from home to them during those times and that the letters they wrote her individually should be removed from the annuals of history.

Constantly in a core of intellectuals, Miss Mayfield never felt that she was living in a truly fantastic era. There was a time when she lived within a few blocks of Zelda and Scott, Hemingway and Hadley, in Paris.

She added, "I could never in those days have ever thought that there would be a course given on Scott at the Sorbonne and one given on Menken and that I would be asked to lecture at them."

Miss Mayfield said she never felt a sense of destiny about her nor about the intellectuals she knew. "They were just like my next door neighbors," she added with a smile.

But they were done for, for Miss Mayfield contends that the Fitzgeralds took their talents and literary life too seriously.

"If you don't have the viseral fortitude to simply go your own

that Scottie's selflessness and humility in the face of the Fitzgerald legend is to be admired since she has great abilities of her own.

Never feeling that she was the stabilizing force of so many intellectuals, Miss Mayfield jokingly says she was stabilized. "I have always had a grand aversion to the literary life or to the theatrical life or what ever it is that people go in for. The moment writers begin to take themselves seriously, they are the most hideous bores on earth."

But Miss Mayfield holds the primary difference between the writer and the artist lies in the difference between introversion and extroversion.

Reflecting on the Menkens, Miss Mayfield said she once won a short story contest while in college and was to be awarded as a prize, a twenty dollar gold piece from H. L. Menken who promptly invited her to dinner.

"The idea of a freshman going to dinner with the bad boy of Baltimore, you can't conceive of what it was like."

So Miss Mayfield's friend escorted here to dinner as a chaperon, and for seven years following Miss Mayfield chaperoned her friend Sara and Menken until they eventually married.

But, Sara Mayfield treasures

way and do your wor... be beguiled down the ... paths that open up ... 'hat's too bad."

As far as So... only daughter ... geralds, Miss ...

... time that are now feeling she lived the past fully and in the hard way.

Educated at the University of Chicago, University of Paris, University of London, and the University of Alabama, she feels she really got her education at the "odyssey of the wondering mind."

At the University of Alabama, she acquired her Master's degree in English and became a lasting friend of Hudson Strode, one-time University English professor and author of several popular travel books.

"I got my literary start because my father had these Rousseauistic ideas about education. He thought all children should work." And as a child Miss Mayfield overcame her household jobs and read such authors as Scott, Dickens and Thackery. She proved to be quite an ingenious thinker however.

Her main job was to churn butter but she soon found that she could accomplish her job by attaching the churner to a sewing machine wheel and peddle the wheel causing the butter to be churned, at which time she was left free to read the novels she loved.

Miss Mayfield was, as a child, a member of secret clubs remembering that at the time the influence of the Civil War was still being felt, especially when she was not allowed to play with the children of 'Black' Republicans.

As a college student, Miss Mayfield felt herself to be very liberal. "I've heard it said that any man or woman who is not a liberal in their youth has no heart; any man or woman who is not a conservative in their old age, has no head."

Though not an advocate of women's lib, Miss Mayfield says that the college students of today are not concerned about their social standing as they were in her day. They are more involved today and much more on top of things.

If the young person is an artist, Miss Mayfield, having lived her life around distinctive members of literary circles, said "that the years of any young struggling artist are terrific then it (success) all comes after you're worn out with the whole darn business."

And so, Sara Mayfield has spent a lifetime living her life and making it memorable and now remains the historian of a couple and a time of the Jazz Age; one of the truly amazing eras of the 20th century.

FIGURE 21. *Crimson White* article about Sara Mayfield

Sara worked hard to establish herself as a literary biographer and was recognized both locally, in the University of Alabama's *Crimson White* newspaper, and nationally, with reviews of her books and an entry in *Contemporary Authors*. (University of Alabama Libraries Special Collections)

featuring "Alabama Celebrities": "Because you are one of Alabama's 'Own' who made it Big in the outside world." The event was modeled on the 1872 Calico Ball, and guests were expected to attend "dressed in stylish calico." No record of whether she attended survives, but she saved the invitation, further proof that her post-Bryce reputation was secure.

In the fall of 1971, having decided to stay in Tuscaloosa after all, Sara moved to Riverside Drive, just west of the university, living in the same set of tree-shaded, two-story brick apartments with ample screened balconies as two of her friends: Alex Sartwell, who worked for the State Geological Survey as a public information officer but loved books and the arts, and Bill McMinn, the philosophy professor who had gotten to know her on campus when she was still in Bryce, had worked with her on one edit of the Mencken book (she wrote a friend that he "literally ripped it to pieces"), and with whom she'd traveled, albeit not very happily, in Europe the previous year.

Her best Christmas present for 1971 was a leather-bound volume of *Exiles* with marbleized end papers, sent to her by her editor at Delacorte Press, Dick Kennedy, with the note, "A merry Christmas and love from all of us." He had sent her the same of *The Constant Circle*, of which she'd written him, "I was dumbstruck with delight." On one of the blank pages in the front of the book, Sara wrote "Sara Mayfield, Christmas 1971."

Chapter 17

"A Sweeping Historical Novel"

Sara is now an Established Writer, proving that her Determination and Orderliness have paid off. Finishing the Mona Lisa Novel. Occasional Entertaining in the Grand Manner.

MORE THAN FIVE YEARS HAD NOW PASSED SINCE SARA HAD LEFT Bryce, that long, strange dream in that "green-barred hell," and she had proved that she could make it on the outside. Having worked hard to establish herself as a successful writer and literary biographer, with two books to her name and an entry in *Contemporary Authors*—a sure sign of having arrived as an author of national stature, Sara resumed the social life of a woman of "old family" around Alabama. Her neighbor Alex Sartwell, who had relatives in Montgomery like Sara did, walked past as she was sitting on the porch with an old friend and was hailed with the words: "Cabbages and kings, come let us talk of Montgomery things."

In Tuscaloosa, Sara had a number of old and new friends, including Miss Willie White, "the famous doll lady of Tuscaloosa," a collector who had a cottage near Sara's apartment. (Miss Willie had visited the Sesame Club at Bryce as a guest speaker, with her "large collection of dolls," an event Sara reported in the *Bryce News* in 1952.) On occasion, Sara and her buddies would take to the road, as one night when they drove thirty miles down the dark highways outside Tuscaloosa to a restaurant called the Cotton Patch—a rustically decorated, Old South–themed place popular with the university crowd and famed for its fried chicken, easygoing "brown bag" policy on liquor, and African American waitresses in Mammy costumes—and "thence to see the antebellum houses in Eutaw by moonlight," singing into the night all the way home. Although she was sympathetic, in a general way, with desegrega-tion, Sara was still in many ways a creature of her Old-South upbringing. Un-like many of her contemporaries, Virginia Foster Durr and Juliette Hampton Morgan among them, she never became active in civil rights efforts, perhaps because during the key years of the movement she was hospitalized, fighting what she saw—however solipsistically—as her own civil rights battle to be released. (A letter she wrote to a literary agent in 1963, while still in Bryce, gives some flavor of her very mildly progressive but extremely paternalistic attitudes in regard to race: "Two days ago, when Wallace was inauguerated [*sic*] he made a fire-eating segregation speech that left this place seething with so many rumors, counter rumors, and counter counter rumors that it is impossible to get anything done. But it is a black man's fight and a redneck's war, and I have no patience and no part in it and no time to listen to the question of integration here at the U. of A. being debated pro and con. It's fatuous and fantastic for Confederates who were reared in a negro mammy's lap to want to start another civil war over sitting beside a colored person in the library or classroom."[1] About the same time, she had described in her journal a conversation with a friend who had heard rumors about the Klan in Tuscaloosa: "Bob said that the local segregationists had already mapped out what they plan to do if the integrationists attempt to enroll Negroes at the U. of A., i.e. shoot the Negroes as fast as they register them. This is so barbarous, brutal, defiant that [it] is hard to believe it could be thought, much less said in a supposedly civilized community.")

Sometimes she entertained in style, as when she cohosted a cocktail party with her pal Waverly Barbe, a library studies professor at UA, at Waverly's home in Tuscaloosa's historic district. They even sent out invitations, dark-bordered, cream-colored, on heavy cardstock:

Sara Mayfield and Waverly Barbe
invite you for
Cocktails
Saturday, the thirteenth of November
Six-thirty to eight-thirty
13 Audubon Place
Regrets only

For such parties Sara would hire a waiter to pass around hors d'oeuvres in what one friend called "the Grand Manner." Other parties were more intimate, with candlelight and good wines. She and Waverly often had a drink together at the end of the day (what she called his "five-o-clock news cast"), and she wrote fondly of him to a friend that "since Waverly is admittedly non compos scribinis, I'll add his love to mine." While she was traveling in Europe in 1970, she had written asking him to open her mail to see whether she had received a royalty check for *The Constant Circle*: "Please open all my mail, extract, and deposit all checks. I regret to say that I have no private life and hence no secrets—at least, from you."

One Valentine's Day, she threw a big party at the University Club. She wore a long red dress and welcomed her guests, among them longtime friend Ruby Folsom, the sister of former governor Big Jim Folsom and the mother of Cornelia, George Wallace's second wife; Ruby had sent a telegram to Bryce when Sara's brother died. There were surplus funds for parties now. Sara had begun earning money from her writing again with the publication of *The Constant Circle*, but other income came in as well. Alex Sartwell recalled that "sometime in the early 70's coal in Alabama became like black gold and the big coal companies really geared up around Jasper . . . where Judge Mayfield had bought up coal rights and all of a sudden, Sara found herself extremely wealthy. People would actually ask me how much money Sara had. . . . She didn't discuss it with me but Sara would call me because I was over at the Geological Survey and ask me about mineral rights and I would ask people who could help her and she was always very grateful to me for it."[2] Sara also occasionally sold lumber from her land, jointly owned with her nephew.

There was even a little money from the movies. Hollywood had shown some interest in *Exiles*. As the *Tuscaloosa News* reported in March 1972 ("Sara Mayfield Signs Movie Option"), Sara had signed an option agreement with well-known actor-turned-producer Helmut Dantine. When Liza Minnelli came to Tuscaloosa for the UA Homecoming Concert in the fall of 1973, it was Sara she asked to speak to backstage. Minnelli was thinking of playing Zelda and wanted to talk to an expert on the subject. Sara had had her doubts about Liza's resemblance to Zelda, but, she told an interviewer, after the show, "I went backstage, and by then she had her makeup off and the resemblance to Zelda was quite noticeable. Of course, she is not blonde as Zelda was, but I think she might be able to play the part."[3]

It was gratifying to have a star asking to speak to her, and Sara would not have wanted *not* to be asked. But a part of her shrank from having a public presence. Her young writer friend Johnny Greene wrote that when Sara went to other towns to speak, she "paid a fair price to get through those ordeals, and they took more out of her finally than the public gave her in return." He also wrote, with insight: "I believe Sara feared being misunderstood, and for that reason she spoke from prepared texts that were frequently too erudite for her audiences. She would often slip into an upper-class or British pronunciation of words some listeners found charming for the 'lady writer' Sara never wanted to be, but other listeners found disconcerting. Her excessively 'fine' manners were part of her same scheme. They protected her long enough to get through situations and return to the safety of her home, her typewriter and her notebooks."[4] Sara once wrote of herself that "beyond the routine parlour tricks that every Confederate girl learns, I suppose I am rather timid, especially about public appearance."

Sara still got up and did yoga every morning, and she sometimes swam and played golf and tennis. She even claimed to have given up drinking and smoking. (In 1970, she had written to Matthew Bruccoli, who was trying to quit, himself, "I stopped for fourteen years and wish I had never started again. I had an aunt who used to say, 'Smoking is a nasty, dirty, expensive habit, and I love it.'") In Bryce, Sara had realized the importance of what she called "psychosomatic hygiene" in maintaining her equilibrium, and routines worked for her, keeping her habits and her thought processes on track. Especially when she was working on a big project, she had a set writing pattern, getting up at 5:00 a.m., working until lunch, taking a brief nap, and then working until early evening. She went to bed right after supper and read until 10:00 or so, usually a biography or a book related to whatever she was working on. She liked to have younger helpers to do some of the leg work for her books, and her friend Caroline Plath, with whom she'd traveled in Europe, said that "she would get people to help her, but didn't quite want to pay or whatever, but she was used to having people in attendance." Caroline found herself slipping into the role of assistant but pulled away, later saying "I didn't want that role."[5] Sara's cousin Burdette and Cannie Mayfield's daughter, Camella, did help Sara extensively with her work, typing up manuscripts, running errands, and generally supporting Sara's literary life. Although Sara could take others' efforts on her behalf for granted, at least some of the time she paid Camella for her work. Camella, who admired Sara and appreciated her encouragement, had grown up knowing her older cousin as a Bryce patient, and later described her, diplomatically, as having "a different outlook" and, being, perhaps, "not totally 100% accurate" all the time. Although Camella had not been afraid to visit Sara in Bryce, since her father worked there, she also recognized that while Sara "thoroughly thought she was getting a bum deal" by being there, she did have what Camella called "mental problems."[6]

Caroline Plath, who was romantically involved with philosophy professor Bill McMinn, tried to describe Sara's personality in an interview conducted after her death: "She was arrogant; she was autocratic; she could be a snob; and yet she could also go the other way, too. She had very different personalities, which we all do, I guess." Around old Montgomery families, "Sarah would just pivot to that also—language, the whole manners and everything. But, I don't think she was at home with that." Where Sara was comfortable, said Plath, was "being around Bill, being in an environment especially of male intellectuals." A loosely evolving gang would meet at Pete's Restaurant near the university, moving from coffee to lunch to beer and bars. Afternoons blended into evenings. Out on the town with Bill and Caroline, crowded around a table, smoke wreathing the circle of friends, Sara enjoyed lively company and conversation. Caroline also remembered her as having "a coyness and a flirtatiousness" and how she would sometimes flirt with young men: "She would be very stimulated by the conversation and sort of revert to . . . the young maiden in a way. She still had that fire in her." Sometimes when Sara drank, though, "She would sort of go off to another zone a little bit. She would revert to an earlier age and wear a different mask, a different persona. . . . It was some of the special enigmas of Sarah and Sarah's behavior in these different realities that Sarah would float in." Finally, said Caroline, "I'm not certain where the real core of Sarah lay, or if anybody knew the real core of Sarah. Perhaps even Sarah didn't. We all knew so many parts of her." She added, however, that Sara "was a woman who tried to step out of her time and out of the south and the world that had been so rich for her but also held her back and was part of what was destroying so many of her family. . . . She had so many talents."[7]

Sara had one book more to finish and publish, a book forty years in the making. Although she had begun a major rewrite of the Mona Lisa manuscript in the spring of 1966—"ripping out all the flashbacks, rewriting the entire first part, recasting the rest of it so that the whole thing is told from Mona Lisa's point of view, making drastic cuts, and suturing in splices"— and had made her trip to Italy for atmosphere and further research in 1967, she did not complete the final draft of the novel until after she had finished the Mencken and Fitzgerald books. When a final draft was ready for editing, her publisher asked her instead to redirect her energies to the proposed

biography of Tallulah's early years, which she was calling "All My Love, Tallulah." With another biography of Bankhead by first-time biographer and future literary forger Lee Israel in the works (Israel's book would be published
in 1972), it was decided the biography should be pushed forward in line,
which Sara found horribly similar to her race to the finish line with Nancy
Milford. Writing to novelist Elise Sanguinetti, Sara bemoaned her plight:
"Don't let the whims and idiocies of publishers get you down. I could a tale
unfold about my present one that would curl your hair. He had me spend
my entire much-needed vacation in Spain last Spring revising the 'Mona
Lisa.' . . . Then he suddenly decides that he wants a book on Tallulah Bankhead, for which I contracted to do, done pronto. . . . Will anymore I have to
say about publishers be written on asbestos paper." Her reasons for wanting
to publish "Mona Lisa" first were also more personal and psychological: she
wrote to her agent, "I need a respite from the twenties and the tragedies of
my friends."

Once again, it was back to the archives. Always forward-looking in regard to scientific and technological inventions, she began learning to use a
computer at the Huntingdon College/Alabama State University Educational
Computing Service while doing research in Montgomery in 1973. Sara had
access to the Bankhead family papers at the state archives as well as other
letters from Tallulah, and had also gotten to know Cal Schumann, a friend of
Tallulah's who had recorded hundreds of conversations with her toward the
end of her life. She had visited Cal in Baltimore in 1971, writing in a thank-
you note, "From the hosting that you do in your charming apartment, I know
that you are a past grand master of the art. I spent a lively evening there
between you, Jack Daniels, and the fabulous recordings." She worked hard
on the book, turning in the first four chapters, on "the early London years,"
to her new editor, Rutledge Carpenter, with the following note: "You have
doubtless heard the story of the producer who called in the scenario writer. 'A
good movie should have religion, royalty, action, and sex. Those are the necessary elements for any hit. A few days later the perfect scenario writer handed
in his script: "My God,' said the duchess. 'Let go my leg.' These four chapters
have all those elements plus the Cinderella motif." Despite Sara's assertions
about the sauciness of her book, the publisher wrote to her and her agent in
December: "We felt that the first half of the manuscript on Tallulah . . . did
not contain her private life as an adult and that it would be madness to bring
it out in competition with the full life, no matter how unofficial the other
biography is. . . . We were sure that the private sources available to the author

would produce a story of her personal adult life as well as her public life." For "personal adult life," read "sex life," but Sara was dishing no dirt, and the book was killed. A completed typescript of "All My Love, Tallulah" rests in her papers in the Special Collections library at the University of Alabama, a book meant to round out a trio of Sara's books on her childhood friends, but finally an orphan manuscript without a publisher.

Hearing the news, the ever-loyal Betty Adler wrote Sara to affirm her decision: "Muckrakery & debunking have their place, but dirty for its own sake is worse than pornography. You are too much a lady to write for venom or hatred." Meanwhile, the Montgomery lady ranks—or at least some of them—closed to Lee Israel, with one Montgomery friend writing Sara: "A few weeks ago some woman named Lee called me for information of Tallulah—It seems she too, is planning a book—I assured her that I know really nothing, as I certainly had no intention of telling any of the tales I knew—The girl really had a sweet, fine side and a stranger could easily write a very unsympathetic story—I think she ended up talking to Julia Garland."

With the Tallulah book sidelined, the Mona Lisa book moved back up to first in line at the publisher's. In this historical novel about Leonardo da Vinci, Sara focused on the model for the Mona Lisa, Lisa del Giocondo (née Gherardini). Seeking to rescue the flesh-and-blood historical woman and her life, even fictionally, from being merely an image of a lady with an enigmatic smile, Sara wrote her agent of "the sad, sad fact that literally all that is known of her is that she was the daughter of Ser Antonio Maria de Noldo Gherardini, the wife of Francesco Giocondo, the mother of a child who died in infancy, that she was painted by Leonardo and rumored to have been loved by Cardinal Giovanni de Medici." The absence of information about Lisa gave her free rein to invent. Sorting out the complicated plotting and allegiances among the various powerful families of Italy suited Sara's sense of intrigue and mirrored the myriad, interwoven strands of connectedness she saw among the rich and powerful of Alabama.

Despite Sara's enthusiasm for the subject and her writing multiple revisions, when it came time to move forward with publication, the book still needed work. Sara's friend Johnny Greene, having left Tuscaloosa for New York to attend Columbia Journalism School, got a phone call at school one day from Sara's editor at Grosset and Dunlap. Standing in the din of the J-School newsroom, the story he heard from the editor was this: Sara had authorized Johnny to edit the book, which had already been rejected by multiple publishers, and if he refused, the publisher was done with it. Greene asked the advice of a journalism faculty member who told him: "If a writer believes in another writer, he has to do everything humanly possible to help that writer get published. Sara Mayfield did that for you. Are you dumb enough to think you can do anything less?"[8]

Sara had become so frustrated with her copy editors over their suggested and unapproved changes (she was, for instance, unwilling "to have direct quotes from Leonardo and others translated into Madison Avenue lingo") she had been ready to drop the whole project. She wrote her agent, "I know this has been the most troublesome novel that you ever handled." She did agree to "tone down" the love scenes, which apparently were considered too risqué by the editors. In the finished book, there is a fair amount of hand-holding and eye-gazing between Leonardo and Mona Lisa, and a number of references to obligatory marital sex and to husbands who keep mistresses, but only two scenes are explicitly sexual. In the first, Lisa and her friend Cecilia, who is in training to become a nun, take a day trip to the archaeological site of Paestum, in southern Italy near Salerno, to see the Greek temple ruins. The day being hot, they take off their clothes for a swim and afterward stretch out nude on the beach in "a secluded cove." In a brief love scene, Lisa admires Cecilia's body, and Cecilia calls Lisa "captivating . . . irresistible." Then, "Cecilia drew her into her arms. The buds of Lisa's breasts flowered at her touch. A swift fountain of emotion rose from the center of her body as their lips met and clung.

"Lisa's pagan delight in the embrace struck a sudden chord of fear in Cecilia. 'It's time for us to go,' she said, flushed and breathless." The two are silent and awkward as they get dressed, and Cecilia wonders aloud, "Do you suppose that's what the Mother Superior calls 'carnal joy'?" Lisa responds, "What do you want to do, confine carnal joy within respectable bounds? . . . What's the body without the soul or the soul without the body? You can't divide yourself into halves like a peach." Here, Lisa, who "was earthborn and . . . had never denied her heritage," sounds remarkably like Sara.[9]

The second scene that might have been deemed objectionable is an orgy performed for the amusement of guests at a banquet given by Cesare Borgia. Based on an actual event known as the Chestnut Ball, fifty footmen dance with fifty courtesans in a "wild Italian dance," with the courtesans flinging off their clothes as the dance gets wilder. Cesare decrees that a "richly furred mantle" will be given to the courtesan who collects the most chestnuts as the guests toss them to the floor, and that "three elegant silk mantles with caps and boots to match" will be given to the footman who can "ride the greatest number of posts with the courtesans." Lisa is appalled and wants to leave, but Cesare insists that she stay, as they are "umpires" for the contest.

Johnny Greene must have done a good job of smoothing out any uneven places in the text, even handling proofreading and checking the galleys to be sure everything had been entered correctly. The book, a quite readable and entertaining novel, received respectful and fairly positive reviews when it was published in 1974. An Associated Press wire review that ran in smaller newspapers all over the country called it a "very good" historical novel: "Because of our ignorance of Mona Lisa herself, the novelist can take her unscathed through the violence, sex, cruelty and artistic cataract of the late 15th and early 16th century Italy of the Medici, Borgias, Sforzas and the other Renaissance families who managed to combine the functions of great art patrons and the modern mafia. As Miss Mayfield tells her story, this ordeal was needed to mature Mona Lisa physically, mentally and spiritually into the only woman who could catch Leonardo's mind and imagination."[10] *Kirkus Reviews* was less positive, asserting that "Sara Mayfield sentimentalizes the famed painting that is her biography's centerpiece" by creating a story of Leonardo and Mona Lisa that reduces the painting to merely a love story and "ignores the intelligence of the entire portrait . . . everything that really amazes in the painting."[11]

Closer to home, *Anniston (AL) Star* writer Tom Gordon, who had interviewed Sara for the *Star* in August 1973, called the book "a sweeping historical novel." He goes on: "If Miss Mayfield has done her homework, and I think she has, Lisa Gherardini was something else. Lisa entranced many, including Leonardo, and endured an unhappy marriage, poisoning and constant intrigue. Through it all she managed to remain both enigmatic and alluring." Coincidentally, also on the book page in the *Star* for that day was a brief review of *Bits of Paradise: 21 Uncollected Stories by F. Scott and Zelda Fitzgerald.* The reviewer says the value of the book is that "an effort has been made for the first time to separate Zelda's own works from those which actually were collaborations." He goes on: "Unfortunately, none of the stories in this book by either of the authors are particularly good, but the ones attributed to Zelda are valuable for the light they shed upon this unhappy woman."[12] Sara might well have smiled her own Mona Lisa smile as she read both reviews.

Only the Associated Press reviewer dared to write of Leonardo's sexuality in relation to Lisa: "The fact that so little is known about Mona Lisa herself rules out straight biography. But this gives a novelist an opening. Miss

Mayfield's thesis is that Mona Lisa was the only woman who could make the homosexual Leonardo almost become a heterosexual."[13] Throughout her life, Sara had struggled with questions of sexuality, generally in a veiled way; it is possible that writing a book in which a homosexual was capable of heterosexual love may have worked as a kind of wish fulfillment for her, but it is more likely that the character of Lisa, who could enjoy both Cecilia and Leonardo, more closely expressed her own sexuality. In the spirit of the unique love she felt for Elisabeth Thigpen Hill, Sara dedicated *Mona Lisa*, "For the house of 'Thee-and-I' past and present."

Sara also used the character of Lisa to address some of her lifelong concerns about women's roles. Raised and educated by her father, Lisa is brave, clever—perhaps too clever for her times—and able to hold her own in intellectual arguments. But she speaks to da Vinci about what she mockingly calls her "proper province . . . to buy an ell of lawn, to transplant my iris before the rain, put fresh lavender in the sheets, hem my new satin dress, and tell the laundress not to starch my husband's linen stiff. . . . To think beyond that safe domestic round is madness for a woman—or so most men think."[14] Madness for a woman. Or capable, perhaps, of causing madness in a woman.

In late fall of the year *Mona Lisa* came out, Sara appeared in Huntsville, Alabama, in a talk sponsored by the Huntsville Literary Association, but the event, as the promotional poster promised, was to be not about her new novel but rather "an evening of reflections on the days with F. Scott and Zelda . . . New York . . . Paris . . . Montgomery, Ala."[15] Sara dressed formally for the gathering, wearing a dark velvet top and a long skirt with a black background and squares of glittery gold. Her jewelry shone as well: circular gold earrings, a starburst pendant, a gold pinky ring on her right hand. Her hair was short, white, and waved, her eyebrows dark, her lips red. As a concession to necessity, a functional cord holds her reading glasses. In one photo from the event, she holds forth to a small crowd after her talk, speaking thoughtfully. In another, standing over a desk where a younger woman speaks to her, she leans in, engaged, smiling slightly, paying close attention to whatever the woman is saying. Clearly, she is a presence, a person you might be drawn to talk to, her face lined with age but bright with intelligence and curiosity.

The very next week, November 18, 1974, "A Conversation with Sara Mayfield," produced by the University of Alabama Center for Public Television, ran statewide on Alabama Public Television. This was in the era of "appointment TV"—before streaming, before digital recording, even before widespread VHS tape recording, so anyone who wanted to watch the show would

FIGURE 22. Sara Mayfield at a book signing

In 1974, the year her historical novel *Mona Lisa* was published, Sara Mayfield spoke to the Huntsville (AL) Literary Association about her literary life. (Cynthia Denham)

have sat down at 10:00 p.m. that Monday and paid attention.[16] The show, airing just after the publication of Sara's new novel, would have been good publicity. Sadly, it is lost to time; no copies exist, and if they did, the equipment to play that old film would be very hard to find.

Now both a biographer and a novelist, Sara thought she might have one last project in her. While in Bryce, she had worked on an essay titled "Shakespeare and the Pembrokes" covering what Sara called "Shakespeare's Lost Years," arguing that Shakespeare had the Pembroke family as patrons. Always fascinated by strong women, Sara was especially interested in Mary Sidney, Countess of Pembroke, poet, literary patron, and the sister of poet Philip Sidney, and she planned to write her biography. The Mary Sidney Society's webpage describes the society as "an educational and literary organization founded on the premise that Mary Sidney Herbert, Countess of Pembroke, wrote the works attributed to William Shakespeare," and perhaps this persistent though not widely accepted assertion reminded Sara of Scott's use of Zelda's writings. In the summer of 1976, she took a final trip abroad, a research trip to England, traveling at least part of the time with a female friend; among her souvenirs of the trip is a color booklet on Wilton House, in Salisbury, "Home of the Earls of Pembroke for over 400 years." The booklet is inscribed "For Sara, In memory of a wonderful day, warm love, Louisa" and dated July 9, 1976. Two days later, paraphrasing Shakespeare, Louisa inscribed a booklet on Penshurst Place in Tonbridge, Kent: "For Sara, she is tiny but she is mighty. With all love—Louisa."

After her visit to Wilton House, Sara wrote to the Earl of Pembroke's secretary asking about unpublished letters or documents related to her subject. Although a book about Mary Sidney had been published in 1912, Sara was again in communion with the cultural zeitgeist; a new book on the writer was in the works. Gary Waller's *Mary Sidney, Countess of Pembroke: A Critical Study of Her Writings and Literary Milieu* would be published in 1979. Sara enjoyed the research and she loved having a project in the works, but knowing what it had taken out of her to do the other two biographies (and an unpublished third), it was too much of a slog to contemplate. When, on a visit back to Tuscaloosa, Johnny Greene tried to engage her with the idea of writing "a long New Yorker style profile of a colorful Tuscaloosa character," she replied: "The only things I write anymore are checks."[17]

Chapter 18

"Sara Mayfield Dies; Was Author"

Concludes Sara's Story. The Loss of Liz. Assessments by Friends, and a Summing-Up.

THE FALL OF 1976 BROUGHT THE LOSS OF SARA'S OLDEST, DEAREST friend. Elisabeth Thigpen Hill died on October 18. Liz was seventy-four; Sara had just turned seventy-one. In an undated letter from sometime in the 1970s, Sara had tried to explain, in abstract, philosophical terms, using Plato's *Symposium*, the Bible (1 Cor. 13, on love) and the Sanskrit Devi Bhaga-vata, how individual love of a beautiful thing can lead to the love of all beauty, and how truly loving one person can open the door to a love of all beings. That concept was, for her, "a basic intrinsic part of my thinking, *modus vivendi*, and past history." And that beloved one, for her, was Elisabeth. The letter begins with an affirmation of her love for Elisabeth and continues, referring to whatever it was that happened in Cornwall when they were young and whatever it was Margaret Booth said about it: "when we were very young, we had a deep psychic trauma inflicted on us. You've had to deal with it in your way and I in mine; you immersed yourself in your home and family and I in work. No one who has never been forced by fate to practice that kind of stern immolation . . . can ever realize just what it takes—or just what it takes out of you—or appreciate the will power and endurance that it takes to conquer the death wish that is the inevitable result of that kind of immolation. The older one grows, the more aware one is of the beauty and nobility of character of those who succeed in doing it and the more one loves them." Losing Liz meant losing her first, best, longest love, the friend she idealized and whose mere existence made Sara feel less alone, "as noble a friendship as exists in this wicked world."

In addition to emotional losses, Sara had to cope with failing health in her last years—breathing problems, recurrent coughing, fluid retention, and sciatica. The fall in Ibiza in 1970 had left her with permanent leg damage, as well. As always, trying to make light of troubles, she had written to Liz of the brace she had to wear strapped onto the injured leg, "It is a charming little device, a pair of what look like football shoes, gray laced with brown, attached to a pair of steel stanchions. I'm sure that it must have been invented by Torquemada and used extensively during the Spanish Inquisition, but I can walk and drive a car with it . . . even if it limits my orbit to daytime activities, for you can imagine how chic it would look with a cocktail or an evening dress." One of Sara's doctors was a woman, an unusual achievement for 1970s Alabama—which Sara surely admired, and she remembered Sara as a caring person despite her physical ailments: when the doctor's car broke down and Sara heard about it, she insisted that the doctor borrow her car rather than having to drive her husband's truck.[1]

Depending on how she was doing, Sara had sitters and sometimes a nurse, had someone in to cook for her, and relied on friends and family to help run errands or simply visit. Alex Sartwell said that Sara had "a definite early twentieth century antebellum attitude toward servants, and class structure in general." He recounted the story of a maid named Julia who worked for him, Bill McMinn, and Sara. He once suggested that because Julia had a bad leg, Sara shouldn't ask her to do things she couldn't do, and "Sara snapped . . . 'Servants should be able to do what servants do.'"[2]

It was during these last years that her nephew, James "Jeff" Mayfield, the only living son of her brother, came back into her life. While in Bryce, she had sent him birthday presents and generally doted on him as much as circumstances would allow, writing one day in her journal after his mother had brought the boy by for a visit, "He is such a precious lamb and looked too sweet in a little striped shirt and blue denim pants with a red handkerchief in his pocket." He returned from college in Arizona and lived in Tuscaloosa for a time around 1978, where, as an adult, he visited his aunt in her Riverside Drive apartment. He became interested in photography because of her, going with her to the darkroom in Woods Hall on the UA campus, the place she had developed photos while still in Bryce.[3] They owned some land jointly, land he had inherited through his father, and in Sara's final will (there had been several), she made him, as her closest living relative, her primary heir and executor.

Sara, still defending her hard-won declaration of sanity, wrote that should anyone try to break the will, "I . . . direct that any member of my immediate family who attempts to impugn my sanity or contest my Will shall be automatically disinherited." Second, Sara asked that her remains be donated to the anatomy department at the University of Alabama in Birmingham then cremated. Her ashes were to be buried in the family plot "with no funeral or ceremony other than to have the attending Minister read the Burial Service from the old Book of Common Prayer and the Thirteenth Chapter of I Corinthians from the Holy Bible." This was the passage she had encouraged Liz to read on the varieties of love—what should, she said, be *agape* where the translation is usually "charity." It begins: "Though I speak with the tongues of men and of angels, and have not charity, I am become as sounding brass, or a tinkling cymbal" and ends: "For now we see through a glass, darkly; but then face to face: now I know in part; but then shall I know even as also I am known. And now abideth faith, hope, charity, these three; but the greatest of these is charity."

Sara died on January 10, 1979. The day before, Sara's cousin Camella had told her she was pregnant; the baby girl, who would be born just a day after Sara's birthday in September, she named after Sara.[4] Sara's death made the front page of the *Tuscaloosa News*, "Sara Mayfield Dies; Was Author," and was also noted in the *Birmingham Post*, "Rites Today in Tuscaloosa for Sara Mayfield, Novelist," and the *New York Times*, "Sara Mayfield, Wrote Biography of Mencken." The *Times* was the only paper to note, getting the dates a bit wrong, that "between 1946 and 1966 Miss Mayfield was a patient at Bryce State Hospital in Tuscaloosa." And if you can read triumph between the lines, it is there in the next sentence: "Her book about Mr. Mencken was published after her release."[5] Unlike the many patients who died while in Bryce and were then buried in one of the cemeteries on or near the Bryce property, their graves becoming difficult to locate as the years passed, Sara's ashes were buried in a family plot in Evergreen Cemetery, in the shadow of UA's Bryant-Denny Stadium, in its own way a shrine to football.

One old friend in particular did not make it to the funeral. Johnny Greene, who had become a contributing editor for *Harper's Magazine*, heard about her death when he was paged in the Washington, DC, airport, en route from New York to New Orleans. He briefly agonized about whether to change his plans and dash to Tuscaloosa for the funeral. Finally, he "remembered too many pieces of fiction and nonfiction by Southern writers that opened with characters taking trains and planes and buses to funerals. The form was now a stock cliché Sara would insist I avoid. I would go instead to New Orleans and remember Sara there."[6]

Two Tuscaloosa friends assessed her life in different ways. Caroline Plath found inspiration in Sara's example: "So often I have gone and looked at how Sara struggled, how she lived with debilitating disease and her body waning and her destructive behavior against her body. Still, she lived at a level where she still interacted and kept going. It didn't cripple her emotionally. Maybe she had been through the worst of that in Bryce. So I have learned a lot from her and her rebounding. If you would measure a life, I think Sarah's life was very full, very rich, and I think she really made the most of life."[7] Alex Sartwell, however, thought she had "led a fairly unhappy life because she never realized the idea of herself," suggesting that her travels and her journalistic work being cut short had limited her life. Perhaps the difference in perception lay in Caroline seeing an older woman and identifying with her, or perhaps Alex, as an Alabamian rather than a transplant like Caroline, had a different insight into Sara in light of her culture and family. He remembered her "wonderful infectious laugh" and that she was "sharp as a tack—not affectionate—keeping her distance from people."[8] For Sara's namesake, Camella's daughter Sara, the famous cousin she never met was evoked in her childhood by a party dress of Sara's that was kept in a box in the living room. The white silk dress, heavily beaded, evoked the glamour of times gone by, the allure of an occasion special enough for such a dress.

Sara Mayfield, the youngest of the four Montgomery girls, was the last to go. She had written of the other three, Sara Haardt Mencken, Zelda Sayre Fitzgerald, and Tallulah Bankhead, as though her particular charge in life was to defend and memorialize those friendships and their times. Sara had accepted that the Tallulah book would not be published, but of all her many writing projects she did regret that the ambitious autobiographical novel she worked on over the decades would never see the light. The novel used the material of her life and her friends' lives, in a work that took many forms and several titles over the decades, with plans ranging from a single novel to five. She described the full planned sequence this way: "There never has been, and probably never will be, in my life and times such a wonderful hunk of raw material for an American *Remembrance of Things Past* or *Alexandria Quartet*. It would begin with 'The Gold-Plated Heel,' in Montgomery of the Twenties, the story of a Confederate belle who marries a Jazz Age laureate and is vivisected in his novels and destroyed by him, heart and mind. When the sanitarium in which he has put her away burns down, she saves her

FIGURE 23. Sara Mayfield in 1971

Sara Mayfield in 1971, shortly after the publication of *Exiles from Paradise*, her book on the Fitzgeralds. She would publish one more book before her death in 1979, a historical novel, *Mona Lisa* (1974). (*Graphic [Tuscaloosa, AL]*; University of Alabama Libraries Special Collection)

traditions and her friends from the holocaust at the expense of her life. Then 'Uncertain Glory,' in which an academic spinster tell[s] the story [of] Kay Marchmont, who marries the man the aforesaid belle was in love with and leaves him to revert to type and to the plantation in the Troubled Thirties and succeeds in stirring up a Confederate hornet's nest by running an unemployment colony during the depression. And so on, through 'Out of Our Hearts,' in which Kay's mentor, a liberal critic, wages war [on] New Deal liberalism in the Forties and in the fight gains a reputation as an archconservative, a satire on Southern politics. 'The Queen Bee,' Kay Marchmont's story told from the point-of-view of the socially ambitious wife of the superintendent of the State Hospital. 'The Unbalanced Virgin,' in which Kay Marchmont tells her own story." Aspects of Sara's and her friends' lives are clearly evident in this description, but she was working in a fictional mode, mixing and matching characters and plot lines. Kay Marchmont, as the stand-in for Sara, is named similarly: a short name with a long *a*, followed by a month and a geographical designation: for May, March; for -field, -mont. Her life indeed was "a wonderful hunk of raw material" but she could not, finally, wrestle it into a publishable narrative, either as memoir or as fiction. Her narrative skill she poured into the lives of her friends, telling their stories as she saw them, and into the story she told others of her life, weaving a pattern that was complex and lively, choosing the strands that went together best and laying aside some others—"the truth, not the whole truth, but the truth."[9]

As a child of Montgomery's elite, a southern daughter, Sara was less famous than her friend Zelda but fared better, being seen as a writer in her own right, finding a way to be an independent woman, surviving and overcoming mental illness and the Bryce hospital years. She may have lived, as she wrote, "between headlines and deadlines," but it was a life fully felt and deeply experienced. Through adventure and adversity, Sara kept her own kind of faith, and if she chose to see her life the way she thought it needed seeing, with a little shine on the dull or dingy parts, a little skip and whistle past the dark corners, who can blame her? She did, finally, survive to tell the tale.

Afterword

LIKE A MIST RISING OFF THE NEARBY BLACK WARRIOR RIVER, THE legend of Sara Mayfield seemed to be in the air when I moved to Tuscaloosa for graduate school in creative writing at the University of Alabama, only seven years after her death: in stories of how she slept in the nearby Bryce mental hospital by night and went to the university library, lunches, concerts, by day. How she was friends with Zelda Sayre Fitzgerald, Tallulah Bankhead, H. L. and Sara Haardt Mencken. The older professors had known her as a patient, visiting on campus; they drank with her at local bars after her release from the hospital. One, along with his girlfriend, a bookstore owner, traveled to Europe with her. In Sara's version of the story, the psychiatrists decided early on that she was perfectly sane, so she had a great deal of freedom while remaining technically committed. Eventually, Sara's spin became the standard story.

In the 1980s, when I arrived, Tuscaloosa still felt like a sleepy southern university town. I learned about its history in bits and pieces. Spelled "Tuskaloosa" in earlier days (from two Muskogean words meaning "warrior" and "black"), it was named after a sixteenth-century Indian chief who lost a battle to Hernando de Soto. It had lost its status as state capital in the nineteenth century and settled for being home to the state university and the state mental institution instead, the one next to the other, cheek by jowl.

In those early days of hearing stories about Sara Mayfield, about old Tuscaloosa, I wondered: how did a woman who grew up the privileged child of an Alabama state supreme court justice and became a successful writer get committed to the state mental hospital for nearly two decades? How on earth did she keep her mind alive, and how did she manage to end her life so triumphantly, with meaningful work, some acclaim, and friends who cared about her?

Learning that Sara had left all her papers to the UA Special Collections library, I began to contemplate a book about her, which, all these years later, has come to fruition. Investigating her life, I thought of the women of my own southern family, in Arkansas, rather than Alabama: my beautiful, clever, artistic aunt Pat. My mother, Pat's admiring, adoring younger sister, a poet who raised two daughters while keeping her creative spark alive, sometimes with writing, sometimes with inventively themed birthday parties. Their mother, who painted, taught piano, even hosted a local radio show in the late forties and early fifties. As I walk around my house now, I am greeted in each room by evidence of these women's artistry: the watercolor of a harbor by my grandmother in the guest room, the still life by Aunt Pat in the kitchen, the signed print of an abstract titled "The Red Morning" by my mother's first cousin Jo that I wake to every day.

I realized that my curiosity about Sara was in part curiosity about how the women in my family had navigated the need for creative expression while trying to fulfill what they had been taught to expect of themselves: to be traditional wives and mothers, putting others first. Excavating boxes in search of material that might shed light on those women I think of as my creative forebeings (the "bears" part of the word was originally "be-ers"), I found a newspaper clipping from January 1973 when my football-coach grandfather was inducted into the Arkansas Sports Hall of Fame and my mother accepted the award on his behalf. (He had died a decade earlier, just before my younger sister was born.) My widowed grandmother would have been in California by then, remarried, in 1970, to her childhood sweetheart. My aunt Pat had died in 1969, so my mother would have been the one to represent the family. At the ceremony she gave a short speech, in which she said of her father that he was a "belligerent humanitarian" who always wanted to help when there was a need but "heaven help anyone who tried to praise him for it."[1]

The newspaper article quoted what was said after her speech by the emcee, Frank Morris: "'I've heard a lot of women talk,' Morris said when Mrs. Horne finished, 'but at last I heard a woman say something.'"[2] I imagined my mother, who had an MA in English and was an accomplished writer, torn between smiling agreeably at the joke and wincing with frustration and perhaps even humiliation as she was simultaneously praised for her words and put down for her gender, and of the internal conflict that created.

Trying to find entry points into Sara's life and times, I imagined a past in which her family had encountered mine. It is entirely possible that Sara met one or both of my great uncles while visiting Annapolis, as they were midshipmen during the time she was at Goucher. It is a mildly head-spinning proposition to imagine Sara flirting with my handsome Uncle Jack, or even chatting with Jo, my grandmother, at Annapolis visiting her brothers, as the two young women powdered their noses.

> The slightly older Jo: "You're here for the dance?"
> Sara: "Yes, I'm up from Goucher for the weekend. You?"
> Jo: "Visiting my brothers, the Thach boys. I graduated from
>   Galloway, in Arkansas."
> Sara: "Oh, my mother was from Little Rock! Susie Martin."
> Jo: "I know some Martins . . ."

And so they'd be off, finding the connections, looking for potential distant cousinhood. And almost a hundred years later, the granddaughter of one of those women would be writing about them both.

Further back, I could imagine Sara's grandmother meeting my great-grandmother in Arkansas, at some Episcopal Church Women event. I grounded what I didn't know in what I did, and then I learned everything I could about Sara, comparing different versions of events, keeping in mind for both my own telling and others' that, as Adrienne Rich wrote in *Of Woman Born*, "I am keenly aware that any writer has a certain false and arbitrary power. It is *her* version, after all, that the reader is reading at this moment, while the accounts of others—including the dead—may go untold."

I also went looking for models of the kind of book I wanted to write but could not yet fully envision. One book, Nuala O'Faolain's *The Story of Chicago May*, was a revelation, the way she incorporated her own knowledge of Irish culture into her investigation of the life of one Irish immigrant, a woman who lived a life of crime in the US and abroad, but, after becoming an avid reader in prison, ultimately claimed her own story and wrote her memoirs. O'Faolain's book unlocked something within, creating a moment of epiphany as I lay propped up in bed reading in the little cottage my husband and I had rented for a vacation in Wellfleet, Massachusetts, far from our home near Alabama's Black Belt region. Maybe I'd put the book down for a minute to think, or to rest my eyes. Perhaps I was reading the section about May's imprisonment in Aylesbury jail in England for attempted murder, in which O'Faolain writes, "She saw sane women being taken off to the asylum for the criminally insane at Broadmoor. And she was terrified of Broadmoor."[3] I don't remember that part perfectly. What I do remember is sitting bolt upright because a thought had just moved through my mind like the book you push in the bookshelf that opens the door to the secret tunnel: my fascination with Sara must have found an echo in what my mother had told me once, briefly, without further discussion, of how she lived with the legacy of a (male) doctor who told her, when her sister was ill with undiagnosed thyroid disease that caused lethargy and depression, "If you don't have your sister committed, whatever happens to her is on your head." My mother, to her credit, didn't follow his advice, but when her sister, in a weakened physical state, died in the hospital from double pneumonia in her late thirties, the thyroid disease finally diagnosed, but too late, my mother lived not only with that grief but with the unwarranted guilt of wondering if there was something she could have done to save her sister—was what happened, indeed, "on her head"? Our two families lived only a couple of miles apart in Little Rock, Arkansas, and we often visited my aunt, divorced, the mother of three, with the sisters staying in the kitchen to talk while the children were sent outside to play. Why couldn't she have changed the course of events, figured out a way to make things turn out differently? Why did the doctors fail her sister?

In April 1994 my mother was dying of a brain tumor. Each day, it seemed, we lost a little more of her. But some days she got back some of herself, even some of what she'd lost along the way of life. During a good period, between surgeries, on a weekend I was there visiting, she was up in the middle of the night, going through an old file cabinet, looking for what—the rejection slips from magazines and publishers I'd find after she was gone, directions for one of the helpful little gadgets her mother sent her before she had died, just a few months earlier?

Perhaps she was looking for the place she kept her guilt, so she could throw it away. The next morning, waking, she told me, "I don't owe her a life."

Was the "her" her mother, or her sister? I thought at the time she meant her mother, that she'd failed her by failing to save her sister. But maybe it was her sister—the prettier, smarter big sister, whom she somehow couldn't bring back from the brink of illness. Either way, it was one of a series of realizations she had while dying, a kind of fierce forgiveness of herself.

Near the end of my mother's life, we stood in her living room near the front door of her house out in the country and she said, almost didn't say but then did, "I wonder what my life would have been like if I had devoted myself to writing" and I, desperate for her life and choices and family to have mattered, and not wanting to hear the loss and regret implied in that statement, said "Your life is your art." She smiled and was pleased with the statement—"That should be my epitaph"—but we didn't talk about death and we also didn't talk anymore about writing, and I didn't ask the questions I might have asked.[4] In exploring the life of Sara Mayfield, I've come to see that I was also trying to better understand the women of my family, those gracious, warm women who could make any room feel comfortably welcoming, who hid their private sorrows and regrets, who never spoke of their compromises and sacrifices. The unspoken past was only perceptible in melancholic tints of the air, on certain days, in certain moods, and hard to fathom.

The further I went in researching Sara's story, the more convinced I became hers was a story that needed telling, not because, as I initially imagined, it fit into a clean narrative of a conservative family cruelly oppressing their wayward daughter, but because of the messy complexity of Sara's life, the intermingling of the familial, the individual, the sexual, the psychological, the cultural, and the literary, and because of the light her struggles might shed on those of others. The more I came to know Sara Mayfield through her letters and diaries, written over a seventy-year period, the more I came to admire her determination to lead a meaningful, productive, creatively rich life, despite whatever obstacles she faced.

I could see the themes: family conflict, survival, the enduring power of art. But how to tell it, and how to do her justice?

Driving through the University of Alabama campus one day, I turned onto the road that ran past the green lawns of Bryce Hospital and found myself behind a car whose vanity license plate read:

MAYFLD

Sign from the universe or wonderful random coincidence? It didn't matter. I decided to claim it either way. I followed Sara's lead whenever I could, trying to tell her story honestly while respecting her efforts to be in control of her life's narrative. I lived with Sara for years, as biographers do, made sense of her dense handwriting and watched it get worse over the years, the words hunching forward like a line of women walking into a stiff wind. I studied her assessing eyes in photographs, walked the streets she walked—in Tuscaloosa and Montgomery and Paris and London—in a kind of time-daze, overlapping then and now.

As I finished this book, I was several months older than my mother was when she died, half a year older than Sara when she left the hospital. I could feel in my bones what it would be like to learn this was the end of my life, and I could imagine what it would feel like to start over. There are things we can absorb intellectually but have to grow into to fully understand.

Engaging so deeply with another person's life, I came to see that while an individual's history can be assembled, chock full of facts, and that facts do and should matter, it is the stories we tell about each other and ourselves that matter most in shaping who we become. And yet we must be very careful in that shaping: human stories are always complicated, and when we oversimplify them, we run the risk of limiting others and ourselves. To find the full expression of those who came before us, the big, imperfect picture that can free us from impossible expectations, we must pay attention to which stories don't get told, learn to sense the presence of those we've never heard. To coax out stories from their hiding places, we must notice where the woman doing the telling smoothly elides into another, her eyes flickering sideways for a moment and then back to her listener. Where the gaps are, the quiet, shadowed places. However difficult, that's where the rich complexity of life lies, not in making up tidy endings but in asking, again and again: "and then?"

Acknowledgments

I WORKED ON THIS BOOK OVER A NUMBER OF YEARS, WHILE SIMULTA-
neously completing other book projects, and many people helped me with
source material, interviews, manuscript critiques, and encouragement. Although it is impossible to name everyone, I thank and acknowledge all of
those who patiently gave their ears and eyes to help this book come into being. First on the list is my husband, Don Noble, who never stopped believing
that I would finish this project, even when I faltered. He now knows almost
as much about Sara Mayfield as I do.

A further but inevitably partial list includes the following:

For permission to access and quote from the Mayfield papers and Sara
Mayfield's Bryce hospital records, and for his insights into his aunt, James J.
Mayfield IV, Sara Mayfield's nephew and her literary executor.

For sharing Mayfield stories and insights, Sara Mayfield Glassman, Sara's
namesake and cousin, and her mother, Camella Mayfield.

For all their helpful feedback on my drafts and for years of writerly moral
support, special thanks to Rachel Dobson, Katie Lamar Jackson, Jay Lamar,
Bebe Barefoot Lloyd, and Wendy Reed. For encouragement along the way,
thanks also to Rick and Nancy Anderson, Dianne Baker, T. J. Beitelman,
Kim Cross, Mark Dawson, Jennifer Fremlin, William Gantt, Jane Green,
May Lamar, Joanne Mann, Katherine Patterson, Jacqueline Trimble, Frances
Tucker, and Ed and Julia Williams.

For their belief in me, I thank my family, especially my father, Allan Horne,
who read parts of this manuscript early on, and my sister, Mary Horne, and
cousins Angela Bocage and Joseph Bocage Few.

For conversations about Sara and her times, thanks to Sue Blackshear,

Barbara Broach, Nancy Callahan, Temo Callahan, Cynthia Denham, Ric Dice, Dwight Eddins, Camille Elebash, Louise Faircloth (with thanks to Billy Field for connecting us), Michael Florence, Wayne Greenhaw, Aileen Kilgore Henderson, Isabel Thigpen Hill, Marcia Lehman, Nancy Loeb (who did early work on researching Sara's life), Norman McMillan, Robert Mellown, Gloria Narramore Moody, David Nelson, Isabel Oldshue, Emmett Parker, Howell Raines (for sharing memories of Sara Mayfield and Tuscaloosa in the sixties), Alvin Rosenbaum (for sharing memories of Sara's visits to his family home), Luther Richardson, Brenda Childs See (for sharing memories of her aunt, Thelma Trainham, a nurse at Bryce), Mike Williams, and Willita Zoellner. Thanks to Stan Murphy for his timely advice and support and for sharing stories of his parents, Jay and Alberta Murphy. According to Alberta Murphy's obituary, "The legal theory of a 'constitutional right to treatment' for residents of mental institutions [was developed] . . . one evening in her living room in a discussion among Alberta and Jay Murphy, visiting attorney George Dean, and Dr. Ray Fowler, then chair of the University of Alabama department of psychology," which led to the landmark *Wyatt v. Stickney* case and sweeping reforms in mental institutions in Alabama and nationwide. Thanks to Martha Bace and Mary Bess Paluzzi for help with files relating to Sara Mayfield, including interviews done by Katherine Alexander with T. Earle Johnson, Caroline Plath, and Alex Sartwell, and to Katherine Alexander for the work she did in preserving recollections by Sara's friends. Thanks to Patti McGee Brown for the memories she posted online. Special thanks to Sue Paul, one of the original archivists of Sara's papers, who shared memories of her husband, Waters Paul, and of Sara's Bryce days, and encouraged me in completing this project; although she died in 2022, before this book could be published, she helped bring Sara's story full circle. All of these conversations and interviews greatly helped me to understand the Tuscaloosa of Sara Mayfield's time.

This project would not have been possible without the dedicated assistance of the staff of the W. S. Hoole Special Collections Library at the University of Alabama, led by Jessica Lacher-Feldman for the first part of my project and then by Lorraine Madway.

Thanks to scholars and writers who provided insights into Sara Mayfield's world, including Dean Bonner, for sharing his essay "Seeking Asylum"; Caitlin Burns, whose paper "'To Whom It May Concern': A Rhetorical Analysis of Sara Mayfield's Diaries from 1948–65" helped me appreciate the specific rhetorical strategies and contexts of Sara's Bryce diaries; Patricia Foster, for her encouragement at a crucial stage of the manuscript; Koula Svokos Hartnett, author of *Zelda Fitzgerald and the Failure of the American Dream for Women*, for her enthusiastic support and her interviews with those who knew Sara Mayfield; Barry Mason, for sending me photos of where Sara's flat would have been in London, near Virginia Woolf's house; Wayne Flynt, author of *Alabama: The History of a Deep South State*, for his understanding of Alabama culture and history, and his ability to communicate that understanding clearly and eloquently; Steven Goldleaf for sharing his entry on Fitzgerald books from the *St. James Guide to Biography*; Kat Meads, for sharing her play on Zelda Fitzgerald, "Matched"; Paige Miller, the University of Alabama Women and Gender Resource Center; Elizabeth Findley Shores, author of *Earline's Pink Party: The Social Rituals and Domestic Relics of a Southern Woman*; Mary Stanton, for her biography of Juliette Hampton Morgan, *Journey to Justice*, which was invaluable for helping me understand the atmosphere of Montgomery during the bus boycott. Thanks to John Crowley for early encouragement on this project. Thanks to David Hardin, Archivist at the National Archives at St. Louis, for looking for Sara Mayfield's personnel records. Steve Davis, archivist at Bryce Hospital, helped me understand the wards and layout of the hospital during the years Sara was there. Thanks to Robin McDonald for helping with photographs and for his fine design work on my article on Sara Mayfield that appeared in *Alabama Heritage* in 2016, and to the staff members of the Alabama Department of Archives and History, the Special Collections Department at the Enoch Pratt Free Library, and the Special Collections and Archives Department at Goucher Library, who assisted with photographs and permissions. Thanks to the legal staff of the Authors Guild and to Sarah F. Henson for guidance on legal matters.

A special thanks to the Clancy Sigal (1926–2017), writer, who worked with R. D. Laing on mental health treatment reform in London in the 1960s, and who wrote me in an email exchange: "You nail it re Sara. Just keep going. And avoid 'diagnostic' labels. Just keep to her actual experience. Being in the bug house 17 years could drive any of us nuts. . . . No secret dealing with the mad, no golden key. Just listen, listen, have patience and don't get crazy yourself out of sympathy."

Parts of this manuscript, in different versions, have been published in *Alabama Heritage* magazine and the *Peauxdunque Review*, for which the essay was the runner-up in the Tennessee Williams Literary Festival, creative nonfiction category. I delivered a talk on Sara Mayfield and Zelda Fitzgerald for the 2013 International Fitzgerald Society conference and the 2017 Society of Alabama Archivists meeting. A version of the talk on Sara Mayfield and Zelda Fitzgerald was published as "Sara Mayfield: Zelda's Southern Biographer," in 2022 in *The Romance of Regionalism in the Work of F. Scott and Zelda Fitzgerald: The South Side of Paradise* (Lexington Books), edited by Kirk Curnutt and Sara A. Kosiba. Thanks to those conference organizers, editors, and publishers for their confidence.

I thank Rand Brandes and Lenoir-Rhyne University for my time at LRU as visiting writer-in-residence in the spring semester of 2018, during which time I completed valuable work on this manuscript.

I owe a great debt to Gretchen McCullough and to the three anonymous peer reviewers for the University of Alabama Press for reading this book in draft and offering invaluable criticism and suggestions for revisions at a critical point in the completion of the book.

I am grateful to my copy editor, Anne R. Gibbons. Her expertise in matters of style and syntax made this book better, and the graceful way in which she worded suggestions for improvement made her a joy to work with.

Finally, I thank the staff of the University of Alabama Press, especially Jon Berry, Carol Connell, Claire Lewis Evans, Kelly Finefrock-Creed, Michele Myatt Quinn, Lori Lynch, and Dan Waterman. Claire Lewis Evans intelligently and supportively shepherded this work into a publishable manuscript. I could not ask for a more supportive, professional, and conscientious team to work with.

Notes on Sources

A s I state in my author's note I relied primarily on the Sara Mayfield Papers in the W. S. Hoole Special Collections Library at the University of Alabama, her Bryce Patient Records, and on her two books about the Menckens and the Fitzgeralds. However, because Sara Mayfield was not always a reliable narrator of events, whenever possible I have checked her version against other contemporaneous accounts, in newspaper articles, through interviews, and in other books on the subject. The books, articles, and web resources that proved helpful in writing each chapter appear below, in order of first use; full citations for those sources are provided in the bibliography. In addition, published works quoted directly are cited in the endnotes, as are a few significant quotations from unpublished materials.

CHAPTER 1
Works that were helpful in writing this chapter include: *The Life of James Jefferson Mayfield*, by Henry Holman Mize; "A Brilliant Wedding," *Arkansas Gazette*, July 1, 1897; "Susie Fitts Martin Mayfield," *A Register of the Officers and Students of the University of Alabama; Who Was Who in Alabama*, vol. 1, by Henry S. Marks; *Dictionary of Alabama Biography*, by Thomas McAdory Owen; "Judge Mayfield Drops Dead at Radio Party," *Montgomery Advertiser*, January 2, 1927; "Chitlins and Caviar: Montgomerian Returns" (Column), by Wayne Greenhaw, *Alabama Journal, 1969–70*; "Colonial Dames Entertained At Tea by Mrs. E. L. Robinson," *Mobile Register*, April 10, 1948; "Mrs. Susie Fitts Martin Mayfield," *National Society of the Daughters of the American Revolution, vol. 28*; "Alabama," *Encyclopedia Britannica*, 11th ed., vol. 1; "Children of the Alabama Judiciary," by Marie Bankhead Owen, *Montgomery*

Advertiser, March 26, 1911; "Belle of Letters: Sara Mayfield's Days," by Tom Gordon, *Anniston (AL) Star*, August 26, 1973; *Journey toward Justice: Juliette Hampton Morgan and the Montgomery Bus Boycott*, by Mary Stanton; "'The Lightning Route': The Development of the Electric Streetcar and Its Effect on Montgomery, 1885–1900," by Mary Ann Neeley, *Boll Weevil Review: Essays from Central Alabama's Past*; "Montgomery," by Mary Ann Oglesby Neeley, *Encyclopedia of Alabama Online*; *Zelda's Story*, in *Flappers: Six Women of a Dangerous Generation*, by Judith Mackrell; "The Literary World's Sara Mayfield," by Despina Vodantis, *Crimson White*, July 19, 1971; "Little Lady," by Sara Haardt, *Southern Souvenirs: Selected Stories and Essays of Sara Haardt*; Ancestry.com. *US City Directories, 1821–1989*; Federal Census 1910; *Outside the Magic Circle*, by Virginia Foster Durr; US Passport Applications 1795–1925, National Archives and Records Administration; New York Passenger Lists 1820–1957; *Intimate Matters: A History of Sexuality in America*, by John D'Emilio and Estelle B. Freedman; *The Eleventh House: Memoirs*, by Hudson Strode; personals column, *Montgomery Advertiser*, Sept. 29, 1922; "The Palm Court," Plaza Hotel; *Donnybrook Fair* 1921, Goucher College Archives.

CHAPTER 2

Works that were helpful in writing this chapter include: "Books and Authors," by James T. Bready, *Baltimore Sun*, Sept. 11, 1965; *Goucher Kalends* clipping, vol. 28, no. 5; "The Literary World's Sara Mayfield," by Despina Vodantis, *Crimson White*, July 19, 1971; "Remember When: The City's Glitterati Met at 412 North Howard Restaurant," by Frank Rasmussen, *Baltimore Sun*, April 6, 1997; *Zelda Fitzgerald: Her Voice in Paradise*, by Sally Cline; *The Gatsby Affair*, by Kendall Taylor; *Alabama in the Twentieth Century*, by Wayne Flynt; "The New Woman: Changing Views of Women in the 1920s," by Estelle B. Freedman, *Journal of American History*, vol. 6, no. 2 (Sept. 1974); *Historical Statistics of the United States, Colonial Times to 1970, Part 1*; *A Turn in the South*, by V. S. Naipaul; "The Alabama Climate Report," vol. 3, No. 12, Alabama Climatology Office; "History of St. John's," St. John's Episcopal Church; *Journey toward Justice*, by Mary Stanton; *Writing a Woman's Life*, by Carolyn Heilbrun.

CHAPTER 3

Works that were helpful in writing this chapter include: "Judge Mayfield Drops Dead at Radio Party," *Montgomery Advertiser*, Jan. 2, 1927; *Hugo Black of Alabama*, by Steve Suitts; "The Unveiling of the Memorial to Judge James Jefferson Mayfield," *Alabama Law Journal*, 1927–28; Lethargic Encephalitis," *Public Health Reports (1896–1970)*; "Encephalitis Lethargica Information Page," National Institutes of Health; "Encephalitis Lethargica: 100 Years after the Epidemic," by Leslie A. Hoffman and Joel A. Vilensky, *Brain: A Journal of Neurology*; "The Mann Act," PBS.org; *One Hundred Years of Marriage and Divorce Statistics, 1867–1967*, US Department of Health, Education, and Welfare; "How City Welcomed Amelia Earhart," by Victoria Bartlett; "FAQ: *A Room of One's Own*"; *Tallulah!* by Joel Lobenthal; "The Obscenity Trial of Miss Radclyffe Hall's novel 'The Well of Loneliness'—16 November 1928," British Newspaper Archive Blog, Nov. 15, 2013; "Echoes from a Golden Age: Sara Recalls Idols of '20s," by Don Chapin, *Huntsville (AL) Times*, Nov. 1974; "Plays of the Month," *Play Pictorial*, Sept. 1929; "Sara (Martin) Mayfield," Gale Literature: *Contemporary Authors*; *Sexual Reckonings: Southern Girls in a Troubling Age*, by Sarah K. Cahn.

CHAPTER 4

Works that were helpful in writing this chapter include: *Crazy for You: The Making of Women's Madness*, by Jill Astbury; letter from H. L. Mencken to Sara Haardt, Jan. 11, 1927, Goucher College Digital Archives; *Journey toward Justice*, by Mary Stanton; "Sara (Martin) Mayfield," Gale Literature: *Contemporary Authors*; "The Literary World's Sara Mayfield," by Despina Vodantis, *Crimson White*, July 19, 1971; "Sayre Is Victim of Long Illness," *Birmingham News*, Nov. 18, 1931; "The Muse and the Maker: Gender, Collaboration, and Appropriation in the Life and Work of F. Scott Fitzgerald and Zelda Fitzgerald," by Ashley Lawson, *F. Scott Fitzgerald Review*; "F. Scott Fitzgerald," Baltimore Literary Heritage Project; "Top Ten Weather Events in the 20th Century for Alabama," NOAA; "1932 Deep South Tornado Outbreak," Wikipedia; "Ruby Pickens Tartt: Citizen of the World," by Philip Beidler and Elizabeth Buckalew, *Alabama Heritage*; "John Lomax," Wikipedia; "Ruby Pickens Tartt," *Encyclopedia of Alabama Online*; *Thirteen Loops: Race, Violence, and the Last Lynching in America*, by B. J. Hollars; "A. T. Harden 'Hardin,' Dan Pippen Jr. and Elmore Clark," Digital Repository Service, Northeastern University Library.

CHAPTER 5

Works that were helpful in writing this chapter include: "Ross Clemo Treseder," Prabook.com; "Rum Rush," *Time* magazine, Dec. 4, 1933; "Books and Authors," by James T. Bready, *Baltimore Sun*, Sept. 11, 1965; Gloria

Narramore Moody, telephone interview with the author; "Thomas Lovell Beddoes," citing H. W. Donner, ed., *Plays and Poems of Thomas Lovell Beddoes*, Wikipedia; *Grimoires: A History of Magic Books*, by Owen Davies; *Some Sort of Epic Grandeur*, by Matthew Bruccoli; "Road Show (musical)," Wikipedia; "Adrienne Morrison," IMDB.com.

Chapter 6

Works that were helpful in writing this chapter include: New York Harbor Parks, Sandy Hook, Fort Hancock; "Franklin D. Roosevelt Day by Day," FDR Library Online; "Danzig," US Holocaust Museum website; "Bedside Note of President Franklin D. Roosevelt Regarding the Invasion of Poland by Germany, 09/01/1939," National Archives and Records Administration; "German Army Attacks Poland; Cities Bombed, Port Blockaded; Danzig Is Accepted into Reich," *New York Times*, Sept. 1, 1939; "Children of the Alabama Judiciary," by Marie Bankhead Owen, *Montgomery Advertiser*, March 26, 1911; "A Look Back at What Things Used to Cost," farmersalmanac.com; "Six Months of War," *New York Times*, March 3, 1940; Camille Elebash, interview with author; *Pepys' Diary and the New Science*, by Marjorie Hope Nicolson; "Frank A. F. Severance" (Obituary), *New York Times*, May 20, 1979; "Garden Club Members to Discuss Plans for Christmas Season," *Tuscaloosa News*, Dec. 10, 1939; "History of Psychology: The Birth and Demise of *Dementia Praecox*," by Margarita Tartakovsky, Psychcentral.com; "V Sign: The V for Victory Campaign and the Victory-Freedom Sign," Wikipedia; "Britain's Battle of the Air: 'V' Symbol a Radio Contribution, Article in 'Saturday Evening Post' Reveals," *Broadcasting*, April 13, 1942; "Colonel Britton and the 'V-for-Victory' Campaign," *Army Talks*, Sept. 16, 1945; "'Mr. V.,' a British Melodrama with Leslie Howard, Opens at Rivoli," *New York Times*, Feb. 3, 1942; *Mrs. Whaley and Her Charleston Garden*, by Emily Whaley.

Chapter 7

Works that were helpful in writing this chapter include: "Robert Rice Reynolds," North Carolina History Project; "Lurton Blassingame, 84, Agent" (Obituary), *New York Times*, Apr. 13, 1988; Louise Faircloth, interview with author; Gloria Narramore Moody, telephone interview with author; *Zelda*, by Nancy Milford; "Hampton Roads in 1941: Ready for War," *Daily Press* online; *Mud on the Stars*, by William Bradford Huie, and *Rachel's Children*, by Harriet Hassell.

CHAPTER 8
Works that were helpful in writing this chapter include: *Encyclopedia of US-Latin American Relations*, by Thomas M. Leonard; National Personnel Records Center; David Hardin, Archivist, National Archives at St. Louis, personal correspondence with author; "The Writers' War Board: Writers and World War II," by Robert Thomas Howell, LSU Digital Commons; "Fighting the Fires of Hate: America and the Nazi Book Burnings," US Holocaust Museum; "Klauber's Victory Vs. WWB," *Variety*, June 13, 1945; "San Francisco," *Encyclopedia of the United Nations and International Agreements*; "The Day is New: Dawn to Darkness in Mexico City" (film), US Office of Inter-American Affairs; *Mexican Political Biographies, 1935–2009*, by Roderic Ai Camp; "Blumenthal, Alfred Cleveland. Divorced," Milestones, *Time*, Sept. 10, 1945; "Foundation of the Law Firm of Mayfield and Harris with Offices in the Searcy Building," *Tuscaloosa News*, Nov. 29, 1953; "Beware of Japanese Balloon Bombs," by Linton Weeks, NPR.org; "Georgia Lloyd" (Obituary), *Chicago Tribune*, Feb. 23, 1999; "Ely Culbertson: American Bridge Player," *Encyclopedia Britannica Online*; Guggenheim Fellows, 1945, Guggenheim Foundation.

CHAPTER 9
Works that were helpful in writing this chapter include: Camille Elebash, personal interview with author; "Mrs. F. Scott Fitzgerald, Widow of Author, among Those Killed," *Mobile Press Register*, March 11, 1948; "Died: Zelda Sayre Fitzgerald, 48, Invalid Wife of Jazz Age Novelist F. Scott Fitzgerald," *Time*, March 22, 1948; *Zelda*, by Nancy Milford; *To Kill a Mockingbird*, by Harper Lee; *Farmer's Almanac*, 1948; "Colonial Dames Pay Tribute to Mrs. Mayfield," *Mobile Register*, April 15, 1948; "Colonial Dames Entertained at Tea by Mrs. E. L. Robinson," *Mobile Register*, April 10, 1948; "Files Cross Bill in Custody Suit," *Gulfport (AL) Daily Herald*, April 23, 1949; *Safire's Political Dictionary*, by William Safire; *Alabama in the Twentieth Century*, by Wayne Flynt; "Eugenics: Compulsory Sterilization in 50 American States," Lutz Kaelber, presentation at the 2012 Social Science History Association Meeting; "Eugenics In Alabama," by Gregory Michael Dorr, *Encyclopedia of Alabama Online*; "Shock the Gay Away: Secrets of Early Gay Aversion Therapy Revealed," by Jamie Scot, *Huffington Post*, June 28, 2013.

CHAPTER 10
Works that were helpful in writing this chapter include: "Electroconvulsive Therapy: A History of Controversy, but Also of Help," by Jonathan

Sadowsky; "A Brief History of Electroconvulsive Therapy," by Raheem Suleman; Luther Richardson, personal interview with author; Steve Davis, Bryce historian, email communication with author; Visitors Guide Map produced by Tuscaloosa Chamber of Commerce, 1950; *The Lute Player: A Novel of Richard the Lionhearted*, by Norah Lofts; "Greater Mental Health Support in State Urged," *Tuscaloosa News*, Sept. or Oct. 1952; *The Letters of a Victorian Madwoman*, by John S. Hughes; "Subversive Apologia," by Fredrick E. Vars, *Law and Psychology Review*; Recovery in the USA: From Politics to Peer Support," by Laysha Ostrow and Neal Adams, *International Review of Psychiatry*; "*Wyatt v. Stickney*: A Landmark Decision," by Lauren Wilson Carr, *Alabama Disabilities Advocacy Program Newsletter*; US School Yearbooks, Murphy High School, 1937, Ancestry.com; "Called Crazy for Racial Beliefs," *Chicago Defender*, April 5, 1952; "Death Plunge Ends Tortured Life of Pretty Model," *Atlanta Constitution*, Feb. 20, 1955; "Former Model, Inmate at Bryce, Is Captured," *Anniston (AL) Star* June 12, 1949; "Legal Explanation of the Week," *Jet*, April 10, 1952.

CHAPTER 11

Works that were helpful in writing this chapter include: "Judge's Death in Montgomery Held 'Undoubtedly' Suicide," *Atlanta Daily World*, April 5, 1956; *US City Directories, 1822–1995*, Ancestry.com; *Alabama Divorce Index, 1950–59*, Ancestry.com; "J. Mayfield Fatally Shot," *Anniston (AL) Star*, April 4, 1956; "Blame Judge's Suicide on Segregation Issue," *Chicago Defender*, April 14, 1956; "Poor Health 'Partially' Blamed by Mayfield in His Suicide Note," *Anniston (AL) Star*, April 6, 1956; "Law in a White Man's Democracy: A History of the Alabama State Judiciary," by Robert J. Norrell, *Cumberland Law Review*; *Journey toward Justice*, by Mary Stanton; "A History of the Alabama Appellate Courts." Alabama Judicial System; "William Stanley Hoole: A Man of Letters," by Elizabeth Hoole McArthur, *Alabama Heritage*; Sue Paul, personal interview with the author; "A Science Odyssey: People and Discoveries: Drug for Treating Schizophrenia Identified, 1952," PBS.org; "Fifty Years Chlorpromazine: A Historical Perspective"; Camille Elebash, personal interview with author; "Voices and Visions: Bryce Historical Committee Members Explore Their Hopes for Bryce," *Listen*; "God Knows Where I Am," by Rachel Aviv, *New Yorker*; "Yoga Pioneers: How Yoga Came to America," by Holly Hammond, *Yoga Journal*.

CHAPTER 12
Works that were helpful in writing this chapter include: "Living Wright," by Sarah Pirch, *Alabama Journey*; "Political Melodrama Way Down South," by Orville Prescott, *New York Times*, Mar. 13, 1964; "Class Notes/Deaths," *Vanderbilt Magazine* 82, no. 4 (Fall 2001); "Paid Notice: Deaths, Landman, Sidney James," *New York Times*, Jan. 2, 2001.

CHAPTER 13
Works that were helpful in writing this chapter include: Clancy Sigal, personal correspondence with author; "Clancy Sigal, Novelist Whose Life Was a Tale in Itself, Dies at 90," by Sam Roberts, *New York Times*, July 21, 2017; "Clancy Sigal Obituary," by Kim Howells, *Guardian (Manchester)*, July 25, 2017; "Former Judge Wiley Hill's Rites Held at Montgomery," *Birmingham Post-Herald*, June 18, 1963; Norman McMillan, personal interview with author; *Goucher Alumnae Quarterly*, Summer 1964.

CHAPTER 14
Works that were helpful in writing this chapter include: *Zelda Fitzgerald and the Failure of the American Dream for Women*, by Koula Svokos Hartnett; Mike Williams, personal interview with the author; "Going Once, Going Twice: John F. Kennedy's Diary as a Young Journalist to Be Auctioned," by George Lemoult, WGBH News, Mar. 24, 2017; "The Rochambeau Apartments."

CHAPTER 15
Works that were helpful in writing this chapter include: "Critic Mencken's Old Friend Gets 'Head Start' On Book," *Tuscaloosa News*, Jan. 13, 1966; "Curtains Come Down on 'Room with a View,'" by Patricia Clough, *Independent* (UK), July 8, 1993; "Miss Mayfield Writes about Zelda, Scott," by Dolph Tillotson, *Tuscaloosa News*, Apr. 5, 1969; "Author from Anniston to Autograph Books," *Anniston (AL) Star*, Oct. 21, 1968; "The Aftermath of Mencken," by Edmund Wilson, *New Yorker*, May 31, 1969; "Ruined by the Uplift," by Geoffrey Wolff, *Washington Post*, Sept. 3, 1968; "Alabama Library Association Handbook: History: Alabama Author Awards"; "Literary Associate Speaks at LC," *Hilltop News*, Apr. 15, 1969; "77th Goucher College Alumnae Reunion to Be Held June 20–22," *Baltimore Sun*, June 6, 1969; "Guide to the Francis P. Squibb Papers, 1894–2003," University of Chicago Library.

CHAPTER 16

Works that were helpful in writing this chapter include: "Nancy Milford," Gale Literature: *Contemporary Authors*; *Zelda*, by Nancy Milford; *The Time of Their Lives: The Golden Age of Great American Book Publishers*, by Al Silverman; "Tuscaloosan at Large," by Warren Koon, *Tuscaloosa News*, n.d.; interview with Alex Sartwell by Katherine Alexander; "Scott's Editor, Zelda's Friend," by Aaron Latham, *Washington Post*, Dec. 19, 1971; "The Iceberg," by Zelda Fitzgerald, *New Yorker* Dec. 20, 2013; "Did Zelda Inspire Scott's Creativity?" by Ronald C. Hood, *New Orleans Post-Crescent*, Aug. 15, 1971; "Attis Adonis Osiris Fitzgerald and Co.," by Robert M. Adams, *New York Review of Books*, Jan. 27, 1972; "The Literary World's Sara Mayfield," by Despina Vodantis, *Crimson White*, July 19, 1971; Robert Mellown, personal interview with author; "Publisher's Letter," *People*, Sept. 23, 1985; "Avoiding Stock Clichés and Missing Sara's Funeral," by Johnny Greene, *Alabama Alumni News* and *Menckeniana*; "Chitlins and Caviar: Montgomerian Returns," by Wayne Greenhaw, *Alabama Journal*, n.d., circa 1969–70; interview with Caroline Plath by Katherine Alexander.

CHAPTER 17

Works that were helpful in writing this chapter include: *Bryce News*, Apr. 5, 1952, Mayfield Papers; Pauline Jones Gandrud Papers, William Stanley Hoole Special Collections Library, University of Alabama; interviews with Caroline Plath and Alex Sartwell by Katherine Alexander; "Sara Mayfield Signs Movie Option," *Tuscaloosa News*, Mar. 19, 1972; "Echoes from a Golden Age: Sara Recalls Idols of '20s," by Don Chapin, *Huntsville (AL) Times*, Nov. 1974; "Avoiding Stock Clichés and Missing Sara's Funeral," by Johnny Greene, *Alabama Alumni News* and *Menckeniana*; "Sara Mayfield's Days," by Tom Gordon, *Anniston (AL) Star*, Aug. 26, 1973; "Tuscaloosan at Large," by Warren Koon, *Tuscaloosa News*, n.d.; Sara Mayfield Glassman, telephone interview with author; Camella Mayfield, telephone interview with author; "Lee Israel, Literary Forger" (Obituary), *Telegraph (UK)*, Feb. 24, 2015; "Mona Lisa Flamboyant," by Ronald C. Hood, *Hattiesburg (MS) American*, Oct. 6, 1974; "Mona Lisa: The Woman in the Portrait," *Kirkus Reviews*, Aug. 1, 1974; "Mona Lisa's Smile Still Baffling," by Adele M. Allison, *Pittsburgh Press*, Jan. 11, 1976; "Lisa behind a Smile," by Tom Gordon, *Anniston (AL) Star*, Sept. 29, 1974; "The Fitzgeralds as Collaborators," *Anniston (AL) Star*, Sept. 29, 1974; Cynthia Denham, email interview with author; "Author Mayfield Spotlighted," *Mobile Register*, Nov. 16, 1974.

CHAPTER 18

Works that were helpful in writing this chapter include: "Elisabeth Thigpen Hill," Findagrave.com; Isabel Oldshue, telephone interview with author; interview with Caroline Plath by Katherine Alexander; interview with Alex Sartwell by Katherine Alexander; James Jefferson Mayfield IV, telephone interview with author; Sara Mayfield Glassman, telephone interview with author; "Sara Mayfield Dies; Was Author," *Tuscaloosa News*, Jan. 11, 1979; "Rites Today in Tuscaloosa for Sara Mayfield, Novelist," *Birmingham Post*, Jan. 13, 1979; "Sara Mayfield, Wrote Biography of Mencken," *New York Times*, Jan. 15, 1979; "Avoiding Stock Clichés and Missing Sara's Funeral," by Johnny Greene, *Alabama Alumni News* and *Menckeniana*; "The Literary World's Sara Mayfield," by Despina Vodantis, *Crimson White*, July 19, 1971.

Notes

CHAPTER 1

1. Sara Mayfield, "Strange Possession," MS, Mayfield Papers, Box 1227, Folder 7.

2. Sara Mayfield, *Exiles from Paradise* (New York: Delacorte, 1971), 42, 71; Sara Mayfield Patient File, Bryce Hospital: "Family History: General Social Adjustment."

3. Sara Haardt, "Little Lady," *Southern Souvenirs: Selected Stories and Essays of Sara Haardt*, Ann Henley, ed. (Tuscaloosa: University of Alabama Press, 1999), 86–87; Mayfield, *Exiles*, 12.

4. Virginia Foster Durr, *Outside the Magic Circle* (Tuscaloosa: University of Alabama Press, 1985), xi.

5. Harold T. Council to Sara Mayfield, Dec. 2, 1969. Mayfield Papers, Box 1221, Folder 281.

6. D'Emilio and Freedman, *Intimate Matters*, 240.

7. Sara Mayfield, draft of *The Constant Circle*, 80, Mayfield Papers, Box 1228, Folder 15.

8. D'Emilio and Freedman, *Intimate Matters*, 130, 21, 129, 193–94, 226.

9. Mayfield, *Exiles*, 91–92.

10. Hudson Strode, *The Eleventh House: Memoirs* (New York: Harcourt Brace Jovanovich, 1975), 98.

11. Sara Mayfield, draft of *The Constant Circle*, 9, Mayfield Papers, Box 1228, Folder 12.

12. Flynt, *Alabama in the Twentieth Century*, 268.

CHAPTER 2

1. Sara Mayfield to her father, Oct. 17, 1922, Mayfield Papers, Box 1220, Folder 180.

2. *Goucher College Weekly*, Dec. 20, 1922, Goucher College Digital Archives.

3. Sara Mayfield, *The Constant Circle* (Tuscaloosa, AL: Fire Ant Books, an imprint of University of Alabama Press, 2003), 1–5, 21–25; James T. Bready, "Books and Authors," *Baltimore Sun*, Sept. 11, 1965, Mayfield Papers; Frank Rasmussen, "Remember

When: The City's Glitterati Met at 412 North Howard Restaurant," *Baltimore Sun*, Apr. 6, 1997.

4. H. L. Mencken to Sara Haardt, Jan. 11, 1927, Goucher College Digital Archives; Mayfield, *Constant Circle*, 59–60, 62–63.

5. Carl Bode interview with Sara Mayfield, c. late 1960s, Mayfield Papers, Box 1227, Folder 16.

6. Bready, "Books and Authors." *Baltimore Sun*, Sept. 11, 1965, Mayfield Papers.

7. Mayfield, *Exiles*, 43.

8. Mayfield, *Exiles*, 43.

9. Sally Cline, *Zelda Fitzgerald: Her Voice in Paradise* (New York: Arcade Publishing, 2003), 39–41; Kendall Taylor, *The Gatsby Affair: Scott, Zelda, and the Betrayal That Shaped an American Classic* (Lanham, MD: Rowman and Littlefield, 2018), 19–21; Mayfield, *Exiles*, 23.

10. D'Emilio and Freedman, *Intimate Matters*, 186, 257.

11. Mayfield, *Constant Circle*, 83.

12. Anne Firor Scott, *The Southern Lady: From Pedestal to Politics, 1830–1930* (Chicago: University of Chicago Press, 1970), 181, 210; Flynt, *Alabama in the Twentieth Century*, 267–68; Estelle B. Freedman, "The New Woman: Changing Views of Women in the 1920s," *Journal of American History*, 6, no. 2 (Sept. 1974): 377.

13. *Historical Statistics of the United States, Colonial Times to 1970*, Part 1. US Census.

14. Siddons quoted in V. S. Naipaul, *A Turn in the South* (New York: Knopf, 1989), 42; Scott, *The Southern Lady*, 226.

15. Mayfield, *Constant Circle*, 77.

16. Sara Mayfield to John Sellers, June 30, 1940, Mayfield Papers, Box 1220, Folder 193.

17. Mayfield, *Exiles*, 107–8.

18. Mayfield, *Exiles*, 108–12.

19. Mayfield, *Exiles*, 113–14.

20. Carolyn Heilbrun, *Writing a Woman's Life* (New York: Ballantine, 1988), 48–51.

CHAPTER 3

1. "Judge Mayfield Drops Dead at Radio Party," *Montgomery Advertiser*, Jan. 2, 1927, 1.

2. "The Unveiling of the Memorial to Judge James Jefferson Mayfield," 3 Ala. L.J. (Tuscaloosa) 249 (1927–28).

3. "Lethargic Encephalitis," *Public Health Reports* (1896–1970), 34, no. 14 (1919): 681–83, JSTOR; "Encephalitis Lethargica," NIH.gov; Leslie A. Hoffman and Joel A. Vilensky, "Encephalitis Lethargica: 100 Years after the Epidemic," *Brain: A Journal of Neurology*, 140, no. 8 (Aug. 1, 2017): 2246–51.

4. "Family History: General Social Adjustment," Mayfield Patient File, Bryce.

5. *One Hundred Years of Marriage and Divorce Statistics, 1867–1967*, US Department of Health, Education, and Welfare.

6. Scott, *The Southern Lady*, 216.

7. Mayfield, *Exiles*, 126–27.

8. D'Emilio and Freedman, *Intimate Matters*, 190–93.

9. Mayfield, *Exiles*, 137.

10. Don Chapin, "Echoes from a Golden Age: Sara Recalls Idols of '20s," *Huntsville (AL) Times*, Nov. 1974.

11. Sara Mayfield, "All My Love, Tallulah" MS, chap. 10, p. 72, Mayfield Papers, Box 1226, Folder 5.

12. Sara Mayfield, "Living in London," pp. 5–6, 8–9, Mayfield Papers, Box 1225, Folder 36.

13. "Plays of the Month," *Play Pictorial* 53, no. 318, Sept. 1929, ix, British Periodicals online.

14. "The Obscenity Trial of Miss Radclyffe Hall's novel 'The Well of Loneliness'—16 November 1928," British Newspaper Archive Blog, Nov. 15, 2013.

15. D'Emilio and Freedman, *Intimate Matters*, 201.

16. "Family History," under the heading "Sexual Development," Mayfield Patient File, 1940.

17. Sarah K. Cahn, *Sexual Reckonings: Southern Girls in a Troubling Age* (Harvard University Press, 2007), 10.

18. Sara Mayfield, "Living in London," Mayfield Papers, Box 1225, Folder 36.

CHAPTER 4

1. Jill Astbury, *Crazy for You: The Making of Women's Madness* (Oxford University Press, 1996), 3–4.

2. Mayfield, *Constant Circle*, 157–58.

3. Mayfield, *Constant Circle*, 157.

4. Carl Bode interview with Sara Mayfield, c. late 1960s, Mayfield Papers, Box 1227, Folder 16.

5. Mayfield, *Exiles*, 171.

6. Mayfield, *Exiles*, 190–91.

7. Ashley Lawson. "The Muse and the Maker: Gender, Collaboration, and Appropriation in the Life and Work of F. Scott Fitzgerald and Zelda Fitzgerald," *F. Scott Fitzgerald Review* 13 (2015): 100.

8. Mayfield, *Exiles*, 197–98.

9. Mayfield, *Exiles*, 196–97.

10. Sara Mayfield, "Strange Possession" MS, Mayfield Papers, Box 1227, Folder 5.

11. Sara Mayfield, "Strange Possession," Mayfield Papers, Box 1227, Folder 5.

12. Astbury, *Crazy for You*, 29.

13. Siddons quoted in V. S. Naipaul, *A Turn in the South* (New York: Knopf, 1989), 42.

CHAPTER 5

1. "Rum Rush," *Time* magazine, Dec. 4, 1933.

2. Mayfield Papers, Box 1227, folder 8. SM's description: "The subsequent account of National Distillers, made as a deposition to my brothers [*sic*] February 25, 1935, is a record of the incidents from which the following conclusions can be inferred."

3. Mayfield, *Constant Circle*, 212, 216.

4. Mayfield, *Exiles*, 225–26.

5. Mayfield, *Exiles from Paradise*, 173.

6. "Thomas Lovell Beddoes," citing H. W. Donner, ed. *Plays and Poems of Thomas Lovell Beddoes* (London: Routledge and Kegan Paul, 1950), Wikipedia.

7. "Family History: Religion and Standards," Mayfield Patient File, Bryce Hospital.

8. "Family History: Religion and Standards," Mayfield Patient File, Bryce Hospital.

9. Mayfield, *Constant Circle*, 112.

10. Mayfield, *Exiles*, 248–50.

11. Sara Mayfield to Margaret Mitchell, Dec. 5, 1939, Mayfield Papers, Box 1220, Folder 192.

12. Matthew Bruccoli, *Some Sort of Epic Grandeur*, rev. ed. (Columbia: University of South Carolina Press, 2002), 445.

CHAPTER 6

1. "Bedside Note of President Franklin D. Roosevelt Regarding the Invasion of Poland by Germany, 09/01/1939," National Archives and Records Administration.

2. Thomas Maier, "Joseph Kennedy's Lesson to Today's Pot Investors," *Newsday* online, Nov. 14, 2014.

3. "Garden Club Members to Discuss Plans for Christmas Season," *Tuscaloosa News*, Dec. 10, 1939, Google News.

4. Margarita Tartakovsky, "History of Psychology: The Birth and Demise of *Dementia Praecox*," review of *American Madness: The Rise and Fall of Dementia Praecox*, by Richard Noll, Psychcentral.com, June 22, 2012.

5. Mayfield, *Constant Circle*, 146.

6. Emily Whaley, *Mrs. Whaley and Her Charleston Garden* (Chapel Hill, NC: Algonquin Books, 1997), 147.

CHAPTER 7

1. Carl Bode interview with SM, c. late 1960s, p. 25, Mayfield Papers, Box 1227, Folder 16.

2. Douglas Walter Bristol Jr., "Terror, Anger, and Patriotism: Understanding the Resistance of Black Soldiers during World War II," in *Integrating the U.S. Military: Race, Gender, and Sexual Orientation since World War II*. Douglas Walter Bristol Jr. and Heather Marie Stur, eds. (Baltimore: Johns Hopkins University Press, 2017), 10–35.

3. "Summary of Patient's Remarks," Oct. 8, 1940, Mayfield Patient File.

4. William Bradford Huie, *Mud on the Stars*, reprint (Tuscaloosa: University of Alabama Press, 1996), 88.

5. Harriet Hassell, *Rachel's Children*, reprint (Tuscaloosa: University of Alabama Press reprint edition, 1990), 282.

CHAPTER 8

1. Thomas M. Leonard, *Encyclopedia of U.S.–Latin American Relations* (Washington, DC: CQ Press, 2012), 314, Google Books.

2. National Personnel Records Center; David Hardin, Archivist, National Archives at St. Louis, personal correspondence with author, June 30, 2017; Robert Thomas Howell, "The Writers' War Board: Writers and World War II, Vols. 1 and 2," LSU Digital Commons; "Writers' War Board," Wikipedia; "Fighting the Fires of Hate: America and the Nazi Book Burnings," US Holocaust Memorial Museum.

3. George Lemoult, "Going Once, Going Twice: John F. Kennedy's Diary As a Young Journalist to Be Auctioned," WGBH News, Mar. 24, 2017.

4. Interview with Caroline Plath, Aug. 4, 1993, Katherine Alexander, Oral History Project for UA class with Cully Clark, author's personal copy.

5. "Ely Culbertson," *Encyclopedia Britannica Online*.

6. Mayfield, *Constant Circle*, 256.

7. Mayfield, *Exiles from Paradise*, 284.

CHAPTER 9

1. Sara Mayfield to Dr. S. H. Darden, n.d., but approx. Jan. 1949 because she says she has been in Bryce for ten months, Patient Files, Bryce Hospital.

2. M. H. (Matt) Rothert to Sara Mayfield, Feb. 4, 1948, Mayfield Papers, Box 1221, Folder 281.

3. Nancy Milford, *Zelda* (New York: Harper and Row, 1970), 52, based on an interview with Gerald Murphy, who heard the account from the Fitzgeralds.

4. Harper Lee, *To Kill a Mockingbird* (Philadelphia: J. B. Lippincott, 1960), 13–14.

5. Louise Faircloth, interview with author at Pine Valley Assisted Living Facility, Tuscaloosa, AL, May 23, 2009.

6. John S. Hughes, "Commitment Law, Family Stress, and Legal Culture: The Case of Victorian Alabama," in *The Constitution, Law, and American Life: Critical Aspects of the Nineteenth-Century Experience*, Donald G. Nieman, ed. (Athens: University of Georgia Press, 1992), xv; Megan Testa, MD, and Sara G. West, MD, "Civil Commitment in the United States," *Psychiatry*, 7, no. 10 (Oct. 2010); Substance Abuse and Mental Health Services Administration (SAMHSA), "Civil Commitment and the Mental Health Care Continuum: Historical Trends and Principles for Law and Practice," 2019; "Timeline: Treatments for Mental Illness, 1950s–1992," *American Experience: A Brilliant Madness*.

7. "Colonial Dames Entertained at Tea by Mrs. E. L. Robinson," *Mobile Register*, Saturday, Apr. 10, 1948.

8. Sara Mayfield to Garrett R. Lane, Lane Tile and Marble Co., Dec. 16, 1948, Mayfield Papers, Box 1220, Folder 201.

9. Sara Mayfield to Dr. P. B. Mayfield, June 18, 1948. Mayfield Papers, Box 1220, Folder 201.

10. "Tribunal Voids Anti-Picketing Laws in Alabama," Apr. 22, 1940 (no source, no page), Mayfield Papers, Box 1217, Folder 48; 310 US 88, Thornhill v. Alabama (No. 514), Argued: Feb. 29, 1940, Decided: Apr. 22, 1940, 28 Ala. App. 527; 189 So. 913, reversed; "Mayfield Says Elector Charges Wholly False," *Tuscaloosa News*, Nov. 22, 1948, clipping in Box 1217, Folder 48, Mayfield Papers.

11. D'Emilio and Freedman, *Intimate Matters*, 129.

12. Flynt, *Alabama in the Twentieth Century*, 214–15.

13. Lutz Kaelber, "Eugenics: Compulsory Sterilization in 50 American States," presentation at the 2012 Social Science History Association Meeting; Gregory Michael Dorr, "Eugenics in Alabama," *Encyclopedia of Alabama Online*.

14. Jamie Scot, "Shock the Gay Away: Secrets of Early Gay Aversion Therapy Revealed," *Huffington Post*, June 28, 2013, updated Feb. 2, 2016.

15. John S. Hughes, *The Letters of a Victorian Madwoman* (University of South Carolina Press, 1993), 16, 18, 1, 242, 6; Superintendent J. T. Searcy to Gov. Joseph F. Johnston, Jan. 1, 1896, reproduced in Hughes, *Letters of a Victorian Madwoman.* 59–60.

16. Hughes, *Letters of a Victorian Madwoman*, 19–20.

CHAPTER 10

1. Jonathan Sadowsky, "Electroconvulsive Therapy: A History of Controversy, but Also of Help," *The Conversation*, Jan. 13, 2017; Raheem Suleman, MD, "A Brief History of Electroconvulsive Therapy," *American Journal of Psychiatry Residents' Journal*, Sept. 2020.

2. "Life Expectancy in the U.S., 1900–1998."

3. Visitors Guide Map produced by Tuscaloosa Chamber of Commerce, 1950, Mayfield Papers, Box 1217, Folder 10.

4. Norah Lofts, *The Lute Player: A Novel of Richard the Lionhearted* (New York: Doubleday, 1951), 317, 318.

5. "Greater Mental Health Support in State Urged," a story about Dr. Margaret Quayle of the UA Psychological Services Clinic speaking to the Rotary Club, *Tuscaloosa News*, Sept. or Oct. 1952, Mayfield Papers.

6. Hughes, *Letters of a Victorian Madwoman*, 8.

7. Fredrick E. Vars, "Subversive Apologia," *Law and Psychology Review*, 35 (Spring 2011): 109–19, Criminal Justice Abstracts with Full Text, EBSCOHost Discovery Service.

8. Lauren Wilson Carr, "Wyatt v. Stickney: A Landmark Decision," Alabama Disabilities Advocacy Program Newsletter, July 2004.

9. Carr, "Wyatt v. Stickney."

10. "Ricky Wyatt," *Listen* Magazine, 14, no. 3 (Winter 2009): 25–27; Deborah Jane Belcher, "Minimum Moral Rights: Alabama Mental Health Institutions and the Road to Federal Intervention, a Thesis Submitted to the Graduate Faculty of Auburn

University in Partial Fulfillment of the Requirements for the Degree of Masters of Arts, Auburn, Alabama, Dec. 19, 2008."

11. Carr, "Wyatt v. Stickney."

12. Ira DeMent, quoted in Carr, "Wyatt v. Stickney."

13. Quoted in Carr, "Wyatt v. Stickney."

14. Carr, "Wyatt v. Stickney"; "Wyatt v. Stickney," 325 F. Supp. 781 (M.D. Ala. 1971), 334 F. Supp. 1341 (M.D. Ala 1971), 344 F. Supp. 373 (M.D. Ala. 1972), sub nom Wyatt v. Aderholt, 503 F. 2d 1305 (5th Cir. 1974); "The Legacy of Wyatt," Minnesota Council on Developmental Disabilities; Jack Bass, *Taming the Storm: The Life and Times of Judge Frank M. Johnson, Jr., and the South's Fight Over Civil Rights* (New York: Anchor Books, 1993): 278, Google Books; Megan Testa, MD, and Sara G. West, MD, "Civil Commitment in the United States," *Psychiatry*, 7, no. 10 (Oct. 2010).

15. "Death Plunge Ends Tortured Life of Pretty Model," *Atlanta Constitution* (1950–68), Feb. 20, 1955, ProQuest Historical Newspapers.

16. "Legal Explanation of the Week," *Jet*, Apr. 10, 1952: 19, Google newspapers; "Called Crazy for Racial Beliefs," *Chicago Defender*, Apr. 5, 1952: 1, ProQuest Historical Newspapers.

17. "Death Plunge Ends Tortured Life of Pretty Model," *Atlanta Constitution*.

18. Ancestry.com, *Cook County, Illinois Marriage Index, 1930–1960*, Ancestry.com.

19. *Jet* (magazine), Mar. 3, 1955, Google newspapers; *Chicago Daily Tribune*, Feb. 18, 1955, ProQuest Historical Newspapers.

CHAPTER 11

1. *The Atlanta Journal and the Atlanta Constitution* (1950–68), June 6, 1954, ProQuest Historical Newspapers.

2. Mary Stanton, *Journey toward Justice: Juliette Hampton Morgan and the Montgomery Bus Boycott* (Athens: University of Georgia Press, 2006), 150, 187.

3. "J. Mayfield Fatally Shot," *Anniston Star*, Apr. 4, 1956, ProQuest Historical Newspapers.

4. "Blame Judge's Suicide on Segregation Issue," *Chicago Defender (national edition) (1921–67)*, Apr. 14, 1956: 2, ProQuest Historical Newspapers: Chicago Defender (1910–75).

5. "Judge's Death in Montgomery Held 'Undoubtedly' Suicide," *Atlanta Daily World*, Apr. 5, 1956, ProQuest Historical Newspapers.

6. "Poor Health 'Partially' Blamed by Mayfield in His Suicide Note," *Anniston Star*, Apr. 6, 1956.

7. "Before Rosa Parks, a Teenager Defied Segregation on an Alabama Bus," National Public Radio, Mar. 2, 2015.

8. Robert J. Norrell, "Law in a White Man's Democracy: A History of the Alabama State Judiciary," 32 Cumb. L. Rev. 135 2001–2.

9. "Fifty Years Chlorpromazine: A Historical Perspective."

10. Rachel Aviv, "God Knows Where I Am," *New Yorker*, May 30, 2011.

CHAPTER 13

1. T. Earle Johnson, interview with Katherine Alexander, Aug. 5, 1993, UA oral history project.

2. Clancy Sigal to author, personal correspondence by email, June 2, 2017.

3. Sam Roberts, "Clancy Sigal, Novelist Whose Life Was a Tale in Itself, Dies at 90," *New York Times*, July 21, 2017.

4. "Former Judge Wiley Hill's Rites Held at Montgomery," *Birmingham Post-Herald*, June 18, 1963, Clipping in Mayfield Papers, Box 1222, Folder 366. "Hill was found dead at home early Sunday by his wife. He was 63. Coroner Charles Willis said death was caused by a self-inflicted 12-gauge shotgun wound."

5. Elisabeth Thigpen Hill to Sara Mayfield, Dec. 1958, Mayfield Papers.

6. Allen Rankin, article on Dr. Charles Thigpen, "On the Approaching Occasion of His 85th Birthday," *Montgomery Advertiser*, Dec. 10, 1950, Clipping in Mayfield Papers, Box 1227, Folder 5.

7. Sara Mayfield to Norman Moon, Dec. 14, 1964, Box 1220, Folder 218.

8. Sara Mayfield Patient File, Dec. 22, 1964. Sam Darden (SHD).

CHAPTER 14

1. James T. Bready, "Books and Authors," *Baltimore Sun*, Sept. 11, 1965, Mayfield Papers.

2. Case no. 12334, Circuit Court of Tuscaloosa County, Mayfield Patient File.

CHAPTER 16

1. Howell Raines, telephone interview with author, Oct. 4, 2018.

2. Al Silverman, *The Time of Their Lives: The Golden Age of Great American Book Publishers* (New York: Truman Talley Books, 2008), 234–37.

3. Alex Sartwell, Aug. 3, 1993, interview with Katherine Alexander for Oral History Project for UA class.

4. Scottie Fitzgerald Smith to Sara Mayfield, Feb. 22, 1971, Mayfield Papers, Box 1223, Folder 494.

5. Scottie Fitzgerald Smith to Sara Mayfield, June 9, prob. 1970, Mayfield Papers, Box 1223, Folder 494.

6. Aaron Latham, "Scott's Editor, Zelda's Friend," *The Washington Post*, Dec. 19, 1971.

7. Mayfield, *Exiles*, 168.

8. Milford, *Zelda*, 172.

9. Mayfield, *Exiles*, 114–16.

10. Michael Florence, interview with author, Apr. 4, 2009; Sara Mayfield, *Exiles*, 148.

11. Despina Vodantis, "The Literary World's Sara Mayfield," *Crimson White*, 81, no. 5, July 19, 1971.

12. Alex Sartwell, Aug. 3, 1993, interview with Katherine Alexander, Oral History Project for UA class.

13. "Publisher's Letter," *People*, Sept. 23, 1985.

14. Johnny Greene, "Avoiding Stock Clichés and Missing Sara's Funeral," *Alabama Alumni News* (1979) and *Menckeniana*, 71 (1979): 14–15.

15. Vodantis, "The Literary World's Sara Mayfield."

CHAPTER 17

1. Letter from Sara Mayfield to Madeleine Boyd, Mayfield Papers, Letter Files, Jan. 16, 1963.

2. Alex Sartwell, Aug. 3, 1993, interview with Katherine Alexander, Oral History Project for UA class.

3. Don Chapin, "Echoes from a Golden Age: Sara Recalls Idols of '20s," *Huntsville (AL) Times*, Nov. 1974.

4. Greene, "Avoiding Stock Clichés."

5. Caroline Plath, Aug. 4, 1993, interview with Katherine Alexander, Oral History Project for UA class.

6. Camella Mayfield, telephone interview with author, Mar. 7, 2007.

7. Caroline Plath, Aug. 4, 1993, interview with Katherine Alexander, Oral History Project for UA class.

8. Greene, "Avoiding Stock Clichés."

9. Sara Mayfield, *Mona Lisa: The Woman in the Portrait* (New York: Grosset and Dunlap, 1974), 84–87.

10. Ronald C. Hood, "Mona Lisa Flamboyant," *Hattiesburg (MS) American*, Oct. 6, 1974, NewspaperArchive.com.

11. "Mona Lisa: The Woman in the Portrait," review, *Kirkus Reviews*, Aug. 1, 1974.

12. Tom Gordon, "Lisa behind a Smile," review, *Anniston Star*, Sept. 29, 1974, NewspaperArchive.com.

13. Ronald C. Hood, review, "Mona Lisa Flamboyant," *Hattiesburg (MS) American*.

14. Mayfield, *Mona Lisa*, 243.

15. "Echoes from the Golden Age: The 20s," mimeographed flyer, author's personal collection, courtesy of Cynthia Denham.

16. "Author Mayfield Spotlighted," *Mobile Register*, Nov. 16, 1974, America's Historical Newspapers.

17. Greene, "Avoiding Stock Clichés."

CHAPTER 18

1. Isabel Oldshue, May 3, 2017, telephone interview with author.

2. Alex Sartwell, Aug. 3, 1993, interview with Katherine Alexander, Oral History Project for UA class.

3. James J. Mayfield IV, telephone interview with the author, May 27, 2009; personal interview with the author, May 10, 2012.

4. Sara Mayfield Glassman, Mar. 17, 2017, telephone interview with author.

5. "Sara Mayfield Dies; Was Author," *Tuscaloosa News*, Jan. 11, 1979; "Rites Today

in Tuscaloosa for Sara Mayfield, Novelist," *Birmingham Post*, Jan. 13, 1979; "Sara May-field, Wrote Biography of Mencken," *New York Times*, Jan. 15, 1979: D9, ProQuest Historical Newspapers.

6. Greene, "Avoiding Stock Clichés."

7. Caroline Plath, Aug. 4, 1993, interview with Katherine Alexander, Oral History Project for UA class.

8. Alex Sartwell, Aug. 3, 1993, interview with Katherine Alexander, Oral History Project for UA class.

9. Vodantis, "The Literary World's Sara Mayfield."

AFTERWORD

1. Jim Bailey, "'Hall' Finds Phones Fun: Inductee Coleman Says Hands Full on the Field," *Arkansas Gazette*, Saturday, Jan. 20, 1973.

2. Bailey, "'Hall' Finds Phones Fun."

3. Nuala O'Faolain, *The Story of Chicago May* (New York: Riverhead Books, 2005), 196.

4. The first part of this paragraph also appeared in an essay in a volume edited by Susan Cushman, *A Second Blooming: Becoming the Women We Are Meant to Be* (Mercer University Press, 2017).

Bibliography

Books

Annis, J. Lee. *Big Jim Eastland: The Godfather of Mississippi.* Jackson: University Press of Mississippi, 2016. Google Books.

Appignanesi, Lisa. *Mad, Bad, and Sad: Women and the Mind Doctors.* New York: W. W. Norton, 2008.

Astbury, Jill. *Crazy for You: The Making of Women's Madness.* Oxford: Oxford University Press, 1996.

Ball, Howard. *Hugo L. Black: Cold Steel Warrior.* Oxford: Oxford University Press, 1996.

Bass, Jack. *Taming the Storm: The Life and Times of Judge Frank M. Johnson Jr. and the South's Fight over Civil Rights.* New York: Anchor Books, 1993. Google Books.

Bristol, Douglas Walter, Jr. "Terror, Anger, and Patriotism: Understanding the Resistance of Black Soldiers during World War II." In *Integrating the U.S. Military: Race, Gender, and Sexual Orientation since World War II.* Edited by Douglas Walter Bristol Jr. and Heather Marie Stur. Baltimore: Johns Hopkins University Press, 2017.

Bruccoli, Matthew. *Some Sort of Epic Grandeur,* rev. ed. Columbia: University of South Carolina Press, 2002.

Cahn, Sarah K. *Sexual Reckonings: Southern Girls in a Troubling Age.* Cambridge: Harvard University Press, 2007.

Camp, Roderic Ai. *Mexican Political Biographies, 1935–2009,* 4th ed. Google Books.

Catalog of Copyright Entries, Part 1 © Group 3: Dramatic Compositions and Lectures and Motion Pictures. (Mona Lisa play.) Vol. 19, 1946. Google Books.

Chisholm, Hugh, ed. "Alabama." *Encyclopedia Britannica,* 11th ed., 1910. 1: 459. Google Books.

Churchwell, Sarah. *Careless People: Murder, Mayhem, and the Invention of* The Great Gatsby. London: Virago Press, 2013.

Cline, Sally. *Zelda Fitzgerald: Her Voice in Paradise,* 1st ed. New York: Arcade, 2003.

Crowther, Hall. *An Infuriating American: The Incendiary Arts of H. L. Mencken.* Iowa City: University of Iowa Press, 2014.

Curnutt, Kirk, and Sara A. Kosiba. *The Romance of Regionalism in the Work of F. Scott and Zelda Fitzgerald: The South Side of Paradise.* Lanham, MD: Lexington Books, 2022.

Davies, Owen. *Grimoires: A History of Magic Books.* Oxford: Oxford University Press, 2010. Google Books.

D'Emilio, John, and Estelle B. Freedman. *Intimate Matters: A History of Sexuality in America,* 1st ed. New York: Harper and Row, 1988.

Donaldson, Scott. *The Impossible Craft: Literary Biography.* University Park: Pennsylvania State University Press, 2015.

Donnybrook Fair (Goucher yearbook). Goucher College Digital Library, Donnybrook Fair Yearbook Collection.

Durr, Virginia Foster. *Outside the Magic Circle: The Autobiography of Virginia Foster Durr.* Tuscaloosa: University of Alabama Press, 1990.

Flexner, James Thomas. *Maverick's Progress: An Autobiography.* New York: Fordham University Press, 1996.

Flynt, Wayne. *Alabama in the Twentieth Century.* Tuscaloosa: University of Alabama Press, 2004.

Fowler, Therese Ann. *Z: A Novel.* New York: St. Martin's Press, 2013.

Gary, Amy. *In the Great Green Room: The Brilliant and Bold Life of Margaret Wise Brown.* New York: Flatiron Books, 2016.

Haardt, Sara. "Little Lady." *Southern Souvenirs: Selected Stories and Essays of Sara Haardt.* Edited by Ann Henley. Tuscaloosa: University of Alabama Press, 1999.

Hartnett, Koula Svokos. *Zelda Fitzgerald and the Failure of the American Dream for Women.* New York: Peter Lang, 1990.

Hassell, Harriet. *Rachel's Children.* Reprint, Tuscaloosa: University of Alabama Press, 1990.

Heilbrun, Carolyn. *Writing a Woman's Life.* New York: Ballantine, 1988.

Hemingway, Ernest. *A Moveable Feast.* New York: Charles Scribner's Sons, 1964.

Hobson, Fred. *Mencken: A Life.* New York: Random House, 1994.

Holland, Barbara. *They Went Whistling: Women Wayfarers, Warriors, Runaways, and Renegades.* New York: Pantheon Books, 2001.

Hollars, B. J. *Thirteen Loops: Race, Violence, and the Last Lynching in America.* Tuscaloosa: University of Alabama Press, 2011.

Hughes, John S. "Commitment Law, Family Stress, and Legal Culture: The Case of Victorian Alabama." In *The Constitution, Law, and American Life: Critical Aspects of the Nineteenth-Century Experience.* Edited by Donald G. Nieman. Athens, GA: University of Georgia Press, 1992.

———. *The Letters of a Victorian Madwoman.* University of South Carolina Press, 1993.

Huie, William Bradford. *Mud on the Stars.* Reprint, Tuscaloosa: University of Alabama Press, 1996.

Laughlin, Clara E. *So You're Going to Paris!* London: Methuen, 1924.

Lee, Harper. *To Kill a Mockingbird.* Philadelphia: J. B. Lippincott, 1960.

Leonard, Thomas M. *Encyclopedia of U.S.–Latin American Relations.* Washington, DC: CQ Press, 2012. Google Books.

Lobenthal, Joel. *Tallulah! The Life and Times of a Leading Lady.* New York: Regan Books, 2004.

Lofts, Norah. *The Lute Player: A Novel of Richard the Lionhearted.* New York: Doubleday, 1951.

Mackrell, Judith. "Zelda's Story." In *Flappers: Six Women of a Dangerous Generation.* London: Macmillan, 2013. Kindle.

Mainwaring, Marion. *Mysteries of Paris: The Quest for Morton Fullerton.* Hanover, NH: University Press of New England, 2001.

Marks, Henry S. *Who Was Who in Alabama.* Huntsville, AL: Strode Publishers, 1972.

Mayfield, Sara. *The Constant Circle: H. L. Mencken and His Friends.* Reprint, Tuscaloosa: Fire Ant Books, an imprint of University of Alabama Press, 2003.

———. *Exiles from Paradise: Zelda and Scott Fitzgerald.* New York: Delacorte, 1971.

———. *Mona Lisa: The Woman in the Portrait.* New York: Grosset and Dunlap, 1974.

McIntyre, Rebecca Cawood. "Zelda Sayre Fitzgerald and Sara Martin Mayfield: Alabama Modern." In *Alabama Women: Their Lives and Times.* Edited by Lisa Lindquist Dorr and Susan Youngblood Ashmore. Athens: University of Georgia Press, 2017.

Mead, Marion. *Bobbed Hair and Bathtub Gin: Writers Running Wild in the Twenties.* Orlando, FL: Harcourt Books, 2004.

Milford, Nancy. *Zelda.* New York: Harper and Row, 1970.

Mize, Henry Holman. *The Life of James Jefferson Mayfield.* MA thesis, University of Alabama, 1935. W. S. Hoole Special Collections Library at the University of Alabama.

Mizener, Arthur. *The Far Side of Paradise: A Biography of F. Scott Fitzgerald.* Boston: Houghton Mifflin, 1951.

Moore, Honor. *The White Blackbird: A Life of the Painter Margarett Sargent by Her Granddaughter.* New York: Viking, 1996.

Moorehead, Caroline. *Iris Origo: Marchesa of Val d'Orcia.* Boston: David R. Godine, 2002.

Naipaul, V. S. *A Turn in the South.* New York: Knopf, 1989.

Neeley, Mary Ann Oglesby. "Montgomery." *Encyclopedia of Alabama Online.*

Nicolson, Marjorie Hope. *Pepys' Diary and the New Science.* Charlottesville: University Press of Virginia, 1965.

O'Faolain, Nuala. *The Story of Chicago May.* New York: Riverhead Books, 2005.

Owen, Thomas McAdory. *Dictionary of Alabama Biography.* Chicago: S. J. Clarke, 1921.

Owen, Thomas McAdory, and Marie Bankhead Owen. "Thigpen, Charles Alston." In vol. 4 of *History of Alabama and Dictionary of Alabama Biography.* Google Books.

Pachter, Marc, ed. *Telling Lives: The Biographer's Art*. New Republic Books: Washington, DC., 1979.

Rich, Adrienne. Foreword, *Of Woman Born: Motherhood as Experience and Institution*. W. W. Norton, 1995.

Rodgers, Marion Elizabeth, ed. *Mencken and Sara: A Life in Letters*. New York: McGraw-Hill, 1987.

Safire, William. *Safire's Political Dictionary*. Oxford: Oxford University Press, 2008.

Salmond, John A. *The Conscience of a Lawyer: Clifford J. Durr and American Civil Liberties*. Tuscaloosa: University of Alabama Press, 1990.

"San Francisco." *Encyclopedia of the United Nations and International Agreements*. Milton Park, UK: Taylor and Francis, 1990. Google Books.

Scheper-Hughes, Nancy. *Saints, Scholars, and Schizophrenics: Mental Illness in Rural Ireland*. Berkeley: University of California Press, 2001.

Seaton, George W. *What to See and Do in the South: How to Get the Most Out of Your Trip*. New York: Prentice-Hall, 1941.

Shores, Elizabeth Findley. *Earline's Pink Party: The Social Rituals and Domestic Relics of a Southern Woman*, 2nd ed. Tuscaloosa: University of Alabama Press, 2017.

Silverman, Al. *The Time of Their Lives: The Golden Age of Great American Book Publishers*. New York: Truman Talley Books, 2008.

Some University of Alabama Poets: Sixth Series. Chi Delta Phi. Birmingham, AL: Birmingham Printing Co., 1931.

Stanton, Mary. *Journey toward Justice: Juliette Hampton Morgan and the Montgomery Bus Boycott*. Athens: University of Georgia Press, 2006.

Strode, Hudson. *The Eleventh House: Memoirs*. New York: Harcourt Brace Jovanovich, 1975.

Taylor, Kendall. *The Gatsby Affair: Scott, Zelda, and the Betrayal That Shaped an American Classic*. Lanham, MD: Rowman and Littlefield, 2018.

Turnbull, Andrew. *Scott Fitzgerald: A Biography*. New York: Charles Scribner's Sons, 1962.

Wagner-Martin, Linda. *Telling Women's Lives: The New Biography*. New Brunswick, NJ: Rutgers University Press, 1994.

Walsh, Elsa. *Divided Lives: The Public and Private Struggles of Three Accomplished Women*. New York: Simon and Schuster, 1995.

Ward, Mary Jane. *The Snake Pit*. New York: Signet Books, 1948.

Whaley, Emily. In conversation with William Baldwin. *Mrs. Whaley and Her Charleston Garden*. Chapel Hill, NC: Algonquin Books, 1997.

Whitely, Opal. *The Singing Creek Where the Willows Grow: The Mystical Nature Diary of Opal Whitely*, rev ed. With a biography and an afterword by Benjamin Hoff. New York: Penguin, 1986.

Williams, Tennessee. *A Streetcar Named Desire*. New York: Signet Books, 1947.

Winchester, Simon. *The Professor and the Madman: A Tale of Murder, Insanity, and the Making of the* Oxford English Dictionary. New York: HarperCollins, 1998.

Winokur, George, MD, and Ming T. Tsuang, MD, PhD. *The Natural History of Mania, Depression, and Schizophrenia.* Washington, DC: American Psychiatric Press, 1996.

SELECTED ARTICLES AND WEB RESOURCES

Adams, Robert M. "Attis Adonis Osiris Fitzgerald and Co." *New York Review of Books,* Jan. 27, 1972.

"Aesthetic Club." By Paula Kyzer Taylor. *Encyclopedia of Arkansas Online.*

Alabama, US, Deaths and Burials Index, 1881–1974. Ancestry.com.

Alabama Authors. "Sara Mayfield." University of Alabama Libraries Online.

"Alabama Climate Report, Sept. 12, 2013." The National Space Science & Technology Center.

Alabama Divorce Index, 1950–59. Ancestry.com.

"Alabama Judge, 45, Is Ruled a Suicide." *New York Times,* Apr. 5, 1956. America's Historical Newspapers.

"Alabama Judge Kills Self; Cites Race Issue Worry." *Chicago Daily Defender (daily edition) (1956–1960),* Apr. 5, 1956. ProQuest Historical Newspapers.

"Alabama Library Association Handbook: History: Alabama Author Awards."

Allison, Adele M. "Mona Lisa's Smile Still Baffling." *Pittsburgh Press,* Jan. 11, 1976: 47. Google News.

"A. T. Harden 'Hardin,' Dan Pippen Jr., and Elmore Clark." Digital Repository Service, Northeastern University Library, Civil Rights and Restorative Justice.

"Author from Anniston to Autograph Books." *Anniston (AL) Star,* Oct. 21, 1968.

"Author Mayfield Spotlighted." *Mobile Register,* Nov. 16, 1974. America's Historical Newspapers.

Aviv, Rachel. "God Knows Where I Am." *New Yorker,* May 30, 2011.

Bain, Roy. "Critic Mencken's Old Friend Gets 'Head Start' on Book." *Tuscaloosa News,* Jan. 13, 1966. Sara Mayfield Papers. W. S. Hoole Special Collections Library at the University of Alabama.

"Bedside Note of President Franklin D. Roosevelt Regarding the Invasion of Poland by Germany," Sept. 1, 1939. National Archives and Records Administration.

"Before Rosa Parks, a Teenager Defied Segregation on an Alabama Bus." *All Things Considered,* National Public Radio, Mar. 2, 2015.

"Blame Judge's Suicide on Segregation Issue." *Chicago Defender* (national edition), Apr. 14, 1956. ProQuest Historical Newspapers.

"Blumenthal, Alfred Cleveland. Divorced." Milestones. *Time,* Sept. 10, 1945.

Bode, Carl. Unpublished interview with Sara Mayfield. N.d., ca. late 1960s. Sara Mayfield Papers. W. S. Hoole Special Collections Library at the University of Alabama.

"Bowl Championship Series, 1979." ESPN.

Bready, James H. "Books and Authors." *Baltimore Sun,* n.d., ca. 1965. Clipping in Sara

Mayfield Papers. W. S. Hoole Special Collections Library at the University of Alabama.

"A Brilliant Wedding." *Arkansas Gazette*, July 1, 1897. Newspapers.com.

Broadcasting Magazine Archives. Apr. 13, 1942. "Britain's Battle of the Air: 'V' Symbol a Radio Contribution, Article in 'Saturday Evening Post' Reveals." Radiohistory.com.

Brown, Ivor. "Re-Enter the Actor." *Saturday Review: Politics, Literature, Science, and Art*, (Sept. 1, 1929): 146. British Periodicals.

Brown, Melissa. "Governor Robert Bentley Celebrates Grand Opening of New Bryce Hospital Facility." May 21, 2014. AL.com.

Bryer, Jackson R. "A Planned Campaign to Exonerate Zelda." *Baltimore Sun*, Sept. 26, 1971.

Byron, Lindsay. *PhD for Hire* (blog). My Research. "'The Straightest Story Ever Told in Alabama': Two Eccentric Women Tell of One Southern Mental Hospital, 1890–1965."

"Called Crazy for Racial Beliefs." *Chicago Defender (national edition)*, Apr. 5, 1952. ProQuest Historical Newspapers.

Carr, Lauren Wilson. "Wyatt v. Stickney: A Landmark Decision." *Alabama Disabilities Advocacy Program Newsletter*, July 2004.

Chapin, Don. "Echoes from a Golden Age: Sara Recalls Idols of '20s." *Huntsville (AL) Times*, Nov. 1974.

Cissell, Jordan. "Alabama's Desegregation Leaders Recall Struggles, Eventual Victories." *Crimson White*, Mar. 4, 2013.

"Clancy Sigal." Obituary. *Guardian* (US edition), July 25, 2017.

"Class Notes/Deaths." *Vanderbilt Magazine* 82, no. 4 (Fall 2001).

Clough, Patricia. "Curtains Come Down on 'Room with a View.'" *Independent* (UK), July 8, 1993.

"Colonial Dames Entertained at Tea by Mrs. E. L. Robinson." *Mobile Register*, Apr. 10, 1948.

"Colonial Dames Pay Tribute to Mrs. Mayfield." *Mobile Register*, Apr. 15, 1948.

Cook, Joan. "Lillian Greneker, 95; Made Mannequins with Movable Parts." *New York Times*, Feb. 6, 1990.

Cox, David R. "The King Story." Letter to the Editor. *Washington Post*, Feb. 29, 2000.

"Cox-Mayfield-Sutley House [Carson Place]." National Register of Historic Places Inventory—Nomination Form.

"Danzig." US Holocaust Museum.

"Dauphin Island's First Bridge, 1955–1979." Dauphin Island, AL: Archive of Historical Data, Books, Maps and Other Materials.

Davies, Tom. "Betty Wason—2002." Indiana Journalism Hall of Fame.

"The Day Is New: Dawn to Darkness in Mexico City." YouTube. US Office of Inter-American Affairs.

"Death Plunge Ends Tortured Life of Pretty Model." *Atlanta Constitution*, Feb. 20, 1955. ProQuest Historical Newspapers.

"Died: Zelda Sayre Fitzgerald, 48, Invalid Wife of Jazz Age Novelist F. Scott Fitzgerald." *Time*, Mar. 22, 1948.

"Dodgie: Goodbye Grande Dame." Mcalpinehouse.com.

Donnybrook Fair Yearbook Collection. Goucher College. Digital Collection. https://goucher.contentdm.oclc.org/digital/collection/p16235coll5/id/8777/.

Dorr, Gregory Michael. "Eugenics in Alabama." *Encyclopedia of Alabama Online*.

Dullea, Georgia. "A Pastoral Life Resists Change Only 32 Miles from Manhattan." *New York Times*, June 17, 1973.

"EJI Dedicates Marker for Lynching Victims in Tuscaloosa County, Alabama." Equal Justice Initiative, Mar. 7, 2017.

"Elisabeth Thigpen Hill." Findagrave.com.

"Eloise J. Tarwater." Obituary. *Tuscaloosa News*, Feb. 1, 2001.

"Ely Culbertson: American Bridge Player." *Encyclopedia Britannica Online*.

"Encephalitis Lethargica." NIH.gov.

"FAQ: *A Room of One's Own*." UAH.edu.

Federal Census 1910. Ancestry.com.

"Fifty Years Chlorpromazine: A Historical Perspective." NIH.gov.

"Fighting the Fires of Hate: America and the Nazi Book Burnings." US Holocaust Museum.

"Files Cross Bill in Custody Suit." *Gulfport (AL) Daily Herald*, Apr. 23, 1949. Newspaper Archive.

Findagrave.com.

"Former Model, Inmate at Bryce, Is Captured." *Anniston (AL) Star*, June 12, 1949. Newspaper Archive.

"Frank A. F. Severance." Obituary. *New York Times*, May 20, 1979.

"Franklin D. Roosevelt Day by Day." Aug. 24, 1939. FDR Library Online.

Fitzgerald, Zelda. "Eulogy of the Flapper." *Metropolitan Magazine*, Apr. 1922.

———. "The Iceberg." *New Yorker*, Dec. 20, 2013.

"The Fitzgeralds as Collaborators." *Anniston (AL) Star*, Sept. 29, 1974. Newspaper Archive.

"Five Will Be Inducted into Alabama HOF." *Tuscaloosa News*, Oct. 5. 1995.

"Folsom's Success Story Grows as Three Candidates Sweep In." *Atlanta Journal-Constitution*, June 6, 1954. ProQuest Historical Newspapers.

"Former Judge Wiley Hill's Rites Held at Montgomery." *Birmingham Post-Herald*, June 18, 1963. Clipping in Box 1222, Folder 366, Mayfield Papers. W. S. Hoole Special Collections Library at the University of Alabama.

"Foundation of the Law Firm of Mayfield and Harris with Offices in the Searcy Building." *Tuscaloosa News*, Nov. 29, 1953. Google News.

"Frances Benjamin Johnston—Biographical Overview and Chronology." Prints and Photographs Reading Room, Library of Congress.

Freedman, Estelle B. "The New Woman: Changing Views of Women in the 1920s." *Journal of American History*. Vol. 6, no. 2 (Sept. 1974).

"Freemasons: Politician Members in Alabama." PoliticalGraveyard.com.

"F. Scott Fitzgerald." Resources: Writers. Baltimore Literary Heritage Project.

Gandrud, Pauline Jones. Papers. William Stanley Hoole Special Collections Library at the University of Alabama.

"Garden Club Members to Discuss Plans for Christmas Season." *Tuscaloosa News*, Dec. 10, 1939. Google News.

"Georgia Lloyd." Obituary. *Chicago Tribune*, Feb. 23, 1999.

"German Army Attacks Poland; Cities Bombed, Port Blockaded; Danzig Is Accepted into Reich." *New York Times*, Sept. 1, 1939.

Gordon, Tom. "Belle of Letters: Sara Mayfield's Days." *Anniston (AL) Star*, Aug. 26, 1973.

———. "Lisa behind a Smile." *Anniston (AL) Star*, Sept. 29, 1974.

Goucher Alumnae Quarterly, Summer 1964, 42, no. 4, 41–42. Goucher Digital Library.

"Greater Mental Health Support in State Urged." *Tuscaloosa News*. Sept. or Oct. 1952. Sara Mayfield Papers. W. S. Hoole Special Collections Library at the University of Alabama.

Greene, Johnny. "Avoiding Stock Clichés and Missing Sara's Funeral." *Alabama Alumni News* (1979) and *Menckeniana* 71 (1979).

Greenhaw, Wayne. "Chitlins and Caviar: Montgomerian Returns." (Column.) *Alabama Journal*, ca. 1969–70. Clipping in Box 1236, Folder 23, Sara Mayfield Papers, W. S. Hoole Special Collections Library at the University of Alabama.

Guggenheim Fellows, 1945. Internal website search. Guggenheim Foundation.

"Guide to the Francis P. Squibb Papers, 1894–2003." University of Chicago Library.

Hammond, Holly. "Yoga Pioneers: How Yoga Came to America." *Yoga Journal*, Aug. 29, 2007.

"Head of Transradio Tells FCC of Start." *New York Times*, Oct. 17, 1941, 24. ProQuest Historical Newspapers.

"Herbert Samuel Moore." Obituary. *Washington Post*, Jan. 26, 1994.

Historical Statistics of the United States, Colonial Times to 1970. Part 1. US Census.

"History of St. John's." St. John's Episcopal Church (Montgomery).

"A History of the Alabama Appellate Courts." Alabama Judicial System.

H. L. Mencken to Sara Haardt. Letter. Jan. 11, 1927. Goucher College Digital Archives.

Hoffman, Leslie A., and Joel A. Vilensky. "Encephalitis Lethargica: 100 Years after the Epidemic." *Brain: A Journal of Neurology*, 140, no. 8 (Aug. 1, 2017): 2246–51.

"Home/Why Sheppard Pratt." Sheppard Pratt History. Sheppardpratt.org.

Hood, Ronald C. "Did Zelda Inspire Scott's Creativity?" *New Orleans Post-Crescent*, Aug. 15, 1971.

———. "Mona Lisa Flamboyant." *Hattiesburg (MS) American*, Oct. 6, 1974. NewspaperArchive.com.

"How City Welcomed Amelia Earhart." Victoria Bartlett. Hampshire and Isle of Wight. BBC, Nov. 11, 2009.

Howell, Robert Thomas. "The Writers' War Board: Writers and World War II." Vols. 1 and 2. LSU Digital Commons.

"James Henry Hammond Advocates Slavery." PBS.

"J. Mayfield Fatally Shot." *Anniston (AL) Star*, Apr. 4, 1956. ProQuest Historical Newspapers.

Johnston, Josephine. "The Ghost of the Schizophrenogenic Mother." *AMA Journal of Ethics*, 15, no. 9, Sept. 2013.

"Judge Mayfield Drops Dead at Radio Party." *Montgomery Advertiser*, Jan. 2, 1927.

"Judge's Death in Montgomery Held 'Undoubtedly' Suicide." *Atlanta Daily World*, Apr. 5, 1956. ProQuest Historical Newspapers.

Kaelber, Lutz. "Eugenics: Compulsory Sterilization in 50 American States." Presentation at the 2012 Social Science History Association Meeting.

Kazek, Kelly. "Spooky, Dilapidated Searcy Hospital Complex Was State's First Asylum for Black Patients." Sept. 8, 2016. AL.com.

"Klauber's Victory Vs. WWB." *Variety*. June 13, 1945. Archive.org.

Latham, Aaron. "Scott's Editor, Zelda's Friend." Review of *Dear Scott/Dear Max*, edited by John Kuehl and Jackson Bryer, and *Exiles from Paradise*, by Sara Mayfield. *Washington Post*, Dec. 19, 1971.

Lawson, Ashley. "The Muse and the Maker: Gender, Collaboration, and Appropriation in the Life and Work of F. Scott Fitzgerald and Zelda Fitzgerald." *F. Scott Fitzgerald Review* 13 (2015).

"Lee Israel, Literary Forger." Obituary. *Telegraph* (UK), Feb. 24, 2015.

"The Legacy of Wyatt." Minnesota Council on Developmental Disabilities.

"Legal Explanation of the Week." *Jet*, Apr. 10, 1952. Google News.

Lemoult, George. "Going Once, Going Twice: John F. Kennedy's Diary as a Young Journalist to Be Auctioned." WGBH News. Mar. 24, 2017.

"Lethargic Encephalitis." *Public Health Reports (1896–1970)*, 34, no. 14 (1919): 681–83. JSTOR.

"Life Expectancy in the U.S., 1900–1998." University of Berkeley.

"Literary Associate Speaks at LC." *Hilltop News*, 11, no. 2 (Apr. 15, 1969).

"A Look Back at What Things Used to Cost." *Farmers' Almanac Online*.

"Lurton Blassingame, 84, Agent." Obituary. *New York Times*, Apr. 13, 1988.

Maier, Thomas. "Joseph Kennedy's Lesson to Today's Pot Investors." *Newsday*, Nov. 14, 2014.

"Major Peyton Spotswood Mathis Jr." Obituary. Dignity Memorial.

"The Mann Act." PBS.org.

Mayfield, Sara. "The F. Scott Fitzgeralds in Paris: Reminiscences." *Comment: The University of Alabama Review*, Winter 1965.

———. "On Breaking One's Neck." *Smith Monthly: Intercollegiate Issue*, Mar. 1924, 33, no. 5.

———. "The 'Robin Hood' of Corsica." *Baltimore Sun*, July 28, 1929. ProQuest Historical Newspapers.

———. "Spirit of Sincere Faith Pervades Conference Air." *Birmingham News*, n.d. Clipping in Box 1219, Folder 129, Sara Mayfield Papers. W. S. Hoole Special Collections Library at the University of Alabama.

"Mayfield Book Defends Zelda in 'Exiles from Paradise.'" *Graphic* (Tuscaloosa, AL), July 22, 1971. Clipping in Box 130, Folder 15, Sara Mayfield Papers. W. S. Hoole Special Collections Library at the University of Alabama.

"Mayfield Says Elector Charges Wholly False." *Tuscaloosa News*, Nov. 22, 1948. Clipping in Box 1217, Folder 48, Sara Mayfield Papers.

McArthur, Elizabeth Hoole. "William Stanley Hoole: A Man of Letters." *Alabama Heritage*, Winter 2008.

McWilliams, Richebourg Gaillard. "History of Beautiful Dauphin Island; Origin of Street Names." n.d. Dauphin Island History Online.

"Mencken, H. E." Ernest A. and Madeleine E. Boyd Collection. Georgetown University Archival Resources.

"Mental Hospitals in Ala. Ordered to Desegregate." *Afro American,* Feb. 22, 1969. Google News.

"Minimum Moral Rights: Alabama Mental Health Institutions and the Road to Federal Intervention." Deborah Belcher. A Thesis Submitted to the Graduate Faculty of Auburn University in Partial Fulfillment of the Requirements for the Degree of Master of Arts, Auburn, Alabama, Dec. 19, 2008.

"Mona Lisa: The Woman in the Portrait." *Kirkus Reviews*, Aug. 1, 1974.

"Mrs. F. Scott Fitzgerald, Widow of Author, among Those Killed." *Mobile Press Register*, Mar. 11, 1948.

"Mrs. Mayfield's Choice Recipes Will Appear in the News Daily." *Tuscaloosa News*, Sept. 26, 1947.

"Mrs. Susie Fitts Martin Mayfield." *National Society of the Daughters of the American Revolution*, vol. 28. Ancestry.com.

"'Mr. V.,' a British Melodrama with Leslie Howard, Opens at Rivoli." *New York Times*. Feb. 3, 1942.

"Nancy Milford." Gale Literature: *Contemporary Authors*.

Nedelman, Michael. "Doctors Thought She Was Psychotic, but Her Body Was Attacking Her Brain." CNN. Sept. 25, 2017.

Neeley, Mary Ann. "'The Lightning Route': The Development of the Electric Streetcar and Its Effect on Montgomery, 1885–1900." *Alabama Review* 40 (Oct. 1987): 243–58.

New York Harbor Parks. Sandy Hook. Fort Hancock.

New York Passenger Lists 1820–1957. Ancestry.com.

"1932 Deep South Tornado Outbreak." Wikipedia.

Norrell, Robert J. "Law in a White Man's Democracy: A History of the Alabama State Judiciary." 32 *Cumberland Law Review* 135: 2001–2002.

"Obituary: Peyton S. Mathis Jr., BE '40, Home to Montgomery." *Vanderbilt Magazine*, Mar. 23, 2015.

"The Obscenity Trial of Miss Radclyffe Hall's Novel 'The Well of Loneliness'—16 November 1928." British Newspaper Archive Blog, Nov. 15, 2013.

Ostrow, Laysha, and Neal Adams. "Recovery in the USA: From Politics to Peer Support." *International Review of Psychiatry*, Feb. 2012, 24, no. 1: 70–78.

Owen, Marie Bankhead. "Children of the Alabama Judiciary." *Montgomery Advertiser*, Mar. 26, 1911. World Newspaper Archive.

"Paid Notice: Deaths, Landman, Sidney James." *New York Times*, Jan. 2, 2001.

Panhorst, Michael W. "Confederate Monument on Capitol Hill." *Encyclopedia of Alabama Online.*

"Papers of Lillian Louise Lidman Greneker, 1890–1990." Harvard Library Online.

Penley, Gary. *Della Raye: A Girl Who Grew Up In Hell and Emerged Whole*. Gretna, LA: Pelican Publishing, 2002.

Piper, Henry Dan. "Exiles from Paradise." *American Literature*, Nov. 1, 1972, 44, no. 3: 512–13.

Pirch, Sarah. "Living Wright." *Alabama Journey*, Jan./Feb. 2010.

"Plays of the Month." *Play Pictorial*, Sept. 1928. British Periodicals.

"Poor Health 'Partially' Blamed by Mayfield in His Suicide Note." *Anniston (AL) Star*, Apr. 6, 1956.

Prescott, Orville. "Political Melodrama Way Down South." *New York Times*, Mar. 13, 1964. ProQuest Historical Newspapers.

"Publisher's Letter." *People*, Sept. 23, 1985.

Rankin, Allen. Article about Dr. Charles Thigpen, "On the Approaching Occasion of His 85th Birthday." *Montgomery Advertiser*, Dec. 10, 1950. Clipping in Box 1227, Folder 5, Sara Mayfield Papers. W. S. Hoole Special Collections Library at the University of Alabama.

Rasmussen, Frank. "Remember When: The City's Glitterati Met at 412 North Howard Restaurant." *Baltimore Sun*, Apr. 6, 1997.

Review of *Exiles from Paradise*. *Library Journal*, July 1971, 96: 2306.

"Ricky Wyatt." *Listen* magazine, 14, no. 3 (Winter 2009).

"The Rise and Fall of American Madness." Blog. Harvard University Press, Jan. 30, 2012.

Ritchie, Douglas. Obituary. "Douglas Ritchie, 62, B.B.C.'s Col. Britton." *New York Times*, Dec. 16, 1967.

"Rites Today in Tuscaloosa for Sara Mayfield, Novelist." *Birmingham Post*, Jan. 13, 1979.

"Road Show (musical)." Wikipedia.

"Robert Rice Reynolds." North Carolina History Project.

Roberts, Sam. "Clancy Sigal, Novelist Whose Life Was a Tale in Itself, Dies at 90." *New York Times*, July 21, 2017.

"The Rochambeau Apartments." Baltimore Heritage.

Roney, Marty. "World War II Flier Laid to Rest after Seventy Years." *USA Today*, Jan. 3, 2015.

"Ross Clemo Treseder." Prabook.com.

"Ruby Pickens Tartt." *Encyclopedia of Alabama Online*.

"Ruby Pickens Tartt: Citizen of the World." Philip Beidler and Elizabeth Buckalew. *Alabama Heritage* (Winter 2008).

"Rum Rush." *Time*, Dec. 4, 1933, 22, no. 23: 63.

Sadowsky, Jonathan. "Electroconvulsive Therapy: A History of Controversy, but Also of Help." *The Conversation*, Jan. 12, 2017.

"Samuel H. Darden Jr., M.D." Obituary. *Tuscaloosa News*, May 20, 2001.

"Sara (Martin) Mayfield." Gale Literature: *Contemporary Authors*, 2003.

"Sara Mayfield, Wrote Biography of Mencken." *New York Times*, Jan. 15, 1979. ProQuest Historical Newspapers.

"Sara Mayfield Dies; Was Author." *Tuscaloosa News*, Jan. 11, 1979. Google News.

"Sara Mayfield Signs Movie Option." *Tuscaloosa News*, Mar. 19, 1972.

"Sayre Is Victim of Long Illness." *Birmingham News*, Nov. 18, 1931.

"A Science Odyssey: People and Discoveries: Drug for Treating Schizophrenia Identified, 1952." PBS.

Scot, Jamie. "Shock the Gay Away: Secrets of Early Gay Aversion Therapy Revealed." *Huffington Post*, June 28, 2013, updated Feb. 2, 2016.

"77th Goucher College Alumnae Reunion to Be Held June 20–22." *Baltimore Sun*, June 6, 1969. ProQuest Historical Newspapers.

Shooting the Past (film). 1999. Written and directed by Stephen Poliakoff.

Short, K. R. M. "Hewing Straight to the Line: Editorial Control in American News Broadcasting, 1941–42." *Historical Journal of Film, Radio, and Television* 1: 2, 1981, Taylor and Francis Online.

Showalter, Elaine. "Unwell, This Side of Paradise." Review of *Zelda Fitzgerald: Her Voice in Paradise*, by Sally Cline, and *Dear Scott, Dearest Zelda: The Love Letters of Scott and Zelda Fitzgerald*, edited by Jackson R. Bryer and Cathy W. Barks. *Guardian* (UK), Oct. 5, 2002.

"Six Months of War." *New York Times*, Mar. 3, 1940, Sec. 9.

Slowe, Betty. "Looking Back: July 6." *Tuscaloosa News*, July 5, 2015.

Substance Abuse and Mental Health Services Administration (SAMHSA). "Civil Commitment and the Mental Health Care Continuum: Historical Trends and Principles for Law and Practice," 2019.

Suitts, Steve. *Hugo Black of Alabama*. Montgomery: NewSouth Books, 2005.

Suleman, Raheem, MD. "A Brief History of Electroconvulsive Therapy." *American Journal of Psychiatry Residents' Journal*, Sept. 2020.

"Susie Fitts Martin Mayfield." *A Register of the Officers and Students of the University of Alabama, 1831–1901*, p. 408. Google Books.

Tartakovsky, Margarita. "History of Psychology: The Birth and Demise of *Dementia*

Praecox." Review of *American Madness: The Rise and Fall of Dementia Prae-cox*, by Richard Noll. Psychcentral.com.

Testa, Megan, MD, and Sara G. West, MD. "Civil Commitment in the United States." *Psychiatry*, Oct. 2010: 7, no. 10.

"Thomas Lovell Beddoes." Citing *Plays and Poems of Thomas Lovell Beddoes*. Edited by H. W. Donner. London: Routledge and Kegan Paul, 1950. Wikipedia.

Tillotson, Dolph. "Miss Mayfield Writes about Zelda, Scott." *Tuscaloosa News*, Apr. 5, 1969.

"Timeline: Treatments for Mental Illness." PBS *American Experience: A Brilliant Madness*.

"Today in Met History: February 4." The Metropolitan Museum of Art.

"Top Ten Weather Events in the 20th Century for Alabama." National Weather Service.

"Transradio Head Says Dies Report Misrepresents News Link with Nazis." *Christian Science Monitor*, Nov. 22, 1940. ProQuest Historical Newspapers.

"Tribunal Voids Anti-Picketing Laws in Alabama." Apr. 22, 1940. (No source, no page.) Clipping in Sara Mayfield Papers. W. S. Hoole Special Collections Library at the University of Alabama.

"Unveiling of the Memorial to Judge James Jefferson Mayfield." 3 Ala. L.J. (Tuscaloosa) 249 (1927–28).

US City Directories, 1821–1989. Ancestry.com.

US Department of Health, Education, and Welfare. *One Hundred Years of Marriage and Divorce Statistics, 1867–1967*. DHEW Publication No. (HRA) 74-1902. Dec. 1973.

US Passport Applications 1795–1925. National Archives and Records Administration. Ancestry.com.

US School Yearbooks. Murphy High School (Mobile, AL), 1937. Ancestry.com.

Vars, Fredrick E. "Subversive Apologia." *Law and Psychology Review*, Spring 2011, 35: 109–19. Criminal Justice Abstracts with Full Text, EBSCOHost Discovery Service.

Velasquez-Manoff, Moises. "When the Body Attacks the Brain." *Atlantic*, July/Aug. 2016.

Visitors Guide Map. Tuscaloosa Chamber of Commerce, 1950. Sara Mayfield Papers. W. S. Hoole Special Collections Library at the University of Alabama.

Vodantis, Despina. "The Literary World's Sara Mayfield." *Crimson White*, 81, no. 5, July 19, 1971.

"Voices and Visions: Bryce Historical Committee Members Explore Their Hopes for Bryce." *Listen*, Winter 2009: 11. ADMH Office of Consumer Relations.

"V Sign: The V for Victory Campaign and the Victory-Freedom Sign." Wikipedia.

Warren, Dale. "(Signed) F. S. F." *Princeton University Library Chronicle*, Winter 1964. JSTOR.

Weather History Archive, 1948. Zip code 35405 [Tuscaloosa, AL]. Almanac.com.

Weeks, Linton. "Beware of Japanese Balloon Bombs." National Public Radio. Jan. 20, 2015.

Weinstein, Dina. "50 Years of Integration Began with Jewish Student's Editorial." *Forward* Online, Feb. 4, 2013.

White, Gail. "Breaking Down in the South." *The Gift of Experience: Atlanta Review 10th Anniversary Anthology*. Edited by Daniel Veach. Spring/Summer 2005.

Whitlock, Kelli. "The First Footsteps: The Beginning of Coeducational Studies at UA." *Tuscaloosa News*, Nov. 15, 1992.

Wilson, Edmund. "The Aftermath of Mencken." *New Yorker*, May 31, 1969.

Wolff, Geoffrey. "Ruined by the Uplift." *Washington Post*, Sept. 3, 1968. ProQuest Historical Newspapers.

Young, Frances, comp. *A History of Dauphin Island under Five Flags, 1699–1989: In Adversity We Thrive*. Dauphin Island, AL. Written in 1988. Updated in 2001.

Zimmerman, Dwight Jon. "The 'V for Victory' Campaign." Defense Media Network. July 8, 2021.

Index

Page numbers in italics refer to figures.

185; and cotton experiments, 62, 63, 78, 82, 85, 100, 117, 121, 122, 158; on daily life at Bryce Hospital, 160–63; "Death and Transfiguration," 158; death of, 238; and death of brother, 153–54; and death of father, 30–31; and death of mother, 152, 154; and death of Sara Haardt Mencken, 66–67; and delusions, 96, 124, 134, 138, 140, 148, 159, 162, 168, 172, 184, 188; and discharge from Bryce Hospital, 170–71, 183; *Earth Takes Its Toll*, 67, 72–73; and electroshock therapy, 132–34; in England, 36–38, 41–42, 235; in Europe, 11–13, 212–14, 228–29; and farm management innovations, 62–63, 85, 126; and Fitzgeralds, 54, 74, 233; and foreign language studies, 69, 163, 166, 168, 202–3; in France, 1–2, 27–28, 38–41; as freelance reporter, 80–82; "The F. Scott Fitzgeralds in Paris," 208; and Goucher College, 15–17, 20, 32, 33, 35–36, 182, 207; guardianship of, 125, 152, 169, 171, 180, 188; guardianship of revoked, 190–91; and habeas corpus, 125, 131, 143, 147, 148, 166–67, 171, 179, 187; and H. L. Mencken, 3, 54, 68, 70–71, 89, 117; at Idlewyld, 60, 68, 83, 100, 119, 123; "If You Kiss a Rogue," 75; income of, 226; in Italy, 201–2; and letters from H. L. Mencken, 23, 93; and letters from Liz Hill, 33; and letters from mother, 17, 135; and letters from Sara Haardt Mencken, 52, 66–67; and letters to father, 17, 26; and letters to H. L. Mencken, 39, 78–79, 92, 98, 99, 116, 128; and letters to Liz Hill, 89, 104, 200, 237; and letters to mother, 16–17, 22, 26, 28, 29, 33, 78, 135–36; and letters to

Sara Haardt Mencken, 42, 45–46, 52; and Liz Hill, 11–12, 33–35, 119–20, 151, 194–98, 207, 217; "Man about Town," 42; marriage of, 24–27, 29, 32–33; and Mason family, 84–85, 128; "Memoirs of Paris," 209; "Mojo," 75, 136; and Nancy Milford, 208–11; and National Distillers, 65–66, 72, 86, 114; and newspaper and paper plant, 120–21, 128–29; in New York, 53–54, 77, 79; "The Odyssey of a Wandering Mind," 38; papers of at University of Alabama library, 3, 156, 230; and paranoia, 97–100, 104–6, 128–29, 134–35, 138–40, 158–59, 163, 168, 169, 180, 188; and paranoid precox, 88; patent applications by, 78, 85, 92, 100, 108–9, 116–17, 128, 158; and photography, 173, 174; and Plastex, 77; and plastic planes, 85, 87–88, 90, 93, 94, 102; and plastics, 87, 90, 121, 122, 126, 128, 158; and plastics plant, 120; on psychological warfare, 87–88, 92, 99, 101, 120, 169; and public appearances, 204, 226–27; "The Question of the Sphinx," 177; and racial sympathy, 118, 225; and release from Bryce Hospital, 1, 98–99, 186, 191–92; reporting for Transradio, 80–82, 103, 110, 115; romantic relationships of, 20–23, 35–36, 39–41, 44–46, 48–49, 116; and Sam Darden, 160–61, 168, 194; on same-sex relationships, 83–84, 167–68; and Sara Haardt Mencken, 19–20, 43, 49, 56, 67, 205, 239, 242; and Scott Fitzgerald, 3, 68, 113; "Shakespeare and the Pembrokes," 235; at Sheppard Pratt Hospital, 91–96; sketches by, *137, 157*; and sleeping sickness, 31–32; social life of, 200, 224–26; "Study Guide for Modern French Painting,"